SOCIAL CONTROVERSY

SOCIAL CONTROVERSY

EDITED BY
WILLIAM PETERSEN AND DAVID MATZA
UNIVERSITY OF CALIFORNIA

"Honesty is an indispensable
quality of a good teacher,
but neutrality is not."

Robert Lekachman

WADSWORTH PUBLISHING COMPANY, INC.,
BELMONT, CALIFORNIA

CONTENTS

4 THE QUALITY OF AMERICAN LIFE

INTRODUCTION

This book relates to one area in the broad field of sociology—the Social Problems of contemporary America. It is designed both for the beginning student and for the literate layman who wants to know something of what is happening in his society—and has been repelled, perhaps, by the jargoned presentation in professional journals or in works that imitate them. Most textbooks in Social Problems do not systematically explore the controversies implicit in such issues as family instability, race relations, crime and delinquency, and mass culture. We believe that a book on social polemics— which juxtaposes conflicting opinions by respected and responsible experts —may prove to be a stimulating introduction to the problems of present-day American society.

The Place of Values in the Social Sciences

A recurrent question among social scientists is whether their fields *can* be sciences in the same sense as physics, zoology, or even meteorology. Some sociologists hold that their discipline is different from other sciences not in its methods of observation and analysis, but only in its subject matter. Others emphasize that since he is also a member of the society he studies, a sociologist faces methodological problems that do not concern a natural scientist, so that if sociology is a science, it is a much more difficult one than its physical or biological counterparts.

One element of this dispute concerns the proper place of values in the social sciences. By the so-called positivist position, the social sciences can and should be value-free. In the view of those we can term the humanists, values form an intrinsic and essential part of social disciplines and neither can nor should be avoided. Some have tried to find a middle ground. In the history of social thought, many leading figures (for instance, Auguste Comte, who coined both *sociology* and *positivism;* Herbert Spencer and most other Social Darwinists; Karl Marx and the several schools of Marxists) have taken partisan positions on social issues and, at the same time, have seen themselves as objective, nonpartisan observers and analysts of these same phenomena.

To this day, the many attempts to resolve the dilemma have been at best only partially successful. And the dilemma is particularly acute in the analysis of social problems, however these are defined.[1] Whatever else it is, a social problem is in part the consequence of a discrepancy between social values and the actual state of a society. One motive in studying it, moreover, is generally to search for efficient modes of prevention, control, and amelioration. How difficult it is to combine such ends with the stance of

[1]Many of the sociologists who have tried to delineate the concept "social problem" have recognized the underlying conflicts in values. This view has been expressed most consistently in a series of articles by Richard C. Fuller, in *Social Forces,* May 1937; *American Journal of Sociology,* November 1938; and, with Richard R. Myers, *American Sociological Review,* February 1941 and June 1941.

the value-free scientist can be illustrated by a recent essay by Robert Merton. With his customary intelligence, he avoids the extremes of both the positivist and the humanist schools, but his effort to find a middle position is not entirely successful. He emphasizes, on the one hand, that "the concept of social dysfunction does not harbor an implied moral judgment"; on the other hand, he warns the reader against assuming that "nothing can be done, through deliberate plan, to reduce the extent to which obsolescent institutions and disorganization work against the realization of values that men respect." In studying a social problem, the sociologist—in his capacity of sociologist—merely introduces "pertinent sociological truths"; he "neither exhorts nor denounces, advocates nor rejects."[2] Is this really the typical behavior of sociologists who analyze, say, the Catholic doctrine of birth control, or racial discrimination, or narcotics peddlers—not to say Nazi genocide? What is more, should it be?

We do not propose to offer one more attempt to reconcile positivism and a professional interest in social amelioration. We would rather suggest that sociology is large enough, heterogeneous enough, to encompass both views. One can work productively in some specialties—formal demography, for instance, or the methodology of survey analysis—without ever engaging one's social values. Social Problems, at the other extreme, defines a specialty in which the scholarly competence of the social scientist overlaps and intertwines with the practical concerns of the intellectual and of the policy-maker. In any interchange among these three types, the contribution of each is likely to be shaped by specific virtues and vices. The policy-maker's practical experience may push him toward bureaucratic caution; the intellectual's concern with basic values, toward ignoring the means of implementing them; the sociologist's skill in social analysis, toward methodological or doctrinal hair-splitting. This can be a useful partnership, thus, but decidedly less so if the sociologist may contribute nothing more than established "sociological truths"—of which, as every sociologist knows, there are precious few.

Characteristics of a Social Problem

A Clash of Views. By the definition that we prefer, social problems exist when they are so defined by the members of a society—initially, usually, by intellectuals, social scientists, or policy-makers, but eventually by at least one broad stratum of the society. Underlying each social problem, that is to say, is generally a difference of opinion, a clash of views. When Gunnar Myrdal entitled his classic work on Negro-white relations "an American dilemma," he intended to emphasize that this problem is fundamentally one of reconciling the egalitarian American creed with the Southern doctrine of white supremacy. One can describe the degradation of Negroes by documenting their lower status by such indices of discrimination as income, occupation, education, health, and neighborhood; but the plight of the Negro is defined as a social problem only because of the opposition between two value systems: white supremacy, which insists on this differentiation, and democratic liberalism, which finds the Negroes' degradation reprehensible.

[2]Robert K. Merton, "Social Problems and Sociological Theory," in Merton and Robert A. Nisbet, eds., *Contemporary Social Problems* (New York: Harcourt, Brace, 1961).

Similarly, one can document "the tragedy of waste" with a multitude of objective data, as Stuart Chase did in the book of that title; but the social problem, the "tragedy," exists only for those who believe that rational efficiency is the prime social virtue. If one maintains, with Kenneth Galbraith, that in an "affluent society" the effort to increase the gross national product is itself mistaken, then Chase's jeremiads against waste lose much of their pertinence.

Topicality. The second key characteristic of a social problem is its immediate relevance to the present scene. A look through the textbooks in the field over so short a period as the last twenty-five or thirty years would be enough to demonstrate that there is no necessary continuation in any of the subjects covered. Several decades ago poverty was the dominant theme; today it is discussed in one section of a chapter on dependency or has disappeared altogether. The quality of public education, to take another example, has been a matter of professional concern among teachers as long as there were public schools; it has become a social problem only recently.

The Essays Selected

Thus, the issues included in this book were selected because they have recently given rise to a clash of views. Sometimes the specific subjects (for example, immigration restrictions and McCarthyism) might not appear to be of current concern; but these subjects exemplify persistent problems—in these cases, a just immigration policy and the dilemmas in trying to maintain both internal security and personal liberty.

The articles are grouped into four parts, beginning with institutions of socialization, *The Family and Education;* continuing with instances of faulty socialization and the institutions set up to cope with them, *Law, Liberty, and Lawlessness;* shifting to *Ethnic Minorities,* the subcultures most strikingly involved in the study of social problems; and ending on the broadest theme, *The Quality of American Life.*

Each selection was made with the idea of presenting the best argument available, and not merely as a façade of tolerance. In choosing the articles, we have tried, and we think successfully, to hold our own views in abeyance. We have also tried to find essays that combine scholarly with literary competence; while professional argot has its place, it is not in this book.

The selections were determined by negative as well as positive criteria. Some rather obvious choices have been omitted—sometimes because they are *too* obvious; the issues of capital punishment and socialized medicine, for instance, have been debated for so many decades that contending parties now talk past each other. We have passed over polemics that are mainly of interest to professional sociologists. We have excluded all controversies that pertain mainly to political or economic policies—though in some cases the dividing line from *social* issues has had to be arbitrary. Finally, the coverage has been restricted to domestic issues, thus excluding such policy questions as foreign relations and the modernization of underdeveloped areas. These are important questions, too important to be fitted into a corner of a book that is mainly concerned with other matters.

Following the presentation of each issue are *a list of questions* designed to suggest some of the major points implicit in the selections, and thus to guide subsequent discussions; and *a list of selected readings,* which again includes good arguments for both sides of the issue. Some of the suggested readings are by writers who straddle the issue—although none of these, however excellent in other respects, have been reprinted here. Even when truth is divided between the two sides of a question, we doubt the value of beginning with an unexciting balance of every "on the one hand" with an "on the other hand." If the reader concludes that each antagonist offers a part of the truth, let him do so after he has first heard them both.

We admit to having a point of view on virtually all of the issues included, and in most cases the reader will be able to guess what it is. This does not at all mean, however, that we have a single point of view on *all* of them taken together. We do not regard ourselves as liberals or conservatives, as reactionaries or socialists. To see a social problem from the point of view of a "liberal," say, often means to concentrate on fitting the facts into this particular framework and thus to forgo analysis; and we do not believe this to be a useful exercise.

Up to the French Revolution, which can be taken as the opening of the modern political era, the history of political philosophy knows nothing of liberals and conservatives. There was a clash of principles, yes; of moral, political, and theological principles. And there was a continual clash of interests. But there was no controversy over one's relation to the historical process itself—while it is precisely this relation which is the essential quality of both liberalism and conservatism, just as it is the interpretation of this relation that sets them at odds. . . .

It is, I think, an intuitive recognition of this situation that makes so many—even of our most articulate people—unclear in their own minds as to whether they are proper "liberals" or "conservatives." This confusion is a sign of health, not of decadence; of vigor, not of lassitude.[3]

Varieties of Controversy

Controversy is of various kinds, and our issues have been selected to exemplify several types. Most obviously, there may be a patent difference in values. Is contraception, or divorce, morally legitimate? What are the goals of public education? What is the legitimate function of a court of law? In many cases, no analysis can take us further than the bare confrontation of the two points of view. Gibbons and Davis disagree on birth control, for instance, not out of a misunderstanding, or a lack of facts, or any other easily remediable circumstance. Each position is correctly deduced from divergent premises, and reconciliation would be possible only at the base.

Controversy may be over facts. How widespread was repression during the McCarthy period? Can Johnny read? The issue in such cases is often whether a social problem can be said to exist: is a deviation from the social norm merely an expression of mankind's imperfectibility, or is it a specific social malady that ought to be combatted and, if possible, corrected? More precisely, is the incidence of this deviation low or high, static or growing? A rise in unemployment, for instance, may be the consequence of greater mobility from countryside to city (an example of frictional unemployment) or of the decline of a whole industry, such as bituminous coal mining (structural unemployment). The first type is seen as an inevitable concomitant

[3]Irving Kristol, "Old Truths and the New Conservatism," *Yale Review* (1960), pp. 365–373.

of a healthily growing economy; the second, as a possible symptom of a coming depression.

Controversy may be over the effect of social deviations on the broader society. Even phenomena that the layman would define unhesitatingly as evil have been regarded as useful or "eufunctional" by at least some analysts. On balance, has organized crime been an evil or a blessing in disguise? On balance, have mass media raised or lowered the over-all cultural level? The dispute in such cases is, with a certain oversimplification, between the descendants of the muckrakers, who may understand little about social processes but know what they don't like, and the modern social theorists, who emphasize social integration and thus find a "function" for city bosses, ignorance, prostitution, and almost any other social malady.

Controversy may be over policy. Indeed, in one sense all controversy in Social Problems is over policy; for the ultimate question is always, "What, if anything, should one do about it?" For example, should federal support be extended to parochial schools? Should America's immigration laws be rewritten from a new point of view? Can we solve the problem of homosexuality by revoking the laws prohibiting it? More generally, these issues relate to a broader debate: How much can one control social behavior through formal legislation and courts?

Controversy may be, and perhaps most often has been, over causes of problems. Are stereotypes of minority groups perceptual distortions, or do they also reflect independent social and cultural differences? Is suburban life effecting an excessive cultural conformity? A full understanding of social problems often demands contrasting the several possible perceptions of the same data. Most obviously, analysts are likely to see any social ill within the particular framework of their own academic discipline. Alcoholism, for instance, has been analyzed as primarily the consequence of a physiological proclivity, of a psychological need, or of a cultural or social environment.

Controversy may be over the definition of a deviance—whether as crime, illness, or custom. If the use of narcotics, for example, is defined as the customary behavior of a minority (or allegedly, in some portions of the Orient, perhaps even a majority) of the population, then the implicit attitude is cultural relativism and the corollary policy is tolerance of the custom. If the use of narcotics is defined as illness—that is, as a symptom of either a psychic or a somatic malfunctioning—the appropriate policy is treatment. And if the same act is seen in a legal framework, as a violation of the moral norms embodied in the law, the suitable policy is punishment. This triad— custom:tolerance, illness:treatment, and crime:punishment—is a useful framework for structuring a wide variety of analyses. Thus, delinquency, ordinarily defined as illegality, has also been perceived as the prevalent custom of slum youths; and other analysts diagnose the delinquent as "sick" and prescribe one or another nostrum. Homosexuality and other sexual aberrations are seen by those who practice them as the legitimate customs of a minority; by psychologists as a type of illness (but often with an implied plea for tolerance, as well as treatment); by law-enforcement agencies as crime. How to draw the line in such cases is essentially a moral question, but at least one element in the decision is the very practical matter of whether the proposed policy works. Communities suffering from food-deficiency diseases or malaria were at one time described as lackadaisical, lazy, without ambition; these "national characteristics" are now diagnosed as symptoms of disease—correctly, because with appropriate treatment they disappear. In the area of crime, however, the rehabilitative program has had no similar record of success in "curing" deviants; perhaps its main effect thus far has been to confuse the standards of justice on which the courts of law rest. On the other hand, the attempt to redefine as crime such customary practices as, for example, the consumption of alcoholic beverages resulted in the tragic farce of Prohibition.

Most of these controversies, it must be emphasized, are based on genuine dilemmas. This is true even when the difference is over supposed facts: to echo the phrase that more research is required, though this is ordinarily valid enough, does not immediately resolve anything. Take even so simple a question as whether children learn to read more adequately with phonics or the "look-say" method. In spite of the clear operational criterion of success and by now hundreds of tests to "prove" the greater worth of one or the other method, the dispute continues, if only because the vested interests of every institution tend to be tied up with one or another set of "facts." Sometimes the truth divided between two opposed positions can be nicely split. For example, a California commission has recommended that juvenile offenders be tried in regular courts, with all of the traditional legal protections, to determine whether they are in fact guilty; and that then their cases be transferred to juvenile courts, with their social-work aides, to determine what action is appropriate for the actual offenders. The reader may want to wrestle with other problems, to see whether even in the abstract he can work out such neat compromises. In most cases he will fail; for the controversies exist, and are recorded here, precisely because as yet no such easy answer has been found.

In summary, we have chosen those issues that we consider important and interesting, and therefore worth discussing. These are mostly those that everyone else finds important and interesting, and therefore worth discussing. We have not tried to be original in this respect. Nothing is required to read this book beyond an interest in one's own society, and we hope that interest will be enriched.

A Caveat

Because the selections are mainly restricted to contemporary domestic problems, they cannot ordinarily provide an adequate historical or cross-cultural perspective. In a book or a course that focuses on contemporary American problems, the accomplishments and progress in the United States are by the nature of the endeavor neglected or omitted.

A country with the political stability and industrial development of the United States suffers from no insurmountable weaknesses or crucial malfunctionings. Law and order are challenged by criminals and by extremists, but there is hardly any threat of mob rule or revolution. Adolescents oppose their parents, perhaps more, perhaps less, than they used to; but the essential continuity of the culture is assured. "Mass culture," it is alleged, is overwhelming artistic creativity, but the minimum communication necessary for even a complex urban-industrial society is not endangered. Within its own borders—and thus excluding the dual threat of Communist expansion and atomic war—this country can meet any non-utopian demand on its technical equipment, its institutions, its cultural heritage. The most important question involved is not typically whether the demand can be satisfied but whether it should be, and if so by whom, and at whose expense.

Indeed, the achievements of the United States, whether in economic development or in political and social democracy, are so great that both Communist regimes and underdeveloped countries use them as their guide to future successes. Thus, a book about America's social problems, passing over all of its positive features, must convey an impression of bias. A fully adequate discussion of Negro-white relations in the United States, for example, would include a comparison with, say, the caste system in India, the russified ethnic minorities in the Soviet Union, and apartheid in the Union of South Africa. With such contrasts it would become clear that America's social problems are often of a different type—the struggle to realize civil rights rather than their absence, "mass culture" rather than mass illiteracy, organized gambling rather than banditry and highwaymen.

It would be useful, if space permitted, to furnish not only a cross-cultural but also a time perspective. Sociologists as a group are notoriously ahistorical, but never so much so, perhaps, as when they are analyzing a society's problems. No matter what the specific subject, the current social malady is often (though not typically in the essays we have included) put against an idyllic backdrop of an untroubled pre-industrial community. To idealize the romantic past, the simple rustic, the noble savage, is of course a common mood not only in the social sciences but in literature and politics as well. It should not be surprising that analysts of social problems, concentrating as they do on present faults, should often take deterioration for granted. Unless we insist on a historical context, matters that no longer vex us disappear from view. In the middle of the twentieth century, we see the problem of the aged rather than infant mortality, of overeating and heart disease rather than malnutrition and pellagra, of traffic congestion rather than provincial isolation, and so on.

Some social ills have persisted over a considerable period, of course; but the record of such continuity, particularly the statistical record, is often misleading. Nothing changes so fast in a society undergoing modernization as the various measuring rods by which its effects are gauged. The lawless frontier had no crime statistics and therefore, if one measures lawlessness statistically, no crime.[4] Similarly, divorces went unrecorded during most of the nineteenth century and in any case were uncommon; for in the still loosely integrated federation of states it was simpler to abandon one wife and, somewhere in the untrammeled West, to marry another. Or, as another example, statistics suggest that with the spread of hectic modern life there has been a consequent sharp increase in mental illness. But when the members of one rural community were examined, there was uncovered a high incidence of undiagnosed, unrecorded, and of course untreated mental illnesses of various kinds.[5] Only one study has extended over a long enough period really to measure the effect of urbanization on mental illness; according to its findings, apart from the increased number of old persons and thus

[4]For an interesting commentary, see Daniel Bell, "The Myth of Crime Waves," in *The End of Ideology* (Glencoe, Ill.: Free Press, 1960), ch. 8.
[5]Joseph W. Eaton and Robert J. Weil, *Culture and Mental Disorders: A Comparative Study of the Hutterites and Other Populations* (Glencoe, Ill.: Free Press, 1955).

of senile disturbances, the whole of the past century has seen no rise in the age-specific rates of first admissions to mental institutions.[6]

In this caveat we have suggested that a native American looking at his own country is likely to see social problems out of their context. As a corrective to this tendency, we have appended an article by the anthropologist Horace Miner. Paradoxically, a trained observer can see more of an alien culture than can its own members. The student of social problems would do well to ponder the implications of Miner's analysis.

[6]Herbert Goldhamer and Andrew W. Marshall, *Psychosis and Civilization* (Glencoe, Ill.: Free Press, 1949).

BODY RITUAL AMONG THE NACIREMA

Horace Miner

The anthropologist has become so familiar with the diversity of ways in which different peoples behave in similar situations that he is not apt to be surprised by even the most exotic customs. In fact, if all of the logically possible combinations of behavior have not been found somewhere in the world, he is apt to suspect that they must be present in some yet undescribed tribe. This point has, in fact, been expressed with respect to clan organization by Murdock.[1] In this light, the magical beliefs and practices of the Nacirema present such unusual aspects that it seems desirable to describe them as an example of the extremes to which human behavior can go.

Professor Linton first brought the ritual of the Nacirema to the attention of anthropologists twenty years ago,[2] but the culture of this people is still very poorly understood. They are a North American group living in the territory between the Canadian Cree, the Yaqui and Tarahumare of Mexico, and the Carib and Arawak of the Antilles. Little is known of their origin, although tradition states that they came from the east. According to Nacirema mythology, their nation was originated by a culture hero, Notgnihsaw, who is otherwise known for two great feats of strength—the throwing of a piece of wampum across the river Pa-To-Mac and the chopping down of a cherry tree in which the Spirit of Truth resided.

Nacirema culture is characterized by a highly developed market economy which has evolved in a rich natural habitat. While much of the people's time is devoted to economic pursuits, a large part of the fruits of these labors and

Reprinted from Horace Miner, "Body Ritual Among the Nacirema," *American Anthropologist*, 58:3 (June 1956), 503–507, by permission of the author and the publisher. Horace Miner is a professor of anthropology and sociology at the University of Michigan and the author of articles on comparative social structure and social change.

[1]George P. Murdock, *Social Structure* (New York: Macmillan, 1949), p. 74.
[2]Ralph Linton, *The Study of Man* (New York: Appleton-Century, 1936), p. 326.

a considerable portion of the day are spent in ritual activity. The focus of this activity is the human body, the appearance and health of which loom as a dominant concern in the ethos of the people. While such a concern is certainly not unusual, its ceremonial aspects and associated philosophy are unique.

The fundamental belief underlying the whole system appears to be that the human body is ugly and that its natural tendency is to debility and disease. Incarcerated in such a body, man's only hope is to avert these characteristics through the use of the powerful influences of ritual and ceremony. Every household has one or more shrines devoted to this purpose. The more powerful individuals in the society have several shrines in their houses and, in fact, the opulence of a house is often referred to in terms of the number of such ritual centers it possesses. Most houses are of wattle and daub construction, but the shrine rooms of the more wealthy are walled with stone. Poorer families imitate the rich by applying pottery plaques to their shrine walls.

While each family has at least one such shrine, the rituals associated with it are not family ceremonies but are private and secret. The rites are normally discussed only with children, and then only during the period when they are being initiated into these mysteries. I was able, however, to establish sufficient rapport with the natives to examine these shrines and to have the rituals described to me.

The focal point of the shrine is a box or chest which is built into the wall. In this chest are kept the many charms and magical potions without which no native believes he could live. These preparations are secured from a variety of specialized practitioners. The most powerful of these are the medicine men, whose assistance must be rewarded with substantial gifts. However, the medicine men do not provide the curative potions for their clients, but decide what the ingredients should be and then write them down in an ancient and secret language. This writing is understood only by the medicine men and by the herbalists who, for another gift, provide the required charm.

The charm is not disposed of after it has served its purpose, but is placed in the charm-box of the household shrine. As these magical materials are specific for certain ills, and the real or imagined maladies of the people are many, the charm-box is usually full to overflowing. The magical packets are so numerous that people forget what their purposes were and fear to use them again. While the natives are very vague on this point, we can only assume that the idea in retaining all the old magical materials is that their presence in the charm-box, before which the body rituals are conducted, will in some way protect the worshipper.

Beneath the charm-box is a small font. Each day every member of the family, in succession, enters the shrine room, bows his head before the charm-box, mingles different sorts of holy water in the font, and proceeds with a brief rite of ablution. The holy waters are secured from the Water Temple of the community, where the priests conduct elaborate ceremonies to make the liquid ritually pure.

In the hierarchy of magical practitioners, and below the medicine men in prestige, are specialists whose designation is best translated "holy-mouth-men." The Nacirema have an almost pathological horror of and fascination with the mouth, the condition of which is believed to have a supernatural influence on all social relationships. Were it not for the rituals of the mouth, they believe that their teeth would fall out, their gums bleed, their jaws shrink, their friends desert them, and their lovers reject them. They also believe that a strong relationship exists between oral and moral characteristics. For example, there is a ritual ablution of the mouth for children which is supposed to improve their moral fiber.

The daily body ritual performed by everyone includes a mouth-rite. Despite the fact that these people are so punctilious about care of the mouth, this rite involves a practice which strikes the uninitiated stranger as revolting. It was reported to me that the ritual consists of inserting a small bundle of hog hairs into the mouth, along with certain magical powders, and then moving the bundle in a highly formalized series of gestures.

In addition to the private mouth-rite, the people seek out a holy-mouth-man once or twice a year. These practitioners have an impressive set of paraphernalia, consisting of a variety of augers, awls, probes, and prods. The use of these objects in the exorcism of the evils of the mouth involves almost unbelievable ritual torture of the client. The holy-mouth-man opens the client's mouth and, using the above-mentioned tools, enlarges any holes which decay may have created in the teeth. Magical materials are put into these holes. If there are no naturally occurring holes in the teeth, large sections of one or more teeth are gouged out so that the supernatural substance can be applied. In the client's view, the purpose of these ministrations is to arrest decay and to draw friends. The extremely sacred and traditional character of the rite is evident in the fact that the natives return to the holy-mouth-men year after year, despite the fact that their teeth continue to decay.

It is to be hoped that, when a thorough study of the Nacirema is made, there will be careful inquiry into the personality structure of these people. One has but to watch the gleam in the eye of a holy-mouth-man, as he jabs an awl into an exposed nerve, to suspect that a certain amount of sadism is involved. If this can be established, a very interesting pattern emerges, for most of the population shows definite masochistic tendencies. It was to these that Professor Linton referred in discussing a distinctive part of the daily body ritual which is performed only by men. This part of the rite involves scraping and lacerating the surface of the face with a sharp instrument. Special women's rites are performed only four times during each lunar month, but what they lack in frequency is made up in barbarity. As part of this ceremony women bake their heads in small ovens for about an hour. The theoretically interesting point is that what seems to be a preponderantly masochistic people have developed sadistic specialists.

The medicine men have an imposing temple, or *latipso,* in every community of any size. The more elaborate ceremonies required to treat very sick patients can only be performed at this temple. These ceremonies involve not only the thaumaturge but a permanent group of vestal maidens who move sedately about the temple chambers in distinctive costume and headdress.

The *latipso* ceremonies are so harsh that it is phenomenal that a fair proportion of the really sick natives who enter the temple ever recover. Small children whose indoctrination is still incomplete have been known to resist attempts to take them to the temple because "that is where you go to die." Despite this fact, sick adults are not only willing but eager to undergo the protracted ritual purification, if they can afford to do so. No matter how ill the supplicant or how grave the emergency, the guardians of many temples will not admit a client if he cannot give a rich gift to the custodian. Even after one has gained admission and survived the ceremonies, the guardians will not permit the neophyte to leave until he makes still another gift.

The supplicant entering the temple is first stripped of all his or her clothes. In everyday life the Nacirema avoids exposure of his body and its natural functions. Bathing and excretory acts are performed only in the secrecy of the household shrine, where they are ritualized as part of the body-rites. Psychological shock results from the fact that body secrecy is suddenly lost upon entry into the *latipso*. A man, whose own wife has never seen him in an excretory act, suddenly finds himself naked and assisted by a vestal maiden while he performs his natural functions into a sacred vessel. This sort of ceremonial treatment is necessitated by the fact that the excreta are used by a diviner to ascertain the course and nature of the client's sickness. Female clients, on the other hand, find their naked bodies are subjected to the scrutiny, manipulation, and prodding of the medicine men.

Few supplicants in the temple are well enough to do anything but lie on their hard beds. The daily ceremonies, like the rites of the holy-mouth-men, involve discomfort and torture. With ritual precision, the vestals awaken their miserable charges each dawn and roll them about on their beds of pain while performing ablutions, in the formal movements of which the maidens are highly trained. At other times they insert magic wands in the supplicant's mouth or force him to eat substances which are supposed to be healing. From time to time the medicine men come to their clients and jab magically treated needles into their flesh. The fact that these temple ceremonies may not cure, and may even kill the neophyte, in no way decreases the people's faith in the medicine men.

There remains one other kind of practitioner, known as a "listener." This witch-doctor has the power to exorcise the devils that lodge in the heads of people who have been bewitched. The Nacirema believe that parents bewitch their own children. Mothers are particularly suspected of putting a curse on children while teaching them the secret body rituals. The counter-magic of the witch-doctor is unusual in its lack of ritual. The patient simply tells the "listener" all his troubles and fears, beginning with the earliest difficulties he can remember. The memory displayed by the Nacirema in these exorcism sessions is truly remarkable. It is not uncommon for the patient to bemoan the rejection he felt upon being weaned as a babe, and a few individuals even see their troubles going back to the traumatic effects of their own birth.

In conclusion, mention must be made of certain practices which have their base in native esthetics but which depend upon the pervasive aversion to the natural body and its functions. There are ritual fasts to make fat people thin and ceremonial feasts to make thin people fat. Still other rites are used to make women's breasts larger if they are small, and smaller if they are large. General dissatisfaction with breast shape is symbolized in the fact that the ideal form is virtually outside the range of human variation. A few women afflicted with almost inhuman hypermammary development are so idolized that they make a handsome living by simply going from village to village and permitting the natives to stare at them for a fee.

Reference has already been made to the fact that excretory functions are ritualized, routinized, and relegated to secrecy. Natural reproductive functions are similarly distorted. Intercourse is taboo as a topic and scheduled as an act. Efforts are made to avoid pregnancy by the use of magical materials or by limiting intercourse to certain phases of the moon. Conception is actually very infrequent. When pregnant, women dress so as to hide their condition. Parturition takes place in secret, without friends or relatives to assist, and the majority of women do not nurse their infants.

Our review of the ritual life of the Nacirema has certainly shown them to be a magic-ridden people. It is hard to understand how they have managed to exist so long under the burdens which they have imposed upon themselves.

1

THE FAMILY
AND EDUCATION

IS THE USE OF CONTRACEPTIVES
MORALLY LEGITIMATE?

The population of the world, about 500 million in 1650, grew to about 2,500 million in 1950—or by five times over the three centuries. According to a United Nations estimate, "a world population of between 6,000 and 7,000 million by the end of the century should now be expected almost as a matter of certainty,"[1] unless the conditions favoring growth change radically. These conditions are, simply put, two: (1) the incredibly rapid decline in mortality in underdeveloped areas, and (2) the persistence there of the high fertility that once, when perhaps half of those born died before reaching maturity, had been necessary to maintain the population. Attempts to modernize underdeveloped economies, and thus to raise the people's living conditions, have been seriously impeded by the rapid procreation of new mouths to feed. In the long run—and it is not now so very long—something must give: either the birth rate must come down, or the death rate will be increased by mass famines and epidemics. This is a moral dilemma of literally global relevance.

It *is* a dilemma because in any society fertility and mortality are likely to decline at different rates. All peoples accept a longer life span when it becomes available to them, but the established patterns of procreation are generally protected against change by ethical norms and strong sanctions. After efficient means of contraception were developed, their diffusion was blocked by ignorance (reinforced by illiteracy) and hostility (reinforced by traditionalism). In the West, Roman Catholicism represents the main exponent of the view that the control of births by the most efficient means available is morally impermissible. This prohibition, at least in the United States, is no longer observed by all Catholics. According to a survey of a nationwide sample, 30 per cent of married Catholic women, or their husbands, use methods of birth control condemned by the Church; and among couples not troubled by sterility and married ten years or more, the proportion is half.[2] The effect of any church's dicta on its communicants, it is true, is not a public issue in a pluralist society like ours. What makes it of public concern is the fact that, in areas that it deems to be morally crucial, the Catholic Church tries to shape legislation, foreign-aid programs, and other general social controls to its specific concept of the good.

Father Gibbons is one of the best spokesmen in the United States for the Catholic position on birth control.[3] Opposition to this position is often

---

[1] United Nations, Department of Economic and Social Affairs, *The Future Growth of World Population* (New York, 1958), Population Studies, No. 28, p. 20.

[2] Ronald Freedman, Pascal K. Whelpton, and Arthur A. Campbell, *Family Planning, Sterility, and Population Growth* (New York: McGraw-Hill, 1959), pp. 182–183.

[3] He is the author of considerably longer and more detailed arguments on this matter than the selection included here. See, for example, his "Fertility Control in the Light of Some Recent Catholic Statements," *Eugenics Quarterly*, 3:1 (March 1956), 9–15; 3:2 (June 1956), 82–87.

secularist, based on generalized Western humanitarianism or on a scientist's attempt to avoid all value judgments; and this point of view is represented by Professor Davis's short statement. It is important to note, however, that most Protestant churches have abandoned their earlier antagonism to birth control, and now not only accept it but also advocate it as a morally necessary element of a world with efficient death control. The statement by the United Church of Christ (formed in 1957 by the merger of the Congregational Christian Churches and the Evangelical and Reformed Church) is typical of present-day American Protestant opinion.

THE CATHOLIC VALUE SYSTEM AND HUMAN FERTILITY

William J. Gibbons, S.J.

In a philosophy of life which accords with Catholic thinking, human fertility is not a factor to be isolated from other values. If for purposes of scientific study we consider it apart, this is presumably with the remembrance that man is a unity whose various functions and capacities are ordered by nature to a single end—achievement of beautitude in the life to come. Such is the philosophical and ethical premise from which the Catholic proceeds in his study of fertility. It is a premise shared in substance, if not in every conclusion deducible from it, by all who affirm a rational basis for human conduct. That includes many ethicians of all ages, non-Christian as well as Christian. Such an approach is at once alien to sentimental, positivistic, materialistic interpretations of human behavior.

When making value judgments and determining conduct norms about human reproduction, the Catholic moral thinker emphasizes especially the rational. He knows that nowhere more than in the area of sex is it easier to obscure the reasoning process through undue attention to passion and emotion. Nevertheless in reaching specific conclusions as to the propriety of given conduct, he does not confine himself to deductive reasonings about man's nature, but also takes into account human behavior in a concrete environment. This is not to say that the Catholic ethician or moralist draws rules of behavior from what *is,* but rather that, in principle if not always in practice, he takes into consideration the findings of the natural and social sciences when determining what *ought* to be.

Sound Catholic thought recognizes that if moral science has its own terms of reference and formal object, so too do the social sciences in their various ramifications. No good purpose is served when the moralist over-

Adapted by the author from William J. Gibbons, S.J., "The Catholic Value System in Relation to Human Fertility," in George F. Mair, ed., *Studies in Population* (Princeton: Princeton University Press, 1949), pp. 108–129. Copyright 1949 Princeton University Press. Reprinted by permission of the author and the publisher. Father Gibbons is adjunct assistant professor of sociology at Fordham University and the author of articles on social issues.

steps the bounds of his science and draws inferences as to what *is* from his own conclusions about man's moral obligations in the abstract. Neither is the cause of truth advanced when the student of the social sciences departs from his field of investigations to lay down rules of conduct based primarily or exclusively upon what some men do or wish to do.

By keeping in mind the delimitations of their respective sciences, the moralist and social scientist can get along together. Furthermore, inasmuch as the subject of their study is the same, namely man, they can cooperate in aiding modern men to adapt themselves to their environment, and also modify it in such a way that man's purpose on earth is more readily achieved.

If such mutual understanding and cooperation is objectively possible, how does it come to pass that in certain conclusions concerning the complex of values surrounding human reproduction, the practicing Catholic on occasion finds himself at odds with many manifestly sincere persons who also base their ethical behavior upon a rational foundation? A partial answer may be drawn from what was already said concerning occasional confusions about the limits of the moral and social sciences. But the major explanation for the disagreement, it would appear, must be sought in the Catholic concept of the Church's teaching authority. That authority is not taken as a denial of reason but as its complement and safeguard. The Catholic moralist and social philosopher each approaches his field with the conviction that the Church, by reason of the divine guidance accorded it, is in a position to make definitive decisions regarding questions of human values and moral conduct. These decisions are not arbitrary. Nor are they mere practical norms of behavior consequent to current ecclesiastical policy as it adjusts itself to the contemporary scene. Rather, definitive pronouncements on disputed moral points are conceived as the necessary and supernaturally provided adjuncts to the rules of ethical conduct derived from reason.

Acceptance of these definitive rules, which are at times admittedly irksome to man, is regarded by the Catholic Church as obligatory in conscience, just as much as are the primary dictates of the natural law imprinted on the minds of men. This conclusion derives in turn from the belief that Christ, the Divine Teacher, not only laid down certain explicit rules of conduct Himself, but also left behind a permanent teaching body which would be safeguarded from error when removing authoritatively doubts on specific points of human behavior. Sometimes these moral imperatives accepted by the Catholic conscience are quite explicit. At other times they are clearly deducible from some other definitive pronouncement on doctrine or morals.

Failure to distinguish clearly between the absolute norms of conduct, authoritatively laid down, and the adaptable disciplinary rules of the Church is responsible at times for a feeling among those not of the Catholic faith that sooner or later some adjustment will be made on basic teaching regarding sex, marriage and the family. The fact is that while fuller implications behind certain doctrinal truths are constantly being discovered, the essentials of Catholic belief remain unchanged. The Church never reverses herself on authoritative moral positions any more than she does in the case of doctrine. Individual members do indeed fall short of the ideal, and even cease practicing their religion, but the teaching Church does not therefore modify the body of truth she is assigned to guard.

This, be it noted, is a reasoned position springing from the firm conviction that the Church's authority is not of human origin. Hence the Church, in making moral pronouncements, is not authoritarian, much less totalitarian, in the manner that manmade governments are when they usurp unwarranted authority over the consciences of men. There is a higher law to which even the supreme rulers of the Church must themselves submit. Human beings take justifiable pride in subjecting their conduct to reason, especially in the face of conflicting emotions. In the same light, the Catholic regards his own submission to the teaching Church in its authoritative pronouncements, even though the nonrational part of his nature prompts otherwise. He believes that the pope or a universal council does not make truth, much less modify it at will, but rather clarifies what already is true.

To return more specifically to the position of the Church on human fertility. Man, though composed of body and soul and endowed with a multiplicity of capacities, is a unity. With the animals he shares sense faculties and impulses. Unlike the animals, he is also possessed of a spiritual soul, created by God for eternal existence in heaven. Rational by nature, this composite creature man is capable of regulating his impulses and instincts according to the rules of an objective order, of which his reason becomes progressively aware. He does not create this order out of his mind, which is, unfortunately, at times beclouded by emotion and confused or prejudiced in its approach to moral truth.

Rather, man, in studying the universe about him and in sounding the inner mysteries of his own person, comes to see that God the Creator has endowed man with a nature which must find its perfection in a particular way. This it does through the exercise of intelligence and within the framework of an objective scheme of things which transcends the whim and desire of the individual person. Man, the reasoning animal, recognizes that he has no logical alternative but to embrace and follow the rules of conduct which his nature and the order of creation dictate. To do otherwise, as well he may because of the freedom of choice wherewith he is endowed, is to distort the role assigned him and to risk his eternal salvation. Accordingly, strictly human acts, as distinguished from involuntary responses on the sense level, are always in the concrete moral or immoral. Without morality, man would not be man.

To cite enlightened reason as the guiding norm of moral conduct, is not to deny that the sense and rational levels of man's being can, at any given moment, be oriented in different directions. But in the event of conflict, reason is supposed to win out. Obedience to the rule of reason and to an enlightened conscience may sometimes occasion suffering, even death itself. But sacrifice is integral to man's existence in this world. The need for such sacrifice, men are accustomed to recognize in many departments of life, not excluding the duty of surrendering one's life in defense of the fatherland. There is no law of personal development or of self-expression which negates the moral law, with its individual and social responsibilities. Self-conquest, discipline, the practice of moral restraint are, in the nature of things, the concomitants of a moral life. Nowhere is this more true than in the ordering of sex, a dominant passion of the average man.

Now it should be clear to everyone who understands the physiology of the sexual organs of man, and the psychic reactions connected with them, that these are by nature ordered to one end, namely human reproduction.

The fact that the urge to use these faculties is more or less persistent in the normal person in no way leads to the conclusion that their use can go unregulated by reason. Self-restraint may be difficult, but it is not impossible. The reproductive urge is, of course, so strong in the human race that in the normal course of events the vast majority of men marry. Thus the human species is continued, and the divine directive, "Increase and multiply," is carried out.

Such a development leaves room for a number of individuals to renounce marriage and the legitimate satisfaction of the reproductive urge. The duty to reproduce is incumbent upon the race; not upon every single individual in it. Even though some individuals avail themselves of their freedom not to marry, they can do so with good conscience knowing that relatively few will follow their example. Accordingly, perpetual continence is morally permissible, and may for specific individuals be the better course, when embraced for a good motive or through necessity, without danger to virtue. Perfect chastity, or virginity, Christian tradition teaches, is in itself preferable to marriage, when chosen for appropriate reasons.

Even in marriage itself, temporary continence, for spiritual reasons of penance, self-restraint or dedication to a higher work, is legitimate and praiseworthy, provided the rights of neither party are disregarded. Moreover, in Catholic annals there are recorded marriages of saintly persons who observed perpetual continence by mutual agreement. Whether in all cases this was praiseworthy objectively might perhaps be questioned in cases where offspring were desirable because of serious social considerations. Attention is called here to the moral legitimacy of such continence, to forestall any suspicion that in the case of married persons Catholicism correlates sanctity with the number of children born. At times confusion arises in the minds of some regarding this point, so that the Catholic moral and ascetical tradition may be in part overlooked.

The reproductive function in man is directed toward the family, which is the only institution adapted to the proper care and education of children brought into the world by reason of human fertility. With most of mankind, Catholicism regards the family as a basic unit of society, whose sanctity must be respected under penalty of grave social ills. The begetting and rearing of children is one of the most responsible tasks man could undertake. It is also a sacred task, for not only are the parents cooperating with God in the production of human life; they are also the occasion of God's creating another soul destined for eternal life.

Abuse of sex in any manner whatsoever is considered within the Catholic framework of values as sinful, an offense against the law of nature and of God. The pleasures associated with the use of sex are, as it were, a stimulus and a reward for willingness to accept the responsibilities which are the consequent of human reproduction. To voluntarily seek or accept such pleasures in a manner which excludes by positive action the primary end of marriage is seriously sinful and places man in an inimical relationship to God so long as he remains in an unrepentant state. Catholic moral thinking says in effect that just as man may not violate the law of self-preservation by willfully destroying his health or life, so neither may he make arbitrary use of the reproductive capacity God has given him.

This emphasis upon the primary end of marriage, and upon the relationship of sexual activity to reproduction, is not intended as a denial of other legitimate ends of marriage. Mutual aid and the quieting of concupiscence, to use the traditional terminology, are recognized objectives of married life. These secondary purposes are in fact predominant in the minds of most persons entering upon marriage. Such an orientation need not conflict with sound ethical norms, so long as it implies no positive exclusion of the fundamental reason for marriage as an institution.

Those persons who, throughout the centuries, have regarded marital intercourse for motives other than reproduction as something unlawful, or at least improper, inadequately understand the nature of marriage. The fostering of mutual love, the rendering of the marriage debt, the avoidance of unchastity, are reasonable motives for intercourse and for cohabitation under a common roof. What Catholic moral teaching objects to is not these elements of mutuality or the expression of love and personality, but rather the subversion of the ends of marriage in such wise that the secondary ends become primary, and the primary end is negated in principle or positively excluded in practice.

As a value system, Catholicism endeavors to impress upon men the truth that perfect happiness comes only with the attainment of eternal salvation. Man's temporal life is a testing ground, wherein success is determined on the basis of the individual's readiness to conform to the divine plan. This plan does not forbid what is good for man, but only puts moral restraint upon him to avoid what runs contrary to his nature and destiny. By stressing these truths, Catholic teaching proves itself the convinced defender of human liberty and the opponent of any effort to reduce the human person to the nonrational level, on which impulse would be the internal driving power, and physical force the only ultimate means of external control.

That the mastery of sex is difficult, Catholic teaching fully recognizes. Approaching the matter theologically, it can be said that had Adam and Eve, the first human pair, been obedient to God, they and their children would have continued in the state of original justice. That state, characteristically identified with the possession of the supernatural gift of sanctifying grace, also carried with it certain other gifts, among which integrity is always listed by the theologians. Put briefly, possessed of integrity in the theological sense, man would have been able to regulate his passions without the conflict of tendencies now experienced. Unclouded reason would have ruled, so that present difficulties in keeping the use of sex on a rational level could have been avoided. God, in redeeming fallen man, did not see fit to restore the gift of integrity. But He did assure sufficient grace necessary to keep the moral law; it is up to man to accept it. Difficult as is the observance of chastity, even at times within the married state, it is not beyond man's capacities, provided he avails himself of the sources of grace God has opened up to him.

In the hierarchy of values accepted by the Catholic Church, chastity is regarded as a safeguard of the family. Jacques Leclercq, the French Catholic ethician, has ably summed up the relationship between chastity, continence and married life. He writes:

We speak of chastity and continence. Chastity is the virtue whereby a person brings and keeps the sex instinct under the control of reason. Continence implies chastity, but chastity can exist without continence. In married life, conjugal chastity calls at times for continence and at times merely for moderation.[1]

Thus Leclercq draws attention to the now evident sociological fact that men will progressively lose esteem for sound family life when they have no hesitation in gratifying sexual impulses apart from marriage. Also implied is the further truth, recognized by many psychiatrists and sociologists, that the conceiving of marriage solely as an opportunity for sexual gratification cuts the very foundation from beneath family stability.

Prior to marriage, youth are morally bound to chastity and continence, which not a few, aided by grace, accept with a high degree of spiritual motivation. Nor is this period of premarital chastity a bad thing, even from the psychological and sociological viewpoint. Early marriages are not the unmixed blessing their advocates sometimes make them out to be, nor are they any substitute for the disciplined practice of chastity in youth. Man is made in such a way that the reproductive capacity and urge are present before the emotional and intellectual maturity desirable for responsible family life has been arrived at. If the voluntary acceptance of perfect and perpetual chastity for spiritual reasons implies a degree of virtue of relatively rare occurrence, it does not therefore follow that the observance of chaste continence when circumstances require it is beyond man's moral capacities or harmful to him physically and psychologically.

"The primary end of marriage is the procreation and education of children; the secondary end, mutual comfort and the remedy of concupiscence."[2] That is the reason for the generative organs in man, and the moral justification of marriage as a state of life. Nevertheless, Catholic teaching, properly understood, does not encourage the exercise of the reproductive function in marriage without any regard for how the children born will be brought up. Fully aware of how readily many persons would turn to illegitimate sexual gratification were too many obstacles placed in the way, the Church normally shows herself more disposed to facilitate marriage than to set up barriers. But this does not mean she approves imprudent fertility. Catholicism would be going against the basic ethical principle of subjecting passion to reason were it to praise, for example, the shortsighted abandon of those who regard marriage as a legitimized opportunity for unrestrained sexual gratification. Unfortunately the careless language of some popular writers at times conveys the wrong impression. Both chastity and continence have their place, even within the married state. Nor is the practice of the two unconnected psychologically.

If Christian principles urge chastity and restraint, and hold up virginity as an ideal, that implies no condemnation of marriage. God's creation of a helpmate for Adam and His treatment of the first human pair indicate differently. In the New Testament, Christ raised marriage to the dignity of a sacrament. Thus is the marriage contract of the baptized blessed and made a medium of grace, both at the time of the marriage and in the difficult years that follow.

The sacramental character of marriage is not intended as a cloak for something evil. Catholic belief does not regard concupiscence as sinful, unless

---

[1] Jacques Leclercq, *Marriage and the Family: A Study in Social Philosophy* (New York: Pustet, 1945), p. 98.
[2] Code of Canon Law, Canon 1013, No. 1.

occasioned or yielded to sinfully. Nor does it conceive of intercourse and fertility as sinful. Not the use of marriage but its abuse is wrong. Hence, the married state is in itself something good, and the normal vocation for the great majority of men. It is, however, important that in entering into marriage man recognize the true character of the contract. Not man but God has made the rules which govern it. Adherence to these rules, which is impossible without the practice of chastity, is the safeguard of marriage as an institution.

Before discussing Catholic thinking on human fertility in relation to world population trends, it is desirable to clarify the Church's position on several points which sometimes occasion misunderstanding. The Catholic value system, not only as related to marriage but also to human personality, includes very definite attitudes toward sterilization and birth control.

Direct sterilization, whether for eugenic or simple birth-control purposes, is clearly outside the moral pale so far as Catholics are concerned. This does not imply a desire to see individuals who lack aptitude or discretion bring children into the world without regard for ability to care for them. Among the moral imperatives Catholicism enunciates is that the welfare of the children must be taken into consideration when making use of marriage. But if individuals entering marriage have a heavy moral responsibility in this regard, it still remains true that the physical as well as the spiritual integrity of the human person must be held sacred. The Catholic Church conceives of direct sterilization as an unwarranted attack upon the dignity of the human person. It is in this light that the question of sterilization should be reviewed.

Catholic thinking has always recognized the lawfulness of surgical operations which might deprive the individual of some organ or limb, but which are necessary for preservation of life or proper health. Consequently, there has been no serious question among Catholic moralists about the legitimacy of operations which might result indirectly in sterilization. In specific cases, moralists may question the legitimacy of given techniques because there is doubt about the necessity of the operation or the intention of surgeon or patient. Doctors as a rule tend to play safe, and on occasion go beyond the limits of their science by counselling operations of this sort primarily to avoid what they at times refer to as "complicating pregnancies." Moralists, on the other hand, insist rightly that in a matter of such moment as preserving the integrity of the generative organs, need for an operation resulting in sterility should not be assumed lightly. However, in the present discussion it is neither possible nor necessary to examine in detail the delicate questions of medical ethics.

The problem before us is not indirect sterilization, but rather what is referred to as *direct*. In times past this was often referred to as eugenic sterilization and was advocated for purposes of preventing reproduction by the mentally deficient or the criminally insane. Not infrequently advocates of this sort of sterilization, in urging that it be sanctioned legally and practiced on governmental authority, proved overzealous in their cause. They put forward exaggerated claims as to the extent of mental deficiency and then retreated into doubtful positions by confusing the respective roles of heredity and environment. But there have been other advocates of sterilization who recognized the danger inherent in having so much power over the human person in the hands of public officials, and sought to safeguard the individual by elaborate legislative precautions.

It would be unfair to call into question the sincerity of all proponents of legal sterilization. Many, no doubt, had and still have the interests of society at heart. What they tend to overlook, however, is the essentially moral nature of the question. Not every means of solving social problems is necessarily legitimate, or morally permissible. The full range of human and social values must always be taken into consideration. We are faced again in this instance with the necessity of avoiding an isolated approach to sex or the reproductive function.

Speaking sociologically, widespread recourse to direct sterilization would endanger the individual's right to bodily integrity. It might easily lead to conflicting policies in regard to population, which would resemble too closely those of the Nazis. The German National Socialists presented the spectacle of encouraging sterilization of the so-called unfit while at the same time making quite acceptable the practice of childbearing outside of wedlock. Similar contradictions in social policy can usually be found among those who make a biological rather than a moral approach to the question of human fertility. Social consideration must never be overlooked, least of all by the moralist, but when conflict occurs, Catholic social philosophy insists what is socially expedient must be determined within the framework of definite moral principles.

In seeking, therefore, a solution to problems of economic hardship, population pressure or eugenics, Catholics do not think in terms of sterilization. This does not mean that Catholic social thought overlooks the existence of these problems, but rather that it circumscribes the area in which morally acceptable remedies may be sought. The traditional attitude of the Church toward fertility and the birth rate is primarily a positive and constructive one. In line with Christian thought, children are welcomed because they are new souls destined for eternal life. Leclercq, in his *Marriage and the Family,* puts it thus: "To bring a child into the world under conditions favorable to his development as a human being is one of the greatest works that man can perform. It constitutes the glory of marriage."[3]

The blessing of a fertility conformable to reason is such that, had mankind remained in its original state of innocence, from which excess and lust were absent, virginity and celibacy would have been judged differently than they are today. Their special value in the fallen state of man derives largely from the fact that they help bring passion under the control of reason, and aid the mind in attending to higher things.

Human fertility, since man is a creature of reason and not mere instinct, must be a reasonable fertility. Multiplication of children, as a result of license, or over-indulgence, or improvidence, implies varying degrees of moral guilt, depending on the extent to which the individual is personally responsible, and the relationship which exists between his own unrestrained sexual gratification and the future welfare of the children. The fertility that Christian tradition exalts is, therefore, rational fertility, not, as is sometimes thought, mere multiplication of offspring in itself.

It is to be feared that, on occasion, excessive concentration on the negative side of sex, and on the moral strictures which delimit its use, leads to

[3]Leclercq, *op. cit.,* p. 210.

false or deceptive conclusions. This inadequate approach, which tends to overlook the Church's positive teaching on human reproduction, is not confined to those social scientists who ignore the full range of Christian values; it also extends to some Catholics who become excessively preoccupied with the moral prohibitions their Church makes known to them.

Something needs to be said at this point about the Church's position on artificial birth control. As indicated at the outset of this paper, the prohibition is not a matter of disciplinary legislation, but a firm judgment on the morality of the practice. Such a doctrinal position will not be reversed.

By artificial birth control the Church means the use of any mechanical, chemical, or other procedure resorted to for the purpose of keeping male seed from entering the uterus and/or from reaching the Fallopian tubes. The precise type of contraceptive is not the important issue; neither is the fact that there are different rates of effectiveness. Rendering the sperm nonviable, or impeding its normal motility, is included under the general heading. This moral judgment on contraception does not change because conception occasionally occurs, or may at times be planned. Rather, the moral prohibition extends to each individual use of artificial means designed to frustrate the natural purpose of the act.

Nor is there any contradiction involved in the fact that Catholic moral teaching, while banning the use of contraceptives, in many instances recognizes the legitimacy of marital relations between persons, one or both of whom is incapable of having children. Such would be the case, for instance, with women who have passed the menopause or who are known to be sterile but capable of having intercourse.

The fact that conception will not result from a particular act of intercourse does not render the act unnatural or illicit. In emphasizing this aspect of the natural law, the Church shows conclusively that her first concern is that the reproductive function be not abused by deliberate exclusion of the primary end of marriage, namely the begetting of children. In her capacity as a moral teacher the Church does not positively advise parents as to the number of children they should have; rather she insists that they regulate their married life in accord with reason and not circumvent the law of nature, as clarified by her, because of the persistence of sexual passion.

Catholicism has judgments in the realm of values and morals regarding contraceptive practices other than the employment of mechanical and chemical means. The governing principle enunciated by moralists is that the act of intercourse must be performed in a natural manner and without the interposition of any positive obstacle to conception. Mechanical and chemical means are ruled out under the second part of that principle, which is, in the last analysis, but a more explicit statement of the first part. In accord with the general principle, Catholic moral thinking also objects to the use of the douche, medicated or unmedicated, as a means of contraception. The relative ineffectiveness of this method does not affect the morality. Even when not used with contraceptive intent, the douche, according to qualified moralists, should not be used immediately following intercourse for a period sufficiently long to give the seed a chance to penetrate the uterus. Behind these seemingly fine distinctions lies a genuine concern for safeguarding the natural and moral integrity of the reproductive act.

Because it is not in accord with the natural manner of intercourse, coitus interruptus is also ruled out in the Catholic scheme of values affecting human fertility. It is first referred to in Genesis, where the name of Onan provides a name for the practice. Christian tradition, as it is found in the Catholic Church, merely continued the Old Testament ban on onanism. As modern contraceptive techniques developed, the principle underlying the moral objection to onanism was applied and developed.

The governing norm, whereby various practices in connection with intercourse are evaluated, is the naturalness of the completed act. The likelihood or unlikelihood of conception on any particular occasion does not in itself affect the morality. There are secondary ends of marriage which justify its legitimate use, even though children do not follow. This reasoning gives rise to questions concerning the moral acceptability of periodic continence as a means of regulating the number of children. Not a little confusion exists on this subject, and this extends to Catholic circles.

There are two approaches to the use of the "rhythm" of fertility and sterility, or periodic continence, which should be avoided. One is unrestrained advocacy; the other, outright or implied condemnation. As regards the first, it is an inadequate statement of the case to represent periodic continence as just another form of birth control, whereby families can be planned to suit the purely personal wishes of the parents. But it is no less unsatisfactory to discuss the subject in such a way as to leave the impression that rarely if ever do married couples practice periodic continence without some degree of moral guilt.

Human fertility is supposed to be reasonable fertility, which in turn implies moral restraint in the use of the reproductive faculties. Some such restraint is obviously associated with the use of periodic continence. Hence, provided unchastity be avoided, taking advantage of the rhythm does not militate against the primary end of marriage in the same way as does artificial birth control or other unnatural practices.

Nevertheless, advocacy of periodic continence must never be such as to obscure or ignore the purpose for which marriage was instituted. Such would be the case were the impression left that rhythm is the Catholic answer to the query of the selfish: how to achieve the gratification of marriage, while avoiding its major responsibility.

On the other hand, it is unjustifiable to belittle or condemn the use of periodic continence, as some have done, on the grounds that rarely if ever is the motivation legitimate. The precarious health of a mother, or a well-grounded fear that an additional child cannot be cared for properly, are valid reasons for having recourse to such continence. Nor is the motivation of those to be condemned who look ahead and try to foresee how they will care for future offspring. Such an approach to fertility is rational and legitimate, provided of course the parents avoid the opposite error of thinking the fewer the children the better.

Married couples should understand the difficulties which can attend use of rhythm. In the first place, unless they train themselves to the necessary self-restraint, they may well reduce its effectiveness or else act unchastely. Then, too, a marriage without children, or with only one or two, unless circumstances so dictate, represents an incomplete social institution. Were such marriages common, neither the families nor the community would replace themselves. Finally, where self-mastery is neglected, there may occur psychological stress detrimental to individual or family. These aspects of the matter should not be forgotten when periodic continence is utilized, in the presence of valid reasons, as a means of spacing children or regulating family size. The practice presupposes habitual striving for a reasonable and chaste use of sex within marriage.

The recent social history of our culture indicates that selfishness or other unworthy attitudes can at times be associated even with a morally permissible practice like periodic continence. Instead of a healthy concern that reasonable opportunity be afforded children born into this world, today we can discern on occasion an excessive fear of childbirth and pregnancy, or worry about family living standards to the point where a child is regarded as a tragedy. And some marriages, initially childless voluntarily, later have experienced involuntary childlessness. Thus, an inherently moral regulatory practice is used in some instances for improper motives, or else occasions unhappy side effects.

To what extent to use periodic continence, or whether to use it in a given case, is a question which cannot be resolved by *a priori* reasoning. Catholicism, as a value system, does not tell parents how many children they must have. Moral attitudes vary, spiritual motivation differs, economic and health considerations are not always the same. Unlike some advocates of planned parenthood, the Catholic Church has learned that personal decisions in this matter should be arrived at by the married people themselves. She does not tell them to what extent to use marriage, but declares to them what is morally acceptable and what is not. She counsels them as to the end and nature of marriage, and informs them of their responsibility toward children, and the advisability of moderation. The Church's first concern is that her members do not sin, and then that they should be as reasonable as possible in the ordering of their lives.

The adjustment of moral values and motivation in the use of periodic continence is not always an easy task. Today there are some married couples who justifiably make use of rhythm, and then reveal moral confusion by attempting to justify also their employment on occasion of artificial birth-control techniques. Wrong motivation, combined with excessive desire for sexual gratification, has brought on the confusion. Under these conditions the deeper values of Christian self-discipline and of moderation become obscured.

Yet the spiritual growth of the married couple requires that they learn to integrate into their lives a willingness to accept responsibility and sacrifice, at the same time they acquire reasoned concern for their children's welfare. It should not be forgotten that within the Catholic scheme of values, sacrifice may mean, in practice, complete abstinence in some instances from the use of marriage, when no other solution for a problem can be found. Catholicism, over the centuries, has not attempted to win friends for itself by minimizing the difficulties of chaste living. That is a lesson the married need to learn, as well as the unmarried. Their spiritual development requires a proper understanding of the principle involved.

It is against the background of doctrinal and moral values that the Catholic social scientist approaches problems of population and resources. His faith emphasizes what reason tells him, namely that the material and spiritual wealth of this world is provided for the benefit of all mankind during the brief span of years within which it is allotted individuals to work out their salvation. The temporal is but a stepping stone to the eternal. Man needs material wealth, but not at the price of losing his soul. Hence, as the Catholic sees it, the morally unacceptable in matters of sex, as well as in other departments of life, cannot be used to solve temporal problems. Ecological difficulties arising from population increase or disequilibrium are no exception.

The question of quantity of population in relation to given developed or potential resources is one which can be treated from either a national or a world viewpoint. From the national viewpoint, few Catholic social thinkers acquainted with the facts would deny that some countries are overpopulated in relation to their present resources, or are in danger of becoming so. Puerto Rico, certain countries of Central America, Italy, and portions of Germany where millions of expellees have resettled, are cases in point. From a world viewpoint, contemporary Catholic social thought stresses the desirability of a rational reallocation of natural resources in relation to population, and the urgent need for developing new resources and conserving resources already in use. The world with all its material wealth was made for man, so that the sequestration of its resources by a few individuals or nations, to the detriment of others' rights, is morally indefensible.

It is in accord with Catholic social principles that greater opportunities for movement of peoples should exist. Immigration barriers, when directed less at preservation of social order than at keeping other people from needed resources, are hard to justify. Progressive Catholic social thought accordingly favors adjustment of immigration laws and of other obstacles, so as to permit a better equilibrium between people and resources to develop in an orderly manner. The unity of Christendom in the Middle Ages, however loosely woven it may have been, is something of an indication how the Christian social philosophy looks beyond the local and national community. In line with its doctrinal beliefs, there is no more ardent defender of a world outlook, or of the brotherhood of man, and of human rights, than the Catholic Church. Hence, it is to be expected that well-informed Catholics will appreciate the need for developing a world community in which all men have an opportunity for the satisfaction of temporal needs.

In line with these principles, Catholic social thought regards colonial exploitation of underdeveloped areas, to the detriment of the native populations, as a serious abuse. This is especially true today when the less developed nations stand in great need of learning to use their own resources wisely. Similarly, the Lebensraum theory of Hitler, which saw weaker nations with potential resources as so many opportunities for raising the living standards of National Socialist Germany, was severely condemned in enlightened Catholic circles. The fact that pro-Mussolini elements attempted to justify on moral grounds the conquest of Ethiopia is quite apart from the authentic social teaching of the Church. Even today the nationalism of some Catholics distorts their understanding of ethical norms espoused by Christianity.

But freer movement of peoples cannot be effected, nor natural resources made accessible, without suitable political and economic organization on the international level. This is fully recognized in Catholic social thought, although the Church as such does not make authoritative statements as to the techniques whereby the desired objective can be reached. She merely puts forward the moral principles affecting social organization, and leaves the rest to the political and economic wisdom of men. As a value system, Catholicism will continue to favor reasonable efforts to meet the population and resources problem through international action. Hence, Catholic social thinkers will tend to support development and resettlement projects, reclamation, irrigation and conservation programs, and other morally acceptable plans whereby the world's potential and developed resources can be allocated and distributed to peoples.

There are today, of course, two questions in the minds of all who think about population and resources: (1) Are potential resources adequate to feed the world's people properly for any considerable length of time? (2) If they are adequate, will men make proper use of the resources to achieve the desired result? As a moral and doctrinal teacher, the Catholic Church does not attempt to give authoritative answers to these questions. What she does say is that men may not resort to unacceptable means to limit population, and that they have a serious duty in justice and charity to cooperate in working for increased productivity and a more equitable distribution of material wealth.

In evaluating social behavior, Catholicism takes a midway position between optimism and pessimism. Aware of the fact that original sin has left its effects upon men, and witness over the centuries to the folly, greed, and lust of so many human beings, the Catholic Church does not look for a utopia upon earth. But neither, on the other hand, does she take so pessimistic a view of human nature that no hope remains for improvement of conditions through education and cooperative effort.

Is a positive population policy compatible with the Catholic value system? Precisely because the Catholic value system is so many-sided, there is no simple answer. But some inferences can be drawn from what has already been said.

Beginning negatively, it can be stated that the Church will never give approval to unacceptable methods of population control such as systematic sterilization, legitimized abortion, or dissemination of artificial birth-control information and materials. If, for prudential reasons, she does not always force these issues, that implies no weakening of disapproval, or any yielding to her disobedient members who may resort to the practices.

On the other hand, Catholicism agrees with those sociologists who exert efforts to eradicate legalized prostitution, easy divorce, child marriage, or hasty entrance into matrimony by immature adolescents. Moreover, so long as premarital chastity is properly esteemed, the Catholic value system is not in conflict with the practice of delaying marriage until such time as education has been completed. Actually, in line with all that has been said on the rational use of sex, such delay would in many cases be counselled if there were doubt about the proper support and upbringing of the children. Furthermore, Catholic moral teaching defends the liberty of those who for good reasons do not or cannot marry, insisting merely on their strict obligation to remain chaste and continent, and warning them of the danger of selfishness.

There is another point worth noting, when it comes to discussion of sex practices in some regions where somewhat different values are set on human fertility than we are accustomed to in our milieu. Reference is made to areas where very early marriages or high fertility rates are taken for granted regardless of circumstances, or where the custom of irregular marriages or concubinage is prevalent. The full application of Christian teaching on sex would gradually modify the mores of these areas. Within the Catholic scheme of values, chastity holds high place. That means promiscuity and high illegitimacy rates will be affected where these values are accepted. Marriage will be held in greater esteem, and the practice of chaste continence, when desirable or necessary, will be more readily approved. The conditions in some so-called Catholic countries, which are well known to sociologists and students of population, do not reflect the Church's moral teaching. Rather they indicate how the weaknesses of certain cultural patterns persist despite the introduction of religious values. Genuine Christianization of peoples, then, would indirectly work toward a goal many social planners seek, namely stabilization of marriage and a sense of responsibility in making economic provision for offspring.

It can be anticipated that as the Catholic population generally comes to understand better the economic problems attendant upon too rapid population increase, particularly in countries unprepared to support the burden, adjustments in fertility patterns will occur. A sense of social responsibility should operate in a number of cases, just as a sense of individual responsibility toward their own children is evident with most parents. But such a development will be indirect, and the result of people seeing the social scene as it really is in some countries.

Catholic leadership cannot be expected to advocate or approve propaganda designed solely to frighten couples into planning their families regardless of other considerations. On the one hand, a broadening sense of moral responsibility to family and society should lead individuals and couples to greater self-restraint. On the other hand, it would be wrong and unwise to put undue pressure upon them or to encourage them to morally unacceptable practices or behavior. As always, the Church's first concern in these matters is the spiritual welfare of her members. She has no objection to the prudent diffusion of knowledge gained through the social sciences, so that people will acquire a greater sense of social responsibility, but she does not want to see the family undermined or individuals exposed to the danger of unchastity.

In conclusion, let it be said that the Catholic value system will always place the emphasis upon the primary end of marriage, as was indicated at the outset. At the same time, it does not deny or overlook the other ends of marriage, among which are to be counted the fostering of mutual love and the quieting of concupiscence. Catholicism does not tell married people they must have a high birth rate, but it does warn them about the abuse of marriage and the dangers of undersized families. It opposes selfishness and excessive individualism, whether it be in the use of sex or in the utilization of material wealth. This is done by insisting upon social responsibility, whether it be to the family or to society in general. Catholicism emphasizes today the need for seeking social solutions for problems of productivity and distribution of material wealth. It sees this procedure as the first approach to difficulties presented by pressure of population upon resources. With family life in the state it is in, Catholicism is frankly concerned that profound values inherent in rational human fertility may be lost sight of, being replaced by a selfish seeking of sex gratification without accompanying regard for the welfare of offspring. Finally, the Catholic value system is not opposed to the systematic study of population problems and of fertility patterns, provided regard be had for ethical values. Rather, the Church welcomes such study, especially when it is accompanied by understanding of the moral truths which underlie the proper use of sex and the reproductive capacity.

The rationale of sex indicated above is not exclusively Catholic. It is founded upon sound natural ethics, and is a reasoned position which the Catholic Church has merely defended and, where necessary, clarified.

VALUES, POPULATION, AND THE SUPERNATURAL: A CRITIQUE

Kingsley Davis

Habituated to the statistical handling of tangible facts, modern demographers show little facility in dealing with the ethical realm. They usually ignore ethical values, and if they do touch upon them, they tend to become evaluative themselves or to ascribe to values a significance beyond the capacity of science to understand or measure. Yet values, by almost any definition, are deeply involved in the behavior governing births and deaths in human society, and like other phenomena they are susceptible to scientific analysis. The student of social structure, although more at home in dealing with ethical values than is the demographer, is too often unfamiliar with demographic facts and techniques.

The common belief that values cannot be scientifically studied rests seemingly on their subjectivity and their controversiality. It is hard to get agreement even on a working definition of the term "value," and in consequence discussion is often somewhat confused.

It is worth noting that, in the common meaning of the term, a value can exist quite apart from its embodiment in practice. An alcoholic may believe firmly in the value of abstention. At the risk of seeming elementary, therefore, one should be clear that an ethical or valuational proposition is a statement of preference, not a statement of fact. If this much is agreed upon, a clear distinction can be made between attempts to speak about value systems from the standpoint of an outside observer and, on the con-

Abridged from Kingsley Davis, "Values, Population, and the Supernatural: A Critique," in George F. Mair, ed., *Studies in Population* (Princeton: Princeton University Press, 1949), pp. 135–139. Copyright 1949 Princeton University Press. Reprinted by permission of the author and the publisher. Kingsley Davis is a professor of sociology at the University of California, Berkeley, and the author of books and articles on population, the family, and social theory.

trary, attempts to speak about a value system from the standpoint of an insider who presumably shares the values discussed. The purpose of the latter type is to persuade the reader that the values are "right," utilizing for this end both statements of alleged fact (some supernatural and some natural) and statements of sentiment and attitude. Between the two approaches—that of the observer and that of the believer—there is no reconciliation. To be sure, the scientific observer cannot quarrel with the preferences of the believer; if he does, if he tells the believer what values he *should* have, he ceases to be a scientific observer. However, the observer can, and indeed as a scientist he must, quarrel with any supposedly existential statements he believes to be untrue; and since every value system tends to bolster itself with an alleged description of what the world is actually like, the scientific and the religio-ethical approaches are perpetually at war, despite any facile proclamations to the contrary. For the purpose of the present critique, therefore, Father Gibbons' paper must be viewed as an *example,* not an analysis, of a system of values. It cannot be criticized by an outside observer in terms of the preferences or values it expresses, but solely in terms of the facts it alleges and the logic it employs. The claim, for example, that the church is divinely appointed to exercise authority over the morality of mankind is obviously not susceptible of scientific proof. Anyone who accepts it does so on faith—faith in the supernatural. If one views with scientific scepticism the supernatural propositions of Father Gibbons' paper, the deductions from these propositions also fall down. The only thing left then for our serious consideration is what effect the views of the church may have upon actual demographic behavior.

Ethical and religious formulations of specialized groups may have only a negligible influence on the demographic behavior of the masses. The formulations of a self-contained class of professional theologians or philosophers are generally couched in abstract terms, are usually a few centuries behind the times, take little account of the actual conditions faced by the ordinary person, and in practice are capable of varied interpretations to suit the convenience of the situation. One could not predict from the sacred literature of the Hindus the demographic behavior of the Indian people, any more than one could predict from Catholic doctrine the actual behavior of either medieval or contemporary Catholics. This means not only that other things besides values influence behavior, but also that other values than those mummified in official doctrine are at work.

Reflection on history leaves the impression that the reproductive folkways and mores of the common man have varied more in relation to the conditions of his life than with reference to religious or philosophical doctrine. Although contraception has become a Western folkway, no major religion advocated its use *prior* to its popular adoption. The common people took it over in the face of almost universal ecclesiastical opposition. Today the official Catholic doctrine on this matter is not preventing the widespread use of contraception by Catholics. It seems that, when other factors are similar, Catholics in the United States use contraception slightly less than do Protestants and Jews; but as compared to factors such as degree of urbanization, education, income, etc., the influence of Catholic affiliation is not strong. In Latin America the Catholic views on concubinage and illegitimacy do not prevent these institutions from being widespread. In view of this discrepancy between official religio-ethical values and the actual ones pursued by the people, it seems likely that the hair-splitting distinction between "natural" and "artificial" methods of limiting offspring will have little influence on the behavior of the Catholic masses throughout the world. How long the Catholic clergy will lay down one rule while its parishioners follow another is hard to say. The church is now obviously in a difficult position, and it is quite possible that if new techniques of contraception are invented it may adapt itself to the modern world by giving the new techniques its sanction, finding some acceptable theological reason for doing so and yet forbidding the ones it has already banned.

To people concerned about the misery of densely settled and rapidly increasing agricultural populations, any pronouncement from any major religion is of considerable importance. Even though formal religious doctrine may not exercise a major influence, such people are still looking for help from any quarter which will aid in reducing the fertility of overpopulated regions. Father Gibbons' paper will therefore be read with interest. What does it offer? It emphasizes that the church does not advocate unrestricted reproduction within marriage. This is favorable for the people in question. But it also says that postponement of marriage, the "rhythm" method, and in general "self-control" are the only methods allowable. In view of this extreme limitation on the means, our people concerned with overpopulation may question the sincerity of the church's interest in the population problem, especially since the church makes every effort, through legislative lobbying, to force its restrictions on the general public. The view that people who use mechanical and chemical contraceptives are less self-controlled than those who do not will find scant support from those who are worried about densely settled impoverished regions. It will seem to them that the individuals who have the greatest civic and social responsibility are precisely those who practice efficient contraception, that the aim of such individuals is not to have no children at all, not to have limitless intercourse, but simply to have a socially satisfactory size of family.

Further, many will question whether the substantial body of opinion cited by Father Gibbons as favoring redistribution of the world's resources and freer movement of the earth's people offers any solution to the world's long-range population problem. An equalization of the world's resources as between regions would merely postpone the time of reckoning when either population would have to stop growing or the standard of living would have to decline. Equality does not itself create wealth. It seems beyond question that the earth's human population cannot go on increasing forever. Simple arithmetic will show that in just a few centuries the current rate of increase would cover the earth's crust solidly with human flesh, and eventually the entire substance of the earth would be absorbed into the bodies of human beings. The growth must stop at some point, and there are only two things that can stop it: a decline in fertility or a rise in mortality. If the church persists in forbidding the more efficient means of reducing fertility, it will be open to the accusation that it is really favoring high mortality. The church's position is still reminiscent of the time when death rates were so high that the need was to achieve a fertility high enough to ensure survival. The need today, in many regions at least, is to achieve a fertility low enough to ensure a decent standard of living. For this need the church has an ideal solution—celibacy and continence—but one that is objectionable to many millions on moral and psychiatric grounds and which has never yet been proved workable. As a consequence, another solution has been adopted by the peoples of the West and is being looked for in connection with the peoples of the East.

RESPONSIBLE PARENTHOOD AND THE POPULATION PROBLEM

United Church of Christ

The Council of Christian Social Action of the United Church of Christ affirms the following statement and calls upon the members of our churches to give it earnest thought and prayerful consideration.

A major problem of our time is popularly called "the population explosion." It presently challenges the thinking of political leaders and of social scientists who are engaged in programs to improve the welfare of people everywhere. Technological progress has reduced death rates and improved opportunities for human life to such an extent as to make possible the doubling of the world's population in the last half century, and to give us the expectation of almost tripling our present numbers in another half century. This increasing population demands attention from all, particularly those who are already concerned about the misery and hunger which always accompany population pressures. Christian teaching concerning the rights of people yet unborn demands that we learn how to control population growth. So it is important that the church should speak to this problem.

The problem of population control is related to the institution of the family. Since all children need personal love and nurture, the church must do what it can to support the development of strong family life.

The Christian family begins when two persons are drawn to each other in the covenant of marriage, and the two "become one flesh" (Eph. 5:31). Marriage, in the Christian understanding of it, is a divinely given vocation as well as a free decision on the part of two people. It is a responsible act on the part of two responsible persons. It has its basis, indeed, in nature: it is the response to a mutual attraction of the one for the other. It includes the specifically ethical element of a life-long mutual loyalty. From the perspective of the marriage partners who are ethically serious the marriage bond requires freely given mutual love.

This freely given mutual love will express itself in various ways: in companionship, in acts of selfless service, and in sexual intercourse, all of which are necessary parts of a true marriage. Two purposes are achieved in sexual

Reprinted by permission from Council for Christian Social Action, United Church of Christ, "Responsible Parenthood and the Population Problem," *Social Action,* 26:8 (April 1960), 24–27. This article is a statement adopted by the Council on January 30, 1960.

intercourse: the expression of love between two partners, and the procreation of children. The first of these purposes may be achieved without the other. The procreation of children is a further gift of God, and a sharing in his creation. As was said by an ecumenical study group,

A knowledge of the relation of sexual love to the procreation process gives to a couple the power, and therefore the responsibility, to lift the begetting of children out of the realm of biological accident, or "fate," into the realm of grace where man is free to wait upon God and consciously to respond to his will.[1]

In a responsible Christian marriage there will ordinarily be a willingness to enlarge the family fellowship to include children, and a desire to establish an environment in which children can find security, status, and a sense of being wanted and needed. Questions which need to be asked by every parent relate to how many children they shall have, and at what intervals. These questions need to be answered responsibly as parents carefully consider their economic, spiritual, psychological, and physical ability to make adequate provision for children, to surround them with love and care, and to help them prepare for the opportunities and duties they must meet. The physical and emotional health of the wife-mother and husband-father must also be a major concern.

Since husbands and wives owe a responsibility to other families on the earth, they must take into account the relation of natural resources to the total population. Under present circumstances this means that most couples have not only the right but also the moral obligation to space and limit the number of births. Procreation without regard to the consequences may be as irresponsible as refusal to assume the duties of parenthood.

In considering this problem, husbands and wives who accept the obligation to space and limit the number of their children are confronted with the decision as to the means they will use. Is periodic continence the only morally acceptable method, or may mechanical and chemical barriers to the union of sperm and ovum be employed? We endorse the position taken in 1958 by the Lambeth Conference of the Bishops of the Anglican Communion:

It must be emphasized once again that family planning ought to be the result of thoughtful and prayerful Christian decision. Where it is, Christian husbands and wives need feel no hesitation in offering their decision humbly to God and following it with a clear conscience. The *means* of family planning are in large measure matters of clinical and esthetic choice, subject to the requirement that they be admissible to the Christian conscience. Scientific studies can rightly help, and do, in assessing the effects and the usefulness of any particular means; and Christians have every right to use the gifts of science for proper ends.

There are other problems to be considered in this connection. Christians are deeply concerned about the moral problems of sex relations before marriage, and outside of the marriage bond. From the Christian viewpoint both are violations of God's will as expressed in the moral law. Advocacy of the use of contraceptives by married couples is not an endorsement of promiscuity among the unmarried.

[1]*Responsible Parenthood and the Population Problem,* Report of a Special Ecumenical Study Group, Mansfield College, Oxford, April 12–15, 1959, p. 5.

Nor can we condone the practice of abortion, which is known to be widespread in today's world as a means of preventing the birth of unwanted children. The practice of abortion is a moral as well as a medical and legal problem. Christian conscience cannot approve of abortion as a means of family planning, for it violates personality and involves the destruction of human life.

Another method of controlling conception is sterilization. In some countries voluntary sterilization is endorsed by government, and it has been accepted by some parents who desire to limit the size of their families. In the United States it is sometimes performed with the written consent of husband and wife when the latter's health seems to require it. The whole subject of sterilization is in need of careful study. It should be approached with sympathetic understanding of those factors which make the use of mechanical contraceptives most difficult.

In light of the foregoing considerations, we hold that responsible family planning is today a clear moral duty. We believe that public law and public institutions should sanction the distribution, through authorized channels, of reliable information and contraceptive devices. Laws which forbid doctors, social workers, and ministers to provide such information and service are infringements of the rights of free citizens and should be removed from the statute books. Any hospital which receives public funds should permit doctors to provide all services they consider necessary.

Those who are responsible for international technical-assistance programs should give serious and realistic consideration to the implications of the population explosion in many economically less developed countries. These countries find themselves in a dangerous economic situation because of the rapid decline in death rates brought about by international assistance in medicine and public health. A foreign-aid program which has helped lower the death rates must also be concerned with the birth rate. Yet countries which desire to reduce the resultant population pressure through the encouragement of family planning are receiving little or no assistance on the technical problems involved. This situation imperils their development programs. There is little hope for the success of such efforts unless birth rates are reduced. Therefore those responsible for international technical-assistance programs should include family-limitation helps to those governments requesting them.

We call upon the members of our churches, voluntary agencies, and the government of the United States of America to give serious consideration and active support to these principles.

GUIDES FOR READING AND DISCUSSION

1. Should economic aid to underdeveloped, heavily populated countries be linked to help in setting up effective birth-control programs? If not, how can one avoid the effect of increasing the number of ill-fed, ill-clothed, ill-housed people, rather than raising the level of a more or less static population?

2. Assume for the sake of the argument that with improvements in technology the potential food supply can grow even faster than the population. What impediments, other than technological, are there to the extension of efficient production and distribution of food? Are these impediments aggravated by the growth of the population; and if so, how?

3. In the Introduction (p. 4), the conflict between Gibbons and Davis was designated as irreconcilable, because the two positions are correctly deduced from fundamentally divergent moral premises. Is this description correct? What would have to be adjusted in one or the other position to resolve the controversy?

SUGGESTED ADDITIONAL READINGS

"Population Control," *Law and Contemporary Problems,* vol. 25, no. 3 (Summer 1960), entire issue.

Lee Rainwater, *And the Poor Get Children: Sex, Contraception, and Family Planning in the Working Class* (Chicago: Quadrangle Books, 1960).

Alvah W. Sulloway, *Birth Control and Catholic Doctrine* (Boston: Beacon, 1959).

Christopher Tietze *et al.,* "The Clinical Effectiveness of the Rhythm Method of Contraception," *Fertility and Sterility,* 2:5 (September–October 1951), 444–450.

Alvin Werth and Clement S. Mihanovich, eds., *Papal Pronouncements on Marriage and the Family from Leo XIII to Pius XII* (Milwaukee: Bruce, 1955).

WHAT CONSTITUTES A LEGITIMATE DIVORCE?

A common view, perhaps even the usual one, is that no divorce is wholly legitimate. Since the family is the fundamental social unit, society must protect itself by guaranteeing the stability of that unit. Traditional ethical norms, therefore, permit divorce only under exceptional circumstances, if at all; and those who accept these norms must be deeply concerned over the sharp increase in divorces that has accompanied the rise of modern Western societies. The breakdown of the family, an important cause of the decline of classical civilization, will—according to this point of view—have the same consequence today if remedial steps are not taken.[1]

However prevalent this view, it includes much that is at best unproved. It is not true, first of all, that American divorce rates are exceptionally high compared with those of other societies, particularly those of primitive cultures. Professor Murdock, after making such a comparison, concluded that the American family is definitely more stable than the average. "Current trends could continue without reversal for a considerable period before the fear of social disorganization would acquire genuine justification."[2]

It is not definitely known, secondly, whether in any real sense American divorce rates have been rising since the founding of the Republic. Divorce statistics date only from the middle of the nineteenth century, and even today they are grossly inaccurate. In any case, such records as exist greatly understate the incidence of broken families.

In the colonial period, it was not uncommon for a man to abandon his wife in Europe and marry in America—a practice which probably continued, but at a lesser rate, up through the early years of the twentieth century. Similarly, during the 1800's, the frontier territories served as the meccas of the married who had deserted wife and family in the East.[3]

In short, the first effect of general urbanization was to strengthen the family; for with the end of the frontier, civil norms became somewhat more enforceable throughout the country.

The idea that incompatibility is a just ground for divorce is usually associated with contemporary radical innovators like Bertrand Russell or Judge Lindsey.[4] The argument is presented here, however, in the seventeenth-century words of John Milton. The selection is abridged from a pamphlet entitled, in full, *The Doctrine and Discipline of Divorce, Restored to the Good of Both Sexes, from the Bondage of Canon Law, and Other Mistakes, to the True Meaning of Scripture in the Law and Gospel Compared;*

---

[1]For an extended statement of this argument, see Carle C. Zimmerman, *Family and Civilization* (New York: Harper, 1947).

[2]George Peter Murdock, "Family Stability in Non-European Cultures," *Annals of the American Academy of Political and Social Science*, 272 (November 1950), 195–201.

[3]Paul H. Jacobson, *American Marriage and Divorce* (New York: Rinehart, 1959), p. 89.

[4]See, for example, Ben B. Lindsey and Wainwright Evans, *The Revolt of Modern Youth* (New York: Boni & Liveright, 1925).

Wherein Are Also Set Down the Bad Consequences of Abolishing, or Condemning as Sin, That Which the Law of God Allows, and Christ Abolished Not. Writing as both an advocate of human freedom and a propagandist for the Puritan revolution, Milton set down what sound like hypermodern opinions. He tried, moreover, to base them on the Christian tradition— specifically referring to the Scriptures and to early Christian writers.

The contrary view is given in the words of the Morton Commission, whose report was published in 1956.[5] The report deals specifically with the laws of England and Scotland, but the arguments echo those used throughout the Western world to reinforce impediments to divorce. The dominant group of the Commission saw it as its task to defend the Christian tradition—the same one from which Milton had derived his ideas—against the dissolution of family life implicit in modern society. Some of these traditionalists, however, favored the rather radical innovation of abolishing divorce altogether; in their view, the "inevitable hardships that this would entail" ought to be accepted as the price of the greater happiness and family stability that would also ensue. The whole Commission did not go so far, but it did reject the notion of sinless divorce that some had advocated.

[5]How the Commission was set up is of interest. Several years earlier, Mrs. Eirene White had offered a bill in Parliament, by which a divorce might be obtained by either spouse after seven years of separation—provided there was no prospect of reconciliation. According to this new principle, it would be possible, under stringently restricted circumstances, for a court to grant a divorce without declaring either party to be at fault. "Because her proposals were well received and would have destroyed the doctrine of matrimonial offense, the government offered a Royal Commission as a quid pro quo for the withdrawal of the Bill" (O. R. McGregor, "The Morton Commission: A Social and Historical Commentary," *British Journal of Sociology*, 7:3, September 1956, 171–193). McGregor's article is an excellent critique; see also, at a more popular level, Barbara Wootton, "Holiness or Happiness," *Twentieth Century* (November 1955).

THE DOCTRINE AND DISCIPLINE OF DIVORCE

John Milton

What thing [is] more instituted to the solace and delight of man than marriage? And yet the misinterpreting of some scripture, directed mainly against the abusers of the law for divorce given by Moses, hath changed the blessing of matrimony not seldom into a familiar and coinhabiting mischief; at least into a drooping and disconsolate household captivity, without refuge or redemption. So ungoverned and so wild a race doth superstition run us, from one extreme of abused liberty into the other of unmerciful restraint. For although God in the first ordaining of marriage taught us

Abridged from John Milton, *The Doctrine and Discipline of Divorce,* pamphlet originally published in England in 1643. John Milton (1608–1674), best known for his poetry, also wrote numerous tracts and pamphlets on such subjects as censorship and education.

to what end he did it, in words expressly implying the apt and cheerful conversation of man with woman, to comfort and refresh him against the evil of solitary life, not mentioning the purpose of generation till afterwards, as being but a secondary end in dignity, though not in necessity: yet now, if any two be but once handed in the church, and have tasted in any sort the nuptial bed, let them find themselves never so mistaken in their dispositions through any error, concealment, or misadventure, that through their different tempers, thoughts, and constitutions, they can neither be to one another a remedy against loneliness, nor live in any union or contentment all their days; yet they shall, so they be but found suitably weaponed to the least possibility of sensual enjoyment, be made, spite of antipathy, to fadge together, and combine as they may to their unspeakable wearisomeness, and despair of all sociable delight in the ordinance which God established to that very end. What a calamity is this? and, as the wise man, if he were alive, would sigh out in his own phrase, what a "sore evil is this under the sun!"

All which we can refer justly to no other author than the canon law and her adherents, not consulting with charity, the interpreter and guide of our faith, but resting in the mere element of the text; doubtless by the policy of the devil to make that gracious ordinance become unsupportable, that what with men not daring to venture upon wedlock, and what with men wearied out of it, all inordinate license might abound. It was for many ages that marriage lay in disgrace with most of the ancient doctors, as a work of the flesh, almost a defilement, wholly denied to priests, and the second time dissuaded to all, as he that reads Tertullian or Jerome may see at large. Afterwards it was thought so sacramental that no adultery or desertion could dissolve it; and this is the sense of our canon courts in England to this day, but in no other reformed church else: yet there remains in them also a burden on it as heavy as the other two were disgraceful or superstitious, and of as much iniquity, crossing a law not only written by Moses, but charactered in us by nature, of more antiquity and deeper ground than marriage itself; which law is to force nothing against the faultless proprieties of nature, yet that this may be colorably done, our Savior's words touching divorce are as it were congealed into a stony rigor, inconsistent both with his doctrine and his office; and that which he preached only to the conscience is by canonical tyranny snatched into the compulsive censure of a judicial court; where laws are imposed even against the venerable and secret power of nature's impression, to love, whatever cause be found to loathe: which is a heinous barbarism both against the honor of marriage, the dignity of man and his soul, the goodness of Christianity, and all the human respects of civility.

[It] shall be the task and period of this discourse to prove, first, that other reasons of divorce, besides adultery, were by the law of Moses, and are yet to be allowed by the Christian magistrate as a piece of justice, and that the words of Christ are not hereby contraried. Next, that to prohibit absolutely any divorce whatsoever, except those which Moses excepted, is against the reason of law, as in due place I shall show out of Fagius, with many additions. He therefore who by adventuring shall be so happy as with success to light the way of such an expedient liberty and truth as this, shall restore the much-wronged and over-sorrowed state of matrimony, not only to those merciful and life-giving remedies of Moses, but, as much as may be, to that serene and blissful condition it was in at the beginning, and shall deserve of all apprehensive men (considering the troubles and distempers, which, for want of this in sight, have been so oft in kingdoms, in states, and families), shall deserve to be reckoned among the public benefactors of civil and human life, above the inventors of wine and oil; for this is a far dearer, far nobler, and more desirable cherishing to man's life, unworthily exposed to sadness and mistake, which he shall vindicate. Not that license, and levity, and unconsented breach of faith should herein be countenanced, but that some conscionable and tender pity might be had of those who have unwarily, in a thing they never practiced before, made themselves the bondmen of a luckless and helpless matrimony.

That indisposition, unfitness, or contrariety of mind—arising from a cause in nature unchangeable, hindering, and ever likely to hinder the main benefits of conjugal society, which are solace and peace—is a greater reason of divorce than natural frigidity, especially if there be no children, and that there be mutual consent.

This I gather from the law in Deut. xxiv. 1: "When a man hath taken a wife and married her, and it come to pass that she find no favor in his eyes, because he hath found some uncleanness in her, let him write her a bill of divorcement, and give it in her hand, and send her out of his house," etc. This law, if the words of Christ may be admitted into our belief, shall never, while the world stands, for him be abrogated. First therefore I here set down what learned Fagius hath observed on this law:

The law of God permitted divorce for the help of human weakness. For everyone that of necessity separates, cannot live single. That Christ denied divorce to his own, hinders not; for what is that to the unregenerate, who hath not attained such perfection? Let not the remedy be despised, which was given to weakness. And when Christ saith, who marries the divorced commits adultery, it is to be understood if he had any plot in the divorce.

The cause of divorce mentioned in the law is translated "some uncleanness," but in the Hebrew it sounds, "nakedness of aught, or any real nakedness"; which by all the learned interpreters is referred to the mind as well as to the body. And what greater nakedness or unfitness of mind than that which hinders ever the solace and peaceful society of the married couple? And what hinders that more than the unfitness and defectiveness of an unconjugal mind? The cause therefore of divorce expressed in the position cannot but agree with that described in the best and equalest sense of Moses' law. Which, being a matter of pure charity, is plainly moral, and more now in force than ever; therefore surely lawful. For if under the law such was God's gracious indulgence, as not to suffer the ordinance of his goodness and favor through any error to be seared and stigmatized upon his servants to their misery and thraldom; much less will he suffer it now under the covenant of grace, by abrogating his former grant of remedy and relief.

For all sense and equity reclaims that any law or covenant, how solemn or strait soever, either between God and man, or man and man, though of God's joining, should bind against a prime and principal scope of its own institution, and of both or either party covenanting; neither can it be of force to engage a blameless creature to his own perpetual sorrow, mistaken for his expected solace, without suffering charity to step in and do a confessed good work of parting those whom nothing holds together but this God's joining, falsely supposed against the express end of his own ordinance. And what his chief end was of creating woman to be joined with man, his own instituting words declare, and are infallible to inform us what is marriage, and what is no marriage; unless we can think them set there to no purpose: "It is not good," saith he, "that man should be alone. I will make him a helpmeet for him." From which words, so plain, less cannot be concluded, nor is by any learned interpreter, than that in God's intention a meet and happy conversation is the chiefest and the noblest end of marriage: for we find here no expression so necessarily implying carnal knowledge, as this prevention of loneliness to the mind and spirit of man.

Lest therefore so noble a creature as man should be shut up incurably under a worse evil by an easy mistake in that ordinance which God gave him to remedy a less evil, reaping to himself sorrow while he went to rid away solitariness, it cannot avoid to be concluded that if the woman be naturally so of disposition as will not help to remove but help to increase that same God-forbidden loneliness, which in time draws on with it a general discomfort and dejection of mind, not beseeming either Christian profession or moral conversation, unprofitable and dangerous to the commonwealth; when the household estate, out of which must flourish forth the vigor and spirit of all public enterprises, is so ill-contented and procured at home, and cannot be supported—such a marriage can be no marriage, whereto the most honest end is wanting; and the aggrieved person shall do more manly, to be extraordinary and singular in claiming the due right whereof he is frustrated, than to piece up his lost contentment by visiting the stews, or stepping to his neighbor's bed, which is the common shift in this misfortune; or else by suffering his useful life to waste away, and be lost under a secret affliction of an unconscionable size to human strength. Against all which evils the mercy of this Mosaic law was graciously exhibited.

Marriage is a covenant, the very being whereof consists not in a forced cohabitation and counterfeit performance of duties, but in unfeigned love. Love in marriage cannot live nor subsist unless it be mutual; and where love cannot be, there can be left of wedlock nothing but the empty husk of an outside matrimony, as undelightful and unpleasing to God as any other kind of hypocrisy. So far is his command from tying men to the observance of duties which there is no help for, but they must be dissembled. If Solomon's advice be not over-frolic, "Live joyfully," saith he, "with the wife whom thou lovest, all thy days, for that is thy portion": how then, where we find it impossible to rejoice or to love, can we obey this precept? How miserably do we defraud ourselves of that comfortable portion, which God gives us, by striving vainly to glue an error together, which God and nature will not join, adding but more vexation and violence to that blissful society by our importunate superstition, that will not hearken to St. Paul, 1 Cor. vii, who, speaking of a marriage and divorce, determines plain enough in general, that God therein "hath called us to peace, and not to bondage"! Yea, God himself commands in his law more than once, and by his prophet Malachi, as Calvin and the best translations read, that "he who hates, let him divorce," that is, he who cannot love.

As those priests of old were not to be long in sorrow, or if they were, they could not rightly execute their function; so every true Christian in a higher order of priesthood is a person dedicate to joy and peace, offering himself a lively sacrifice of praise and thanksgiving, and there is no Christian duty that is not to be seasoned and set off with cheerishness; which in a thousand outward and intermitting crosses may yet be done well, as in this vale of tears: but in such a bosom affliction as this, crushing the very foundation of his inmost nature, when he shall be forced to love against a possibility, and to use a dissimulation against his soul in the perpetual and ceaseless duties of a husband; doubtless his whole duty of serving God must needs be blurred and tainted with a sad unpreparedness and dejection of spirit, wherein God has no delight. Who sees not therefore how much more Christianity it would be to break by divorce that which is more broken by undue and forcible keeping, rather than "to cover the altar of the Lord with continual tears, so that he regardeth not the offering any more," rather than that the whole worship of a Christian man's life should languish and fade away beneath the weight of an immeasurable grief and discouragement?

I suppose it will be allowed us that marriage is a human society, and that all human society must proceed from the mind rather than the body, else it would be but a kind of animal or beastish meeting: if the mind therefore cannot have that due company by marriage that it may reasonably and humanly desire, that marriage can be no human society, but a certain formality; or gilding over of little better than a brutish congress, and so in very wisdom and pureness to be dissolved.

But marriage is more than human, "the covenant of God," Prov. ii. 17; therefore man cannot dissolve it. I answer, if it be more than human, so much the more it argues the chief society thereof to be in the soul rather than in the body, and the greatest breach thereof to be unfitness of mind rather than defect of body: for the body can have least affinity in a covenant more than human, so that the reason of dissolving holds good the rather. Again, I answer, that the sabbath is a higher institution, a command of the first table, for the breach whereof God hath far more and oftener testified his anger than for divorces, which from Moses to Malachi he never took displeasure at, nor then neither if we mark the text; and yet as oft as the good of man is concerned, he not only permits, but commands to break the sabbath. What covenant more contracted with God and less in man's power than the vow which hath once passed his lips? yet if it be found rash, if offensive, if unfruitful either to God's glory or the good of man, our doctrine forces not error and unwillingness irksomely to keep it, but counsels wisdom and better thoughts boldly to break it; therefore to enjoin the indissoluble keeping of a marriage found unfit against the good of man both soul and body, as hath been evidenced, is to make an idol of marriage, to advance it above the worship of God and the good of man, to make it a transcendent command, above both the second and first table; which is a most prodigious doctrine.

Christ himself tells who should not be put asunder, namely, those whom God hath joined. A plain solution of this great controversy, if men would but use their eyes. For when is it that God may be said to join? when the parties and their friends consent? No, surely; for that may concur to lewdest ends. Or is it when church rites are finished? Neither; for the efficacy of those depends upon the presupposed fitness of either party. Perhaps after carnal knowledge. Least of all; for that may join persons whom neither law nor nature dares join. It is left, that only then when the minds are fitly disposed and enabled to maintain a cheerful conversation, to the solace and love of each other, according as God intended and promised in the very first foundation of matrimony, "I will make him a helpmeet for him"; for surely what God intended and promised, that only can be thought to be his joining, and not the contrary. So likewise the apostle witnesseth, I Cor. vii. 15, that in marriage "God hath called us to peace." And doubtless in what respect he hath called us to marriage, in that also he hath joined us. The rest, whom either disproportion, or deadness of spirit, or something distasteful and averse in the immutable bent of nature renders conjugal, error may have joined, but God never joined against the meaning of his own ordinance. And if he joined them not, then is there no power above their own consent to hinder them from unjoining, when they cannot reap the soberest ends of being together in any tolerable sort. Neither can it be said properly that such twain were ever divorced, but only parted from each other, as two persons unconjunctive are unmarriable together. A peaceful divorce is a less evil, and less in scandal than hateful, hard-hearted, and destructive continuance of marriage in the judgment of Moses and of Christ.

THE PROPER GROUNDS
OF DIVORCE

The Morton Commission

The Western world has recognized that it is in the best interests of all concerned—the community, the parties to a marriage and their children —that marriage should be monogamous and that it should last for life. It has also always recognized that, owing to human frailty, some marriages will not endure for life, and that in certain circumstances it is right that a spouse should be released from the obligations of marriage. There are, and always have been, differences of view as to whether in such circumstances the marriage tie should be dissolved and the parties set free to enter into new marriages, or whether the parties should merely be legally separated, without dissolution of the marriage tie.

It is obvious that life-long marriage is the basis of a secure and stable family life, and that to ensure their well-being children must have that background. We have therefore had in mind throughout our inquiry the importance of seeking ways and means of strengthening the resolution of husband and wife to realize the ideal of a partnership for life. Nevertheless, we recognize that some marriages will fall short of this ideal and we are all

Abridged from Royal Commission on Marriage and Divorce, *Report,* Cmd. 9678 (London: Her Majesty's Stationery Office, 1956).

agreed that it is right that in certain circumstances divorce should be allowed. There are differences of opinion among us as to the circumstances which would justify dissolution of marriage and as to the effects on the stability of marriage which would result from changes in the existing legal provisions for its dissolution.

This Report will contain no discussion of what may be called the religious aspects of marriage and divorce, but it must not be thought that these aspects have been overlooked. We have had evidence from Christian Churches and other religious bodies and have done our best to weigh that evidence, together with all the other evidence laid before us. We have, however, conceived it to be our duty to examine the problems before us from the point of view of the State, which has to legislate for all its citizens, whatever their religious beliefs may be.

We do not think that the remedy for the problem of marriage failure lies in making divorce more difficult. In our opinion, the roots of the evil go too deep for such a course to be effective in dealing with the tendency to look to divorce as the obvious way out. We had no evidence which suggested that public opinion would support a restriction of facilities for divorce. We were impressed, too, by the fact that witnesses who would, in principle, have favored this course recognized that it would not be practicable, in present circumstances, to adopt it. We ourselves believe that without a radical change in the general attitude towards divorce, to abolish or restrict the scope of any of the present grounds for divorce would be bound to fail in its object of checking breakdown of marriage. People who were minded to get a divorce, and who were prepared if necessary to resort to deception to that end, would usually manage to get one.

We are convinced that the real remedy for the present situation lies in other directions: in fostering in the individual the will to do his duty by the community; in strengthening his resolution to make marriage a union for life; in inculcating a proper sense of his responsibility towards his children. These objectives can only be achieved by education in the widest sense, by specific instruction before marriage, and by providing facilities for guidance after marriage and for conciliation if breakdown threatens.

In both England and Scotland the existing divorce law is founded on what is called, for brevity, the "doctrine of the matrimonial offense." Certain acts (which are termed "matrimonial offenses") are regarded as being fundamentally incompatible with the undertakings entered into at marriage; the commission of these acts by one party to the marriage gives to the other party an option to have the marriage terminated by divorce. With one exception (that of insanity, to which special considerations apply), all the present grounds of divorce, being conduct of a grave nature which cuts at the root of the marriage, conform to this principle.

Some witnesses considered that the existing divorce law should be reframed on the basis of a new principle, which, for convenience, we call the "doctrine of breakdown of marriage." They recommended that the existing grounds of divorce should be abolished and their place taken by a single, comprehensive ground which would allow divorce to be granted if it could be proved that the marriage had irretrievably broken down. These witnesses argued that the matrimonial offenses on which divorce is founded under the present law are not usually the real causes of the breakdown of a marriage but merely its symptoms: that the result of basing the grounds of divorce on symptoms is to deny relief where it should be available because the marriage is completely at an end, and to grant divorce (e.g., for an isolated act of adultery which had been repented of) where there is no reason why the marriage should not continue. They alleged that people deliberately commit offenses, or pretend to commit them, in order to supply grounds for divorce, and suggested that the solution is to require the court to determine in each case whether the marriage has broken down beyond hope of reconciliation.

The majority of those witnesses who supported the doctrine of breakdown of marriage favored the addition to the present law of one or both of the following new grounds:

(i) divorce by the mutual consent of husband and wife;
(ii) divorce at the option of either spouse after a period of separation.

The essential feature of the various proposals for divorce by consent is that husband and wife should be entitled to come before a judge and ask for a divorce simply on the footing that they both seriously desire their marriage to be dissolved, and, if the judge were satisfied that the consent had been freely given, divorce should be granted. Safeguards were suggested designed to prevent divorce on this ground from being lightly obtained. It was argued that the parties to the marriage are in the best position to know if it has failed, and that it follows from the concept of the individual as a free and responsible person that husband and wife should be allowed to terminate their marriage if they are both agreed to take this step. It was said that among the divorces granted under the present law many are in fact divorces by consent, since, in an undefended case, it is very difficult for the court to detect whether there has been collusion; and, further, ground for divorce may be provided by one party in circumstances which do not amount to legal collusion. It was argued that this brings the law into disrepute, because it is regarded as favoring the many who are unscrupulous at the expense of the few who are too scrupulous to resort to an "arranged" divorce. The introduction of divorce by consent would therefore not make divorce any easier than it is at present (since it would merely allow people to do openly what they now do by subterfuge) and, in the view of the witnesses, it would result in an "honest" divorce law which would command the respect of the public.

In putting forward proposals which would allow either spouse to obtain a divorce after the spouses had lived apart for a given period (the suggestions ranged from two to seven years' separation), witnesses had primarily in mind the situation where ground for divorce exists under the present law but the injured spouse has not taken his legal remedy. Such proposals would also enable divorce to be obtained where there is no ground for divorce under the present law. The advocates of proposals on these lines argued that, if a marriage has irretrievably broken down, it is in the interests of the parties to the marriage, of any children of the marriage, and of the community, that the marriage should be ended by divorce, and the parties set free to enter into new marriages, if they so wish. They pointed out that without such freedom illicit unions are formed, and illegitimate children often begotten. In their experience, many of those illicit unions have all the qualities of an enduring marriage and it is a grievous hardship to the parties that they cannot be legally married and have legitimate children. But apart from the individual hardship, it was said to be against the interests of public morality that there should be such illicit unions in that they tend to bring the status of marriage into disrepute.

We of the Commission, with one exception, are all agreed that the present law based on the doctrine of the matrimonial offense should be retained. We differ, however, on whether or not it would be in the interests of the community as a whole that an additional ground should be introduced based on the principle that there should be dissolution of a marriage which has irretrievably broken down. The views of the nine members who are opposed to the introduction of [the doctrine of] the breakdown of marriage follow.

We have rejected the introduction into the law of the principle that a marriage should be ended if it has irretrievably broken down, because, in whatever form that principle might be introduced, it would entail the recognition of divorce by consent. In its more fully developed forms it would also entail the recognition of divorce against the will of a spouse who had committed no recognized matrimonial offense. It is the introduction of either of these elements that we regard as fundamentally objectionable and as containing the seeds of grave damage to marriage as an institution.

We believe that the consequences of providing the "easy way out" afforded by divorce by consent would be disastrous to stability in marriage. The inevitable result would be the granting of divorces in cases where no real necessity for the remedy had arisen. In other words, the divorce rate would be swollen by the failure of marriages which would otherwise have held together with advantage to both parties as well as to children. People would then come to look upon marriage less and less as a life-long union and more and more as one to be ended if things begin to go wrong, and there would be a very real risk that in the end widespread divorce would come to be an accepted feature of our society. As those attitudes spread they would undermine, and ultimately destroy, the concept of life-long marriage.

We believe that it is fundamentally incompatible with the concept of marriage as a union for life for the parties to be free to put an end to it by agreement. It seems to us self-evident that a marriage cannot be the concern only of the partners to it. If there are children, their interests must be considered. But whether there are children or not, the State must be concerned in the maintenance of a marriage and in its dissolution, because the State has an overriding responsibility to ensure, in the interests of the community, that the institution of marriage is upheld. For marriage is not merely a civil contract between the parties to it. It is a status arising out of that contract, and, as a status, it concerns the community as well as the parties. If husband and wife were free to terminate their marriage at pleasure, then marriage would become a purely contractual relationship and the interests of the community would receive no recognition.

To give people a right to divorce themselves would be to foster a change in the attitude to marriage, which would be disastrous for the nation. People would tend to enter marriage more lightly, and with the reservation that, if it were not a success, they could always agree to put an end to it. And when difficulties arose in married life (as happens in most marriages), there would be much less incentive to overcome them. Husband and wife would be tempted to say to each other, "Let us have a divorce and start again." Thus, divorce would increasingly be sought in circumstances where, if a little effort were made, husband and wife could adjust their differences. Such an attitude would be fatal to stability and security in marriage, which in the end would come to be regarded as a temporary relationship, with divorce as a normal incident of life. For this calamity the State would bear the brunt of the responsibility, since, in giving its blessing to divorce by consent, it would in effect have encouraged people to abandon their marriages on the flimsiest provocation.

Our objection to divorce by consent is so fundamental that it cannot be met by the provision of conditions or safeguards, however stringent these might be. Nor can we accept the argument that because the difficulty of getting a divorce leads to perjury, therefore divorce should be made easier. If two people are determined to get a divorce, they may succeed, notwithstanding that the law expressly provides against this. No law can be proof against those who have made up their minds to get around it, and are ready to commit perjury to that end. The only complete cure would be to allow divorce by consent after a separation of three years or less—a solution which we most emphatically reject.

The argument that divorce by consent provides a dignified and honorable means of release is perhaps the most insidious of all. There could be no subtler temptation to divorce than the belief that there was a wholly blameless way of terminating marriage. In our view it is not the function of the law to provide such a means of release; its proper function is to give relief where a wrong has been done. To go beyond this and provide an easy way out would be actively to assist in what can only be regarded as a socially calamitous act.

Witnesses who considered that the existing grounds of divorce should be abolished and their place taken by a single, comprehensive ground argued that divorce would not then be easier to obtain than it is at present; that in fact in some respects it would be more difficult. We do not agree that in practice the proposal would work out in that way. On the contrary, we think that under such a proposal a spouse who wanted to be free of his marriage would as a rule be able to get a divorce.

The fundamental criticism of this proposal is that it would set the court an impossible task. To determine whether or not a marriage had completely broken down is really not a triable issue. If the case were undefended and the petitioner maintained that he would never go back to his spouse, and that the marriage was dead, and if his statement were perhaps supported by the evidence of relatives and friends, we do not see how the court could do otherwise than accept what he said and grant a divorce. This would mean that many divorces would in reality be given merely on the ground of incompatibility or for such defects of temperament as should be regarded as coming within the ordinary wear and tear of married life. It would also mean that it would be open to husband and wife to obtain divorce by consent.

In a contested case the court would be in a similar difficulty. It would be practically impossible for a spouse who wished to resist divorce, perhaps for the sake of the children, to prove that the marriage had *not* broken down, in face of the other spouse's contention that it had. If, for instance, the husband were living with another woman and there were children of that union, it would be very difficult for the court to hold that the marriage had not broken down, however much the wife might argue that, for her part, she regarded it as still intact. Thus this ground is open not only to the objection that it would lead to divorce by consent, but also to the equally grave objection that it would involve divorce against the will of a spouse who was innocent, or mainly innocent, of responsibility for the breakdown.

In conclusion, our examination of the proposals under which breakdown of marriage would be the criterion of divorce has convinced us that it is in the best interests of the community that the matrimonial offense should remain the determining principle of the divorce law. An element of artificiality must be admitted in the doctrine of the matrimonial offense, and the consequential emphasis on legal guilt and innocence; for in real life it is comparatively rare to find all the right on one side and all the wrong on the other. Still, this doctrine provides a clear and intelligible principle; and it makes for security in marriage, because husbands and wives know that they cannot be divorced unless they have committed one of the matrimonial offenses which is ground for divorce. Moreover, these "offenses" are not arbitrary ones; in each case a grave injury has been done, which has cut at the root of the concept of marriage as a partnership for life.

We further believe that in society as it is today people need the external buttress of a system of law which specifies the circumstances in which an individual has the right to ask for his marriage to be dissolved. People have good and bad impulses, and we conceive it to be the function of the law to strengthen the good and to control the bad. We believe that this is the effect of the present law. It acts, for instance, as a strong deterrent to the setting up of illicit unions, because a spouse who is contemplating such a union and his prospective partner both know that there can be no certainty that they will ever be able to marry and have legitimate children.

At the same time, the principle of the matrimonial offense is not rigid: on the contrary, it can be, and has been, adapted to meet the changing views of society on what constitutes a grave matrimonial wrong.

GUIDES FOR READING AND DISCUSSION

1. Are individual happiness and the social good sometimes conflicting principles? If so, how does one choose which principle to follow when there is a conflict?

2. Assuming that "marital offense" is ordinarily a legal fiction, is it nonetheless a useful fiction—one that helps maintain symbolically the idea that family stability may be broken only through the operation of evil?

3. The wide variety of Christian concepts of marriage all derive, in the view of those who hold them, from the same tradition. What does this suggest concerning the utility of traditional values in validating contemporary institutions?

SUGGESTED ADDITIONAL READINGS

Paul W. Alexander, "The Follies of Divorce: A Therapeutic Approach to the Problem," *American Bar Association Journal,* 36 (February 1950), 105–108, 168–172.

"Divorce: A Re-Examination of Basic Concepts," *Law and Contemporary Problems,* vol. 18, no. 1 (Winter 1953), entire issue.

Robert F. Drinan, S.J., "New Approach to Divorce Laws," *Social Order* (April 1949), pp. 145–151.

William J. Goode, *After Divorce* (Glencoe, Ill.: Free Press, 1956).

Paul H. Jacobson, *American Marriage and Divorce* (New York: Rinehart, 1959).

Morris Ploscowe, *The Truth About Divorce* (New York: Hawthorne Books, 1955).

HOW SHOULD ONE TEACH
A CHILD TO READ?

In a country like the United States, it is perhaps inevitable that public schools should be a subject of perennial debate; for no institution is more important. "Popular government without popular education," in the words of James Madison, "is a prologue to a farce or a tragedy." With universal free education as its foundation, America's democratic society has prospered. Millions of immigrants from diverse cultures have been successfully assimilated; and their sons, able to take advantage of the schooling available to them, have often been able to rise above their fathers' low status.

In recent years, however, the eighteenth-century vision of a democratic society based on universal free education has turned a bit sour. In the larger cities, many middle-class parents, if they can afford it, now send their children to private schools, thus withdrawing from a direct, personal effort to help maintain standards in the public schools. Furthermore, in the view of some, this universal education has not produced a higher level of culture; for once they have learned to read, many persons read mainly sports pages and comics.[1] So eminent a personage as Dr. Conant, a former president of Harvard University, has written, as a one-sentence summary of his latest work: "To a considerable degree what a school should and can do is determined by the status and ambitions of the families being served."[2] Schools in well-to-do suburbs, thus, should prepare their charges for college, while those in the slums should concentrate on vocational training. This extremely radical proposal would, in effect, change not only the country's educational system but also its class structure. Advancement in social status depends increasingly on whether the applicant has a degree; thus, if access to college is restricted mainly to those with suitable family backgrounds, the children of poor parents or of Negroes or other minorities will have all of their other disadvantages aggravated.

But is it really necessary to abandon some of the principal concepts underlying democratic government: that virtually all persons are markedly educable; that intelligence is not significantly correlated with ethnic background or even with social class? If pupils of slum schools do not learn very much, the fault may be theirs—or it may be that of the school system. Paradoxically, the end product of the progressive movement in education, whose purpose it was to enhance democracy through the schools, may have been profoundly anti-democratic; for only those schools that concentrate rigorously and efficiently on the single function of teaching can overcome the handicaps of a child whose main environment is a slum home and a slum neighborhood. Progressive education, a philosophy that was once

[1]See the discussion of "mass culture" below, pp. 316–342.
[2]James Bryant Conant, *Slums and Suburbs: A Commentary on Schools in Metropolitan Areas* (New York: McGraw-Hill, 1961), p. 1. In the original the entire sentence is in italics.

radical and creative but is now part of the entrenched educational establishment, sees the major purpose of education as the creation of happy, well-rounded citizens—in a word, life-adjustment.[3] In the traditionalist philosophy of education (once the establishment but now by comparison radical and creative), the major purpose of education is the transmission of the cultural heritage.[4] All too frequently, the dispute is seemingly resolved by the allegation that the methods of each school of thought are suited to achieving its avowed goals. The controversy about method is thus dispensed with, and the citizen is faced with the more difficult task of choosing between two broad, often ill-defined systems of values.

The question of how to teach reading is not so easily begged; and that is one reason that we have chosen to include two essays on what, at first glance, may seem to be a narrow issue, apparently of interest only to professional educators. The dispute between the proponents of the phonics method and the "look-say," or what might be termed the ideographic, method is typically between representatives of, respectively, the traditionalist and the progressive philosophy of education. That the ability to read and write one's own language is a prerequisite to all subsequent education needs no special emphasis, and there are good indications that present schooling is deficient in this respect. For example,

Superintendent of Schools John J. Theobald said yesterday that 10,000 seventh-graders in New York City could not read third-grade books. He also reported that 67,067 of the city's 172,000 junior high school pupils were more than two years behind in reading.[5]

The two articles on methods of teaching reading need no lengthy introduction. Note that Dr. Mackintosh's defense of the "look-say" method is distributed by the federal government's Office of Education. The original version is illustrated—for example, with a smiling moppet looking at a picture book labeled *Television* and exclaiming, "Books are fun! Books are exciting!" Mrs. Lowe's article defending the phonics method is one of the essays in a volume with the depressing title *Tomorrow's Illiterates: The State of Reading Instruction Today.*

[3]See, for example, William Heard Kilpatrick, *Modern Education: Its Proper Work* (Danville, Ill.: Interstate, 1950). Dr. Kilpatrick was second only to John Dewey himself as spokesman for the ideas they shared, and he may have been even more important than Dewey in disseminating these ideas among the teaching profession.
[4]For an elegant, short presentation of this point of view, see Arthur E. Bestor, Jr., "Liberal Education and a Liberal Nation," *American Scholar* (Spring 1952).
[5]*New York Times,* November 15, 1961.

HOW CHILDREN LEARN
TO READ

Helen K. Mackintosh

Whether or not a child learns to read easily and happily depends not only upon the teacher but upon the attitude of the parents toward the child and toward reading. What happens to a child in his preschool years makes a difference in his feelings about reading. Where the child feels secure in being loved by his parents and by other members of the family, and where he has children of his own age to play with who are also interested in books and stories, he is more likely to be socially and emotionally ready for the new experience of school when it comes, and for learning to read.

Although the children who enter the first grade in September may be six years old or nearly six, their differences in other respects may be much wider than the narrow range of their ages. Their intelligence, their ability to use language in speaking, their physical health, their home backgrounds, their experiences in playing and working with other children may vary greatly from child to child.

For these reasons, the teacher recognizes that each child must be treated as an individual; that there are early "starters" and slow "starters" in learning to read. She recognizes that learning to read is not accidental; that she as a teacher must be able to recognize when each child is sufficiently ready to start the reading process from books. She is no magician, and must therefore observe, talk with parents, and possibly use readiness tests to determine when the time is "right."

The good teacher keeps informal records that tell when an individual child asks what certain words say, shows that he is interested in looking at books, reads a story by interpreting what the pictures say, tries to tell stories, and wants to have books that are his own.

But regardless of these records, the teacher herself is probably the most important factor of all. If she is relaxed, if she is patient, if she takes time to learn to know each child as an individual, if she creates a classroom environment which makes a child desire to read, the result in terms of what happens to a boy or girl will be quite different from what would happen if she were another type of person. If she is nervous, if she is concerned about having every child learn to read at the same time, if she is pressured by parents into forcing children to read before they are ready, her attitudes will be reflected in the way children feel and act.

Jersild defines readiness as "the timeliness of what we wish to teach in the light of the child's ability to take it."[1] The child needs to be "ready" from the standpoint of (1) his language and speech habits; (2) his mental maturity; (3) his physical development—such as vision and motor skills; (4)

Abridged from Helen K. Mackintosh, *How Children Learn to Read* (Washington, D.C.: U. S. Government Printing Office, 1952; reprinted 1954, 1957), Bulletin 1952, No. 7. Dr. Mackintosh is Chief of the Elementary Schools Section of the Office of Education, U. S. Department of Health, Education, and Welfare.

[1]Arthur Jersild *et al., Child Development and the Curriculum* (New York: Teachers College, Columbia University, 1946), p. 31.

the breadth and nature of his experiences, especially in relation to his interests in books and reading; and (5) his emotional and social background.

Ruth Strickland says that the average child as he enters first grade has a vocabulary of several thousand words.[2] These may be words that he recognizes when he hears them or words that he himself can use in speaking. They may not all be part of a vocabulary that he understands. Later on, he will acquire a reading vocabulary and a writing vocabulary, in addition to the speaking and hearing vocabularies that he first learns. Some parents keep an informal record of the new words which their children use, as they use them. The child who speaks clearly and distinctly has an advantage over another who talks baby talk. The latter will have difficulty in learning to read until he gets rid of his poor speech habits.

From what we know as a result of scientific studies, the typical child is probably more likely to succeed if he is at least six years and three months of age before he starts to read from books. Others state that the child who is of average mentality may well be six years and six months. Case histories of children with reading difficulties often show that they were forced into reading at some time between five and six years of age.

The child's physical development has an important part to play in his success in reading, particularly in regard to his vision and hearing. Scientific studies show that a child will be more likely to succeed in reading if he can detect likenesses and differences in the appearance of words, can get his clues from beginnings and endings and from the length and shape of the word. Such ability comes with maturity of the organs of vision. Similarly, the child must be able to distinguish between sounds. He needs to be able to match beginning and ending sounds of words with known key words; to select the one word that is different in a list of four or five; and to identify the written symbol of a letter with its sound in a word. Such abilities are dependent upon the quality of the child's hearing, and upon his ability to observe carefully. The teacher can encourage observation by careful questioning.

The breadth of the child's experience with books, and the attitudes that have been cultivated toward books and reading in his home before he comes to school, have a great deal to do with a child's readiness for reading. If a child is slow to express interest, parents should stimulate it by means of experiences.

Whether or not the child is socially and emotionally well adjusted makes a difference, too. If he is happy in his group, not too much smaller or larger physically than the other children, is as well cared for as the others, leaves a happy home to go off to school in the morning, and returns to it at the end of the day—these factors also have to be considered as important. If parents do not get along together, if parents are separated, if parents praise some of the children in the family and scold one, he will be emotionally insecure, and the chances are that he will be more likely to have reading difficulties.

If a teacher is concerned only with the mechanics of reading, with a process designed to make it possible for children to pronounce words glibly,

---

[2]Ruth Strickland, *The Language Arts in the Elementary School* (Boston: Heath, 1951), p. 58.

rather than to get meaning from a printed page, she will not take account of these other factors that really determine in the long run how well the child will be able to read for many purposes throughout the remainder of his life.

The good first-grade teacher observes all the evidences of readiness for reading in each child in her group. At the same time, she works to broaden the experiences and the interests of all the children. Some of the ways that she uses include sharing toys and games; observing pets or looking at growing things in an aquarium or terrarium; taking trips and excursions; looking at still pictures, slides, and filmstrips; preparing a simple food; painting and drawing; building and constructing with blocks and other materials; using simple tools; hearing poetry, telling stories, singing songs, and responding to rhythm; reading labels and signs; and using picture books in the school library and in the classroom.

Children get acquainted with each other, with the teacher, the principal, the custodian, with their building, with their own rooms, with the fact that there are names on the door to help you find your way. Some names are long and some are short. You do some guessing and you let the length and shape of the word help you in deciding what it is.

The teacher may write or print a simple summary of two or three sentences on the board as the children talk; for writing, spelling, and written language expression are closely related to the reading process. Perhaps the story is copied on a chart and is read to them the next day, or some day following when a child who has been absent returns to school.

The teacher waits for the children to accumulate a number of such experiences. Then some day a child remarks, "I know what *that* word says," or "I can read what you wrote," or "I told my mother a story and she wrote it down," or "This is the story I wrote" (it may be a mass of scribbles on paper). Children are becoming accustomed to the sounds of words that they hear over and over again and they know something of how the words look. This is the time when the teacher will probably say, "Can you find the words that tell where we went? Who went with us? What we saw in the park?" The answers will come in the form of sentences that the children recognize as they frame them by placing their hands around them, and then reading aloud. When enough of the words and sentences have been identified, an individual child may read the whole story.

There may be children in the group whose readiness is such that they can read their stories aloud with very little help. The teacher may read and reread these stories as children request them. In the early stages of working with such experience stories, the material may be copied on a large chart which can be kept permanently for the children's own use.

How fast or how slow the teacher proceeds depends upon the needs and abilities of the individual children. Ruth Strickland points out that children may look without seeing and see without comprehending unless they have a background of knowledge and experience, and a teacher who can help them use such experience.[3]

The teacher will find situations in which children can read the chart stories to an audience—a mother, the principal, a visitor, other children in the school. The children themselves may make pictures to illustrate such

[3]*Ibid.*

stories, and thus help to clinch meanings. As they work, their speaking vocabulary will keep ahead of their reading vocabulary, and this is as it should be.

When some children have not fewer than a hundred "sight" words—words that they can recognize, when they see them in print, by matching them with the actual object or a picture or an action—the teacher will start with this group in a preprimer. Here the child will meet some words that are already familiar to him. The vocabularies of the various preprimers are more alike than different since they are based upon studies that have been made of children's word usage, and the frequency of occurrence of words in preprimers now available. One of the real jobs which the teacher has at this point is to help children make the shift from print or manuscript done by hand to printed words in a book. It is because of the likeness between manuscript writing and printing that many teachers prefer this form of writing to the cursive.

Other children will still be working with experiences and the stories that grow out of them. As other small groups are ready for reading, they are introduced to the preprimer; and so the process of forming groups goes on. Such groups are kept flexible so that a child can move from one to another depending upon his own individual progress. There should be no predetermined number of groups. There may be three, or four, or five, depending upon the needs of the children. The number of children in each of such groups will vary, and may be as few as two or three.

As soon as there are three or more groups, the teacher has a problem in knowing how to keep every child at work without resorting to "busy work." However, she can manage if the group is not larger than 20 to 25 children, if she does some planning with the children, and if she provides things to do that children are able to do by themselves.

For example, one first-grade teacher has a large chart made of oak tag on which are listed ten or more things a child can do if he finishes reading the story in his reader, or if he has a free choosing time while she is working with a group. The items on the chart are changed from time to time with the children's help. He may read at the library table; he may watch the turtle so that he can help make a story about him; or practice writing his name; or play in the playhouse in one corner of the room where furniture and objects are labeled; or play with a fist puppet and make it talk; or operate the simple movie-on-a-roll made by last year's first-grade children which has brief titles for each picture. Or he may draw pictures to illustrate a chart story. Some teachers set up centers within the room where each of these activities can be carried on because the materials are there. Signs or labels mark each table so that children know where to look for each activity.

The wise teacher helps children to decide in advance what their choices are going to be, so that in the course of a week or more they will have had a variety of experiences. It is the teacher's responsibility, too, to help children judge or evaluate these experiences to see what their learning value was. All of the experiences described can contribute to reading in some way.

From a preprimer book to other preprimers to first readers are the next steps in the reading process as carried on in the typical classroom in the United States. There are on record, in the form of magazine articles, reports by certain individual teachers to show that some groups of children have been taught to read without the use of reading textbooks.[4] Instead, the teacher has used interesting story books. Where parents are willing, and teachers have imagination and good ideas, further experiments may well be carried on to find new and better ways of teaching children to read.

Whether a child gets as far as reading from a primer while he is in first grade, or whether he is reading easily from several first readers by the end of the year, is a highly individual matter. Some children may not be ready for first readers before the second grade. Neither they, nor their teachers, nor the parents should be critical of a child who is a slow starter, if he has made his best effort. Oftentimes the difficulty is with the adults rather than the child. The typical child should make a spurt in growth in the second year or third year of school, so that he has acquired the basic skills needed in getting thought from the printed page by the time he is nine years old.

In the typical school, teachers are helping children, individually and in groups, to gain skill in reading silently and orally for meaning. No matter how well a child can pronounce words, he has not learned to read unless he can talk intelligently about what he has read. To summarize the story by retelling is not enough. By means of guiding questions such as, "Read far enough to tell who stole the box, *or* where Tom was going, *or* what was in the basket; *or* read the words that tell what Bill's dog was like," the teacher helps children to think, to interpret, and to give reasons for their answers. In order to be able to do these jobs, children must have skill in the mechanics of reading.

In order to be a good reader, a child who grows up in the United States (1) needs to learn to read from left to right; (2) needs to train his eyes so that they move easily back from the end of one line to the beginning of the next; (3) needs to read silently without moving his lips; (4) needs to see words in thought groups of two, three, four, or five rather than singly; (5) needs to recognize familiar words; and (6) needs to have a method for attacking new words.

Since the techniques which the teacher uses to help the child meet the first four needs are somewhat technical and are discussed in textbooks or in articles on reading, they are not analyzed here. But because the skills which the child needs to have—(1) in recognizing words that should be familiar, and (2) in attacking new words—are so widely discussed and often misunderstood, an attempt is made to examine them carefully.

To many mothers and fathers and grandparents the answer to the problems involved in teaching a child to read can be answered by the one word PHONICS. Phonics is defined as a system by means of which a child learns sets of phonograms—word endings by "families" such as *at* in the words *cat, fat, mat, rat;* word beginnings and vowel sounds so that he can apply them to the words he encounters in reading. Such a system presupposes that a child learns his letters first, next puts them together to form words, and lastly hitches the words together in order to make sentences and paragraphs. If such a method really worked, good teachers would be using it today.

[4]Melva Harris, "Beginning Reading Without Readers," *Childhood Education,* 26 (December 1949), 164–167.

As a matter of fact, too much attention to single letters, to the mechanics of word formation, to the sounds of letters, hinders rather than helps a child in the long run if the teacher's purpose is to help him get meaning from the printed page. Such attention to details slows down the act of reading and makes the child so conscious of mechanics that he fails to think of what the words are trying to tell him. The teacher sees to it that there is a proper balance between mechanics and meaning.

Before he begins to read from books, the child has acquired a vocabulary of not fewer than one hundred sight words, words that have been developed through real experiences and that he recognizes when he sees them. He is taught to look carefully at the way the word begins, and the way it ends, as, for example, in the word "tell." Many of the words he learns first are one-syllable words. He therefore looks at the vowel that comes between the beginning and the end of the word. However, he is encouraged to do this without "sounding out" the letters. If he hesitates, the teacher may say, "How does the word begin? With what letter? Can you find a word on the chart we have made that begins like this one? Say that word. [In this case it is the word "take."] Now try the one you are working on." If this help is not enough, she may ask the child to look at the last letter or letters in the word, and if necessary to get help from a key word on the chart. (In this case it is the word "bell.")

Such a chart may be made on a sheet of heavy paper with letters arranged in alphabetical order. After each letter, but filled in only as children actually meet the words and work with them, may be four or five key words, useful to the child in identifying new words. Teachers may refer to such a method of working and to the use of such a chart as functional phonics—phonics which is developed and used as needed in relation to the words that actually occur in the child's reading. Moreover, this chart will help children to know the letters of the alphabet certainly by the end of the first grade.

But the good teacher will not depend upon functional phonics alone, nor will she put it first in her list of helps for the child. First of all she tries to choose material in which the child will meet only a few unfamiliar words. She will encourage the child to look through the whole sentence in which a difficult word occurs, to try to get the meaning from the context; that is, in relation to the words that he does know. She will also encourage the child who has difficulty to look at the pictures as a way of learning what the story is about. And she will certainly help the child to make a best guess as to what the word is from its configuration or length + beginning + ending + appearance of letters above and below the line, as *t, d, b,* or *f, g, y.* Or she may tell the child the word and have him place it in a list for further study.

The big problem for both child and teacher is to relate sound to printed symbols and to meaning. The teacher may play a game with children in which she pronounces very distinctly a series of words, such as *bell, tell, sell, wall, fell, well,* and asks children to raise their hands as soon as they hear a word that doesn't belong. The list of words may then be written down so that children can see them as well as hear them. The job is made easy or more difficult, if the words are ones they know or words they have not met before.

As children meet words of more than one syllable in grades two and three, the teacher helps them to recognize syllables using a simple rule such as, "Every syllable must contain a vowel, or a letter that stands for a vowel. If two consonants (letters other than vowels) come together, one goes with the first syllable, the other with the second." Children are given practice with words that have caused them difficulty, by marking the syllables. This is best done not by rewriting and leaving a space between, or by drawing a vertical line between syllables, but rather by drawing a line beneath each syllable so as not to slow up the eyes in taking in the word. Prefixes, suffixes, double vowels all need special attention, too.

The fact that reading skills have been discussed in detail does not mean that the teacher should attempt to teach them by a drill method. Children should be encouraged to read in a situation in which all the factors are as nearly right as they can be made. If children meet with difficulties, then the teacher must use a variety of methods to help each one solve his own problems, because reading is a highly individual matter. Once the suitable method is found, the child needs enough practice so that the skill is mastered.

Every teacher has a major responsibility in seeing to it that a child's first experience with reading is so satisfying that difficulties are prevented from ever developing. If a child can be successful, especially in the early stages of reading, he is less likely to need remedial help later on. For this reason it is important to see that he reads a great deal of familiar material, but with new purposes set up for each reading. It is equally important that he be prepared for each new step before he attempts it. Children who do not respond to ordinary methods, and who have reached these school years without having acquired the basic skills, may need a more dramatic approach to learning. Experiments with the typewriter have shown that children may have more eagerness for reading if the stories they dictate are typed, and if they have the use of the typewriter. Use of a printing outfit for recording their stories may also stimulate interest. Special care should be given to seating children with handicaps of vision or hearing that cannot be remedied, so that they may have every advantage in seeing and hearing.

Teachers may assume that a child who enters fourth grade has acquired the basic reading skills needed to comprehend or to get thought from the printed page. But it is almost bound to be true that there will be weak children, ones who need encouragement and help, who are reading on a second- or third-grade level. The teacher must begin with them where they are, with easy material, and must offer the same type of help as the primary teacher gives.

Since the intermediate grades in school have been labeled "the period of wide reading," the teacher needs to use the school library or, if there is none, to provide in the classroom a great variety of books of all types which children are encouraged and stimulated to read. Children aged nine to eleven need to develop skill in selecting good books independently and in reading for themselves. The teacher with ingenuity will find many ways to help children locate, select, read, evaluate, and share with others their best-liked books. In this situation children will be applying some of the new skills to be learned during these years.

Important among these new skills are (1) the ability to locate information involving a knowledge of sources; (2) the ability to select material and evaluate it in terms of a purpose; (3) the ability to organize material around a topic or a problem; and (4) the ability to recall. Children may have made some use of these skills in simple form in primary grades.

How can a parent judge whether or not his child is reading up to capacity? Such judgment cannot be made on the basis of whether or not the child can read the book that grandpa gave him for Christmas, or whether or not he knows the alphabet. There are a few simple means which the parent can use to get some idea of how well the boy or girl can read. Can Sue reread aloud at home a story that she first prepared and read at school? Can she read the child's newspaper for which she subscribes at school? Can she read and understand directions for setting up a cardboard playhouse for her dolls? Can she read and use a simple recipe from a child's cookbook for the making of applesauce? Can she read street signs? Does she have a library card and does she bring home books? Does she reread the books that belong to her? Can she find the name and telephone number of a relative in the phone book? These skills range from the simple to the more complex. But these and many others are the kinds of activities that a child will normally carry on at some time during the elementary-school period. The school, the teacher, the parents, and the child himself are all equally interested in having him learn to read comfortably and successfully.

THE WHOLE-WORD AND WORD-GUESSING FALLACY

Helen R. Lowe

Arthur Young, a painter and carpenter, is now twenty-eight years old. He came to me first when he was twenty-four, bringing with him a New York State high-school diploma which certified in impressive Old English type that Arthur Andrew Young had "satisfactorily completed the curriculum requirements prescribed by the Board of Education for the High School and is entitled to this Diploma." He also brought his final report card, certifying that he had received the highest mark—H, for Honor—in English throughout his senior year.

Arthur could not read, even at a primer level. He could not drive a car, because he could not pass the test for a driver's license; he could not

Abridged from Helen R. Lowe, "The Whole-Word and Word-Guessing Fallacy," in Charles C. Walcutt, ed., *Tomorrow's Illiterates: The State of Reading Instruction Today* (New York: Little, Brown & Company, 1961), pp. 87–114. Copyright © 1961 by The Council for Basic Education. Reprinted by permission of Little, Brown & Co.-Atlantic Monthly Press. Mrs. Lowe is director of The William Street Workshop, Glen Falls, New York. She is studying the impact of current educational principles and practices on students of all ages.

read the street signs or traffic directions. He was unable to order from the menu in a restaurant. He could not read letters from his family and he could not write to them. He could not read the mixing directions on a can of paint or the label on a shipment of sheet rock. He had been cheated and swindled in various ways as a consequence of his inability to read.[1]

We went to work. For more than two years he worked with me two or three times a week. It was a slow business, because he needed to learn to spell and write too. It was more than a year before we read a fifth-grade story, a real book, about John Paul Jones. Finally he began to buy *Life* and *Coronet* magazines and struggle through articles which attracted his interest. We read the newspaper, he studied to pass the examination for his driver's license, he discovered that he loved poetry. He began to read letters from his family to me. Finally he read his first adult short story, a not very remarkable piece called "Santa Claus and the Tenth Avenue Kid," which I had selected very specially for him because it was just beyond the range of his experience and understanding, full of implications and allusions strange to him. When we finished it, he said, "I want to read that again. I want to see what it feels like to get all those things as I go along." Arthur had learned to read.

To realize what Arthur is a symbol of, one has only to look at his diminished life, and then at the misrepresentative report card and diploma. That Arthur was not taught to read is a failure on the part of his school and an indictment of many of the accepted purposes, standards, and methods of our system of public education.

I propose to show how hundreds of children taught by the word-recognition method have misread to me; to relate these misreadings to the principles of learning which produced them; and to dissect from the controlling mass of theory and practice the fundamental fallacy of defining and treating the printed word as a symbol of meaning instead of as a symbol of sound.

The essential point to hold in mind when considering this evidence— and this requires a firm hold—is that it *is* evidence. It is not a prediction or guess about the consequences of look-and-say. It is objective records of performance that show how hundreds of students have read and do read today. These bright boys and girls have been taught and they have learned, and when they read like this they are doing precisely what they have been taught to do and precisely what common sense would expect them to do. That this is not reading, in any real sense of the word, would seem indisputable, but it is disputed.

Reading is no longer presented to the beginning reader as a matter of learning how to get from the printed page as exactly as possible the ideas committed to the text by the writer. It has become a process in which the reader projects his imagination, his preferences, his conjectures, his limitations, his inexperience, and his ignorance, using the words he

[1]Every reader of the manuscript of this book expressed skepticism about Arthur Young's honor mark on his report card. Incredible as it may seem, he *did* receive such a mark; Mrs. Lowe submitted a photostatic copy of his report card for his fourth year in high school showing that he received honors in English in each marking period and for a final mark. [Note by the editor of *Tomorrow's Illiterates*.]

chances to recognize—or to mistake—as points of departure for his improvisations and substitutions. This travesty of the achievement that gave man access to the wisdom of the past, that enabled him to enlarge and extend his own experience to levels he could never reach alone in an uncommunicating world—this is not reading.

Man achieved speech long before he invented writing. As he began to try to record and to communicate, he developed two main systems of writing. One was picture writing. This sometimes became ideographic; that is, it developed to become a form of writing in symbols which had lost their explicit pictorial character. These symbols conveyed ideas but not sounds. The other kind of writing which began to evolve was sound or phonetic writing. The invention of an alphabet, from which there is evidence that all alphabets derived, took place about three thousand years ago. An alphabet is a set of characters, each representing a simple or unit sound, with no meaning in itself. From that time on, we have record of the growth of the alphabetic languages and the impetus given to civilization and to the mind of man by this infinitely precise and flexible means of recording language.

No one knowing the history of language or the definition of an ideogram could mistake English for an ideographic language. Ideograms convey ideas but not sounds. We use many ideographic symbols—the arrow, the skull and crossbones, plus and minus signs, 3 or 5 or 9, the dollar sign, the red cross—all clearly conveying meaning and understood by persons who do not even understand each other's spoken language. These are not words, any more than comprehensible gestures are words. Nor are the printed words of the English or any other modern alphabetical language ideograms; that is, symbols of meaning unrelated to sound. The very words "literate," "literacy," "literature" bear testimony to the relation of the letter—*litera*—to reading and writing.

Civilization took a great leap forward when the alphabet was invented. Look-and-say was a reversion to a primitive stage, beyond which English and the other modern alphabetic languages advanced hundreds of years ago. It is difficult for an open mind to believe that those who devised and defended this primitive parody of the invention by which man achieved the ultimate flexibility and effectiveness in communication were entirely innocent in their folly.

I have made a careful study and classification of over a hundred thousand accurately recorded misreadings, which show more than twenty-five distinguishable types of errors characterizing the reading of hundreds of bright normal students of all ages. To simplify this material for presentation, these misreadings have been grouped under four main types.

The first group of recorded errors consists of misreadings which proceed directly from the concept of a word as a visual symbol of an idea, to be recognized by its configuration or total appearance, without awareness of its parts, their sequence, or their function. This includes several easily differentiated types of errors, all clearly the product of whole-word reading, which does not treat letters as symbols of sound. Here are characteristic examples of the simplest type of configuration misreading, where one word is read as another because the two words look alike.

squirrel	*read as*	special
mystery		majesty
equatorial		equilateral
bouquet		banquet
cottage		college
peninsula		penicillin

Here nothing but Look has determined the Say. Such uncomplicated whole-word readings as *futility* for *futurity,* or *feet* for *feel,* must be clearly understood to be not mispronunciations, but ideographic readings which did not come off. The reader often gets the idea, which he has been taught; what he does not get is the word. When this happens the reader has made an association between a visual form and *what it does not mean.*

Now a printed word is exact, in one important sense. It ties the reader to the writer's choice of a certain word. Words stabilize communication, which even the educationists do not explicitly deny to be the purpose of speech and writing. The unrealistic assumption that a word is a visual image conveying an idea belittles both ideas and words. Indeed, Dr. Albert J. Harris tells us that if a word occurs rarely or is not a key word, it does not matter very much whether the reader develops a really accurate comprehension of it or not! To the thoughtful mind there is more than irony in the fact that this opinion is voiced in a chapter of a book entitled *How to Increase Reading Ability.*[2]

A plain illustration of the effect of the ideographic fallacy is the very frequent reading-by-association, where the printed word communicates an idea, expressed in words of the reader's choice arising spontaneously in his mind in response to his perception of the visual pattern. For example:

diphtheria	*read as*	Seppula[3]
snow		cold
fire		stove
milk		bottle
regiment		army
turkey		Thanksgiving
Christmas		Santa Claus

In this kind of reading, a word like *field* triggers a visual image; and the reader, sometimes at a high-school level, says *meadow,* or *pasture, lawn,* or even *park.* Or when he sees the word *milk* he visualizes it as he most often sees it, and without hesitation says *bottle.* If he has grown up on an unmodernized farm, he may even say *bucket,* or *pail,* and while I have never had this happen, it would not be at all surprising if he said *cow.* Rhetorically speaking, this is metonymy, the use of the name of one thing for another to which it has some logical relation: the sign for the thing signified, the container for the thing contained. It is not reading. A frequent variant of this ideographic phenomenon is reading by synonym. Thus we have:

stillness	*read as*	silence
lazybones		sleepyhead
puppy		little dog
fiddle		violin
afraid		frightened

---

[2]Albert J. Harris, *How to Increase Reading Ability* (New York: Longmans, 1956).
[3]The driver of the dog-sledge which carried the diphtheria serum to Nome.

A more complex and at first sight inexplicable variant is the reading by opposites, where we find:

asleep	read as	awake
down		up
mongrel		pedigreed
attendance		absence
north		south

This occurs when the idea established by former contacts with a word is retained in a diffuse, unfocused fashion, and only a hint of the general implication swims into the would-be reader's consciousness. The reader hazards *light* for *dark, winter* for *summer, started* for *stopped,* or *before* for *after,* with deluded consistency. A grotesque variation of this occurs repeatedly when the idea so vaguely recalled is that of some part of the human body. *Arm* is read as *leg, ankles* as *knees, hand* as *head, knee* as *neck, eyebrows* as *elbows,* completely regardless of the utter impossibility of the contortions involved.

Words thus read are often indelibly remembered to mean their exact opposites, and crop up in writing even at a college level. The dislocation of sound and sense which makes it possible for an intelligent eighteen-year-old to write *dark* when he thinks *light* cannot be dismissed by blandly citing the circulation statistics of the American Library Association.

Still another current phenomenon, closely related to the fundamental fallacy of seeking meaning without regard for the particular word, is the habitual paraphrase of the clever, inventive reader. This kind of reading sometimes distorts, sometimes reverses the meaning, and, occasionally, is astonishingly competent—as a paraphrase. Any sort of paraphrase is, at first thought, astonishing, since it must necessarily be based on at least partial comprehension of the passage, *which is then discarded for the reader's version!*

Actually there is little cause for astonishment. This is the transfer of the principle of ideographic reading from the word to the phrase and the sentence. Typical examples of this follow where the idea has sometimes been caught, sometimes distorted, diluted, or missed completely. We have:

What was the cost of the house?	read as	What did he pay for it?
Stop! Stop, Spot!		Complete riot!
into a sizzling frying pan		into a skillet
I'll get you another ticket (for a ride)		I'll take you again
within hauling distance		anywhere
(cougars prey upon) anything that can't defend itself		anything they can get

Burdened to bewilderment by the multiplicity of new and often similar visual patterns, memory produces a flood of random errors where proper names are involved. Proper names are merely designating and identifying sounds. *Dick* designates, and identifies, and may summon a boy, but as a word it conveys no meaning. Proper names suffer so significantly and so spectacularly from whole-word reading that the bizarre items which follow are merely a small selection from crowded files.

Massachusetts	*read as*	Switzerland
Tom		Betty
Washington		Grant
China		Corinth
Africa		America
Mary		Bert
Bethlehem		Baltimore
Asia		Amsterdam

Here is something quite different from the reading from configuration, or from association, synonym, or opposites. This is whole-word reading where the double play—Look to Say to Sense—fails to come off, because memory cannot trigger meaning when there is none.

One of the earliest and most influential of the answers to the inability of look-and-say to produce proficient readers was the restricted vocabulary. Dr. Arthur I. Gates, Professor of Education at Teachers College, Columbia University, urged that all reading texts for the first three grades be based largely on a vocabulary of 1,811 selected words, and that words used in other subjects and in announcements be confined—Dr. Gates's word—as far as possible to the same vocabulary. He also recommended that to develop *language ability* the same words should be used in writing and spelling as well as in reading.[1] It is difficult to see how the concept of reading could be further degraded, or how skill in reading could be made to seem less worth acquiring. Only the very gullible could believe that the limitation of the child's vocabulary could enlarge and stimulate his reading ability.

I have assembled some curious evidence as to how this restricted vocabulary really works and what effect it has upon reading. Careful recording of thousands of reading errors, made by students at all levels and from many different localities, has revealed an odd fact. Certain words were misread with conspicuous frequency by many students, and they were usually misread in exactly the same way. As these words established themselves as practically standardized errors, they were put on a list, which, surprisingly, ceased suddenly to grow longer after it had come to contain 98 words and became known to my students as The Ninety-eight. It was at once evident that these particular mistakes were extremely difficult to eradicate, that they persisted and recurred even at high-school and college level. Reference to Dr. Gates's vocabulary list revealed the extraordinary fact that 73 of these 98 words were among those assigned to be taught in Grade One. That is to say, approximately 75 per cent of these stubborn, ingrained errors, misread almost as standard practice by disabled readers, were among the first words taught, as wholes, with innumerable repetitions, in accordance with the accepted method of teaching beginning reading. Further, 18 more were among those assigned to be taught in the second grade, by that rote recognition which arbitrarily relates a sterile visual image to a taught meaning—or, as with The Ninety-eight—fails wholesale to do so. Thus we have striking evidence that 91 of the 98 words the record shows to have been consistently misread at all

[1] Arthur I. Gates, *A Reading Vocabulary for the Primary Grades* (New York: Teachers College, Columbia University; revised and enlarged, 1935; seventh printing, 1956).

levels, including the high school, are among those which were first and most often presented to the beginning reader for recognition by the whole-word method. Some of these words are *with, when, then, they, how, we, did, of, hand, head, for, said, the, and, from*!

This device of decreasing the child's command of language by restricting his contacts with it had disastrous side effects. Not only was the content of elementary reading texts reduced to an inanity unparalleled in print, but any resort at home to well and normally written children's books was stringently disapproved by the school.

Dr. Gates at one point discusses the extent to which a child may be *entrusted* with miscellaneous children's material at school or at home.[5] The meeting with a new word is now considered a peril to be prevented. One reading expert actually debates whether certain words are "safe" to introduce in the fourth grade.[6] The age of discovery must seem very remote to today's children.

Among the practical solutions devised to solve the problem of teaching children to read by the look-and-say method was the idea of deducing the meaning of words from contextual clues. That the reader has no right to *decide* but must *discover* the meanings of words seemed not to occur to the whole-worders. Certainly it did not deter them from seizing upon this ingenious way to get an idea of sorts from the printed page—and not the idea as expressed by the writer, but one developed by the reader. Children were encouraged to think-what-would-make-sense; and Scott, Foresman, the principal publisher of look-and-say readers, explicitly assures us that if what a youngster figures out makes sense, *he knows he has figured out the right word.* As an example of how this works, we are told that if a child is reading "It began to rain. Sally put up her ———" he would expect the next word to be *umbrella,* whether or not he had ever seen the word before.[7] What he would expect the next word to be if he was not familiar with the word *umbrella* was not predicted. What he does read, shown by repeated experiment, with this sentence separated from the picture of an umbrella, is *rain hood*!

It should be pointed out that substantial parts of many of the standardized reading tests are presented in this predicting-the-probable-outcome form, and obviously the best predicters are rated the best readers—provided they are canny enough to stick to the preformulated predictions and do not free-think too imaginatively. Tests of this sort do not tell simply how well a child can read but illustrate his ability to guess within limits. Furthermore, tests favored by many schools are skillfully constructed not to discover whether the student can read but to demonstrate that he can.[8] Scrutinize carefully the test material supplied with and keyed to the reading texts from which your child is being taught. For an authentic test, give your child some good book by Stevenson or Kipling—or literary work proper for his age—and listen with pencil in hand while he reads to you.

[5]*Ibid.,* p. 4.
[6]Paul McKee, *The Teaching of Reading* (Boston: Houghton Mifflin, 1948).
[7]*When Parents Ask About Reading* (Chicago: Scott, Foresman, Service Bulletin).
[8]California, beset by angry parents and mounting criticism of her ultra-progressive schools, has devised a reading test on which the children of the state score a *year or more* better than they do on the standard national tests!

After the whole-word-guessing from context, undoubtedly the most damaging bit in the look-and-say approach has been the attempt to wrench pictures out of their useful role of contributing vividness and interest to the printed text, and to enlist them to supply specific words that the reader cannot read. Pictures, not words, tell the story in modern beginning-reading texts, and it is to the pictures that the child's attention is directed, and there it is rewarded.

How can the educationists believe that giving the beginning reader dull and uninformative printed words will spark in him a passionate desire to read and read and read? How can he learn to read words when he is taught to look at and think about pictures?

In this connection must be noted the spelling books which present page after page of small pictures with the direction: Spell these *words* to yourself.[9] This is confusion confounded, a fallacy which has lost its way, its identity, its destination. One bright little seven-year-old, dizzy from trying to spell pictures and read ideas, looked at a lively red silhouette of a rat and asked, "I can read that word *animal,* too, can't I, as well as *mouse?"*

Other theories evolved to explain why a child had difficulty in learning to read. One, more directly damaging than most, was the assumption that a substantial percentage—estimated variously from 10 per cent to 35 per cent—of the children entering school suffered from a congenital inability to deal satisfactorily with words, and, specifically, from a congenital inability to learn to read. Well before 1948 I had become convinced that so-called specific reading disability, as indicated conspicuously by reversals and bizarre misreadings, was largely made, and not born. Moreover, for many students referred by school psychologists, psychiatrists, and teachers as severe cases of mixed cerebral dominance, a simpler explanation was easily found, which led to a simple remedy. A failure to develop that was due to hereditary causes would not yield to the simple procedures which I find effective with students from kindergarten to college level. They are told, "Oh, you read backwards? Well, don't. It doesn't work. I'll show you how to read forward." This is not psychotherapy nor yet remedial reading. It is, perhaps, nothing more remarkable than horse sense.

The eager and indiscriminate extension of the blight of mixed cerebral dominance is a striking instance of the increasingly urgent effort to find some kind, any kind, of explanation for the nonreading children crowding the remedial classes. Because a child's introduction to reading consisted of looking at and enumerating, in any order he pleased, the objects in a picture, he looked at words in the same way and read *on* as *no* and *was* as *saw.*

Remedial reading is a misnomer for these frustrated groups, since there is little remedy and less reading involved. What is usually offered is little more than the repetition of the practices and procedures which were responsible for the failure. And the boredom and the inescapable stigma of inferiority do not enhance the charm of learning to read.

There is cogent objective evidence that in only a small percentage of

[9]Mary B. Lambader and William Kottmeyer, *New Goals in Spelling* (St. Louis: Webster Publishing, 1955).

academic failures at any level is there involved any real inability to learn. Two principles of importance can be established from the intensive study of retrieved casualties of the whole-word and word-guessing fallacy. The first is that as a preliminary to any possibility of uninhibited learning there must be established a logical and realistic concept of reading, not simply as a prerequisite to reading in the ordinary sense of the word, but as essential to the whole learning process. The student must recognize that ideas are expressed in and are to be recovered from the words on the printed page. The reader discovers; he may not invent.

The second, closely related to the first and carrying profound neurological implications, is that a subjective concept of reading, in which the reader's experience, his conjectures, his expectation, and his preferences take precedence over the printed *text,* not only produces the disabled reader with whom we are so unhappily familiar, but carries over disastrously into other areas, notably those of mathematics and foreign languages, and, further, induces emotional tensions, conflicts, and a disastrous conviction of inferiority. This damage is not merely a limitation of learning in certain specific academic areas, although it is indeed that. It is an alienation of the learning powers.

Students of excellent abilities are being thrust into the discard of second and third tracks largely on the basis of mediocre marks in tests they could not read accurately. These misshapen and misguided young minds, bewildered, thwarted, disturbed, and inarticulate, are misunderstood by the very nature of their handicap, which cuts them off from communicating with us.

There is still another kind of damage, however, usually complete and irreversible, where not merely the right to learn but the right to live has been abridged. Students who read "the travelworn paper bag" as "twelve onions," and "masses of reddish-gold clouds" as "molasses and radishes" will almost certainly get odd and unfounded ideas about the functioning of the U.N., the properties of liquid helium, and the provisions of their life insurance policies. Students who never learn to read at all—and the record of illiterates discovered among young men drafted during World War II underlines how many of them there are—these discarded young men and women are struggling to make a living, to pursue happiness, with nearly all doors closed to them. For many these doors are closed by the fallacy, the folly, and the fraud which are the subject of this essay. Few of these doors ever open again. Arthur Young's did, only because of his passionate desire, his determination, his patience and pertinacity, and his uncorroded courage.

GUIDES FOR READING AND DISCUSSION

1. What is the range of legitimate educational goals in the United States? Is each goal necessarily related to a particular method? Can the various goals (and methods) be reconciled, and if so how?

2. Does the probable success of phonics or look-say in teaching reading vary with the social class of the pupils? Do the two methods have different effects on the classroom atmosphere?

3. The ability to read is one of the easiest characteristics to test; yet the relative efficiency of various methods still remains a disputed issue. How can one explain this?

SUGGESTED ADDITIONAL READINGS

Arthur Bestor, *Educational Wastelands* (Urbana: University of Illinois Press, 1953); *The Restoration of Learning: A Program for Redeeming the Unfulfilled Promise of American Education* (New York: Knopf, 1956).

John Dewey, *Experience and Education* (New York: Macmillan, 1939).

Martin S. Dworkin, ed., *Dewey on Education: Selections* (New York: Teachers College, Columbia University, 1959).

Rudolph Flesch, *Why Johnny Can't Read* (New York: Harper, 1955); see also the extensive reviews in, among other places, *Time,* January 9, 1956; *Saturday Review,* July 30, 1955.

William Heard Kilpatrick, *Philosophy of Education* (New York: Macmillan, 1951).

Martin Mayer, *The Schools* (New York: Harper, 1961).

Mortimer Smith, *And Madly Teach* (Chicago: Regnery, 1949).

Charles C. Walcutt, ed., *Tomorrow's Illiterates: The State of Reading Instruction Today* (Council for Basic Education; Boston: Little, Brown, 1961).

Paul Woodring, *New Directions in Teacher Education* (New York: Fund for the Advancement of Education, 1957).

SHOULD THE FEDERAL GOVERNMENT
SUPPORT PAROCHIAL SCHOOLS?

Wherever the Roman Catholic Church exists, it has sought to establish a school system paid for out of general taxation but controlled by itself. In the United States, each partial success in this direction, such as publicly financed lunches and buses for parochial schools, becomes the precedent for a new advance. In judging each of these separate issues, then, one should ask where the Church prelates would like to go, what sort of relation between church and state they see as just. The Catholic model for the United States, in our opinion—as in Professor Lekachman's—is not Spain or Ireland, but the democratic, multireligious country of Holland.

In the past history of both the Netherlands and the United States, an established church held special rights and privileges—the Reformed Church in Holland and the Episcopal, Congregationalist, Catholic, or other church in the various American colonies. With the spread of democratic ideals, the favored position of a single church was abolished in both countries, but not in the same way. In the United States, freedom of religion is interpreted negatively. Our basic principle is the separation of church and state, which means that the state shall neither favor any religious group nor hinder its members in the practice of their faith. In the Netherlands, on the contrary, the advantages originally enjoyed by the state church have been granted in principle to all churches, and eventually also to such other quasi-religious groups as the Humanist Society, in proportion to the number of their adherents. The state uses its police power to collect taxes, and then distributes a sizable percentage of the national budget to a wide variety of institutions—schools, hospitals, social-welfare agencies, artistic and scientific institutes, cultural associations, and publications of all types. These institutions function as both public and private bodies: public in the sense that they are financed out of tax funds in order to carry out essential social tasks; private in the sense that they operate in a value context set by one religious or ideological group. It is this system that distinguishes Holland's version of cultural pluralism from that of the United States.

In Holland, the division into Calvinist, Catholic, and "neutral" sectors was established first in public education. Today, political parties, newspapers, radio and television programs, trade unions, farmers' associations, employers' organizations, professional societies, sports clubs and other leisure-time activities—all are also structured along the lines of these three main ideologies. All their lives, from primary school up, the Dutch are taught that they must avoid the *andersdenkenden*—the "different-thinking"—as husbands or wives, as friends, as associates in business or work, as partners in play. Thus, a half inch under the surface of formal relations, one finds antipathies of sometimes amazing virulence.

Of course, Holland is not the United States, and the strong attachment of the Dutch to their religions and their church-affiliated organizations will never be duplicated in full in this country. But implicit in every choice on the relation between church and state is a decision whether to move toward the Dutch system. It is clear that Holland's type of democratic society has important advantages. Its statistics on crime, divorce, suicide, and similar indices of social and psychological health suggest that this is a good society. Those who fit into the system fit in very well; for those who do not, the system is excessively restrictive by present American standards.

Professor Van den Haag argues that public aid should be given to private schools mainly on two grounds: that the parents' freedom of choice, a good thing by democratic standards, would thus be enhanced; and that the "massification" of American society, the trend toward universal sameness, would be combatted. In Professor Lekachman's view, both these points lead to the contrary conclusion. Parents' freedom of choice is greater if it is expressed through wholly private institutions, rather than through those that combine public with private features. And if the diversification of American society is necessary, this goal should not be sought by breaking up what has been the main unifying force of a heterogeneous people—the American public school.

GIVE FEDERAL AID TO PAROCHIAL SCHOOLS

Ernest van den Haag

In one form or another, we all support public education with our taxes. If we have no offspring, we are supposed to benefit nonetheless: other people's children might be more of a nuisance if not kept in school; and there is always the chance that they might learn something useful to us there. (A tenuous justification, but let it go.) Those of us, however, who send our children to private schools pay for the public school they do not use and also for their private school. Is that fair?

Citizens often are taxed for services they spurn: pacifists must pay taxes to support armies they detest, criminals pay to support the police they would rather do without; we are taxed for a bridge even though we prefer to sail across in our own boat. Yet often we can avoid burdening those who do not use the service offered: some taxes are levied only on users or beneficiaries—for instance, amusement or sewer taxes, and various tolls and fees. It would be technically possible to reimburse, or not to tax

Reprinted from Ernest van den Haag, affirmative position in "Federal Aid to Parochial Schools: A Debate," *Commentary* (July 1961), pp. 1–6. Copyright 1961 by the American Jewish Committee. Reprinted by permission of the author and the publisher. Ernest van den Haag is adjunct professor of social philosophy at New York University, professor of sociology at the New School for Social Research, and a practicing psychoanalyst. He is the author of books and articles on education, "mass culture," and world politics.

for the support of public schools, those who prefer private ones; or, we could subsidize private schools at the rate public schools are subsidized—the effect would be almost the same as that of reimbursement. Many other techniques are available to help private education—or those who now shoulder its burden without being relieved of the financial burden of public education. Obviously the issue is not whether we can, but whether we should and do want to help—whether aid to private education is in the public interest, or, at least, not contrary to it.

Taxpayers who send their children to private schools have long been grumbling under their double load. Their dissatisfaction became acute when the Kennedy administration asked Congress to subsidize public education with federal funds, without simultaneously granting a subsidy to private education. This makes the unrequired tax burden of the parents of private-school children still heavier—and it aggravates them. The Roman Catholic Church, which runs the biggest and fastest-growing private-school system in the country, has objected vigorously. Most other religious denominations would benefit less from a subsidy; they don't support many private schools, perhaps because they are reasonably satisfied with the public schools which, after all, reflect a Protestant ethos, if a little more secularized and Americanized than Protestantism in general. There is no gainsaying the ideologically and historically Protestant background of public education. In turn, the Protestant ethos (including the theistic and enlightenment components and the stress on the individual's direct relation to scripture) is shared widely within the Jewish community. Many Jews also favor public schools because separate education of religious groups unavoidably awakens memories of the ghetto. Thus, on the whole, religious non-Catholics have championed the administration's stand. So have many well-meaning people who wish to continue the tradition barring the expenditure of public funds for private schools; some because they favor public schooling, and others because most of the private schools that would benefit from a subsidy would be denominational and the greatest proportion Roman Catholic.

If we turn from motivation to argument, two kinds of questions are raised about public subsidies for private schools: socio-political and moral ones concerned with the development of our culture and the effects subsidies to private and, particularly, denominational education may have; and ones about the constitutionality of a subsidy. Let us first separate the social issue (is it desirable?) from its legal integument (will the courts allow it?).

"Congress shall make no law respecting the establishment of religion or prohibiting the free exercise thereof." The intent of this part of the First Amendment to the Constitution is to guarantee "the free exercise" of religion and conscience by barring "establishment," the legal alliance of organized religion—of churches—with public authority. Such an alliance might make religion a public rather than a private matter and ultimately restrict freedom of conscience.

The Constitution says nothing about education. When the First Amendment was passed, no public-school system existed. (Massachusetts had barely enacted a law making the maintenance of schools compulsory for localities—but attendance was not.) The Constitutional Fathers were not confronted with our problem: shall we support public education only, or private education also? shall we regard church-controlled private schools as mainly educational, or as essentially religious institutions? We can only guess how the Constitutional Convention would have solved these problems. The Supreme Court is in charge of such guessing, but so far it has not been confronted with the issue, so that we can only guess how it would guess.

To be sure, the courts have found unconstitutional the use of public funds for bus transportation of parochial-school children and for tuition payments to specific denominational schools. Even these tangential issues remain muddled, though. And, above all, the real question has never been asked: does the Constitution bar a subsidy that would be equally available to private schools of all denominations, as well as to nondenominational and nonreligious private schools? Clearly, such a subsidy need not "bring about the legal [sic] ascendancy of one sect over another," which Jefferson feared, or the ascendancy of religion in general. There is a world of difference between a subsidy which reduces and one which increases choice, between one available only to religious private schools (or worse, those of a particular denomination) and one equally available to secular ones. So far, the cases submitted to the courts have been of the former kind. No one has tested either whether a limited subsidy would be constitutional— e.g., a subsidy exclusively for science and language teaching in all private schools—if none of the money or service goes into fields affected by religious teaching. Bus transportation and tuition payments benefit religious as well as other instruction. A limited subsidy would not.

It is not necessary actually to subsidize private schools. The subsidy could be paid to the students (directly or by tax reimbursement) or, as part of their tuition, to the school in which they enroll.[1] The Veterans Administration subsidized veterans directly for their living expenses and paid all their tuition to the schools they attended, whether religious or secular, private or public. There was no constitutional challenge. New York State has just started to subsidize all college students regardless of whether they enroll in secular, religious, private, or public institutions. If all accredited private schools are included, rather than just those of a particular church, and if students (or parents) are free to choose, a subsidy can hardly be less constitutional for primary and secondary than for higher education.

There does not seem to be a constitutional bar, then, against subsidizing private schools in some form if the criterion for the subsidy is purely educational and does not favor religious over nonreligious schools, or a particular denomination, and if enrollment in public schools remains available without disadvantage.[2] (Else choice may be restricted rather

[1]Since I favor more strenuous competition between public and private schools, and more freedom of choice for parents, I should be inclined not to subsidize private any less than public schools: the amount it now costs to keep children in public schools would be paid out to any school—public or private—in which parents enroll them provided that scholastic standards are met. But this, though desirable, is not logically implied in discussing a partial federal subsidy, and it calls for more argument than can be presented here.

[2]I forgo discussing minor dodges which I think are unnecessary, such as leasing buildings or services to private schools.

than enlarged.) But if the Supreme Court were to create such a bar tomorrow, it should not be regarded as unsurmountable. In *Plessy* v. *Ferguson,* the Supreme Court declared that "separate but equal" is equal (enough to be constitutional). Fifty-eight years later, in *Brown* v. *Bd. of Education,* the Court found that "separate but equal" is "inherently unequal" and can never be constitutional. In recent times, the Court has often taken much less to change its mind. Thus, should the Supreme Court find all subsidies to private schools unconstitutional—a decision that I would think unjust as well as unlikely—its judgment might delay rather than prevent a subsidy. Let us turn, then, to the decisive social reasons advanced for and against federal aid to private schools.

The use of public funds for private schools may be undesirable though it be constitutional. Whether it is undesirable does not altogether depend on whether private education is. The justification of support must be separated here from the justification of the thing supported.

If we believe private schooling to be altogether contrary to the public interest, we might prohibit it, or make enrollment financially burdensome. However, if we feel that private schools, though not serving the public interest as well as public ones, are still not contrary to it, we might leave the choice to parents on more equal terms than are now offered. One may disapprove of the choice of parents who send their children to private schools, and yet grant their right to make such a choice without suffering all the financial disadvantages they now suffer. The public interest in public education would have to be weighed against the public interest in equity and free parental choice. And the latter may come to weigh more heavily in the balance than it does now.

Thus, even if private schools be undesirable, there may be philosophical reasons for subsidizing them or reimbursing parents. However, there are more conclusive practical reasons for doing so. Private schools are obviously here to stay, even without public subsidy or tax relief. Now, if we grant that schools need a federal subsidy,[3] then certainly private and public schools stand in equal need: most private schools have even less ample financial resources than public schools and as many financial burdens; their pupils require the educational benefits the federal subsidy is designed to yield no less than public-school pupils. Should they be punished for what opponents of private education feel is the obdurate wrong-headedness of their parents? One might oppose the creation of private schools on principle, yet, once they have been created, help the children in them.

To be sure, if private schools are an evil, subsidizing them—though mitigating the evil by improving education for the children already attending—may also encourage it by encouraging enrollments. This dilemma is not unusual, though. For example, measures to subsidize illegitimate children raise analogous questions. We may be opposed to child-bearing outside the public institution of marriage; but once children are conceived under private auspices, we subsidize mothers for the sake of their children, who cannot be blamed for the parental carelessness which we deplore.

---

[3] I am unconvinced of this need, but here I am concerned only with the distribution of the subsidy between private and public schools.

Of course, by relieving present and future unmarried mothers of some of their financial burden, the subsidy encourages illegitimacy in some measure. (The case of prolific parents of families already on relief is similar.) However, most of us feel that the advantages arising to the children and thus to society far outweigh the incidental encouragement of the parental behavior we would prefer to discourage.

Willingness to subsidize unmarried mothers for the sake of their children can be reconciled with unwillingness to subsidize private schools (or religious parents) for the sake of their children only if we believe at least one of the following: (1) The motives causing some parents to prefer private schools are worse than those that cause some to have illegitimate children; the former, therefore, should be punitively deprived—even though the children bear the burden of the deprivation; (2) Withholding a subsidy would be a more effective deterrent in one case than in the other; (3) The social evils of private education are worse than those of illegitimacy.

As to the first, I do not think that even the most adamant opponents of private schools seriously feel that it is better to subsidize illegitimate than private-school children and thus to jeopardize the latter for the sake of some future social advantage. As to the second, financial pressure is no more likely to overcome social or religious than to overcome sexual deviation[1] (the growth of unsubsidized private schools demonstrates as much). And as to the third, there is no evidence for the contention that the social evils of private education are worse than those of illegitimacy; but even if it be true, would not a subsidy help to mitigate the evil? Withholding it surely does not.

I believe I have shown that the case for subsidies is compelling even if one disapproves of private education. But what reasons are there to disapprove of it?

We have a tradition of public education; obviously this per se is no reason for not changing, but it has emotional appeal—though we had traditions of private before we had public education. Tradition is a grab bag. Historically we did not favor the vote for women until we introduced it. We have been for and against witch-hunting, slavery, prohibition, segregation, divorce, etc. What we have mostly favored traditionally is change, unless, that is, we favored no change (which has happened less often). History cannot tell us whether we should subsidize private—or for that matter public—education. It points, as usual, in all directions, and mainly to the past.

Sometimes it is argued that a federal subsidy to private schools would lead to federal control. Certainly an eligibility standard would be required, and we would have to find out whether it is being met. But this is the case where accreditation is concerned too. Control could be vested in local authorities as it is now. I should welcome standards and controls more demanding and more relevant to educational purposes than those now established for accreditation—e.g., minimal curricula and the requirement that a certain percentage of students pass certain tests as a condition for continued subsidization. These things are needed, but not for the sake of the subsidy: though I prefer not to, one could leave them to local and even

[1]That tolerance of sexual deviation has increased more than tolerance of educational deviation suggests a displacement of secularized religious zeal.

private authorities. On the other hand, government power to regulate education does not depend on subsidies, as the courts are busily showing.

Private education is often thought undemocratic. However, in the ordinary sense of the word, there is nothing undemocratic about private, or democratic about public, schools. England—a democracy—has many private schools; the Soviet Union—a dictatorship—has public education exclusively. It is likely that the word "democratic" here is misused to mean "egalitarian" and perhaps also "culturally homogeneous" and "socially cohesive." So interpreted, the issue raises genuinely important questions: How desirable are egalitarianism and homogeneity per se? And how necessary for the cohesion of our society (which is certainly desirable)? How necessary is public education to achieve any or all of these, and how detrimental is private education? Even a treatise could not answer these questions fully. I must confine myself to a few points.

Egalitarianism, though looming rather large in the minds of many, is of little relevance here: a subsidy to private schools is not likely to increase or spread whatever class distinctions private schooling now involves. It may diminish class distinctions by permitting poorer children to attend schools which now only the richer ones can afford.

Cultural differentiation independent of class—or, conversely, the desirability of cultural homogeneity through public schooling—is more important in this context. And it must be conceded that private schools contribute to cultural heterogeneity; at least that often is their purpose. I doubt that a subsidy would materially affect this. Yet, it would give moral approval—at least end opposition—to it. This seems to be the issue. But even if the case for cultural homogeneity were quite appealing, should we use financial pressure—be it effective or not—to achieve it? Permitting or persuading is one thing, but attempting to coerce people into a public school when they would prefer private ones is quite another matter. But let that go. Grant, too, that public education helped in bringing American culture and society to their present development. (Other possibilities existed, to be sure; the Swiss fared pretty well without using a melting pot.) Do we still need that emphasis on cultural homogeneity and these means? Would the generation or perpetuation of some cultural heterogeneity be bad now?

Surely the situation has changed. The very people who oppose help to private schools make the country ring with their complaints about "conformity." Aren't public schools fostering it and private schools—if only by fostering conformity to different ideas—loosening it? Shouldn't we help them because they are different? And if they weren't, what would be the basis for objection?

The public school played a major, though controversial, role in the acculturation of great waves of immigrants. These waves have passed. (The Puerto Ricans are a minor ripple.) Moreover, private schools as they have developed would not do badly in competing with public ones in this respect today. The danger of insufficient "Americanization" through schooling that stresses "un-American" or "non-American" traditions is hardly serious any more. The secular forces of cohesion in the United States are overwhelming. It seems to me that conservation and support of what diversity of cultural tradition remains is likely now, and ultimately, to strengthen them more than insistence on further homogenization. If there is a weak spot in our cohesion, it is not our heterogeneity but our cultural homogeneity; not our religious differences, but the insufficiently transcendent nature of our cohesion, which is influenced by the American standard of living as much as by the idea of America. This is perhaps more likely to be remedied by private than by public schools.

A number of positive things could be said for private schools. Their very independence permits them to be more various in their methods, less uniform in their curricula, more adaptable to the needs of minorities, and more experimental than public schools can afford to be. And taxpayers will continue to profit financially from the existence of private schools: whatever subsidy is granted them is not going to cover costs—nor do proponents demand this. I have neglected these and other arguments in favor of private schools because I thought it quite enough to show that there is no less a reason to help them than to help public schools. To do this, it is enough to show that objections to them, and objections to subsidizing them, cannot be sustained. This I believe I have done.

THE CASE FOR THE PRIMACY
OF THE PUBLIC SCHOOLS

Robert Lekachman

Education is one of the subjects on which nearly all adults feel themselves expert. At the least, they have all been children and the objects of their teachers' energies. Ever after, many adults are convinced that the contents of school curricula and the methods of school administrators and classroom teachers are appropriate subjects of general debate. Nor is this conclusion entirely mistaken, for, though most of the debaters exaggerate the extent of their knowledge, they can scarcely exaggerate the importance of America's schools to the future of democratic society. Discontent with the schools is a good thing, and complacency here may be a greater threat than ignorance.

Because the schools attract so much attention and arouse so many hopes and expectations, the number of goals we ask our schools to reach has steadily increased, from instruction in the basic skills of communication and computation, to training in democracy, vocational preparation, and moral and ethical improvement. In a period of growing religious interest and growing religiosity, this last demand has created a new set of problems. It is all too easy to equate moral behavior with religious symbols and religious instruction and to infer from the equation that the symbols and instruction should be part of the public-school program.

This facile sequence is a serious misinterpretation of the problems of

Reprinted from Robert Lekachman, "An Unreligious View," in Robert Gordis *et al.*, *Religion and the Schools* (New York: Fund for the Republic, 1959), by permission of the author and the Center for the Study of Democratic Institutions (of the Fund for the Republic). Robert Lekachman is an associate professor of economics at Barnard College and the author of books and articles on economic theory and policy.

agreement between the religious and unreligious. In fact, many of the arguments which strain community feelings and reawaken the latent prejudice of Protestant against Catholic and Christian against Jew are the results of a poor understanding of religious meaning. All too frequently, shallow conceptions of the content and claims of religion clash with the equally shallow rival mystiques of unbelievers.

In only two circumstances is the mutual relation between education and religion simple. When the overwhelming majority of the community devoutly adheres to a single religious faith, almost inevitably its educational institutions, public as well as private, will reflect the pervasive cultural, if not religious, impact of this faith. The situation in the Latin American countries probably illustrates such a condition. Alternatively, when the overwhelming majority in a community are either indifferent or hostile to religion, again the problem vanishes, for no responsible person will advocate inflicting false or trivial doctrine upon children.

What of the situations which lie between these extremes? What frictions are caused by the attempt to mingle the religious of many faiths, the indifferent and the hostile? Is not resolution all the more difficult when religious people themselves disagree not alone about the elements of their respective faiths, but also about the dissemination of these elements in schools and colleges? If they remain within constitutional limits, how can local school boards satisfy the demands of some of their critics and allay the apprehensions of the remainder? What gratifies the Christian parents may strike some Jewish parents as covert anti-Semitism, and some irreligious parents as pernicious superstition.

The case is complex enough where the only authority is the local school board. All sorts of unofficial, and probably unconstitutional, arrangements may persist quietly until some dissenter raises a point of conscience, or the federal government appears on the scene both as granter of aid and as regulator of standards. In recent years, the role of government has been limited by the difficulty Congress faces in trying to win the approval both of Catholics who argue that justice demands appropriate support of parochial as well as public schools, and of Protestants, Jews, and agnostics who insist on various grounds—constitutional, civic, or educational—that aid may legitimately go only to the public schools. School buses, free lunches, and an array of other fringe benefits have all been occasions of controversy. So confused have been the battle lines that, at times, opponents of public aid to religious schools have found themselves in the rather strange posture of arguing that free bus transportation for parochial students constituted the establishment of a church. Such are the snares of purely constitutional arguments.

The layman in the law should tread gently or not at all among the conflicting constitutional interpretations of the First Amendment. But it is hard to avoid noting that none of the conflicting groups has stood constitutionally naked in the strife; each has been able to cite favorite Supreme Court utterances, sometimes from the same case. On important issues, the Supreme Court has divided, and its majorities have spoken with different voices on different occasions. As a result, different constitutional principles are clear to different people. Avoiding the law as far as possible, I shall speculate on the civic and political implications of two of the major issues: government aid to religious schools, and the teaching of religion, of some kind, in some degree of dilution, in the public schools.

Take, first, aid to parochial schools. Although some Protestant denominations and some Jewish congregations support their own day schools, only the Roman Catholics enroll throughout the country a substantial proportion of the school-age population in schools oriented around religious doctrine. It must seem to many Catholics that every argument converges to support public assistance to parochial schools. Appealing to the thrifty, there is the fiscal fact that the existence of the parochial-school system saves many millions of dollars annually for local communities. The parochial school seems to perform the public work of instruction in basic skills and knowledge, and practice in group cooperation, at no cost to the public. In addition, the parochial school offers the religious atmosphere and doctrinal teaching which the public school cannot offer. At a time when most Americans pay at least lip service to the values of religion, is not Catholic education actually a means of insuring better instruction than nonreligious schools can offer? Under the circumstances, it seems doubly hard on Catholics to make them pay for their own schools and also for public schools inferior to them which offer services they cannot conscientiously accept.

These are simple appeals to justice, but there is a more complete argument for justice which derives from natural-law doctrine. If all men share a common nature—and Catholicism is not alone in this assumption—then we can infer certain persistent truths from this nature. One of these truths is the right of the parent to supervise the education of his child, who is a creation of the family, not of the state. Because of their own limited training and other preoccupations, most parents must delegate this right. The parent who is content with the public school delegates the education of his child to that school, and empowers the state to collect taxes from him and to use these taxes for support of the public-school system. Moved by a different educational ideal, the Catholic parent delegates his parental right to the parochial school in which his child acquires an education permeated by Catholic values and Catholic beliefs. When the state treats the Catholic parent equitably, therefore, it distributes some of the taxes which he has paid to the institution to which, in the free exercise of his parental right, he has sent his child.

This is more than an abstract doctrine, for in Holland, to take one example, arrangements very much like this one are in actual operation. It follows that the present American arrangement is wholly satisfactory only to the parent who prefers the public school to other alternatives. The proponents of this case admit the right of the community to demand of the parochial institution the same levels of attainment in secular subjects, the same degree of preparation of its students, and the same length of attendance as the community demands of its public schools and their students.

How far can this claim be allowed? What opposing principles contradict its applicability? Let it be said, to begin, that not even a democratic community can grant the right of its citizens to pay taxes only for purposes of which these citizens approve. No citizen has an item veto over the expenditures of his government. In consequence, it is a rare person who does not help support activities which he considers unnecessary or even harmful.

Many Americans judge aid to Yugoslavia and Poland as support of communism itself, and some consider expenditure on Nationalist China a harmful luxury. There must be some bachelors and spinsters who resent the payment of school taxes and some economists who, on various arcane grounds, adjudge aid to agriculture a foolish encouragement to a mistaken use of resources. What can the Christian Scientist think of medical research or the anti-vivisectionist of government assistance to medical training? So it has ever gone. In a democracy, the voter has his resources. Among them are elections, and more immediately well-organized pressures which put elected representatives in salutary fear of their electoral lives. Even so, these mechanisms are imprecise. Political parties of consequence are only two, and the voter resigns himself to the foolish use of his money by his government.

But this is far from a complete answer. Sensitive democratic leaders avoid, when they can, scandalizing their followers. While the government of large, complicated political entities frequently offers no alternative to the overriding of individual preferences about the disposal of tax receipts, sometimes alternatives do offer themselves, and the government which does not grasp them is seriously remiss. Is not the present case such an instance? Here is a large group of Americans who are convinced that the community has visited upon them a persistent injustice. In this grievance, they have earned the support of some thoughtful non-Catholics, among them Will Herberg—although Herberg does not consider the present a prudent time for Catholics to press their claim.

Now, the state cannot accept the differing notions of justice held by all the groups which together constitute a political community, partly because it risks its title to govern when it heeds one group only, but also because conceptions of justice differ and any state which endeavored to heed them all would soon be hopelessly involved in inconsistent action. Nevertheless, political prudence and social harmony unite to urge that deeply felt demands for "justice" be gratified, unless injustice is thereby done to other groups (as these groups define injustice), or some overriding social objective justifies refusal.

Therefore, those who wish to deny to parochial institutions public monies cannot retreat to the claim that this has ever been the American way, for, in this respect, the American way may have been mistaken all along. Neither should they take refuge in constitutional interpretation, partly because constitutional interpretations change and partly because they too have some relation to the tides of opinion and the institutional transformations of their time. In the end, opponents of aid to parochial schools must argue their position on its merits.

What are these merits? It used to be said that the public school was a major agent in the American melting pot. The parents who arrived at Ellis Island on their crowded ships spoke many languages, practiced many customs, and cooked their food in many ways. In the public schools, their children learned the same English as the children of earlier immigrants, worshiped the same heroes, adopted the same tribal habits, and yearned for the same triumphs. If, at the same time, they came to despise their parents and their parents' language and behavior, this, it was felt, was the necessary price of assimilation. Paradoxically, about the time the melting pot had done its work, Americans apparently lost faith in its virtues, for, in the 1920's, they began seriously to restrict immigration into the United States. We all speak English now and think American thoughts, save for some hundreds of thousands of Puerto Ricans whose semi-segregated schools seem the opposite of the schools celebrated in the myth of the melting pot.

In fact, has not the process of assimilation gone much too far for the health of democracy, which lives partly by its unity but partly also by its differences? The rather unpleasant word "pluralism" stresses the differences. It is a sign of a widespread uneasiness about excessive similarity that we are coming to revive, somewhat artificially, many national traditions. The red wine of the Italian immigrant which accompanied his evening meal of spaghetti was despised by his son. It is probably only historical justice that his grandson has self-consciously revived the custom. Much of our advertising adds up to a spurious appeal to the yearning for marginal differentiation, to our desire to be a little different while remaining, by and large, safely the same as other people. The popular conformist outcry against conformity is, one might suppose, no argument for the public school. If it argues for any arrangement, it is for as diversified a set of schools as imaginable, organized according to all manner of principles from Vedanta to vegetarianism. If variety is so hard to achieve, we should not stamp it out in the few places where it shows signs of vigor. Since Catholics, Lutherans, and some Jews want their own schools, perhaps the rest of us should offer them not only money but a vote of thanks as well.

Undoubtedly such considerations must make the proponents of the public school thoughtful. Yet, there is an answer. The heart of the case for the public school is not alone that it makes democracy more workable, but also that it encourages the free formation of many kinds of belief and many varieties of commitment. In a society which aspires to rub along in a democratic fashion, it is a good thing for future citizens to learn early and continuously how to get along with each other even when their beliefs importantly differ. A Catholic may believe of his Protestant friends that their path to salvation is infinitely more difficult than his own, but workable democracy depends upon his coming to know his mistaken brothers, upon his learning to work with them, while critical doctrinal differences are held in suspension. It is desirable for Catholic, Jewish, Protestant, and agnostic children to play and learn with each other. It is particularly important that they do so when the prevailing winds of doctrine emphasize religious affiliation. Since home and church will stress the differences among children, it is appropriate at least, and possibly essential at most, that another influential agency emphasize their similarities. Clearly, this is an argument of degree. It does not imply that all children must go to public schools and none to religious schools or secular private schools. But it is an argument that most children should go to public schools.

Memory tells me that, when I was a child, children who attended parochial school seemed mysterious and disquieting. It was easy to entertain the notion that their lives were very different from mine. Nor do I recall that my reaction was different from that of other public-school pupils. What is different, children tend to resent and distrust. And not only children. Adult distinctions of principle will be more reasonable and more charitable when childish experiences are shared. Democracy depends upon certain kinds of shared experiences and, of these, public education is probably one. Although democracy need not vanish with the collapse of one of these varieties of experience, it will operate less effectively.

But can the public school really be a neutral agency? Is not the preaching of neutrality itself a view of what is valuable, a doctrine in itself? As a matter of sheer logic, the answer is clearly affirmative. If one says in praise of the public school that it teaches an experimental attitude towards truth, even that it judges truth to be evolving and changing, unmistakably such precepts imply that there is no fixed body of truth to communicate about the subjects taught in the school at least, and, by extension, perhaps about other subjects as well.

Not all public schools are addicted to these opinions, at least in this form. But suppose that they were. Would this assumption justify saying that since the public schools cannot be truly neutral about life's vital ends, then we should educate our children in schools which represent the truths we hold dear, and in the public schools only when what is taught in public schools accords with our conceptions in every detail? I think not. Though formally a doctrine, openness forecloses no answers and prevents no commitments. The pupil will not of course hear his parents' religion praised as true, but neither will he hear it ridiculed as false. On ultimate matters, the school does not conceive that it must teach or preach. If it helps children label as ultimate only the ultimate, so much the better, for the hardest thing in the world is to avoid acquiring firm beliefs about individuals, doctrines, races, and nationalities before experience and reflection have justified them. Everything in life—family, friends, church, and innate laziness—conspires to abbreviate the child's exploration of the world and to persuade him to adopt with a sigh of relief the faith of his fathers not only in religion but also in politics, friendship, and taste. At best, the public school postpones some of these choices until they can become the acts of adults rather than the reflexes of children.

The public school is an ally of social tolerance, class fluidity, and the open mind. Therefore, it is an ally of democracy itself. French democracy is a horrible example of the pass to which an overidentification with too many principles can bring a gifted people. So far, the United States is a quite successful illustration of what reluctance to assume fixed positions of principle can achieve. In the end, democracy depends upon the cooperation of people who, at least in theory, find each other's principles intolerable and have only recently got over the habit of fighting wars over them. Any agency which suggests that tentative approaches to principle in most human affairs are best, that different principles may have some justification, does much to raise the quality of a democratic society. In such a society, diverse opinions, freely chosen, flourish, and peculiarity is held to be a virtue.

What are the practical implications of this position? I shall state them flatly: public support of parochial education is inadvisable; the right of churches and other groups to maintain educational institutions which meet the standards of the community is a part of freedom of opinion and freedom of religion; advantages already extended to religious and other private schools, such as tax exemption, should in logic be retrieved, but in practice left undisturbed. Anyone convinced by my case for public education will not wish to promote religious or other private schools. Equally, anyone attached to the constitutional and libertarian values of democracy cannot deny the right of churches to sponsor their own schools.

A healthy democracy encourages the activity of all manner of voluntary groups intermediate between individuals and government. And, although any church may protest being classified with temporal institutions like clubs, societies, and unions, which make no supernatural claims, it is hard to see how a democratic society can otherwise classify churches. Finally, social harmony and a decent respect for established practice imply that the issue of tax exemption should not be raised.

The wave of interest in religion in recent years has been accompanied by a wish to enlist the public schools in this revival. Justification has ranged from the exceedingly naive to the intellectually sophisticated, from a simple identification of theistic belief with democracy, after the fashion of President Eisenhower, to the argument that, at a minimum, religion cannot be ignored in studying history, art, literature, and sociology. In a general atmosphere where religion is esteemed vaguely as a good thing, it seems silly to deny this good thing, like any other good thing, to our children.

Much of this feeling—religiosity, not religion—attaches itself less to the doctrinal practices of a given faith than to its inclusion within the single affirmative term religion. Posters which urge citizens to attend the churches of their faith innocently underline the unimportance of which faith it is.

The practical problems which these free-floating sentiments have created, reawakened, or intensified revolve around three themes. One is the matter of religious symbols. Is it appropriate, in the public schools, to display religious symbols? If it is, what symbols shall they be: those of common Christianity, or of the broader Judaeo-Christian tradition? A second debate concerns released time. Is it appropriate to schedule some unit of time in the school week for the study of religion under the guidance of clergymen of the different faiths? If it is, how shall the program be administered? Finally, in the school curriculum, what shall be the relation of religion to secular subjects? Is it possible to teach religiously neutral history?

What can be said about the display of religious symbols: crèches, copies of the Ten Commandments, Christmas trees, religious art, and the like? In the first place, it is difficult to imagine that children from irreligious homes can avoid hurt and embarrassment when symbols to which their parents are either indifferent or hostile are pressed upon them in an important part of their daily environment. It is equally hard to see anything but ill will as the effect of this identification. How important should these feelings bulk in the decisions of local school boards? Even in the most tolerant of democracies, minorities are not the same as majorities. Majority disapproval is one of the penalties of minority status. One of its gratifications, presumably, is the demonstration of courage and independence which maintenance of one's position generates. If it is indeed true, as church-attendance statistics suggest but do not prove, that most Americans believe in God, and if they wish to proclaim that belief before their children in every way possible, does it not deny them the right freely to exercise their own opinions when a minority by its pressure prevents the display of these symbols?

Here is one of the numerous instances in which the case for both sides is strong. Minorities should not be coerced and majorities should not be thwarted. These good principles frequently cannot be applied simultaneously. If the case were only as it has been stated in the preceding paragraph, then good will would frequently produce logically unsatisfactory, but existentially acceptable, compromises. In deference to the majority wish for some religious practice, on the one hand, and the minority wish to have as little as possible, on the other, religious symbols might be minimized.

But it is a real question whether this particular issue is fairly understood. An agnostic should advise the religious and even the crypto-religious with trepidation; yet it is truly hard to understand how the fuss over ritual mention of God in the Pledge of Allegiance, or Bible reading, or the like, can frequently accompany genuine religious involvement. It seems evident that the communicant who is deeply attached to his faith can cheerfully accept neither an alternative ritual nor a weakened, watered-down, innocuous compromise among faiths, some religion-in-general which approximates the relation to true religion that Prohibition near-beer bore to real beer. A religious revival marked by painful thought and deep emotion will not discover in these flaccid gestures anything but a confusion of genuine religious feeling. A child is brought no nearer to reverence by hearing a few verses of the Bible than by reading the legend on his coins, "In God We Trust."

In recent years, released-time programs have become increasingly popular in large cities. As frequently operated, children armed with the written permission of their parents are conducted to churches or synagogues an hour or so a week, where clergymen and rabbis instruct them in the tenets of their respective faiths. Children whose parents do not wish them to participate generally spend the period studying. Since the time appropriated is part of the regular school day, attendance is taken and reported to teachers in the public schools. To that degree, the disciplinary mechanism of the school is enlisted in the service of the released-time program. After a considerable amount of litigation, the constitutionality of such programs, provided that they do not actually use school property, seems to be established.

Constitutionality is not the same as advisability. From the standpoint of the irreligious, religion deserves no special privileges, and there is no question that released-time programs do amount to a privilege. If the privilege is extended to religion on the ground that to some religion is a good thing, then why not extend it in any direction indicated by other groups which consider that other activities are good things? Why not allow parents addicted to the arts to use the time for instruction in the violin or the piano? Or in the values of trade unionism? Or the merits of the Chamber of Commerce? Logic, if not custom, suggests that released-time programs open the door to their own extension and to claims of competing programs.

At the risk of tediousness, I must again express my wonder at the attachment of some religious groups to these programs. The time at stake is short and the implicit admission to children as well as to skeptical adults that the religious influence of parents and clergymen is so weak that the compulsion of the school is essential seems a damaging price to pay for an hour or two a week. Like the urgent desire to bring religious symbols into the school, released-time programs symbolize shallowness alike of thought, commitment, and confidence. Their existence is, or should be, of more concern to the truly religious than to the indifferent.

When the opposition between the religious and the irreligious is accurately understood, both released time and religious symbols appear in their proper perspective as essentially minor, although exceedingly aggravating issues. Much more serious is the question of what school curricula should do in history, literature, and art classes about religion as an influence upon events and culture. At one extreme it is possible to argue along with some Catholic educators that the schools must operate on the basis of a general theistic assumption, in accordance with the beliefs of the society they serve. At the other extreme is the statement that religion must be exposed as superstition and that the only criteria of truth are those which scientific method sets as the model of experimental investigation.

Since in practice the implications of alternative theistic positions are more different from each other than general theistic belief is from the lack of such belief, it is not at all plain what such an assumption on the part of the schools could possibly mean in the construction of courses and the day-to-day operations of the teacher. Does God intervene directly into events and into men's characters? On such questions the religious disagree. If it is assumed that God does not so intervene, then history taught on this theistic premise may not necessarily differ very much from history taught on no theistic premise whatsoever, or on the premise that God is an unverified hypothesis. Such affirmations would seem to serve only purely ritualistic purposes.

What of the other extreme position? The sort of scientific positivism which it implies has fallen out of fashion even among scientists. It is possible to be an agnostic and still feel that there are mysteries in human existence which no amount of laboratory experiment can elucidate. Equally, it is possible to infer that some of these mysteries relate to the esthetic and the emotional, which yield little return to the controlled experiment. This position is a great deal more common than scientific positivism.

Because the extremes can be excluded, the middle is not thereby clearly defined or adequately justified. Better-balanced arguments about the curriculum of the public schools center on what should be taught about the role of religion as a part of the history and culture of Western society. Whatever he may believe about the validity of religion's claims, no reasonable person can ignore the importance of religion as a motive to action, explanation of behavior, and inspiration to self-sacrifice. The Massachusetts Bay Colony was founded neither for gold nor for turkey dinners. God does appear in the Declaration of Independence, though not in the Constitution, and the name of God has been invoked by American presidents from Washington on. John Brown acted out of religious commitment, and Franklin Roosevelt was a devout churchgoer. The manifestations of religion in our history have covered the complete spectrum from the mainspring of men's action to the grace notes of behavior.

If this were all, there would be no problem. Of course it is not all. Particularly in the elementary schools, the problem is one of selection, of catching the interest of the child with the vivid detail which summarizes and fails to falsify a good deal of history. By astute selection, it is easily possible for a devout teacher to convey the impression that religious principles have always guided good Americans. It is, I should think, a little harder but still perfectly possible to demonstrate that ours is a purely secular society, the leaders of which were either irreligious or religious only in a purely formal sense. A teacher is a person, not a reciter of syllabi, and even the syllabi are written by persons equipped with their full complement of prejudices.

Since there is nothing certain about historical interpretations, and teachers must select from an almost infinite number of concrete details, it is hard to see a complete remedy in the simple proposition that the teacher should strive to accord religion its proper place in history: both authorities and teachers disagree among themselves.

Two illustrations suggest something of the practical difficulties. In Southern schools, our bloody war of 1861–1865 is commonly referred to as the War Between the States. In Northern schools, it is the Civil War. The distinction in terminology indicates a basic difference in attitude toward one of the most thoroughly investigated episodes in any nation's history. It may still be the practice of textbook writers to provide alternative accounts of the Civil War (I went to a Northern school) for Northern and Southern consumption. Take as a second illustration so durable a staple as the Reformation. Surely this term is general enough. Yet, Catholic schools and some historians treat of the Protestant Revolt and the Catholic Reformation. Once more the difference in terminology signalizes a basic divergence of attitude.

If it is naive to expect impartial history, in which religious and secular motives are accorded each their appropriate weight, what is the solution? It cannot be the omission of either category of influence. As much for the irreligious as for the religious, it is a bad answer to skip hastily over anything which concerns religion, as it is said some teachers and some schools tend to do. Since avoidance of offense is avoidance of teaching, it is no fit goal for a teacher. Although the answer is neither simple nor entirely satisfactory, it must serve. In the first place, the responsible teacher owes it to himself and his students to identify his convictions and his biases, and to make some allowance for them in preparing material and teaching classes. This does not amount to saying that he must deliberately teach a view of events which his conscience tells him is untrue or incomplete. But it does suggest the appropriateness, at least in classes for older children, of indicating to them what views their teacher cherishes. A child should learn as soon as he is able to understand the lesson that truth is complex and colored by the personality of the individual who tries to grasp it.

In the second place, indoctrination is a smaller danger when teachers are themselves of varied background, drawn from all the major denominations and from those who profess no religious belief. Although it should not be the deliberate aim of any school system to select its teachers according to their religious faith, school systems which hire according to merit may hope to achieve variety. This diversity is advantageous to all parties. It is good for the religious and the irreligious alike to understand how the world looks to people of different beliefs. It is good for them intellectually, and it is good for them socially and ultimately politically. Honesty is an indispensable quality of a good teacher, but neutrality is not.

Throughout this essay, my concern has been with the position of the irreligious at a time when shallow conceptions of religion lead to the easy equation of democracy and theistic belief (as though believers had not accommodated themselves to every known variation of political organization), and to self-righteous endeavors to force ritualistic expressions of that equation upon the schools. As I reflect on what I have said, I am convinced that my argument lies not with the religious but with those whose feeble conceptions of faith travesty the rigor of the traditional religions. I hope for common ground between the skeptic and the believer on a number of positions.

Much more than the unbeliever, the adherent of religion must be dissatisfied with school exercises which satisfy no religious needs, but only pay tribute to a public mood. Just as an admirer of Shakespeare would much prefer that *King Lear* not be taught at all if it must be taught out of Classic Comic Books, so must a thoughtful believer regard much of what passes for religious enlightenment in the public schools. For, by the very nature of the case, the kind of religious activity which is possible in a public school attended by children of many faiths must represent some least common denominator. While the finding of a common denominator is entirely sensible in dealing with fractions, it is unlikely that many religions would care to regard their own tenets as fractional world views. As an unbeliever, I consider religion to be much too important in human history to see it reduced to a patriotic exercise in the classroom.

Released-time programs at least possess the merit of dignified doctrinal exposition in houses of worship by clergymen committed to the truth of what they preach. To this unbeliever at least, the damage to the public school is much less when released-time programs are the only overt introduction of religious activity into the public schools. Once more, however, should not religion be too important to the religious to employ secular mechanisms and the resented disciplines of the public school to coerce students into churches? Is there not here a recognition of failure, of inability to lead the child away from some out-of-school diversion into a church or synagogue? Clearly, if such is the case, the remedy for lack of parental conviction and deficient clerical leadership cannot really be an hour or two a week of enforced religious instruction.

Nor do I think that much of an issue between the religious and irreligious exists in how the curriculum should deal with religion. It is shocking to think that anyone, whatever his beliefs, could contemplate simply not talking about the impact of religious belief upon human history. Although I have hinted at the great practical difficulties in the way of giving religion its proper weight, I do not believe that divisions about the treatment of these difficulties need follow the lines of belief or doubt.

The issue which remains between some of the religious and practically all of the unbelieving is financial aid to parochial schools. It is obviously accurate to refer to only some of the religious because Protestants and Jews seem generally to oppose public aid, whether or not they maintain their own parochial school. Here there is a real difference of opinion about the meaning of justice and the ends of education. The fact that as a matter of prudence most Catholics do not care to press their demands should not conceal the existence of their deep conviction in the justice of their case and their consequent feeling that the community does not value properly what Catholic education does.

It is clear how I think that this issue should be settled. The public school is too valuable to encourage alternatives to it. Although this is a genuine issue, public debate on it has been confused and, all too frequently, prejudiced. In part, the low quality of the public argument has been the consequence of the mass of irrelevant controversy which has raged over Christmas plays, crèches, displays of the Decalogue, Christmas carols, Hanukkah candles, and the like. Properly perceived, the issue for Catholics and other believers is whether their conception of religion demands that secular education be permeated with a theistic ethic or whether separation between religious and secular instruction is best for both. It is in this framework that debate about public aid to religious schools stands the best prospect of intelligent resolution.

GUIDES FOR READING AND DISCUSSION

1. According to Van den Haag, the public school reflects a Protestant ethos; in contrast, Lekachman considers the public school a neutral agency. Which view is more nearly correct? What do the distinguishing terms really mean?

2. Public support to private institutions implies some sort of minimum control: at the very least, the private school should not contradict generally accepted norms. What limits to financial aid—in addition to purely instructional standards —and what kinds of controls would be appropriate? Is there truth in the adage "Who pays the piper calls the tune"?

3. In the melting-pot society of the United States, the universal culture is generally expressed through public institutions, while subcultures are expressed through private churches, associations, clubs, etc. If a significant change was made in this division, how would group relations be affected? Specifically, would there be more or less anti-Semitism, say, if all Jews went to exclusively Jewish schools?

SUGGESTED ADDITIONAL READINGS

Robert McAfee Brown and Gustave Weigel, S.J., *An American Dialogue* (New York: Doubleday-Anchor, 1961).

Robert Gordis *et al., Religion and the Schools* (New York: Fund for the Republic, 1959).

Evarts B. Greene, *Religion and the State: The Making and Testing of an American Tradition* (Ithaca, N.Y.: Great Seal Books, 1959).

Vashti C. McCallum, *One Woman's Fight*, rev. ed. (Boston: Beacon Press, 1961), with the text of the Supreme Court decision in her case appended.

Victor S. MacKinnon, "Freedom?—or Toleration?" *Public Law* (Winter 1959), pp. 374–395.

Leo Pfeffer, *Church, State, and Freedom* (Boston: Beacon Press, 1953).

"Religion and the State," *Law and Contemporary Problems*, vol. 14, no. 1 (Winter 1949), entire issue.

"The State and Sectarian Education," *National Education Association Research Bulletin*, vol. 34, no. 4 (December 1956).

2

LAW, LIBERTY, AND LAWLESSNESS

WHAT ARE THE SOCIAL CONSEQUENCES
OF ORGANIZED CRIME?

The distinguishing characteristic of organized crime, as well as the main reason for its resilience in the face of periodic exposés and condemnations, is that it serves a voluntary clientele, whereas conventional crime preys on coerced or unwitting victims. Organized crime is in the business of producing goods and services prohibited by law and abhorred by some sectors of the community, but demanded by a considerable number of consumers. Traditionally, this demand has been greater among Catholics than among Protestants, greater in slums than in middle-class residential areas, and greater in large cities than in rural areas.

The specific services that organized crime offers have fluctuated in their importance. The unlicensed production of alcoholic beverages, although still a considerable source of income in dry counties and states, is obviously less important than during the Prohibition period. Racketeering, or the intrusion of criminal elements into business and labor, is still widespread, but has probably also declined relative to other forms of organized crime. Narcotics have always been relatively unimportant, except as a symbol of organized crime's reprehensible character. Prostitution was once a major service of organized crime; but contrary to the general tendency toward increasingly centralized control, it is now largely run by independent entrepreneurs. Gambling, illegal in all but a few American jurisdictions, has thus become by far the most lucrative endeavor of organized crime.

What is the meaning of organized crime in the United States? What part has it played in American life? What have been its moral and social consequences? Though it may surprise a person who has read about crime only in the newspapers, authorities have offered widely divergent answers to such questions. In the first of the two selections reprinted here, the Massachussets Senate Commission argues that organized crime corrodes the moral fiber of politics and individual citizens. Daniel Bell, on the other hand, suggests that organized crime has given members of minority groups an opportunity to rise to higher, and ultimately legitimate, positions in society.

ORGANIZED CRIME AND
ORGANIZED GAMBLING

Massachusetts Senate Commission

This Commission's first assigned task is to determine whether organized crime and organized gambling exist and, if so, to what extent. All

Abridged from Commonwealth of Massachusetts, Special Commission Revived and Continued for the Purpose of Investigating Organized Crime and Other Related Matters, *Report,* No. 107, May 1957.

other tasks within the Commission's mandate will depend on the findings on this basic question.

[Two] factors are both basic and common to every criminal organization and to organized crime as this Commission sees it. The first is the capacity of the illegal activities to produce money. The second is their capacity, through repetition and continuity, to produce a continuing flow of money in which all concerned can participate. Illegal supply of the American thirst tapped a golden stream, and a continuing one, and produced powerful criminal organizations. Repeated bank-robbing operations by gangs or groups have been part of our history. Many fields, large and small, could be named to which a flow of money has attracted criminal organizations.

But there is no such organization of all or most of the forms of crime which are attracted by a steady money flow. There are "bosses" who have their henchmen and gangs of substantial size. Though they may operate in particular fields or segments—or more than one—there is no controlling syndicate, board, or boss of all organized crime. Such an organization would be too big and too vulnerable, and is unnecessary to making money. It is not the leaders—the generals, colonels, captains, and their subordinates —who are basically significant to organized crime. Leaders come and go; associations are fluid and frequently changed. Control rests on and comes through money. The foundation stone of organized crime—the all-important fact—is not the presence of transient leaders, but the continuing existence of an army, mob, or pool from which the criminal with an idea and money can draw recruits for the mission of a night, of months, or of years. This army, mob, or pool is a brotherhood, knit in a patchwork organization, not by leaders, but by a desire for money without work and by a readiness, in varying degrees, to violate society's laws to that end.

This brotherhood is organized crime.

Though founded on acts, violent or otherwise, of career-criminals, organized crime is not a type or quantity of crime. Crime is specific. Organized crime is general. They differ much as do an unjust imprisonment and slavery. The heavy impact of unjust imprisonment is borne by the individual. The heavy impact of slavery is borne by society. A particular crime, influenced by passion, drunkenness, poverty, ignorance, or circumstances which might make a good man bad or a bad man worse, commonly reflects primarily the individual's failure to overcome his individual weakness. Organized crime reflects the failure of society to overcome its own inherent weaknesses.

The members of [the organized-crime] community who follow this way of life are identifiable. They are individuals whose urge for money and aversion to the drudgery of available occupations within the law transcend or subvert principle. The law-abiding citizen follows gainful employment to satisfy his needs and desires by money. He and his business or job are regulated by his principles, and, where necessary, by laws or regulations imposed in the common interest of society. The member of the organized-crime community aims likewise to satisfy needs and desires with money, but there the comparison stops. Organized crime is by nature beyond society's regulation; and its few self-imposed regulations are for the common interest of those in the business of opposing the common interest of society.

The backbone of the organized-crime community is made up of those who eschew honest employment for careers not recognized in our economic system or referred to in our laws except in statutes defining crimes against the person, property, public justice, public peace, public health, chastity, morality, decency, or good order. It also includes persons, who, while not career-criminals, participate on the fringe in criminal activity or, with guilty mind, profit directly or indirectly therefrom. It is to be noted, moreover, that members of the community are by no means engaged exclusively in activities of organized crime. Many are engaged or employed, in varying degrees, in lawful occupations. But all, from center to fringe, are racketeers, though the term is not generally applied when a particular individual is segregated from the class.

Few, if any, of these persons engage in all varieties of crime. There are fields of concentration in crime as elsewhere. Some bookies have told the Commission they would have nothing to do with guns, prostitution, or narcotics. Some gunmen think bookies take candy from babies. But prostitutes and narcotics dealers have engaged in the gaming rackets, and bookies have had to do with guns and prostitution and narcotics. It is doubtless true that some racketeers would work rather than live by some crimes. There may well be degrees of lack of principle. But it may be questioned whether the principle of the racketeer is as firm as the pride which the honest workman in adversity swallows to take a job not worthy of his ability and experience. The racketeer's willingness to swallow his principle could only be tested if he lost his income; and his versatility in crime may properly lead society to presume that the swallow would be accomplished with little gagging.

One thing is certain about this community, from center to fringe. It is ruled by money. In the center are those who found no success or disdained success within the law. On the fringe are those who, with money earned in mediocre success within the law, invest in ventures outside the law. Between center and fringe are varied combinations of "racket" and "legitimate" money. Money and ability to control it are the powers in organized crime. Beside them the power of the gun is secondary and auxiliary. Money is the life blood of organized crime, and money which finds itself in the underworld has a way of circulating there. If a dollar paid to a bookie, a narcotics peddler, a prostitute, or stolen from a bank could, on its route through and out of the underworld, be traced by endorsements reciting who paid it to whom and for what, it would show the interrelationships among crimes and criminals better than any investigation. It would show how vocal money is in the underworld. It would demonstrate more forcefully than this Commission can that the unlawful activity which draws the most money into the underworld is the prime source of power in organized crime and the most serious threat to society.

The prime source of power based on money lies in illegal gaming. The resolve establishing this Commission to investigate organized crime singled out organized gambling for special mention. Since organized illegal gambling is obviously organized crime, the special mention must be construed as emphasis, not differentiation. The Commission had no preconceived ideas on any phase of its assigned subjects. It first sought light from the enforcement authorities of the Commonwealth, police and prosecuting officials. It was told by all that gambling is the major problem, although the question as to organization was not so clear. The files and reports of the Kefauver Committee and of other investigations established illegal gambling as the major problem elsewhere. The Commission has found in its own work that no matter with what career-criminal or with what field of crime an investigation starts, it is sure to run into gambling—sooner, not later. This was the exact experience in the so-called Corridor Justice Probe of 1949, in which a special commissioner was designated by the Supreme Judicial Court to look into irregularities in the matter of bail bonds. There more testimony was received on gambling than on any other crime, all of it relevant to the matter under investigation. Further, the interrelationships between career-criminals are such that an inquiry starting with one field of crime will surely go on to all the others. The commerce or industry of organized crime and the people engaged in it may, for some purposes, be divided and classified. But, if the problem to society is under consideration, division and classification are meaningless. Organized crime and its community constitute and present one entire problem.

The business of off-track betting on licensed pari-mutuel horse races has built-in guarantees of profit. An important element of profit is, queerly enough, guaranteed to the illegal horse player by the law he breaks. The operators never pay more than the pari-mutuel price fixed at the track; and they commonly pay less. But track prices are fixed after the lawful share of the State, and the track and the lawful "breakage" are "taken off the top." The "take out" of State and track aggregates on the average about 14 per cent of the total handle. Breakage, the odd cents resulting after the lawful "take outs," is not repaid to bettors but is shared equally by State and track; it varies with the number of winning tickets, but is somewhat less than 1½ per cent of the handle. Since off-track odds are never greater than track prices, an amount equal to State and track "take out" and breakage goes "off the top" to the operator. It is, moreover, to be noted that reduction of the minimum bet from $2 to 50 cents results in a higher percentage of breakage. In Massachusetts, where State and track share equally in lawful take out and breakage, the illegal operation is guaranteed twice the percentage return from total play which accrues to the lawful track, and from which largely the track must operate and maintain its plant, pay its purses, and cover its many business expenses, including taxes. Assuming illegal volume of $700,000,000 to $850,000,000, and an arbitrary average of 15½ per cent "off the top," the unlawful industry can count on $108,-500,000 to $131,750,000 minimum gross earnings from this element alone. Against these figures may be set expenses of small rental and payroll obligations, no plant except a second-hand adding machine, telephone and wire-service charges, and a few miscellaneous. It seems clear that substantial profits are guaranteed to the racket operator by operation of the law he flouts.

But this guaranteed return "off the top" is not enough for the operators. At the track, after "take out" and breakage, the odds are fixed by the cumulative effect of the bets, and the entire pool is repaid to the holders of winning tickets. The bookmakers in this area do not risk the long prices on horse bets which may result from the lawful system on which their bootlegging rests. They have fixed the maximum prices they will pay at 20–1 to win, 8–1 for place, and 4–1 for show, no matter what the odds at the track. Out-of-state sources have advised the Commission that, unlike in Massachusetts and New Hampshire, odds for win may pay as high as 30–1 or 50–1, and that the price situation here indicates a regulation of competition— perhaps an agreement in restraint of unlawful trade. Be that as it may, it is plain that fixing by bookmakers of maximum odds lower than track prices means a further withholding from the bettors—an additional retention "off the top" of the pool.

Similarly the operator can and does refuse bets, which the track cannot do. Having fixed maximum prices, he can select the risks he will accept and can limit the amount of any risk he will take. In other words, he can heavily weight the play he backs in his own favor. As all agree, "no one can beat the horses," even through the pari-mutuel machines where the odds are mathematically made by all bets, and where about 84½ per cent of the total bet is returned by the track to the bettors as a class. By selection of risks and limitations on play, the unlawful operator can assure a higher percentage of losing bets and higher returns to himself. He runs no pool, takes a large share "off the top," takes affirmative steps to see that "no one can beat the horses," and relies on his losing customers not only to pay the winners but to add to his own earnings.

Description of these business methods should make it plain that not only are the gross revenues of unlawful off-track horse play huge, but the net profits are at least commensurate. If, hit hard in one week, a bookmaker pays out of profits of previous weeks, he looks forward confidently to the next, for he knows the odds are always in his favor. He may go broke—not because his profit is small but because, like some not in the rackets, he spends more than he makes. Financial disaster in unlawful booking is rare.

The Commission is satisfied that, from the point of view of profits as well as revenues, the racket is lucrative in the extreme.

Organized unlawful gambling is big business statewide in the Commonwealth. Some thirty different products [are] distributed by the rackets which make up the business. Practically each one of these rackets should be in itself a distinct subject of investigation if its extent, its financial aspects, the specific groups and individuals comprising its personnel, and its social impact are to be presented in detail and appraised. The Commission has set forth about them but a fraction of the facts which could be developed, documented, and published. Further, these particular rackets, though the major forms of unlawful gaming, are by no means the only ones which in the Commonwealth flourish by offering a chance at a prize for a price.

The Commission believes, however, that enough has been shown to make certain fundamentals crystal clear. The business in every form it takes shows common characteristics. No form of the product is worth the money paid for it. In every form the customer or player, who may think he is taking a fair and reasonable risk or gamble, is being cheated to a degree beyond his comprehension. In fact, his chance at a prize is minute, whatever the prize. The business in each of its forms is thoroughly dishonest. Figures and formulas can indicate its size, but only facts about the people who operate in it, their records and the things they have done and will do to take money from the unsuspecting, can depict its utter sordidness.

As to the size of the business, enough has been shown to establish its huge power to draw money from the economy. Lacking the statistics available from legitimate business, and in a world where books of account are a liability, not an asset, and, if kept, are dishonestly kept and concealed, the Commission has sought to understate rather than exaggerate. It has estimated the volume of off-track horse betting at upwards of three-quarters of a billion dollars; but it believes this one racket to be at least a billion-dollar business. It believes one hundred million dollars conservative for the dog-betting phase of the business. Expert opinion expressed by informed racketeers places the volume of sports betting second only to the total off-track play. The Commission would show no surprise if this figure was placed at around half a billion dollars. It is inconceivable that, with the numbers pools, the lotteries of all sorts, the coin-machine racket, and all the others, the total annual take of organized illegal gambling does not equal or exceed two billion dollars.

Let him who doubts the position of this unlawful business in the Commonwealth's economy compare the figures and estimations developed in this report with officially compiled figures for all retail sales of merchandise of all kinds in Massachusetts. For the year 1954, retail sales here by every establishment having a payroll of any kind totalled $5,202,282,000. The Commission believes that the unlawful revenues of organized gambling reach at least two-fifths of this figure for legitimate, essential business.

There are set forth below similar figures for retail sales in Massachusetts during 1954 of legitimate businesses dealing in the most common articles of necessity and use:

Food stores	$1,280,372,000
Eating, drinking places	420,511,000
General merchandise	553,809,000
Apparel, accessories stores	394,859,000
Furniture, home furnishings, appliance dealers	240,097,000
Automotive group	820,295,000
Drug stores	162,807,000
Jewelry stores	52,691,000
Liquor stores	140,470,000
	$4,065,911,000

Let it be noted that the Commission is convinced that the unlawful gaming take equals or exceeds the total retail sales by stores which provide food, apparel and accessories, and furniture and home appliances. Put another way, the Commission is convinced that this unlawful take equals or exceeds total retail sales of dealers in automobiles and automotive equipment, general merchandise, apparel and accessories, and furniture and appliances; that it substantially exceeds the total for all retail sales of food stores and eating and drinking places; and that it is about fifteen times the total of all retail sales of liquor stores. If it be said that these conclusions of the Commission represent only convictions, it must also be recognized that they represent informed convictions based on known facts and opinions of experts.

That so huge an industry with such huge revenue can flourish in defiance of law is the basis for the solid lack of respect of gaming operators for the law and its enforcement. They find in it an element of stupidity which they would not tolerate in their business. It provokes in them a firm feeling that officialdom and the public are not serious when they speak of the evils of lotteries and gambling; that the law talks out of both sides of its mouth; and that only certain individuals in the law-enforcement business are dangerous to them.

The basic finding of this Commission is that, as illustrated by organized illegal gambling, organized crime has evolved into a state of society which amounts to lawlessness. The existence and the extent of illegal gaming has become a part of the commerce of the Commonwealth and, with its wealth, forms the basis of power for all organized crime. This state of society, this commerce, is attributable to three general conditions within society of tolerance, hypocrisy, and corruption.

Any attack on this state of society must begin by an attack on the specific conditions which go to make up the general conditions. The task will be a long and difficult and continuous one. It will never completely succeed, but it not only is worth trying but must be tried, or this Commonwealth must confess itself to be without ambition.

CRIME AS AN AMERICAN
WAY OF LIFE

Daniel Bell

In the 1890's the Reverend Dr. Charles Parkhurst, shocked at the open police protection afforded New York's bordellos, demanded a state inquiry. In the Lexow investigation that followed, William Travers Jerome staged a set of public hearings that created sensation after sensation. He badgered "Clubber" Williams, First Inspector of the Police Department, to account for wealth and property far greater than could have been saved on his salary; it was earned, the Clubber explained laconically, through land speculation "in Japan." Captain Schmittberger, the "collector" for the "Tenderloin precincts"—Broadway's fabulous concentration of hotels, theaters, restaurants, gaming houses, and saloons—related in detail how protection money was distributed among the police force. Crooks, policemen, public officials, businessmen, all paraded across the stage, each adding his chapter to a sordid story of corruption and crime. The upshot of these revelations was reform—the election of William L. Strong, a stalwart businessman, as mayor, and the naming of Theodore Roosevelt as police commissioner.

It did not last, of course, just as previous reform victories had not lasted. Yet the ritual drama was re-enacted. Thirty years ago the Seabury investi-

Abridged from Daniel Bell, "Crime as an American Way of Life, *Antioch Review,* 13:2 (Summer 1953), 131–154. Reprinted by permission of the author and the Antioch Press. Daniel Bell is a professor of sociology at Columbia University, and the author of books and articles on industrial and political sociology.

gation in New York uncovered the tin-box brigade and the thirty-three little McQuades. Jimmy Walker was ousted as Mayor and in came Fiorello La-Guardia. Tom Dewey became district attorney, broke the industrial rackets, sent Lucky Luciano to jail, and went to the governor's chair in Albany. Then reform was again swallowed up in the insatiable maw of corruption until in 1950 Kefauver and his committee counsel Rudolph Halley threw a new beam of light into the seemingly bottomless pit.

How explain this repetitious cycle? Americans have had an extraordinary talent for compromise in politics and extremism in morality. The most shameless political deals (and "steals") have been rationalized as expedient and realistically necessary. Yet in no other country have there been such spectacular attempts to curb human appetites and brand them as illicit, and nowhere else such glaring failures. From the start America was at one and the same time a frontier community where "everything goes," and the fair country of the Blue Laws. At the turn of the century the cleavage developed between the Big City and the small-town conscience. Crime as a growing business was fed by the revenues from prostitution, liquor, and gambling that a wide-open urban society encouraged and that a middle-class Protestant ethos tried to suppress with a ferocity unmatched in any other civilized country. Catholic cultures have rarely imposed such restrictions and have rarely suffered such excesses. Even in prim and proper Anglican England, prostitution is a commonplace of Piccadilly night life, and gambling is one of the largest and most popular industries. In America the enforcement of public morals has been a continuing feature of our history.

Crime, in many ways, is a Coney Island mirror, caricaturing the morals and manners of a society. The jungle quality of the American business community, particularly at the turn of the century, was reflected in the mode of "business" practiced by the coarse gangster elements, most of them from new immigrant families, who were "getting ahead," just as Horatio Alger had urged. In the older, Protestant tradition the intensive acquisitiveness, such as that of Daniel Drew, was rationalized by a compulsive moral fervor. But the formal obeisance of the ruthless businessman in the workaday world to the church-going pieties of the Sabbath was one that the gangster could not make. Moreover, for the young criminal, hunting in the asphalt jungle of the crowded city, it was not the businessman with his wily manipulation of numbers but the "man with the gun" who was the American hero. "No amount of commercial prosperity," once wrote Teddy Roosevelt, "can supply the lack of the heroic virtues." The American was "the hunter, cow-boy, frontiersman, the soldier, the naval hero"—and in the crowded slums, the gangster. He was a man with a gun, acquiring by personal merit what was denied him by complex orderings of stratified society. And the duel with the law was the morality play par excellence: the gangster, with whom ride our own illicit desires, and the prosecutor, representing final judgment and the force of the law.

Yet all this was acted out in a wider context. The desires satisfied in extra-legal fashion were more than a hunger for the "forbidden fruits" of conventional morality. They also involved, in the complex and ever shifting structure of group, class, and ethnic stratification, which is the warp and woof of America's "open" society, such "normal" goals as independence through a business of one's own, and such "moral" aspirations as the desire for social advancement and social prestige. For crime, in the language of the sociologists, has a "functional" role in the society, and the urban rackets —the illicit activity organized for continuing profit, rather than individual illegal acts—is one of the queer ladders of social mobility in American life. Indeed, it is not too much to say that the whole question of organized crime in America cannot be understood unless one appreciates (1) the distinctive role of organized gambling as a function of a mass-consumption economy; (2) the specific role of various immigrant groups as they, one after another, became involved in marginal business and crime; and (3) the relation of crime to the changing character of the urban political machines.

As a society changes, so does, in lagging fashion, its type of crime. As American society becames more "organized," as the American businessman became more "civilized" and less "buccaneering," so did the American racketeer. In the America of the last fifty years the main drift of society has been toward the rationalization of industry, the domestication of the crude self-made captain of industry into the respectable man of manners, and the emergence of a mass-consumption economy. The most significant transformation in the field of "institutionalized" crime in the 1940's was the increasing importance of gambling as against other kinds of illegal activity. And, as a multi-billion-dollar business, gambling underwent a transition parallel to the changes in American enterprise as a whole. This parallel was exemplified in many ways: in gambling's industrial organization (e.g., the growth of a complex technology such as the national racing-wire service and the minimization of risks by such techniques as lay-off betting); in its respectability, as was evidenced in the opening of smart and popular gambling casinos in resort towns and in "satellite" adjuncts to metropolitan areas; in its functional role in a mass-consumption economy (for sheer volume of money changing hands, nothing has ever surpassed this feverish activity of fifty million American adults); in the social acceptance of the gamblers in the important status world of sport and entertainment, i.e., "café society." And in seeking to "legitimize" itself, gambling had quite often actually become a force against older and more vicious forms of illegal activity.

Jimmy Cannon once reported that when the gambling raids started in Chicago the "combine" protested that, in upsetting existing stable relations, the police were only opening the way for ambitious young punks and hoodlums to start trouble. Nor is there today, as there was twenty or even forty years ago, prostitution of major organized scope in the United States. Aside from the fact that manners and morals have changed, prostitution *as an industry* doesn't pay as well as gambling. Besides, its existence threatened the tacit moral acceptance and quasi-respectability that gamblers and gambling have secured in the American way of life. It was, as any operator in the field might tell you, "bad for business."

The criminal world of the 1940's, its tone set by the captains of the gambling industry, is in startling contrast to the state of affairs in the decade before. If a Kefauver report had been written then, the main "names" would have been Lepke and Gurrah, Dutch Schultz, Jack "Legs" Diamond, Lucky Luciano, and, reaching back a little further, Arnold Rothstein, the czar of the underworld. These men (with the exception of Luciano, who was involved in narcotics and prostitution) were in the main "industrial racketeers." Rothstein, the model for Wolfsheim, the gambler in F. Scott

Fitzgerald's *The Great Gatsby,* had a larger function: he was, as Frank Costello became later, the financier of the underworld, the pioneer big businessman of crime who, understanding the logic of coordination, sought to *organize* crime as a source of regular income. His main interest in this direction was in industrial racketeering, and his entry was through labor disputes. At one time, employers in the garment trades hired Legs Diamond and his sluggers to break strikes, and the Communists, then in control of the cloakmakers union, hired one Little Orgie to protect the pickets and beat up the scabs; only later did both sides learn that Legs Diamond and Little Orgie were working for the same man, Rothstein.

Rothstein's chief successors, Lepke Buchalter and Gurrah Shapiro, were able, in the early thirties, to dominate sections of the men's and women's clothing industries, of painting, fur dressing, flour trucking, and other fields. In a highly chaotic and cut-throat industry such as clothing, the racketeer, paradoxically, played a stabilizing role by regulating competition and fixing prices. When the NRA came in and assumed this function, the businessman found that what had once been a quasi-economic service was now pure extortion, and he began to demand police action. In other types of racketeering, such as the trucking of perishable foods and waterfront loading, where the racketeers entrenched themselves as middlemen—taking up, by default, a service that neither shippers nor truckers wanted to assume—a pattern of accommodation was roughly worked out, and the rackets assumed a quasi-legal veneer. On the waterfront, old-time racketeers performed the necessary function of loading—but at an exorbitant price; and this monopoly was recognized by the union and the shippers, and tacitly by the government.

But in the last decade and a half, industrial racketeering has not offered much in the way of opportunity. *Like American capitalism itself, crime shifted its emphasis from production to consumption.* The focus of crime became the direct exploitation of the citizen as consumer, largely through gambling. And while the protection of these huge revenues was inextricably linked to politics, the relation between gambling and "the mobs" became more complicated.

While Americans made gambling illegal, they did not in their hearts think of it as wicked—even the churches benefited from the bingo and lottery crazes. So they gambled—and gamblers flourished. Against this open canvas, the indignant tones of Senator Wiley and the shocked righteousness of Senator Tobey during the Kefauver investigation rang oddly. Yet it was probably this very tone of surprise that gave the activity of the Kefauver Committee its piquant quality. Here were some Senators who seemingly did not know the facts of life, as most Americans did. Here, in the person of Senator Tobey, was the old New England Puritan conscience poking around in industrial America, in a world it had made but never seen. Here was old-fashioned moral indignation, at a time when cynicism was rampant in public life.

Commendable as such moralistic fervor was, it did not make for intelligent discrimination of fact. Throughout the Kefauver hearings, for example, there ran the presumption that all gamblers were invariably gangsters. This was true of Chicago's Accardo-Guzik combine, which in the past had its fingers in many kinds of rackets. It was not nearly so true of many large gamblers in America, most of whom had the feeling that they were satisfying a basic American urge for sport and looked upon their calling with no greater sense of guilt than did many bootleggers. After all, Sherman Billingsley did start out as a speakeasy proprietor, as did the Kreindlers of the "21" Club; and today the Stork Club and the former Jack and Charlie's are the most fashionable night and dining spots in America (one prominent patron of the Stork Club: J. Edgar Hoover).

The S & G syndicate in Miami, for example (led by Harold Salvey, Jules Levitt, Charles Friedman, Sam Cohen, and Edward [Eddie Luckey] Rosenbaum), was simply a master pool of some two hundred bookies that arranged for telephone service, handled "protection," acted as bankers for those who needed ready cash on hard-hit books, and, in short, functioned somewhat analogously to the large factoring corporations in the textile field or the credit companies in the auto industry. Yet to Kefauver, the S & G men were "slippery and arrogant characters. . . . Salvey, for instance, was an old-time bookie who told us he had done nothing except engage in bookmaking or finance other bookmakers for twenty years." When, as a result of committee publicity and the newly found purity of the Miami police, the S & G syndicate went out of business, it was, as the combine's lawyer told Kefauver, because the "boys" were weary of being painted "the worst monsters in the world." "It is true," Cohen acknowledged, "that they had been law violators." But they had never done anything worse than gambling, and "to fight the world isn't worth it."

Most intriguing of all were the opinions of James J. Carroll, the St. Louis "betting commissioner," who for years had been widely quoted on the sports pages of the country as setting odds on the Kentucky Derby winter book and the baseball pennant races. Senator Wiley sought to pin Carroll down on his contributions to political campaigns:

SENATOR WILEY: Now this morning I asked you whether you contributed any money for political candidates or parties, and you said not more than $200 at one time. I presume that does not indicate the total of your contributions in any one campaign, does it?
MR. CARROLL: Well, it might, might not, Senator. I have been an "againster" in many instances. I am a reader of *The Nation* for fifty years and they have advertisements calling for contributions for different candidates, different causes. . . . They carried an advertisement for George Norris; I contributed, I think, to that, and to the elder LaFollette.

Carroll, who admitted to having been in the betting business since 1899, was the sophisticated—but not immoral!—counterpoint to moralist Wiley. Here was a man without the stigmata of the underworld or underground; he was worldly, cynical of official rhetoric, jaundiced about people's motives; he was an "againster" who believed that "all gambling legislation originates or stems from some group or some individual seeking special interests for himself or his cause."

Asked why people gamble, Carroll distilled his experiences of fifty years with a remark that deserves a place in American social history: "I really don't know how to answer the question," he said. "I think gambling is a biological necessity for certain types. I think it is the quality that gives substance to their daydreams."

In a sense, the entire Kefauver materials, unintentionally, seem to document that remark. For what the committee revealed time and time again was a picture of gambling as a basic institution in American life, flourishing openly and accepted widely. In many of the small towns, the gambling joint is as open as a liquor establishment. The town of Havana, in Mason County, Illinois, felt miffed when Governor Adlai Stevenson intervened against local gambling. In 1950, the town had raised $15,000 of its $50,000 budget by making friendly raids on the gambling houses every month and having the owners pay fines. "With the gambling fines cut off," grumbled Mayor Clarence Chester, "next year is going to be tough."

Apart from the gamblers, there were the mobsters. But what Senator Kefauver and company failed to understand was that the mobsters, like the gamblers, and like the entire gangdom generally, were seeking to become quasi-respectable and establish a place for themselves in American life. For the mobsters, by and large, had immigrant roots, and crime, as the pattern showed, was a route of social ascent in American life.

The Italian community has achieved wealth and political influence much later and in a harder way than previous immigrant groups. Early Jewish wealth, that of the German Jews of the late nineteenth century, was made largely in banking and merchandising. To that extent, the dominant group in the Jewish community was outside of, and independent of, the urban political machines. Later Jewish wealth, among the East European immigrants, was built in the garment trades, though with some involvement with the Jewish gangster, who was typically an industrial racketeer (Arnold Rothstein, Lepke and Gurrah, etc.). Among Jewish lawyers, a small minority, such as the "Tammany lawyer" (like the protagonist of Sam Ornitz's *Haunch, Paunch and Jowl*), rose through politics and occasionally touched the fringes of crime. Most of the Jewish lawyers, by and large the communal leaders, climbed rapidly, however, in the opportunities that established and legitimate Jewish wealth provided. Irish immigrant wealth in the northern urban centers, concentrated largely in construction, trucking, and the waterfront, has, to a substantial extent, been wealth accumulated in and through political alliance, e.g., favoritism in city contracts.[1]

Control of the politics of the city thus has been crucial for the continuance of Irish political wealth. This alliance of Irish immigrant wealth and politics has been reciprocal; many noted Irish political figures lent their names as important window-dressing for business corporations (Al Smith, for example, who helped form the U.S. Trucking Corporation, whose executive head for many years was William J. McCormack, the alleged "Mr. Big" of the New York waterfront), while Irish businessmen have lent their wealth to further the careers of Irish politicians. Irish mobsters have rarely achieved status in the Irish community, but have served as integral arms of the politicians, as strong-arm men on election day.

[1] A fact which should occasion little shock if one recalls that, in the nineteenth century, American railroads virtually stole 190 million acres of land by bribing Congressmen, and that more recently such scandals as the Teapot Dome oil grabs during the Harding administration, consummated, as the Supreme Court said, "by means of conspiracy, fraud and bribery," reached to the very doors of the White House.

The Italians found the more obvious big-city paths from rags to riches pre-empted. In part this was due to the character of the early Italian immigrant. Most of them were unskilled and from rural stock. Jacob Riis could remark in the nineties, "The Italian comes in at the bottom and stays there." These dispossessed agricultural laborers found jobs as ditch-diggers, on the railroads as section hands, along the docks, in the service occupations, as shoemakers, barbers, garment workers, and stayed there. Many were fleeced by the "padrone" system; a few achieved wealth from truck farming, wine growing, and marketing produce; but this "marginal wealth" was not the source of coherent and stable political power.

Significantly, although the number of Italians in the United States is about a third as high as the number of Irish, and of the thirty million Catholic communicants in the United States, about half are of Irish descent and a sixth of Italian, there is not one Italian bishop among the hundred Catholic bishops in this country or one Italian archbishop among the twenty-one archbishops. The Irish have a virtual monopoly. This is a factor related to the politics of the American church; but the condition also is possible because there is not significant or sufficient wealth among Italian Americans to force some parity.

The children of the immigrants, the second and third generation, became wise in the ways of the urban slums. Excluded from the political ladder—in the early thirties there were almost no Italians on the city payroll in top jobs, nor in books of the period can one find discussion of Italian political leaders—and finding few open routes to wealth, some turned to illicit ways. In the children's court statistics of the 1930's, the largest group of delinquents were the Italian; nor were there any Italian communal or social agencies to cope with these problems. Yet it was, oddly enough, the quondam racketeer, seeking to become respectable, who provided one of the major supports for the drive to win a political voice for Italians in the power structure of the urban political machines.

This rise of the Italian political bloc was connected, at least in the major northern urban centers, with another important development which tended to make the traditional relation between the politician and the protected or tolerated illicit operator more close than it had been in the past. This is the fact that the urban political machines had to evolve new forms of fund-raising, since the big business contributions, which once went heavily into municipal politics, now—with the shift in the locus of power—go largely into national affairs. (The ensuing corruption in national politics, as recent Congressional investigations show, is no petty matter; the scruples of businessmen do not seem much superior to those of the gamblers.) One way that urban political machines raised their money resembled that of the large corporations which are no longer dependent on Wall Street: by self-financing—that is, by "taxing" the large number of municipal employees who bargain collectively with City Hall for their wage increases. So the firemen's union contributed money to O'Dwyer's campaign.

A second method was taxing the gamblers. The classic example, as *Life* reported, was Jersey City, where a top lieutenant of the Hague machine spent his full time screening applicants for unofficial bookmaking licenses. If found acceptable, the applicant was given a "location," usually the house or store of a loyal precinct worker, who kicked into the machine treasury a high proportion of the large rent exacted. The one thousand bookies and their one thousand landlords in Jersey City formed the hard core of the political machine that sweated and bled to get out the votes for Hague.

A third source for the financing of these machines was the new, and often illegally earned, Italian wealth. This is well illustrated by the career of Costello and his emergence as a political power in New York. Here the ruling motive has been the search for an entree—for oneself and one's ethnic group—into the ruling circles of the big city.

Frank Costello made his money originally in bootlegging. After repeal, his big break came when Huey Long, desperate for ready cash to fight the old-line political machines, invited Costello to install slot machines in Louisiana. Costello did, and he flourished. Together with Dandy Phil Kastel, he also opened the Beverly Club, an elegant gambling establishment just outside New Orleans, at which have appeared some of the top entertainers in America. Subsequently, Costello invested his money in New York real estate (including 79 Wall Street, which he later sold), the Copacabana night club, and a leading brand of Scotch whiskey.

Costello's political opportunity came when a money-hungry Tammany, starved by lack of patronage from Roosevelt and LaGuardia, turned to him for financial support. The Italian community in New York has for years nursed a grievance against the Irish and, to a lesser extent, the Jewish political groups for monopolizing political power. They complained about the lack of judicial jobs, the small number—usually one—of Italian congressmen, the lack of representation on the state tickets. But the Italians lacked the means to make their ambition a reality. Although they formed a large voting bloc, there was rarely sufficient wealth to finance political clubs.

During the Prohibition years, the Italian racketeers had made certain political contacts in order to gain protection. Costello, always the compromiser and fixer rather than the muscle-man, was the first to establish relations with Jimmy Hines, the powerful leader of the West Side in Tammany Hall. But his rival, Lucky Luciano, suspicious of the Irish and seeking more direct power, backed and elected Al Marinelli for district leader on the Lower West Side. Marinelli in 1932 was the only Italian leader inside Tammany Hall. Later, he was joined by Dr. Paul Sarubbi, a partner of gangster Johnny Torrio in a large, legitimate liquor concern. Certainly, Costello and Luciano represented no "unified" move by the Italians as a whole for power; within the Italian community there are as many divisions as in any other group. What is significant is that different Italians, for different reasons and in various fashions, were achieving influence for the first time. Marinelli became county clerk of New York and a leading power in Tammany. In 1937, after being blasted by Tom Dewey, then running for district attorney, as a "political ally of thieves . . . and big-shot racketeers," Marinelli was removed from office by Governor Lehman. The subsequent conviction by Dewey of Luciano and Hines, and the election of LaGuardia, left most of the Tammany clubs financially weak and foundering. This was the moment Costello made his move. In a few years, by judicious financing, he controlled a bloc of Italian leaders in the Hall—as well as some Irish on the upper West Side and some Jewish leaders on the East Side—and was able to influence the selection of a number of Italian judges. The most notable incident, revealed by a wire tap on Costello's phone, was the "Thank you, Francisco" call in 1943 by Supreme Court judge nominee Thomas Aurelio, who gave Costello full credit for his nomination.

It was not only Tammany that was eager to accept campaign contributions from newly rich Italians, even though some of these *nouveaux riches* had "arrived" through bootlegging and gambling. Fiorello LaGuardia, the wiliest mind that melting-pot politics has ever produced, understood in the early thirties where much of his covert support came from. (So, too, did Vito Marcantonio, an apt pupil of the master: Marcantonio consistently made deals with the Italian leaders of Tammany Hall—in 1943 he supported Aurelio and refused to repudiate him even when the Democratic party formally did.) Joe Adonis, who had built a political following during the late twenties, when he ran a popular speakeasy, aided LaGuardia financially to a considerable extent in 1933. "The Democrats haven't recognized the Italians," Adonis told a friend. "There is no reason for the Italians to support anybody but LaGuardia; the Jews have played ball with the Democrats and haven't gotten much out of it. They know it now. They will vote for LaGuardia. So will the Italians."

Adonis played his cards shrewdly. He supported LaGuardia, but also a number of Democrats for local and judicial posts, and became a power in the Brooklyn area. His restaurant was frequented by Kenny Sutherland, the Coney Island Democratic leader; Irwin Steingut, the Democratic minority leader in Albany; Anthony DiGiovanni, later a councilman; William O'Dwyer, and Jim Moran. But, in 1937, Adonis made the mistake of supporting Royal Copeland against LaGuardia, and the irate Fiorello finally drove Adonis out of New York.[2]

LaGuardia later turned his ire against Costello, too. Yet, Costello survived and reached the peak of his influence in 1942, when he was instrumental in electing Michael Kennedy leader of Tammany Hall. Despite the Aurelio fiasco, which first brought Costello into notoriety, he still had sufficient power in the Hall to swing votes for Hugo Rogers as Tammany leader in 1948. In those years many a Tammany leader came hat-in-hand to Costello's apartment or sought him out on the golf links to obtain the nomination for a judicial post.

During this period, other Italian political leaders were also coming to the fore. Generoso Pope, whose Colonial Sand and Stone Company began to prosper through political contacts, became an important political figure, especially when his purchase of the two largest Italian-language

---

[2]Adonis, and associate Willie Moretti, moved across the river to Bergen County, New Jersey, where, together with the quondam racketeer Abner "Longie" Zwillman, he became one of the political powers in the state. Gambling flourished in Bergen County for almost a decade, but after the Kefauver investigation the state was forced to act. A special inquiry in 1953, headed by Nelson Stamler, revealed that Moretti had paid $286,000 to an aide of Governor Driscoll for "protection" and that the Republican state committee had accepted a $25,000 "loan" from gambler Joseph Bozzo, an associate of Zwillman. Moretti was later murdered, and Adonis deported to Italy.

dailies (later merged into one), and of a radio station, gave him almost a monopoly of channels to Italian-speaking opinion of the city. Through Generoso Pope, and through Costello, the Italians became a major political force in New York.

That the urban machines, largely Democratic, have financed their heavy campaign costs in this fashion rather than having to turn to the "moneyed interests" explains to some degree why these machines were able, in part, to support the New and Fair Deals without suffering the pressures they might have been subjected to had their source of money supply been the business groups.[3] Although he has never publicly revealed his political convictions, it is likely that Frank Costello was a fervent admirer of Franklin D. Roosevelt and his efforts to aid the common man. The basic measures of the New Deal, which most Americans today agree were necessary for the public good, would not have been possible without the support of the "corrupt" big-city machines.

There is little question that men of Italian origin appeared in most of the leading roles in the high drama of gambling and mobs, just as twenty years ago the children of East European Jews were the most prominent figures in organized crime, and before that individuals of Irish descent were similarly prominent. To some extent statistical accident and the tendency of newspapers to emphasize the few sensational figures give a greater illusion about the domination of illicit activities by a single ethnic group than all the facts warrant. In many cities, particularly in the South and on the West Coast, the mob and gambling fraternity consisted of many other groups, and often, predominantly, of native white Protestants. Yet it is clear that in the major northern urban centers there was a distinct ethnic sequence in the modes of obtaining illicit wealth and that, uniquely in the case of the recent Italian elements, the former bootleggers and gamblers provided considerable leverage for the growth of political influence as well. A substantial number of Italian judges sitting on the bench in New York today are indebted in one fashion or another to Costello; so too are many Italian district leaders—as well as some Jewish and Irish politicians. And the motive in establishing Italian political prestige in New York was generous rather than scheming for personal advantage. For Costello it was largely a case of ethnic pride. As in earlier American eras, organized illegality became a stepladder of social ascent.

To the world at large, the news and pictures of Frank Sinatra, for example, mingling with former Italian mobsters could come somewhat as a shock. Yet to Sinatra, and to many Italians, these were men who had grown up in their neighborhoods and who were, in some instances, bywords in the community for their helpfulness and their charities. The early Italian gangsters were hoodlums—rough, unlettered, and young (Al Capone was only twenty-nine at the height of his power). Those who survived learned to adapt. By now they are men of middle age or older. They learned to dress conservatively. Their homes are in respectable suburbs.

[3]This is an old story in American politics. Theodore Allen, a gambler and saloon keeper, whose American Mabille was an elegant music hall and bordello (he once told a Congressional investigating commitee that he was the wickedest man in New York), gave Republican Boss Thurlow Weed a campaign contribution of $25,000 for the re-election of Abraham Lincoln in 1864.

They sent their children to good schools and sought to avoid publicity.[4] Costello even went to a psychiatrist in his efforts to overcome a painful feeling of inferiority in the world of manners.

As happens with all "new" money in American society, the rough and ready contractors, the construction people, trucking entrepreneurs, as well as racketeers, polished up their manners and sought recognition and respectability in their own ethnic as well as in the general community. The "shanty" Irish became the "lace curtain" Irish, and then moved out for wider recognition.[5] Sometimes acceptance came first in established "American" society, and this was a certificate for later recognition by the ethnic community, a process well illustrated by the belated acceptance in established Negro society of such figures as Sugar Ray Robinson and Joe Louis, as well as leading popular entertainers.

Yet, after all, the foundation of many a distinguished older American fortune was laid by sharp practices and morally reprehensible methods. The pioneers of American capitalism were not graduated from Harvard's School of Business Administration. The early settlers and founding fathers, as well as those who "won the West" and built up cattle, mining, and other fortunes, often did so by shady speculations and a not inconsiderable amount of violence. They ignored, circumvented, or stretched the law when it stood in the way of America's destiny and their own—or were themselves the law when it served their purposes. This has not prevented them and their descendants from feeling proper moral outrage when, under the changed circumstances of the crowded urban environments, latecomers pursued equally ruthless tactics.

Ironically, the social development which made possible the rise to political influence sounds, too, the knell of the rough Italian gangster. For it is the growing number of Italians with professional training and legitimate business success that both prompts and permits the Italian group to wield increasing political influence; and increasingly it is the professionals and businessmen who provide models for Italian youth today, models that hardly existed twenty years ago. Ironically, the headlines and exposés of "crime" of the Italian "gangsters" came years after the fact. Many of the top "crime" figures had long ago forsworn violence, and even their income, in large part, was derived from legitimate investments (real estate in the case of Costello, motor haulage and auto dealer franchises in the case of Adonis) or from such quasi-legitimate but socially respectable sources as gambling casinos. Hence society's "retribution" in the jail sentences for Costello and Adonis was little more than a trumped-up morality that disguised a social hypocrisy.

[4]Except at times by being overly neighborly, like Tony Accardo, who, at Yuletide 1949, in his elegant River Forest home, decorated a 40-foot tree on his lawn and beneath it set a wooden Santa and reindeer, while around the yard, on tracks, electrically operated skating figures zipped merrily around while a loudspeaker poured out Christmas carols. The next Christmas the Accardo lawn was darkened; Tony was on the lam from Kefauver.

[5]The role of ethnic pride in corralling minority groups is one of the oldest pieces of wisdom in American politics; but what is more remarkable is the persistence of this identification through second- and third-generation descendants, a fact which, as Samuel Lubell noted in his *Future of American Politics,* was one of the explanatory keys to political behavior in recent elections.

Apart from these considerations, what of the larger context of crime and the American way of life? The passing of the Fair Deal signalizes, oddly, the passing of an older pattern of illicit activities. The gambling fever of the past decade and a half was part of the flush and exuberance of rising incomes, and was characteristic largely of new upper-middle-class rich having a first fling at conspicuous consumption. This significant new stratum in American life is not rich in the nineteenth-century sense of enormous wealth, but consists largely of middle-sized businessmen and entrepreneurs of the service and luxury trades, who by the tax laws have achieved incomes often much higher than the managers of the super-giant corporations. They were the chief patrons of the munificent gambling casinos. During the war decade when travel was difficult, gambling and the lush resorts provided important outlets for this social class. Now they are settling down, learning about Europe and culture. The petty gambling, the betting and bingo which relieve the tedium of small-town life, or the expectation among the urban slum dwellers of winning a sizable sum by a "lucky number" or a "lucky horse," goes on. To quote Bernard Baruch: "You can't stop people from gambling on horses. And why should you prohibit a man from backing his own judgment? It's another form of personal initiative." But the lush profits are passing from gambling as the costs of coordination rise. And in the future it is likely that gambling, like prostitution, winning tacit acceptance as a necessary fact, will continue on a decentralized, small-entrepreneur basis.

But passing, too, is a political pattern, the system of political "bosses" which in its reciprocal relation provided "protection" for, and was fed revenue from, crime. The collapse of the "boss" system was a product of the Roosevelt era. Twenty years ago Jim Farley's task was simple; he had to work only on some key state bosses. Now there is no longer such an animal. New Jersey Democracy was once ruled by Frank Hague; now there are five or six men each "top dog," for the moment, in his part of the state or faction of the party. Within the urban centers, the old Irish-dominated political machines in New York, Boston, Newark, and Chicago have fallen apart. The growth of suburbs and satellite towns, the breakup of the old ecological patterns of slum and transient belts, the rise of functional groups, the increasing middle-class character of American life, all contribute to this decline.

With the rationalization and absorption of some illicit activities into the structure of the economy, the passing of an older generation that had established a hegemony over crime,[6] the general rise of minority groups to social position, and the breakup of the urban boss system, the pattern of crime we have discussed is passing as well. Crime, of course, remains as long as passion and the desire for gain remain. But the kind of big,

---

[6] In 1959, the Justice Department set up a special group to study the "crime syndicates." The group found, in a preliminary report, that the old crime leaders have eschewed violence and "created the appearance of successful businessmen" by entering legitimate business. It is quite possible that in many of these areas (trucking, vending, restaurants, entertainment) these old mobsters are able, by various means, to gain competitive advantages. But the significant thing, sociologically, is that these new areas are legitimate business, and this may not mean, as the Justice Department construes it, the "infiltration" of mobsters into new crime areas, but their attempt to gain quasi-respectability.

organized city crime, as we have known it for the past seventy-five years, was based on more than these universal motives. It was based on certain characteristics of the American economy, American ethnic groups, and American politics. The changes in all these areas means that, in the form we have known it, it too will change.

GUIDES FOR READING AND DISCUSSION

1. It is now a matter of general agreement that the attempt to define social drinking as vice during the Prohibition era resulted in a great impetus to organized crime. Does this mean that other types of vice (gambling, prostitution, narcotics, etc.) should be legalized? How should this decision be made? Where should one draw the line?

2. If Bell is correct in his contention that organized crime afforded one route up for ethnic minorities, still it was not the usual route. What were the legitimate avenues of mobility? What in your opinion probably determined how any particular group, or individual, rose by one route rather than another?

3. The point is often made that business activities, with the pretense of public service and the actual pursuit of profit, do not differ fundamentally from organized crime. Is illegality a minor attribute; is there no important distinction here?

SUGGESTED ADDITIONAL READINGS

E. J. Hobsbawm, *Social Bandits and Primitive Rebels* (Glencoe, Ill.: Free Press, 1960).

Illinois Crime Survey (Chicago: Illinois Association for Criminal Justice, 1929).

Estes Kefauver, *Crime in America* (Garden City, N.Y.: Doubleday, 1951).

Morris Ploscowe, ed., *Organized Crime and Law Enforcement*, 2 vol. (New York: Grosby Press, 1952–53).

United States Senate, *Third Interim Report of the Special Committee to Investigate Organized Crime in Interstate Commerce*, Report No. 307 (Washington, D.C.: U.S. Government Printing Office, 1951).

William F. Whyte, Jr., *Street-Corner Society* (Chicago: University of Chicago Press, 1943).

DOES THE JUVENILE COURT
EXERCISE JUSTICE?

The causes of juvenile delinquency have been a subject of perennial debate. Biological, psychological, and sociological factors have been suggested, and the specific theories over the past century and a half number several hundred. With no attempt to give a complete list, but only to suggest the range, one might cite the following alleged causes: head shape; endocrine balance; character of the nervous system; body-type; intelligence; various neurotic syndromes; ego-failure, culminating in an inability to make realistic decisions; the hostility of working-class (or especially minority) children to the dominantly middle-class standards of public schools; the absence of realistic opportunities for lower-class youth after graduation; the prolonged sexual abstinence presumably required during adolescence; parental neglect or, on the contrary, parental overindulgence or parental inconsistency—combining both factors in an unreasonable pattern. Some of these supposed causes are less popular now than they once were, but nothing like consensus has been achieved. The unfortunate fact is that law-enforcement agencies must operate on the basis of incomplete knowledge and divided opinion, even though any rational system of administering justice ought to rest on a reasonably firm answer to causal questions.

In advanced literate nations, the norms governing sanctions are embodied in legal statutes, which are enforced mainly by the police and courts of law. Both of these, but especially the courts, are responsible for protecting the community, for maintaining standards of morality, and for upholding the principle of justice. Judicial agencies have also long aspired to restore offenders to the respectable community, but during the past several decades this goal of rehabilitating the offender has been sought in part through major revisions in judicial procedure. These innovations have occasioned a considerable controversy, represented in the two papers reprinted here.

Although no two juvenile courts are exactly alike, one can describe the ideal features of two main types—the *traditional legalistic court* and the so-called *socialized court*. Legalistic courts operate under an adversary system, by which a state's attorney and a defense counsel plead a case before a judge and/or jury. The purpose of the trial is to determine whether the defendant in fact committed the crime with which he is charged. Great stress is placed on formal proceedings and rules of evidence, very little on information regarding the defendant's character and background. If he is convicted, the defendant is subject to fine, imprisonment, or execution. The punishment fits the crime, not the particular individual.

Socialized courts usually exercise jurisdiction either over juveniles, both neglected or dependent and delinquent or criminal; or over family law;

or, in some jurisdictions, over both juvenile and domestic problems in one omnibus court. Its methods of procedure have made greatest inroads in the juvenile court. Here, the adversary system is replaced by one or more social workers' reports, which emphasize information regarding the character and background of all parties. The judicial procedure is informal; rules of evidence do not apply. The purpose of the hearing is to determine whether a serious problem exists—whether, for example, a child requires help—and to provide the means to meet the needs of the individuals involved.

The controversy over the proper functions of the court reflects much more than a difference concerning the causes of crime. It would be a serious mistake, thus, to suppose that those who use sociological or psychological theories to explain delinquency, divorce, or other social pathologies therefore support the socialized court, while those holding biological theories support the traditional court. The controversy between proponents of the two types of court is rooted rather in ethical differences, differences in the understanding of justice. In the traditional view, such a concept as "individualized justice," to use Judge Schramm's term, is self-contradictory, for the essence of Western justice is equality before the law. In an occasional, exceptional case, holding the defendant responsible for what he has done irrespective of his race, social class, family, and the like, may *not* do him full justice. In such a case the ordinary justice of common law is tempered with the extraordinary justice of the equity court. In the view of the socialized court's proponents, however, equity should be not an exceptional feature—restricted, as it is now, to a certain type of court—but the general norm applicable in *all* courts. As Judge Schramm points out, important revisions in formal procedures have already spread from juvenile to criminal courts.

Many supporters of the socialized court, although well aware of its shortcomings, view its faults not as dilemmas inherent in the very idea of individualized justice, but as remediable administrative defects.[1] The contrast in point of view comes out more clearly when Judge Schramm's relatively uncritical and enthusiastic advocacy is countered by Professor Allen's prudent skepticism. Present knowledge, Allen points out, often does not furnish an adequate basis for therapy or rehabilitation; and if we insist nevertheless on seeking these goals, we may sacrifice justice to a promissory note with no due date.

[1]For one such guarded defense of the socialized court, see Sol Rubin, *Crime and Juvenile Delinquency* (New York: Oceana, 1961), ch. 4 and 5.

PHILOSOPHY OF THE
JUVENILE COURT

Gustav L. Schramm

Fifty years ago in Chicago, American children received the advantage of the first juvenile court. It was created to protect and guide them, to correct them and help them to grow into useful, happy, and desirable citizens. According to Roscoe Pound, this was the most significant advance in the administration of justice since the Magna Charta was signed in 1215. In the document of Runnymede, Dean Pound points out, the principles of human freedom were set forth. In Chicago, in 1899, a group of Chicago lawyers outlined the first philosophy and objectives of the juvenile court. They set forth the principles of personalized justice.

Fifty years of experience have reaffirmed the principles adopted by that Chicago group. Today this strengthened philosophy of personalized justice and the principle of freedom from oppression stand as two of America's most cherished traditions, to be used by all the world as mankind seeks to live in peace and good will. All about us is the evidence of force, fear, and confusion, but in this land a child's court leads to a better understanding of human dignity, of the growth of personality, of opportunities, and of appreciation of the wants and needs of others. It is a child's court that has led to changes in attitudes and in methods of justice.

The court, acting for the state as a parent, was to recognize the individuality of the child and adapt its orders accordingly. There was legal precedent for this basic idea in the English tradition of the court of equity. A duty of such a court was (and always should be) to see that neglected and abused children were given a chance under protection of the court to grow into useful citizenship.

Functions of the court were broadened logically and wisely. The age when a child is capable of responsibility was studied. If children under seven years were considered under the old Common Law as incapable of criminality, then why not those of eight, nine, or ten years of age? Was it not obvious that criminal courts, which were designed for adults, were not the proper ones to treat children in their growing years? Hence this group of delinquent children could be added to the others already protected by equity courts, the dependent and neglected children. The men of Chicago recognized the principle that children could not in practice be held accountable for their behavior as adults for the simple but valid reason that they are not adults.[1]

Abridged from Gustav L. Schramm, "Philosophy of the Juvenile Court," *Annals of the American Academy of Political and Social Science*, 241 (January 1949), 101–108, by permission of the Academy. Gustav Schramm was, until his recent death, Judge of the Juvenile Court in Alleghany County, Pittsburgh, Pennsylvania.

[1]"The fundamental idea of the [juvenile-court] law is that the state must step in and exercise guardianship over a child found under such adverse social or individual conditions as develop crime. . . . It proposes a plan whereby he may be treated, not as a criminal, or legally charged with crime, but as a ward of the state, to receive practically the care, custody and discipline that are accorded the neglected and dependent child, and which, as the act states, 'shall approximate as nearly as may be that which should be given by its parents.'" *Report,* Committee of Chicago Bar, 1899.

The first juvenile court stimulated thinking about the need of children for legal protection. It brought about new developments in court administration and in function. It began serving children not for prescribed periods of time but for whatever length of time was necessary to help the child. It created administrative machinery for service which would be fluid in that it would change services and adjust them to changing conditions and needs of the children in its charge.

It seems almost self-evident to declare that the juvenile court, protector of children needing help, should follow through in providing this help. Yet there are some who would restrict the juvenile court to a role of "legal determination" and would give executive bodies the administrative responsibilities. Much of the difference in opinion concerning juvenile courts and their proper functions and spheres of activity stems from lack of understanding that this court has the same approach and philosophy as any other equity court. People try to judge the changing pattern of juvenile procedure according to the old yardstick of "an eye for an eye." "Why shouldn't children pay in kind for the grief, anxiety, pain, and inconvenience suffered by others whom they wrong?" they ask. Punishment is the remedy, they argue, not realizing that a juvenile court does not mete out mere punishment, but it corrects children as a parent would. There is no conflict between the state and the child. The state accepts the child into its protection and seeks to help the child to grow into a useful citizen.

Not all juvenile courts are alike. There are courts rich in tradition, in philosophy, and in skill, and there are courts impoverished by legislation, inadequate staffs, lack of facilities, and absence of community cooperation and support. In such latter instances the children suffer as they do when serious defects prevail in homes.

The idea that people are different is the very foundation of the philosophy represented by the juvenile court. We call that philosophy personalized and individualized justice. Each person is an entity within himself, having basic rights and privileges as do all children, but having different needs according to circumstance and personality. In all juvenile-court procedure there is nothing more difficult than properly to identify this difference, to explore it to its conclusion, and to set forth a course of treatment that will be most effective.

In a juvenile court the phrase "individualized justice" means "individualized treatment." It is exactly the opposite to the panacea or elixir viewpoint of one medicine for all suffering from a disease, the medicine given in the same quantity and at the same time. In juvenile court, Tommy and Johnny differ in reaction and in absorption of the treatment prescribed. It does not mean that the court ignores, from case to case, certain general considerations such as procedure, channels, institutions, or social obligations. It means that in the systematic consideration of each problem, coordination of resources and skills in behalf of the child must and does follow.

Individualization means that the problems of Tommy and Johnny, although the boys were referred to the court on identical complaints, must be separated when considered by the court. The judge also must adapt himself to each personality in "countenance, speech and tone of voice."[2] Individualization means that the court will not generalize, or ridicule, or abuse or arbitrarily display its power; but will seek to elicit from family and child a willingness to work out with the court and its representatives the difficulties confronting them. When justice is translated in a child's mind into the relationship between "me and the judge," and when the interest of the court is demonstrated in the personal interest of a man who represents the court and its authority and, in the larger sense, society itself, the entire process becomes humanized.

This approach demands that the court make definite impressions on all parties who have been gathered in the interest of a child. Each person who is in court represents the community, a social interest. Each must carry back to the community an impression that what he contributed was recognized as important by the court; that the judge gave his point of view consideration. We feel that each person who appears in court should carry out with him positive impressions of good faith; faith as evidenced by the discussion and uncovering of all the facts; faith as exemplified by trust in the judicial and ethical integrity of the court's personnel; faith in the court even when decisions are contrary to the interested party's wishes. The public must carry away the impression that decisions are not made routinely or arbitrarily, nor are they made in haste or anger. It is our hope that they take with them the impression that the court's decision is in the best interests of the child; that the findings represent an opportunity for improvement rather than a means for despair.

Group cases, where several children have been apprehended by the police for having participated in one or a series of illegal acts, are one of the most frequent challenges to this individualized approach. Group cases do not evolve into group decisions. Proper variations in the court's findings are accepted when the differences are analyzed in terms of *this* child's needs, *its* personality, *its* social and moral environment. Such differences would be difficult if the emphasis of the court were on the offenses rather than on the troubled children, on their past rather than on their future.

The socialization of justice, as Roscoe Pound has propounded in many articles[3] and lectures, not only looks for the common good but also seeks remedies, skills, and resources outside of the courts which may be used in the fulfillment of these objectives. The word "socialization" takes on its traditional, semantic meaning of group participation as well as that of group use. The labels—juvenile delinquency, dependency, and neglect— are tools and devices used to initiate the proceedings and to focus the problem. But an accompaniment to this court's procedures goes not only to the resources of the court for investigation of factors that led to the present problems, but also to the mobilization of all skills whose aim it is to revitalize the community and its members.

The juvenile court is in a position to accept leadership in coordinating various community resources. It has a strategic role in the logistics of a

[2]Gustav L. Schramm, "The Judge Meets the Boy and His Family," National Probation Association, *Yearbook*, 1945, pp. 182–194.
[3]Roscoe Pound, "The Rise of Socialized Criminal Justice," National Probation Association, *Yearbook*, 1942, pp. 1–22; "The Juvenile Court and the Law," *ibid.*, 1944, pp. 1–22; "The Future of Socialized Justice," *ibid.*, 1946, pp. 6–18.

society's battle for the less fortunate youth in trouble before the public. The medical profession, the psychologists and the psychiatrists, the sociologists and the social workers, the group and recreational leaders, the ministers, the educators, and the policemen,[4] all have something to contribute which will be positive from their point of view. Only in the juvenile court can their individual contributions be integrated and strengthened.

In the juvenile courts of today, after the facts of a child's problems have been established, the analysis of causes and the evaluation of remedies take the foreground. An examination of even the simplest case will show that behavior, whether socially approved or not, is colored by every experience of the individual from the time of his birth to the present.

Many people, particularly zealots who are promoting some pet idea of social control, will advance unit cures and panaceas. A playground, a course in manual training, mental examinations for all, the erection of better housing, fishing trips, the creation of another committee, a juvenile night club, and innumerable other devices have many advocates and promoters. The writer has approved most of these as projects, but they are single approaches to prevention and rehabilitation. We know that many people persist in their beliefs in panaceas in spite of evidence to the contrary. Lags in knowledge of scientific findings and their application seem to be inevitable.

A juvenile court is an integral part of any community program of services to children. The exact relationship may vary with the community resources, the experience of the community, and the effectiveness of the cooperation between groups. While the administrative area of the court need not be duplicated exactly in any two communities, there are three basic premises that are universally applicable.

1. The court has residual powers. It is charged by the law to protect the state as well as to determine the best interests of a child in trouble. Wherever there are gaps the court should attempt directly or indirectly to see that needed service is provided. Wherever adequate facilities are available the court should be careful not to duplicate but to make full and profitable use of them. The court should be as alert as a resourceful parent to make the most of what the community has to offer to meet *this* child's problems.

2. As a court, the juvenile court carries with it broad public support for its ideals. It can therefore give status to the specialized branches of the arts and sciences whose skill the court needs. Social work, psychiatry, psychology, and sociology, as they contribute to the solution of a child's problems, receive through the court public encouragement and support. Such professional groups are neither minimized nor belittled because of their aid, since in their demonstration of cooperation and in the proof of their integration they can justify the public support they receive. There should be no rivalries. The juvenile court as a court of equity is not a competitor, but society's lawful integrator of skills for public service to troubled children.

---

[4]Gustav L. Schramm, "Police-Juvenile Court Teamwork in Pittsburgh, Pa." *FBI Law Enforcement Bulletin,* July 1948, pp. 7–9.

Courts are generally called upon to settle legal disputes of two parties, plaintiff and defendant. Courts of equity functioning within the judicial process have been able over the centuries to develop the techniques of determining many-sided problems. Their administrative arm has enabled them to follow through in all directions needed and for as long as necessary to come to an equitable conclusion. Juvenile courts, as courts of equity, are thus uniquely fitted by experience and by authority to meet the public demand for fair dealing under the law for all concerned in the welfare of a child—the community, the parents, and the child.

3. The juvenile court has, in the half-century of its existence, amply demonstrated to the informed community the wisdom and the advantages of personalized justice for children. These same principles will be more and more accepted until they are adapted to adults as well. Such developments in the adult field as indeterminate sentence, probation, behavior clinics, and pre-sentence investigations owe their acceptance to the demonstration made by the juvenile court. Just as in other areas, such as our labor laws, "a little child shall lead them."

Juvenile courts are the least understood and the most misunderstood of the courts of our land. Their unique philosophy, procedures, and approach are features that not all segments of the population, even of the legal profession and the bench, have fully perceived as yet. In our traditional courts the emphasis is on "Did you or did you not?"; not on "Why, under what circumstances, and what can be done to help?"

It is only half a century since the Chicago group launched the juvenile-court movement in the United States. In this period every state in the Union has made statutory provisions based on the fundamentals propounded by the originators. It is in the day-to-day carrying out of those fundamentals that much yet remains undone. Some courts by implementations have kept pace with experience and have brought about progressive changes; some have been able to incorporate the findings of many fields of social and medical science into their processes of treatment and diagnosis. There are up-to-date models, aging models, and obsolescent ones.

We who work in the field of personalized justice have many responsibilities to the past and to the future. Our juvenile courts are far from perfect. They are changing as experience accumulates. New discoveries and techniques in diagnosis, prediction, and treatment will modify our practices. Those of us responsible for administration of justice realize that our responsibilities do not rest solely with our actions within our courts or derive from the specialists in the community who give us help and cooperation. We have a great obligation to tell and retell to the public what we are doing, what we have done, and what we hope to do. We have the duty to point up community weaknesses and to cooperate in overcoming them.

It is the right of the public to expect us to make an accounting. They should know our effectiveness in dealing with children, our methods, and our objectives. Likewise, it is the right of the public to demand that we be willing to learn; that we constantly improve ourselves to the end that every child shall gain by it. In the field of interpretation we should approach the public with pride for the past, with strength for the present, and with hope for the future. In humility we should remember that we act as custodians of this heritage since it was first pronounced in Chicago.

In humility we must seek to inform the public so that this heritage may have its fullest use and effect upon children and, in due time, upon mankind generally.

CRIMINAL JUSTICE AND THE REHABILITATIVE IDEAL

Francis A. Allen

Although one is sometimes inclined to despair of any constructive changes in the administration of criminal justice, a glance at the history of the past half-century reveals a succession of the most significant developments. Thus, the last fifty years have seen the widespread acceptance of three legal inventions of great importance: the juvenile court, systems of probation, and systems of parole. During the same period, under the inspiration of Continental research and writing, scientific criminology became an established field of instruction and inquiry in American universities and in other research agencies. At the same time, psychiatry made its remarkable contributions to the theory of human behavior described as criminal. These developments have been accompanied by nothing less than a revolution in public conceptions of the nature of crime and the criminal, and in public attitudes toward the proper treatment of the convicted offender.[1]

This history, with its complex developments of thought, institutional behavior, and public attitudes, must be approached gingerly; for in dealing with it we are in peril of committing the sin of oversimplification. Nevertheless, despite the presence of contradictions and paradox, it seems possible to detect one common element in much of this thought and activity, which I shall describe, for want of a better phrase, as the rise of the rehabilitative ideal.

The rehabilitative ideal is itself a complex of ideas which, perhaps, defies completely precise statement. The essential points, however, can be articulated. It is assumed, first, that human behavior is the product of antecedent causes. These causes can be identified as part of the physical universe, and it is the obligation of the scientist to discover and to describe

Abridged from Francis A. Allen, "Criminal Justice, Legal Values, and the Rehabilitative Ideal," *Journal of Criminal Law, Criminology, and Police Science*, 50:3 (September-October 1959), 226–232; and "The Borderland of the Criminal Law," *Social Service Review*, 32:2 (June 1958), 107–119. Copyright 1958, The University of Chicago. Reprinted by permission of the author, the *Journal of Criminal Law, Criminology, and Police Science*, and The University of Chicago Press. Francis A. Allen, a professor of law at the University of Michigan, has written widely on the administration and philosophy of criminal law.
[1]These developments have been surveyed in Allen, "Law and the Future: Criminal Law and Administration," *Northwestern Law Review*, 51 (1956), 207–217. See also Albert Harno, "Some Significant Developments in Criminal Law and Procedure in the Last Century," *Journal of Criminal Law, Criminology, and Police Science*, 42 (1951), 427–467.

them with all possible exactitude. Knowledge of the antecedents of human behavior makes possible an approach to the scientific control of human behavior. Finally, and of primary significance for the purposes at hand, it is assumed that measures employed to treat the convicted offender should serve a therapeutic function, that such measures should be designed to effect changes in the behavior of the convicted person in the interests of his own happiness, health, and satisfactions, and in the interest of social defense.

There is, of course, nothing new in the notion of reform or rehabilitation of the offender as one objective of the penal process. But the modern expression of the rehabilitative ideal must be sharply distinguished from earlier versions. The most important differences, I believe, are two. First, the modern statement of the rehabilitative ideal is accompanied by, and largely stems from, the development of scientific disciplines concerned with human behavior, a development not remotely approximated in earlier periods when notions of reform of the offender were advanced. Second, and of equal importance for the purposes at hand, in no other period has the rehabilitative ideal so completely dominated theoretical and scholarly inquiry, to such an extent that in some quarters it is almost assumed that matters of treatment and reform of the offender are the only questions worthy of serious attention in the whole field of criminal justice and corrections.

This narrowing of interests should put us on our guard. No social institutions as complex as those involved in the administration of criminal justice serve a single function or purpose. Social institutions are multi-valued and multi-purposed. Values and purposes are likely on occasion to prove inconsistent and to produce internal conflict and tension. A theoretical orientation that evinces concern for only one or a limited number of purposes served by the institution must inevitably prove partial and unsatisfactory. In certain situations it may prove positively dangerous.

The rise of the rehabilitative ideal has dictated what questions are to be investigated, with the result that many matters of equal or even greater importance have been ignored or cursorily examined. This tendency can be abundantly illustrated. Thus, the concentration of interest on the nature and needs of the criminal has resulted in a remarkable absence of interest in the nature of crime. This is, indeed, surprising, for on reflection it must be apparent that the question of what is crime is logically the prior issue: how crime is defined determines in large measure who the criminal is who becomes eligible for treatment and therapy.[2] This disinterest in the definition of criminal behavior has afflicted the lawyers quite as much as the behavioral scientists. Even the criminal-law scholar has tended, until recently, to assume that problems of procedure and treatment are the things that "really matter." Only the issue of criminal responsibility as affected by mental disorder has attracted the consistent attention of the nonlawyer, and the literature reflecting this interest is not remarkable for

[2]Cf. Henry Hart, "The Aims of the Criminal Law," *Law and Contemporary Problems,* 23 (1958), 401–441.

its cogency or its wisdom. In general, the behavioral sciences have left other issues relevant to crime definition largely in default.[3]

The absence of widespread interest in other areas is not to be explained by any lack of challenging questions. Thus, what may be said of the relationships between legislative efforts to subject certain sorts of human behavior to penal regulation and the persistence of police corruption and abuse of power?[4] Studies of public attitudes toward other sorts of criminal legislation might provide valuable clues as to whether given regulatory objectives are more likely to be attained by the provision of criminal penalties or by other kinds of legal sanctions. It ought to be re-emphasized that the question, what sorts of behavior should be declared criminal, is one to which the behavioral sciences might contribute vital insights. This they have largely failed to do, and we are the poorer for it.

Another example of the narrowing of interests that has accompanied the rise of the rehabilitative ideal is the lack of concern with the idea of deterrence—indeed the hostility evinced by many modern criminologists toward it. This, again, is a most surprising development.[5] It must surely be apparent that the criminal law has a general preventive function to perform in the interests of public order and of security of life, limb, and possessions. Indeed, there is reason to assert that the influence of criminal sanctions on the millions who never engage in serious criminality is of greater social importance than their impact on the hundreds of thousands who do. Certainly, the assumption of those who make our laws is that the denouncing of conduct as criminal and providing the means for the enforcement of the legislative prohibitions will generally have a tendency to prevent or minimize such behavior. Just what the precise mechanisms of deterrence are is not well understood. Perhaps it results, on occasion, from the naked threat of punishment. Perhaps, more frequently, it derives from a more subtle process wherein the mores and moral sense of the community are recruited to advance the attainment of the criminal law's objectives.[6] The point is that we know very little about these vital matters, and the resources of the behavioral sciences have rarely been employed to contribute knowledge and insight in their investigation. Not only have the criminologists displayed little interest in these matters, some have suggested that the whole idea of general prevention is invalid or worse.[7] We

[3]There are a few exceptions. Dr. Hermann Mannheim, of the London School of Economics, has manifested intelligent interest in such matters; see especially his *Criminal Justice and Social Reconstruction* (London: Kegan Paul, Trench, Trubner, 1946). The late Professor Edwin Sutherland's studies of "white-collar crime" may also be mentioned; see *White-Collar Crime* (New York: Dryden, 1949); also Marshall B. Clinard, *The Black Market* (New York: Rinehart, 1952). Professor Sutherland's efforts in this field, however, in my judgment are among the least perceptive and satisfactory of his many valuable contributions. Cf. Robert Caldwell, "A Re-examination of the Concept of White-Collar Crime," *Federal Probation,* 22 (March 1958), 30–36.

[4]An interesting question of this kind is now being debated in England centering on the proposals for enhanced penalties for prostitution offenses made in the recently issued Wolfenden Report. See L. Fairfield, "Notes on Prostitution," *British Journal of Delinquency,* 9 (1959), 164–173. See also below, pp. 127–144.

[5]But see Johs Andenaes, "General Prevention—Illusion or Reality?" *Journal of Criminal Law, Criminology, and Police Science,* 43 (1952), 176–198.

[6]This seems to be the assertion of Baron Raffaele Garofalo. See his *Criminology,* Robert Wyness Millar, trans. (Boston: Little, Brown, 1914), pp. 241–242.

[7]Thus, speaking of the deterrent theory of punishment, the authors of a leading textbook in criminology assert: "This is simply a derived rationalization of revenge.

are thus confronted by a situation in which the dominance of the rehabilitative ideal not only diverts attention from many serious issues, but leads to a denial that these issues even exist.

We should not overlook the fact that, in many areas, our basic difficulties still lie in our ignorance of human behavior in its infinite complexities. Heavy burdens are placed on the police function, for example, by the problem of drunkenness and alcoholic addiction, but in large measure we handle these problems so badly because we do not know how to handle them better.[8] To be sure, there is much room for improvement in such matters as the facilities and surroundings in which persons detained for drunkenness are confined. No doubt, on a selective basis, individuals could be salvaged who are presently not receiving the sympathetic and intelligent attention that might prove sufficient to the attainment of that happy result. But a fundamental solution to the problems posed by alcoholism awaits further understanding of the affliction and the devising of reasonably reliable, inexpensive, and expeditious therapy. Unless I misread the literature of the field, we are still far from these desirable goals, despite the substantial quantity of impressive and creative research now being carried forward.[9] What is true of alcoholism is true of such areas as narcotic addiction, although it must be conceded that it requires more than a reference to scientific ignorance to justify the absurdities of current efforts to control the narcotics traffic in the United States.[10]

Ignorance, of itself, is disgraceful only as far as it is avoidable. But when, in our eagerness to find "better ways" of handling old problems, we rush to measures affecting human liberty and human personality, on the

---

Though social revenge is the actual psychological basis of punishment today, the apologists for the punitive regime are likely to bring forward in their defense the more sophisticated, but equally futile, contention that punishment deters from [sic] crime." Harry E. Barnes and Negley Teeters, *New Horizons in Criminology*, 2nd ed. (Englewood Cliffs, N.J.: Prentice-Hall, 1954), p. 337. The context in which these statements appear also deserves attention.

[8]In this connection, the development of public-financed clinics for the treatment and rehabilitation of the alcoholic should be noted. An outstanding example is the pioneering experiment made in the District of Columbia, Public Law 347 (80th Congress, 1st sess.), 61 Stat. 744 (1947), D.C. Code §§24-501 to 24-514. An interesting appraisal of experience under the law may be found in Leopold E. Wexberg, M.D., "The Outpatient Treatment of Alcoholism in the District of Columbia," *Quarterly Journal of Studies on Alcohol*, 14 (September 1953), 514-524. The author says, *inter alia:* "The relief for police, courts, and penal authorities has not materialized. . . . The destitute alcoholic, who is at the same time the chronic repeater at the court, can be reached only to a small degree by an outpatient facility." For a report on the Connecticut clinics, see Martha Brunner-Orne, M.D., Frederick T. Iddings, and John Rodrigues, "A Court Clinic for Alcoholics," *ibid.*, 12 (December 1951), 592-600.

[9]See, e.g., Frederick B. Rea, *Alcoholism: Its Psychology and Cure* (London: Epworth Press, 1956), pp. 40-41: "We have now examined three main types of theory concerning the cause of alcoholic addiction. None has proved adequate to fit all the facts." See also the following articles from *Quarterly Journal of Studies on Alcohol*: Wexberg, "Alcoholism as a Sickness," 12 (June 1951), 217-230; Walter L. Boegtlin, M.D., "Treatment of Alcoholism with Adrenal Steroids and ACTH," 14 (March 1953), 28-37; Edwin H. Sutherland, H. G. Schroeder, and C. L. Tordella, "Personality Traits and the Alcoholic: A Critique of Existing Studies," 11 (December 1950), 547-561. An interesting research report recently appeared in a popular periodical: Roger J. Williams, "The Research Frontier," *Saturday Review*, 41:9 (March 1, 1958), 49 ff.

[10]It seems fair to say that American official efforts to deal with the problems of narcotics traffic and addiction are more and more committed to a policy of repression involving sanctions of ever greater severity. For general reference consult "Narcotics: A Symposium," *Law and Contemporary Problems*, 22 (Winter 1957), 1-154.

assumption that we have knowledge which, in fact, we do not possess, then the problem of ignorance takes on a more sinister hue. One of the most alarming aspects of the current agitation for reform of criminal justice and related areas is the apparent willingness of some proponents of reform to substitute action for knowledge, action of the sort that often results in the most serious consequences to the affected individuals. Unfortunately, this is a tendency found too frequently among lawyers of the more "progressive" variety.

An idea tends to lead a life of its own; and modern history is full of the unintended consequences of seminal ideas. The application of the rehabilitative ideal to the institutions of criminal justice presents a striking example of such a development. The rehabilitative ideal has been debased in practice, and the consequences resulting from this debasement are serious and, at times, dangerous.

This proposition may be supported, first, by the observation that, under the dominance of the rehabilitative ideal, the language of therapy is frequently employed, wittingly or unwittingly, to disguise the true state of affairs that prevails in our custodial institutions and at other points in the correctional process. Certain measures, like the sexual psychopath laws, have been advanced and supported as therapeutic in nature when, in fact, such a characterization seems highly dubious. Too often the vocabulary of therapy has been exploited to serve a public-relations function. Recently, I visited an institution devoted to the diagnosis and treatment of disturbed children. The institution had been established with high hopes and, for once, with the enthusiastic support of the state legislature. Nevertheless, fifty minutes of an hour's lecture, delivered by a supervising psychiatrist before we toured the building, were devoted to custodial problems. This fixation on problems of custody was reflected in the institutional arrangements, which included, under a properly euphemistic label, a cell for solitary confinement.[11] Even more disturbing was the tendency of the staff to justify these custodial measures in therapeutic terms. Perhaps on occasion the requirements of institutional security and treatment coincide. But the inducements to self-deception in such situations are strong and all too apparent. In short, the language of therapy has frequently provided a formidable obstacle to a realistic analysis of the conditions that confront us. And realism in considering these problems is the one quality that we require above all others.

There is a second sort of unintended consequence that has resulted from the application of the rehabilitative ideal to the practical administration of criminal justice. Surprisingly enough, the rehabilitative ideal has often led to increased severity of penal measures. This tendency may be seen in the operation of the juvenile court. Although frequently condemned by the popular press as a device of leniency, the juvenile court is authorized to intervene punitively in many situations in which the conduct, were it committed by an adult, would be wholly ignored by the law or would subject the adult to the mildest of sanctions.

---

[11]As I recall, it was referred to as the "quiet room." In another institution a boy was required to stand before a wall while a seventy-pound fire hose was played on his back. This procedure went under the name of "hydrotherapy."

The rise of the rehabilitative ideal, finally, has often been accompanied by attitudes and measures that conflict, sometimes seriously, with the values of individual liberty and volition. As I have already observed, the role of the behavioral sciences in the administration of criminal justice and in the areas of public policy lying on the borderland of the criminal law is one of obvious importance. But I suggest that, if the function of criminal justice is considered in its proper dimensions, it will be discovered that the most fundamental problems in these areas are not those of psychiatry, sociology, social case work, or social psychology. On the contrary, the most fundamental problems are those of political philosophy and political science. The administration of the criminal law presents to any community the most extreme issues of the proper relations of the individual citizen to state power. We are concerned here with the perennial issue of political authority: Under what circumstances is the state justified in bringing its force to bear on the individual human being? These issues, of course, are not confined to the criminal law, but it is in the area of penal regulation that they are most dramatically manifested. The criminal law, then, is located somewhere near the center of the political problem, as the history of the twentieth century abundantly reveals. It is no accident, after all, that the agencies of criminal justice and law enforcement are those first seized by an emerging totalitarian regime. In short, a study of criminal justice is most fundamentally a study in the exercise of political power. No such study can properly avoid the problem of the abuse of power.

The obligation of containing power within the limits suggested by a community's political values has been considerably complicated by the rise of the rehabilitative ideal. For the problem today is one of regulating the exercise of power by men of good will, whose motivations are to help, not to injure, and whose ambitions are quite different from those of the political adventurer so familiar to history. There is a tendency for such persons to claim immunity from the usual forms of restraint and to insist that professionalism and devotion to science provide sufficient protections against unwarranted invasion of individual rights. This attitude is subjected to mordant criticism by Aldous Huxley:

There seems to be a touching belief among certain Ph.D.'s in sociology that Ph.D.'s in sociology will never be corrupted by power. Like Sir Galahad's, their strength is the strength of ten because their heart is pure—and their heart is pure because they are scientists and have taken six thousand hours of social studies.[12]

I suspect that Mr. Huxley would be willing to extend his point to include professional groups other than the sociologists.

There is one proposition which, if generally understood, would contribute more to clear thinking on these matters than any other. It is not a new insight. Seventy years ago, the Italian criminologist Garofalo asserted: "The mere deprivation of liberty, however benign the administration of the place of confinement, is undeniably punishment."[13] This proposition may

[12]Aldous Huxley, *Brave New World Revisited* (New York: Harper, 1958), pp. 34–35.
[13]Garofalo, *op. cit.*, p. 256.

be rephrased as follows: Measures which subject individuals to the substantial and involuntary deprivation of their liberty are essentially punitive in character, and this reality is not altered by the fact that the motivations that prompt incarceration are to provide therapy or otherwise contribute to the person's well-being or reform. As such, these measures must be closely scrutinized to insure that power is being applied consistently with those values of the community that justify interferences with liberty for only the most clear and compelling reasons.

An illustration of these dangers is provided by the sexual psychopath laws, to which I return; for they epitomize admirably some of the worst tendencies of modern practice. These statutes authorize the indefinite incarceration of persons believed to be potentially dangerous in their sexual behavior. But can such persons be accurately identified without substantial danger of placing persons under restraint who, in fact, provide no serious danger to the community? Having once confined them, is there any body of knowledge that tells us how to treat and cure them? If so, as a practical matter, are facilities and therapy available for these purposes in the state institutions provided for the confinement of such persons?[14] Questions almost as serious can be raised as to a whole range of other measures. The laws providing for commitment of persons displaying the classic symptoms of psychosis and advanced mental disorder have proved a seductive analogy for other proposals. But does our knowledge of human behavior really justify the extension of these measures to provide for the indefinite commitment of persons otherwise afflicted? We who represent the disciplines that in some measure are concerned with the control of human behavior are required to act under weighty responsibilities. It is no paradox to assert that the real utility of scientific technique in the fields under discussion depends on an accurate realization of the limits of scientific knowledge.

There are other ways in which the modern tendencies of thought accompanying the rise of the rehabilitative ideal have imperiled the basic political values. The most important of these is the encouragement of procedural laxness and irregularity. In our courts of so-called "socialized justice" one may still observe, on occasion, a tendency to assume that, since the purpose of the proceedings is to "help" rather than to "punish," some lack of concern in establishing the charges against the person before the court may be justified. This position is self-defeating and otherwise indefensible.

For one interested in identifying the dilemmas and perils associated with fundamental redefinition of the system of criminal justice, no development is of greater significance than the juvenile-court movement. This is true both because the problems associated with juvenile misconduct are themselves of pressing urgency and because our efforts to deal with them

---

[14]Many competent observers have asserted that none of these inquiries can properly be answered in the affirmative. See, e.g., Sutherland, "The Sexual Psychopath Laws," *Journal of Criminal Law, Criminology, and Police Science*, 40 (1950), 543–554; Frederick J. Hacker and Marcel Frym, "The Sexual Psychopath Act in Practice: A Critical Discussion," *California Law Review*, 43 (1955), 766–778. See also Paul W. Tappan, *The Habitual Sex Offender* (Report of the New Jersey Commission on the Habitual Sex Offender, 1950).

at the official level, outside the traditional agencies of criminal justice, have identified issues of practice and principle of even broader concern. The establishment of the first juvenile court over a half-century ago was founded on explicit dissatisfaction with the agencies of the criminal law.[15] The measures taken in response were intended to be radical and fundamental. The entire concept of crime was deemed inapplicable to juvenile misconduct; instead, a new label, delinquency, was devised. Provision was made for a new kind of tribunal, non-punitive in orientation, designed to help rather than to punish; and to secure these ends, the resources of psychiatry, social work, and sociological technique were to be employed.[16] These were lofty goals, and one's sympathy with such objectives is in no way inconsistent with a candid recognition that, in practice, they have rarely been fully attained.[17] My purpose, however, is not to appraise the success of the juvenile-court movement. It is, rather, to inquire what matters of general significance can be derived from this long and often conscientious effort.

The essential spirit of the juvenile court has never been better expressed than in a statement made by Judge Edward F. Waite almost four decades ago. According to Judge Waite, the crucial distinction between the traditional criminal court and the juvenile court is that between a court which directs its efforts "to do something *to* a child because of what he *has done*," and a court concerned with "doing something *for* a child because of what he *is* and *needs*."[18] This distinction, so felicitously expressed, points to very real and significant differences in orientation. The difficulty is that too often the distinction between doing something *to* and *for* a child is misconceived and the resulting confusion produces attitudes and procedures inimical not only to the attainment of the proper objectives of the juvenile-court movement, but to the preservation and strengthening of broader human values.

It is important, first, to recognize that when, in an authoritative setting, we attempt to do something *for* a child "because of what he is and needs," we are also doing something *to* him. The semantics of "socialized justice" are a trap for the unwary. Whatever one's motivations, however elevated one's objectives, if the measures taken result in the compulsory loss of the child's liberty, the involuntary separation of a child from his family, or even the supervision of a child's activities by a probation worker, the impact on the affected individual is essentially a punitive one. Good inten-

[15]The first state statute establishing a juvenile court was adopted in Illinois. See "An Act to Regulate the Treatment and Conduct of Dependent, Neglected and Delinquent Children," approved April 21, 1899 (*Ill. Sess. Laws*, 1899, 131).

[16]See the sponsoring *Report of the Committee of the Chicago Bar Association* (1899); Frederick W. Killian, "The Juvenile Court as an Institution," *Annals of the America Academy of Political and Social Science*, 241 (1949), 89–100.

[17]Cf. Tully McCrea, "Juvenile Courts and Juvenile Probation," *NPPA Journal*, 3 (October 1957), 385–391.

[18]The statement in full is as follows: "The Court which must direct its procedure even apparently to do something *to* a child because of what he *has done*, is parted from the court which is avowedly concerned only with doing something *for* a child because of what he *is* and *needs*, by a gulf too wide to be bridged by any humanity which the judge may introduce into his hearings, or by the habitual use of corrective rather than punitive methods after conviction." Edward F. Waite, "How Far Can Court Procedures Be Socialized without Impairing Individual Rights?" *Journal of Criminal Law and Criminology*, 12 (November 1921), 339–347.

tions and a flexible vocabulary do not alter this reality. This is particularly so when, as is often the case, the institution to which the child is committed is, in fact, a penal-custodial establishment. We shall escape much confusion here if we are willing to give candid recognition to the fact that the business of the juvenile court inevitably consists, to a considerable degree, in dispensing punishment. If this is true, we can no more avoid the problem of unjust punishment in the juvenile court than in the criminal court.

There is a second sort of confusion that stems from the distinction between doing something to and for a child. All too often it is forgotten that, for the purpose of determining what a child *is,* it may be highly important to know what he has actually done. For this reason, if for no other, we cannot afford to be careless in establishing the facts of his conduct. The point has broader application than to the procedures of the juvenile court. This interesting case is said to have occurred in California: A defendant was convicted of a sexual offense. Subsequently he was committed as a sexual psychopath following a psychiatric examination. In making their diagnosis the psychiatrists *assumed* that the defendant had committed the sexual act which provided the basis for the criminal conviction. The difficulty was that, as later established, the defendant had all along been the victim of misidentification. Thus, the mistake as to the facts not only resulted in an improper conviction but rendered invalid the psychiatric judgment of the defendant's personality and propensities.[19] However advanced our techniques for determining what an individual *is,* we have not yet approached the point at which we may safely ignore what he has done. What he has done may often be the most revealing evidence of what he is.

Finally, we cannot escape the question of what the child has done, because we cannot prudently ignore the sense of injustice that will surely be engendered in the child by carelessness in establishing the facts of his behavior. A child brought before a tribunal, more or less specifically charged with commission of particular acts, will feel, and I believe will feel properly, that he has the right to receive from the court a sober and cautious weighing of the evidence relating to that issue. He has, in short, a right to receive not only the benevolent concern of the tribunal, but justice. One with reason may inquire as to the value of therapy purchased at the expense of justice.

Courts have occasionally expressed the view that children, being "wards of the state," have no legal rights that the juvenile court is bound to respect.[20] Such an attitude, however, while still revealed frequently enough in practice, is given formal expression less often today than in years gone by. There is, I believe, a wider understanding that the due-process concept represents something more than outmoded ritual or a lawyer's quibble.

[19]Hacker and Frym, *op. cit.,* p. 773.

[20]Thus, in a case in which a fifteen-year-old girl was committed to a reform school merely on the application of her parents, the court said: "The child, herself, having no right to control her own action or to select her own course in life, had no legal right to be heard in these proceedings. Hence, the law which does not require her to be brought in person before the committing officer or extend her the privilege of a hearing on her own behalf cannot be said to deprive her of the benefit of due process of law" (*Rule* v. *Geddes,* 23 App. D.C. 31, 50, 1904). See Monrad G. Paulsen, "Fairness to the Juvenile Offender," *Minnesota Law Review,* 41 (April 1957), 547–576.

This is true, perhaps, because we all—lawyers and non-lawyers alike—have seen enough of the twentieth-century world to render untenable any assumption of the inevitable benevolence of state power. Moreover, at a more practical level, we have had occasion to discover that the exercise of arbitrary and undisciplined power in the juvenile courts has retarded rather than advanced attainment of the objectives of the juvenile-court movement.

What the obligations of decent procedure are in the context of the juvenile court is still a matter of acrimonious debate. There are, it seems to me, certain indispensable conditions. First, we need greater clarity in the definition of the jurisdiction of the juvenile courts. Surely, when great powers over the lives and liberties of persons are granted—even when the persons are merely children—it should be possible to determine with reasonable certainty what the limits of these powers are. This is as important to the conscientious judge who wields the power as to the child or his parents who may be affected by it. Yet it is true that in many jurisdictions the statutory definition of even the basic term "delinquent" or "delinquency" is so amorphous and so all-inclusive that little practical guidance is actually provided.[21] It may be conceded that the definition of "delinquency" can hardly be stated with the precision of a legal description in a real-estate deed, but this does not mean that meaningful and reasonable definition of the powers of the tribunal cannot be achieved.[22]

Second, we must by all means be concerned with the quality and quantity of evidence required to establish the delinquent status of the child. One need not insist that the hearsay rule in all its rigor be bodily transported into juvenile-court proceedings.[23] The essential point is that, before the child can properly be subjected to the drastic powers of the court, more than gossip and rumor is required to establish his legal eligibility for such treatment.[24] This further implies that restrictions must be imposed on the use of social casework reports when the issue is whether the child committed the acts charged against him. If such reports are to be employed at all for this purpose, counsel for the child should be given the names of those supplying information to the investigator and should have

[21]The Illinois definition of the term "delinquent child" illustrates the proposition (*Ill. Rev. Stat.*, 1957, c. 23, §2001). See also Tappan, *Juvenile Delinquency* (New York: McGraw-Hill, 1949), pp. 202–203.

[22]See *A Standard Juvenile Court Act*, 2nd rev. ed. (New York: National Probation and Parole Association, 1949), pp. 16–18.

[23]Cf. Waite, *op. cit.*, p. 343: "Rules of ancient origin, approved or at least tolerated by the citizen whenever he resorts to other legal forums to assert or defend his rights, should not lightly be set aside in juvenile court. The only safe practice is to observe them. If hearsay, for example, has not been found justly admissible in civil disputes and criminal trials, it is no better in juvenile-court proceedings. Exceptions should be made when appropriate, and informal short cuts will often be found agreeable to all concerned; but the exception should always be regarded as an exception. No judge on any bench has more need to be thoroughly grounded in the principles of evidence and more constantly mindful of them than the judge of a juvenile court." For a striking instance of resort to hearsay evidence in a juvenile-court proceeding, see *Holmes' Appeal*, 379 Pa. 599, 109 A. 2d 523 (1954).

[24]There is considerable literature on the point. Among the most helpful are Paulsen, *op. cit.*; Lewis Diana, "The Rights of Juvenile Delinquents: An Appraisal of Juvenile Court Procedures," *Journal of Criminal Law, Criminology, and Police Science*, 44 (January–February 1957), 561–569. See also Tappan, "Unofficial Delinquency," *Nebraska Law Review*, 29 (1950), 547–558.

the right to call such persons into court for cross-examination.[25] If the centuries of experience in the trial of cases before the common-law courts have any lesson to teach, it is that human testimony is often tainted with errors of perception, memory, bias, and prejudice. The most important protections against such errors yet devised—and they are by no means infallible—are confrontation and cross-examination. Out-of-court statements made in private to a caseworker, however useful for other purposes, do not afford an appropriate basis for determining whether the charges made against a child are true or false.

Finally, I believe that the minimum requirements of decent procedure in the juvenile court include recognition of a right to counsel in behalf of the child and perhaps of the child's parents. This is not to deny that many lawyers operate ineffectually in this environment, nor is it possible to deny that lawyers tend to make nuisances of themselves wherever they may be. But there is no reason whatever to doubt that in many cases the attainment of a fair hearing in the juvenile court requires legal representation of the child as insistently as in any other tribunal.[26] There are two further reasons for greater participation by attorneys in juvenile-court proceedings. In the first place, it is good for an institution to have on the premises persons sufficiently independent and sufficiently brash to challenge, on occasion, the assumptions and methods of the institution. I know of no better therapy for the messianic complex. Second, for the bar as a whole to become more familiar with the juvenile court and its problems would probably provide the institution with the support of an important segment of public opinion now too frequently denied it.

[25]See Paulsen, *op. cit.*, pp. 566–567; Bernard Cheriff, "Correct Use of Background Reports in Juvenile Delinquency Cases," *Syracuse Law Review*, 5 (1953–1955), 67–76. See also *People* v. *Lewis*, 260 N.Y. 171, 178, 183 N.E. 353 (1932).
[26]"If substantive norms and methods of procedure are to continue as at present, the child needs legal assistance far more than does the defendant in criminal court. It would be very desirable to have a voluntary or public defender allocated to the juvenile court for his protection" (Tappan, *Juvenile Delinquency*, p. 216). See also Alfred J. Kahn, *A Court for Children* (New York: Columbia University Press, 1943), pp. 100–101.

GUIDES FOR READING AND DISCUSSION

1. Assuming that juvenile courts functioned ideally, would the young people going through them be treated more or less harshly than in the traditional court? What would the juvenile gain, and what would he lose, in the new setting? If you were a defendant, which type of court would you prefer; and why?

2. What is the rationale of the rehabilitative ideal, and what psychological and social axioms underlie it? Is a legal setting in which the defendant's social background is often seen as more important than whether he committed the offense likely to contribute to a "cure"? How do causal theories of delinquency relate to the type of juvenile court considered to be appropriate?

3. Are the principles of the social court, presently applied mostly in juvenile or family courts, equally applicable to all courts of justice? If so, why; if not, why not?

4. The juvenile court, according to various commentators, "mollycoddles" the accused; others argue that it violates the civil rights of the accused. Can both be true of the same court?

SUGGESTED ADDITIONAL READINGS

Paul W. Alexander, "The Family Court of the Future," in National Probation and Parole Association, *Yearbook*, 1951.

David Bordua, *Sociological Theories and Their Implications for Juvenile Delinquency* (Washington: Department of Health, Education, and Welfare, 1960).

Lucien Bovet, *Psychiatric Aspects of Juvenile Delinquency* (Geneva: World Health Organization, 1951).

William McCord, "The Biological Basis of Juvenile Delinquency," in Joseph Roucek, ed., *Juvenile Delinquency* (New York: Philosophical Library, 1958).

Roscoe Pound, "The Rise of Socialized Criminal Justice," in National Probation and Parole Association, *Yearbook*, 1942.

United Nations, Department of Economic and Social Affairs, *Comparative Survey of Juvenile Delinquency*, Part 1: *North America* (New York, 1958). Prepared by Paul Tappan.

Maxine B. Virtue, *Family Cases in Court* (Durham, N.C.: Duke University Press, 1956).

Pauline V. Young, *Social Treatment in Probation and Delinquency* (New York: McGraw-Hill, 1952).

IS THE LEGALIZATION OF
HOMOSEXUALITY WARRANTED?

As we pointed out in the Introduction (pp. 5–6), the triad, custom: tolerance, illness:treatment, crime:punishment, defines the opposed positions in many social polemics. The question debated is usually whether a particular behavior, presently forbidden by law, ought to be legalized. The affirmative argument may be that the practice does no harm; or that the harm is not sufficient to warrant prohibition, which reduces individual privacy; or that whatever harm ensues is the consequence of the law itself. The opponents of legalization ordinarily deny these allegations and affirm the community's right to uphold social standards of decency and morality, even if by invading individual privacy. No one, of course, argues for the legalization of murder or theft or any other crime that is patently harmful and victimizing. The dispute has concerned such offenses as narcotics addition, alcoholism, suicide, and homosexuality—where allegedly the only victim is the person or persons breaking the law.

The following essays exemplify this debate with respect to homosexuality. This aberration, according to Freud, "cannot be classified as an illness"; therefore, psychiatric treatment cannot cure homosexuality but at most can effect "harmony, peace of mind, full efficiency, whether [one] remains a homosexual or gets changed." Moreover, in Freud's view, homosexuality is "nothing to be ashamed of, no vice, no degradation. It is a great injustice to persecute homosexuality as a crime, and cruelty too."[1] In short, according to Freud, homosexuality is a harmless deviation from a cultural norm, latent in all humans and manifest in many during at least a portion of their lives. In recent years the most publicized argument for this view has been Kinsey's.[2] He and his associates identify the moral with the statistical norm; they argue that it is unreasonable to condemn what all or even many persons in fact do. Apart from the ethical or logical worth of this argument, a number of commentators have challenged its empirical base with respect to homosexuality.[3] These commentators point out that a disproportionate number of Kinsey's respondents were unmarried, irreligious, and in the very lowest social class—all social groups that may have a higher percentage of homosexuals than the general population of American males.

One of the most intelligent arguments for the legalization of homosexuality was made by a British government commission, the Wolfenden Com-

---

[1]"Historical Notes: A Letter from Freud," *American Journal of Psychiatry,* 107 (1951), 786–787. Other psychoanalysts, however, have diagnosed homosexuality as a disease; see, for instance, Edmund Bergler, *Homosexuality: Disease or Way of Life?* (New York: Hill & Wang, 1956).

[2]The permissive norm implicit in the larger works on sexual behavior is explicitly stated and defended in Alfred C. Kinsey *et al.,* "Concepts of Normality and Abnormality in Sexual Behavior," in Paul H. Hoch and Joseph Zubin, eds., *Psychosexual Development in Health and Disease* (New York: Grune and Stratton, 1949).

[3]See, for example, A. H. Hobbs and R. D. Lambert, "An Evaluation of 'Sexual Behavior in the Human Male,'" *American Journal of Psychiatry,* 104 (1948), 758–764.

mission, whose report we have abridged. When homosexuality between consenting adults is practiced in private, the majority of the Wolfenden Commission held, it should be tolerated:

> Unless a deliberate attempt is to be made by society . . . to equate the sphere of crime with that of sin, there must remain a realm of private morality and immorality which is . . . not the law's business.

Mr. Adair, one member of the Commission, dissented from this recommendation; and we have appended his major reservation.

Like Mr. Adair, Dr. Cleckley sees homosexuality as a socially injurious malady against which society must protect itself until an effective treatment becomes available. The contrast with the Wolfenden report, or even more with Freud or Kinsey, is sharp. The homosexual, Cleckley argues, is driven by his condition, aggravated by the temptations surrounding him, to make frequent attempts to initiate others. Homosexuality, thus, is not merely a private practice, but also potentially harmful to other persons and to society.

RECOMMENDATIONS CONCERNING HOMOSEXUAL OFFENSES

The Wolfenden Commission

We are concerned, in this part of our inquiry, with homosexual offenses. Any lengthy or detailed study of the nature or origins of homosexuality would, in our view, have fallen outside our terms of reference, even if we had felt ourselves qualified to embark upon it. Nevertheless, since we are concerned also with the treatment of those who have been convicted of homosexual offenses, we have found it necessary to acquaint ourselves with at least the elements of the subject in general, and the following paragraphs set out some of the points and problems which have been raised in our discussions.

Homosexuality is a sexual propensity for persons of one's own sex. This definition of homosexuality involves the adoption of some criteria for its recognition. As in other psychological fields, an inference that the propensity exists may be derived from either subjective or objective data, that is, either from what is felt or from what is done by the persons concerned. Either method may lead to fallacious results. In the first place, introspection is neither exhaustive nor infallible; an individual may quite genuinely not be aware of either the existence or the strength of his motivations and propensities, and there is a natural reluctance to acknowledge, even to oneself, a preference which is socially condemned, or to admit to acts that are illegal and liable to a heavy penalty. Rationalization and self-deception can be carried to great lengths, and in certain circumstances lying is also to be

Abridged from Great Britain, Committee on Homosexual Offenses and Prostitution, *Report,* Cmd. 247 (London: Her Majesty's Stationery Office, 1957), Part Two, ch. 3–5.

expected. Secondly, some of those whose main sexual propensity is for persons of the opposite sex indulge, for a variety of reasons, in homosexual acts. It is known, for example, that some men who are placed in special circumstances that prohibit contact with the opposite sex (for instance, in prisoner-of-war camps or prisons) indulge in homosexual acts, though they revert to heterosexual behavior when opportunity affords; and it is clear from our evidence that some men who are not predominantly homosexual lend themselves to homosexual practices for financial or other gain. Conversely, many homosexual persons have heterosexual intercourse with or without homosexual fantasies. Furthermore, a homosexual tendency may not be manifested exclusively, or even at all, in sexual fields of behavior.

There is the further problem how widely the description "homosexual" should be applied. According to the psychoanalytic school, a homosexual component (sometimes conscious, often not) exists in everybody; and if this is correct homosexuality in this sense is universal. Without going so far as to accept this view in toto, it is possible to realize that the issue of latent homosexuality is relevant to any assessment of the frequency of occurrence of the condition of homosexuality. However, in connection with our recommendations, we are strictly speaking concerned only with those who, for whatever reason, commit homosexual offenses.

In spite of difficulties, there is a general measure of agreement on two propositions: (i) that there exists in certain persons a homosexual propensity which varies quantitatively in different individuals and can also vary quantitatively in the same individual at different epochs of life; (ii) that this propensity can affect behavior in a variety of ways, some of which are not obviously sexual, although exactly how much and in what ways may be matters for disagreement and dispute.

The first of these propositions means that homosexuality as a propensity is not an "all or none" condition, and this view has been abundantly confirmed by the evidence submitted to us. All gradations can exist from apparently exclusive homosexuality without any conscious capacity for arousal by heterosexual stimuli to apparently exclusive heterosexuality, though in the latter case there may be transient and minor homosexual inclinations, for instance in adolescence. According to the psychoanalytic school, all individuals pass through a homosexual phase. Be this as it may, we would agree that a transient homosexual phase in development is very common and should usually cause neither surprise nor concern.

It is interesting that the late Dr. Kinsey, in his study entitled *The Sexual Behavior of the Human Male,* formulated this homosexual-heterosexual continuum on a 7-point scale, with a rating of 6 for sexual arousal and activity with other males only, 3 for arousals and acts equally with either sex, 0 for exclusive heterosexuality, and intermediate ratings accordingly. The recognition of the existence of this continuum is, in our opinion, important for two reasons. First, it leads to the conclusion that homosexuals cannot reasonably be regarded as quite separate from the rest of mankind. Secondly, it has some relevance in connection with claims made for the success of various forms of treatment.

As regards the second proposition, we have already pointed out that a distinction should be drawn between the condition of homosexuality (which relates to the direction of sexual preference) and the acts or behavior resulting from this preference. It is possible to draw a further distinction between behavior which is overtly sexual and behavior, not overtly sexual, from which a latent homosexuality can be inferred.

It must not be thought that the existence of the homosexual propensity necessarily leads to homosexual behavior of an overtly sexual kind. Even where it does, this behavior does not necessarily amount to a homosexual offense; for instance, solitary masturbation with homosexual fantasies is probably the most common homosexual act. Many persons, though they are aware of the existence within themselves of the propensity, and though they may be conscious of sexual arousal in the presence of homosexual stimuli, successfully control their urges towards overtly homosexual acts with others, either because of their ethical standards or from fear of social or penal consequences, so that their homosexual condition never manifests itself in overtly sexual behavior. There are others who, though aware of the existence within themselves of the propensity, are helped by a happy family life, a satisfying vocation, or a well-balanced social life to live happily without any urge to indulge in homosexual acts. Our evidence suggests, however, that complete continence in the homosexual is relatively uncommon—as, indeed, it is in the heterosexual—and that even where the individual is by disposition continent, self-control may break down temporarily under the influence of factors like alcohol, emotional distress, or mental or physical disorder or disease.

Moreover, it is clear that homosexuals differ one from another in the extent to which they are aware of the existence within themselves of the propensity. Some are, indeed, quite unaware of it, and where this is so the homosexuality is technically described as latent, its existence being inferred from the individual's behavior in spheres not obviously sexual. Although there is room for dispute as to the extent and variety of behavior of this kind which may legitimately be included in the making of this inference, there is general agreement that the existence of a latent homosexuality is an inference validly to be drawn in certain cases. Sometimes, for example, a doctor can infer a homosexual component which accounts for the condition of a patient who has consulted him because of some symptom, discomfort, or difficulty, though the patient himself is completely unaware of the existence within himself of any homosexual inclinations. There are other cases in which the existence of a latent homosexuality may be inferred from an individual's outlook or judgment; for instance, a persistent and indignant preoccupation with the subject of homosexuality has been taken to suggest in some cases the existence of repressed homosexuality. Thirdly, among those who work with notable success in occupations which call for service to others, there are some in whom a latent homosexuality provides the motivation for activities of the greatest value to society. Examples of this are to be found among teachers, clergy, nurses, and those who are interested in youth movements and the care of the aged.

We believe that there would be a wide measure of agreement on the general account of homosexuality and its manifestations that we have given above. On the other hand, the general position which we have tried to summarize permits the drawing of many different inferences, not all of them in our opinion justified. Especially is this so in connection with the concept of "disease." There is a tendency, noticeably increasing in strength over recent years, to label homosexuality as a "disease" or "illness." This may be no more than a particular manifestation of a general tendency discernible in modern society, by which, as one leading sociologist puts it, "the concept of illness expands continually at the expense of the concept of moral failure."[1] There are two important practical consequences which are often thought to follow from regarding homosexuality as an illness. The first is that those in whom the condition exists are sick persons and should therefore be regarded as medical problems and consequently as primarily a medical responsibility. The second is that sickness implies irresponsibility, or at least diminished responsibility. Hence it becomes important in this connection to examine the criteria of "disease," and also to examine the claim that these consequences follow.

We are informed that there is no legal definition of "disease" or "disease of the mind"; that there is no precise medical definition of disease which covers all its varieties; that health and ill health are relative terms which merge into each other, the "abnormal" being often a matter of degree or of what is accepted as the permissible range of normal variation; and that doctors are often called upon to deal not only with recognizable diseases, but also with problems of attitude and with anomalies of character and instinct.

The traditional view seems to be that for a condition to be recognized as a disease, three criteria must be satisfied, namely, (i) the presence of abnormal symptoms, which are caused by (ii) a demonstrable pathological condition, in turn caused by (iii) some factor called "the cause," each link in this causal chain being understood as something necessarily antecedent to the next. An example would be the invasion of the body by diphtheria bacilli, leading to pathological changes, leading to the symptoms of diphtheria.

While we have found this traditional view a convenient basis for our consideration of the question whether or not homosexuality is a disease, it must be recognized that the three criteria, as formulated above, are oversimplified, and that each needs some modification. Moreover, there are conditions now recognized as diseases though they do not satisfy all three criteria. Our evidence suggests, however, that homosexuality does not satisfy any of them unless the terms in which they are defined are expanded beyond what could reasonably be regarded as legitimate.

In relation, first, to the presence of abnormal symptoms, it is nowadays recognize that many people behave in an unusual, extraordinary, or socially unacceptable way; but it seems to us that it would be rash to assume that unorthodox or aberrant behavior is necessarily symptomatic of disease if it is the only symptom that can be demonstrated. To make this assumption would be to underestimate the very wide range of "normal" human behavior, and abundant evidence is available that what is socially acceptable or ethically permissible has varied and still varies considerably in different cultures. From the medical standpoint, the existence of significant abnormality can seldom be diagnosed from the mere exhibition of unusual behavior, be this criminal or not, the diagnosis depending on the presence of associated symptoms. Further, a particular form of behavior, taken by itself, can seem to be within the range of the normal but may nevertheless be

[1] Barbara Wootton, "Sickness or Sin," *Twentieth Century*, May 1956.

symptomatic of abnormality, the abnormality consisting in (i) the intensity and duration of the symptoms, (ii) their combination together, and (iii) the circumstances in which they arise. Certain mental diseases, for example, can be diagnosed by the mere association of symptoms to form a recognized psychiatric syndrome, an example of this being schizophrenia, which has no known or generally accepted physical pathology. On the criterion of symptoms, however, homosexuality cannot legitimately be regarded as a disease, because in many cases it is the only symptom and is compatible with full mental health in other respects. In some cases, associated psychiatric abnormalities do occur; and it seems to us that if, as has been suggested, they occur with greater frequency in the homosexual, this may be because they are products of the strain and conflict brought about by the homosexual condition and not because they are causal factors. It has been suggested to us that associated psychiatric abnormalities are less prominent, or even absent, in countries where the homosexual is regarded with more tolerance.

As regards the second criterion, namely, the presence of a demonstrable pathological condition, some, though not all, cases of mental illness are accompanied by a demonstrable physical pathology. We have heard no convincing evidence that this has yet been demonstrated in relation to homosexuality. Biochemical and endocrine studies so far carried out in this field have, it appears, proved negative, and investigations of body-build and the like have also so far proved inconclusive. We are aware that studies carried out on sets of twins suggest that certain genes lay down a potentiality which will lead to homosexuality in the person who possesses them, but even if this were established (and the results of these studies have not commanded universal acceptance), a genetic predisposition would not necessarily amount to a pathological condition, since it may be no more than a natural biological variation comparable with variations in stature, hair pigmentation, handedness, and so on.

In the absence of a physical pathology, psychopathological theories have been constructed to explain the symptoms of various forms of abnormal behavior or mental illness. These theories range from rather primitive formulations like a repressed complex or a mental "abscess" to elaborate systems. They are theoretical constructions to explain observed facts, not the facts themselves; and similar theories have been constructed to explain "normal" behavior. These theoretical constructions differ from school to school. The alleged psychopathological causes adduced for homosexuality have, however, also been found to occur in others besides the homosexual.

As regards the third criterion, that is, the "cause," there is never a single cause for normal behavior, abnormal behavior, or mental illness. The causes are always multiple. Even the invasion of the body by diphtheria bacilli does not of itself lead to the disease of diphtheria, as is shown by the existence of "carriers" of live diphtheria bacilli. To speak, as some do, of some single factor such as seduction in youth as the "cause" of homosexuality is unrealistic unless other factors are taken into account. Besides genetic predisposition, a number of such factors have been suggested—for instance, unbalanced family relationships, faulty sex education, or lack of opportunity for heterosexual contacts in youth. In the present state of our knowledge, none of these can be held to bear a specific causal relationship to any recognized psychopathology or physical pathology; and to assert a direct and specific causal relationship between these factors and the homosexual condition is to ignore the fact that they have all, including seduction, been observed to occur in persons who become entirely heterosexual in their disposition.

Besides the notion of homosexuality as a disease, there have been alternative hypotheses offered by others of our expert witnesses. Some have preferred to regard it as a state of arrested development. Some, particularly among the biologists, regard it as simply a natural deviation. Others, again, regard it as a universal potentiality which can develop in response to a variety of factors.

We do not consider ourselves qualified to pronounce on controversial and scientific problems of this kind, but we feel bound to say that the evidence put before us has not established to our satisfaction the proposition that homosexuality is a disease. Medical witnesses have, however, stressed the point, and it is an important one, that in some cases homosexual offenses do occur as symptoms in the course of recognized mental or physical illness —for example, senile dementia. We have the impression, too, that those whose homosexual offenses stem from some mental illness or defect behave in a way which increases their chances of being caught.

Even if it could be established that homosexuality were a disease, it is clear that many individuals, however their state is reached, present social rather than medical problems and must be dealt with by social, including penological, methods. This is especially relevant when the claim that homosexuality is an illness is taken to imply that its treatment should be a medical responsibility. Much more important than the academic question whether homosexuality is a disease is the practical question whether a doctor should carry out any part or all of the treatment. Psychiatrists deal regularly with problems of personality which are not regarded as diseases, and conversely the treatment of cases of recognized psychiatric illness may not be strictly medical but may best be carried out by non-medical supervision or environmental change. Examples would be certain cases of senile dementia or chronic schizophrenia, which can best be managed at home. In fact, the treatment of behavior disorders, even when medically supervised, is rarely confined to psychotherapy or to treatment of a strictly medical kind. This is not to deny that expert advice should be sought in very many homosexual cases.

The claim that homosexuality is an illness carries the further implication that the sufferer cannot help it and therefore carries a diminished responsibility for his actions. Even if it were accepted that homosexuality could properly be described as a "disease," we should not accept this corollary. There are no prima facie grounds for supposing that because a particular person's sexual propensity happens to lie in the direction of persons of his or her own sex it is any less controllable than that of those whose propensity is for persons of the opposite sex. We are informed that patients in mental hospitals, with few exceptions, show clearly by their behavior that they can and do exercise a high degree of responsibility and self-control; for example, only a small minority need to be kept in locked wards. The existence of varying degrees of self-control is a matter of daily experience— the extent to which coughing can be controlled is an example—and the capacity for self-control can vary with the personality structure or with temporary physical or emotional conditions. The question which is important for us here is whether the individual suffers from a condition which causes diminished responsibility. This is a different question from the question whether he was responsible in the past for the causes or origins of his present condition. That is an interesting inquiry and may be of relevance in other connections; but our concern is with the behavior which flows from the individual's present condition and with the extent to which he is responsible for that behavior, whatever may have been the causes of the condition from which it springs. Just as expert opinion can give valuable assistance in deciding on the appropriate ways of dealing with a convicted person, so can it help in assessing the additional factors that may affect his present responsibility.

Some psychiatrists have made the point that homosexual behavior in some cases may be "compulsive," that is, irresistible; but there seems to be no good reason to suppose that at least in the majority of cases homosexual acts are any more or any less resistible than heterosexual acts, and other evidence would be required to sustain such a view in any individual case. Even if immunity from penal sanctions on such grounds were claimed or granted, nevertheless preventive measures would have to be taken for the sake of society at large, in much the same way as it is necessary to withhold a driving license from a person who is subject to epileptic fits. This is particularly true of the offender who is a very bad risk for recurrence, but is not certifiable either as insane or as a mental defective.

Homosexuality is not, in spite of widely held belief to the contrary, peculiar to members of particular professions or social classes; nor, as is sometimes supposed, is it peculiar to the intelligentsia. Our evidence shows that it exists among all callings and at all levels of society; and that among homosexuals will be found not only those possessing a high degree of intelligence, but also the dullest oafs.

Some homosexuals, it is true, choose to follow occupations which afford opportunities for contact with those of their own sex, and it is not unnatural that those who feel themselves to be "misfits" in society should gravitate towards occupations offering an atmosphere of tolerance or understanding, with the result that some occupations may appear to attract more homosexuals than do others. Again, the arrest of a prominent national or local figure has greater news value than the arrest of, say, a laborer for a similar offense, and in consequence the press naturally finds room for a report of the one where it might not find room for a report of the other. Factors such as these may well account to some extent for the prevalent misconceptions.

Our consideration of the problems we have had to face would have been made much easier if it had been possible to arrive at some reasonably firm estimate of the prevalence either of the condition of homosexuality or of the commission of homosexual acts. So far as we have been able to discover, there is no precise information about the number of men in Great Britain who either have a homosexual disposition or engage in homosexual behavior.

No inquiries have been made in this country comparable to those which the late Dr. Kinsey conducted in the United States of America. Dr. Kinsey concluded that in the United States, 4 per cent of adult white males are exclusively homosexual throughout their lives after the onset of adolescence. He also found evidence to suggest that 10 per cent of the white male population are more or less exclusively homosexual for at least three years between the ages of sixteen and sixty-five, and that 37 per cent of the total male population have at least some overt homosexual experience, to the point of orgasm, between adolescence and old age. Dr. Kinsey's findings have aroused opposition and skepticism. But it was noteworthy that some of our medical witnesses expressed the view that something very like these figures would be established in this country if similar inquiries were made. The majority, while stating quite frankly that they did not really know, indicated that their impression was that his figures would be on the high side for Great Britain.

A recent inquiry in Sweden suggested that 1 per cent of all men were exclusively homosexual and 4 per cent had both homosexual and heterosexual impulses, and we were interested to learn from official sources in Sweden that other information available seemed to indicate that these figures were too low. But here again, there is no evidence that similar inquiries in this country would yield similar results.

Such statistical information as we have been able to obtain about incidence in this country has been extracted almost entirely from criminal and medical records. It is obvious that only a minority of homosexuals, or, for that matter, of those who indulge in homosexual acts, fall into the hands of the police, and it is likely also that only a minority of such persons find their way to the doctor's consulting room. But it is impossible to determine what proportion of the persons concerned these minorities represent; still less, on this evidence, what proportion of the total population falls within the description "homosexual." These figures, therefore, cannot be relied on as an indication of the extent of homosexuality or homosexual behavior among the community as a whole. The only figures relating to the systematic examination of anything like a "normal" sample in this country were provided by one of our witnesses, a psychologist, who had examined one hundred male undergraduates and found that thirty of them had had homosexual trends and fantasies at some time in their lives and that five of these still retained them at the age of 20-plus. Our witness, while certainly not prepared to say that none of the five would outgrow their condition, felt that such a change was unlikely. This sample is, however, neither sufficiently large nor sufficiently representative of the population as a whole to enable any valid conclusions to be drawn.

It is widely believed that the prevalence of homosexuality in this country has greatly increased during the past fifty years and that homosexual behavior is much more frequent than used to be the case. It is certainly true that the whole subject of homosexuality is much more freely discussed today than it was formerly; but this is not in itself evidence that homosexuality is today more prevalent, or homosexual behavior more widespread, than it was when mention of it was less common. Sexual matters in general are more openly talked about today than they were in the days of our parents and grandparents; and it is not surprising that homosexuality should take its place, among other sexual topics, in this wider range of permissible subjects of conversation. Public interest in the subject has undoubtedly increased, with the consequences that court cases are more frequently reported and that responsible papers and magazines give considerable space to its discussion. In general literature, too, there is a growing number of works dealing incidentally or entirely with the subject. All this has no doubt led to a much greater public awareness of the phenomenon and its manifestations. But it does not necessarily follow that the behavior which is so discussed is more widespread than it was before.

It is certainly true also that the number of homosexual offenses known to the police has increased considerably. It does not, however, necessarily follow from these figures that there has been an increase either in homosexuality or in homosexual behavior; still less can these figures be regarded as an infallible measure of any increase which may have occurred during that period. Unlike some offenses (e.g., housebreaking), which, by their nature, tend to be reported to the police as they occur, many sexual offenses, particularly those taking place between consenting parties, become "known to the police" only when they are detected by the police or happen to be reported to them. Any figures relating to homosexual offenses known to the police will therefore be conditioned to a large extent both by the efficiency of the police methods of detecting and recording, and by the intensity of police activity. These factors vary from time to time and from place to place.

Clearly, the more efficient the police methods of detection, the higher the proportion of offenses detected. It was to be expected that the more intensive training given to police officers in recent years, particularly in methods of detection, would result in the discovery of a higher proportion of offenses; but this does not necessarily indicate that more offenses have occurred. We understand, too, that efforts have been made in recent years to improve the methods by which offenses known to the police are recorded, and these may have been reflected in higher figures without any necessary implication of a higher number of offenses. Lastly, the extent to which the police follow up suspicions of homosexual behavior varies considerably as between one police force and another according to the outlook of the senior officers; and sometimes even within a given police force the intensity of action varies from time to time along with the ups and downs of public indignation aroused, or public annoyance caused, by the behavior of the offenders.

In brief, therefore, it would be dangerous to argue from the police statistics alone either that there was an over-all increase or that homosexual behavior was most prevalent in those areas where the number of cases recorded as known to the police was the highest. Most of us think it improbable that the increase in the number of offenses recorded as known to the police can be explained entirely by greater police activity, though we all think it very unlikely that homosexual behavior has increased proportionately to the dramatic rise in the number of offenses recorded as known to the police.

Our medical evidence seems to show three things: first, that in general practice male homosexuals form a very small fraction of the doctor's patients; secondly, that in psychiatric practice male homosexuality is a primary problem in a very small proportion of the cases seen; and thirdly, that only a very small percentage of homosexuals consult doctors about their condition. It is almost impossible to compare the incidence of homosexual behavior with the incidence of other forms of sexual irregularity, most of which are outside the purview of the criminal law and are therefore not recorded in criminal statistics; our impression is that of the total amount of irregular sexual conduct, homosexual behavior provides only a very small proportion. It cannot, however, be ignored. The male population of Great Britain over the age of fifteen numbers nearly eighteen million, and even if the Swedish figures, which are the lowest figures relating to incidence that have come to our notice, are at all applicable to this country, the incidence of homosexuality and homosexual behavior must be large enough to present a serious problem.

Our conclusion is that homosexual behavior is practiced by a small minority of the population, and should be seen in proper perspective, neither ignored nor given a disproportionate amount of public attention. Especially are we concerned that [general] principles of law should apply to those involved in homosexual behavior no more and no less than to other persons.

It is against the foregoing background that we have reviewed the existing provisions of the law in relation to homosexual behavior between male persons. We have found that with the great majority of these provisions we are in complete agreement. We believe that it is part of the function of the law to safeguard those who need protection by reason of their youth or some mental defect, and we do not wish to see any change in the law that would weaken this protection. Men who commit offenses against such persons should be treated as criminal offenders. Whatever may be the causes of their disposition or the proper treatment for it, the law must assume that the responsibility for the overt acts remains theirs, except where there are circumstances which it accepts as exempting from accountability. Offenses of this kind are particularly reprehensible when the men who commit them are in positions of special responsibility or trust. We have been made aware that where a man is involved in an offense with a boy or youth the invitation to the commission of the act sometimes comes from him rather than from the man. But we believe that even when this is so that fact does not serve to exculpate the man.

It is also part of the function of the law to preserve public order and decency. We therefore hold that when homosexual behavior between males takes place in public it should continue to be dealt with by the criminal law.

There is a third class of offense to which we have had to give long and careful consideration. It is that of homosexual acts committed between adults in private. In England and Wales, during the three years ended March 1956, 307 men (300 in England and Wales and 7 in Scotland), guilty, as far as is known, only of offenses committed in private with consenting adult partners, were convicted by the courts.

On the basis of [general] considerations, we have reached the conclusion that legislation which covers acts in the third category we have mentioned goes beyond the proper sphere of the law's concern. We do not think that it is proper for the law to concern itself with what a man does in private, unless it can be shown to be so contrary to the public good that the law ought to intervene in its function as the guardian of that public good.

In considering whether homosexual acts between consenting adults in private should cease to be criminal offenses, we have examined the more serious arguments in favor of retaining them as such. We now set out these arguments and our reasons for disagreement with them. In favor of retaining the present law, it has been contended that homosexual behavior between adult males, in private no less than in public, is contrary to the public good on the grounds that—

(i)   it menaces the health of society;
(ii) it has damaging effects on family life;
(iii) a man who indulges in these practices with another man may turn his attention to boys.

As regards the first of these arguments, it is held that conduct of this kind is a cause of the demoralization and decay of civilization, and that therefore, unless we wish to see our nation degenerate and decay, such conduct must be stopped by every possible means. We have found no evidence to support this view, and we cannot feel it right to frame the laws which should govern this country in the present age by reference to hypothetical explanations of the history of other peoples in ages distant in time and different in circumstances from our own. In so far as the basis of this argument can be precisely formulated, it is often no more than the expression of revulsion against what is regarded as unnatural, sinful, or disgusting. Many people feel this revulsion, for one or more of these reasons. But moral conviction or instinctive feeling, however strong, is not a valid basis for overriding the individual's privacy and for bringing within the ambit of the criminal law private sexual behavior of this kind. It is held also that if such men are employed in certain professions or certain branches of the public service their private habits may render them liable to threats of blackmail or to other pressures which may make them "bad security risks." If this is true, it is true also of some other categories of person: for example, drunkards, gamblers, and those who become involved in compromising situations of a heterosexual kind; and while it may be a valid ground for excluding from certain forms of employment men who indulge in homosexual behavior, it does not, in our view, constitute a sufficient reason for making their private sexual behavior an offense in itself.

The second contention, that homosexual behavior between males has a damaging effect on family life, may well be true. Indeed, we have had evidence that it often is; cases in which homosexual behavior on the part of the husband has broken up a marriage are by no means rare, and there are also cases in which a man in whom the homosexual component is relatively weak nevertheless derives such satisfaction from homosexual outlets that he does not enter upon a marriage which might have been successfully and happily consummated. We deplore this damage to what we regard as the basic unit of society; but cases are also frequently encountered in which a marriage has been broken up by homosexual behavior on the part of the wife, and no doubt some women, too, derive sufficient satisfaction from homosexual outlets to prevent their marrying. We have had no reasons shown to us which would lead us to believe that homosexual behavior between males inflicts any greater damage on family life than adultery, fornication, or lesbian behavior. These practices are all reprehensible from the point of view of harm to the family, but it is difficult to see why on this ground male homosexual behavior alone among them should be a criminal offense. This argument is not to be taken as saying that society should condone or approve male homosexual behavior. But where adultery, fornication, and lesbian behavior are not criminal offenses, there seems to us to be no valid ground, on the basis of damage to the family, for so regarding homosexual behavior between men. Moreover, it has to be recognized that the mere existence of the condition of homosexuality in one of the partners can result in an unsatisfactory marriage, so that for a homosexual to marry simply for the sake of conformity with the accepted structure of society or in the hope of curing his condition may result in disaster.

We have given anxious consideration to the third argument, that an adult male who has sought as his partner another adult male may turn from such a relationship and seek as his partner a boy or succession of boys. We should certainly not wish to countenance any proposal which might tend to increase offenses against minors. Indeed, if we thought that any recommendation for a change in the law would increase the danger to minors, we should not make it. But in this matter we have been much influenced by our expert witnesses. They are in no doubt that whatever may be the origins of the homosexual condition, there are two recognizably different categories among adult male homosexuals. There are those who seek as partners other adult males, and there are pedophiliacs, that is to say, men who seek as partners boys who have not reached puberty.[2]

We are authoritatively informed that a man who has homosexual relations with an adult partner seldom turns to boys, and vice versa, though it is apparent from the police reports we have seen and from other evidence submitted to us that such cases do happen. But pedophiliacs, together with the comparatively few who are indiscriminate, will continue to be liable to the sanctions of criminal law, exactly as they are now. And the others would be very unlikely to change their practices and turn to boys simply because their present practices were made legal. It would be paradoxical if the making legal of an act at present illegal were to turn men towards another kind of act which is, and would remain, contrary to the law. Indeed, it has been put to us that to remove homosexual behavior between adult males from the listed crimes may serve to protect minors; with the law as it is, there may be some men who would prefer an adult partner but who at present turn their attention to boys because they consider that this course is less likely to lay them open to prosecution or to blackmail than if they sought other adults as their partners. If the law were changed in the way we suggest, it is at least possible that such men would prefer to seek relations with older persons, which would not render them liable to prosecution. In this connection, information we have received from the police authorities in the Netherlands suggests that practicing homosexuals in that country are to some extent turning from those practices which are punishable under the criminal law to other practices which are not. Our evidence, in short, indicates that the fear that the legalization of homosexual acts between adults will lead to similar acts with boys has not enough substance to justify

[2]There are reasons for supposing that pedophilia differs from other manifestations of homosexuality. For example, it would seem that in some cases the propensity is for partners of a particular age rather than for partners of a particular sex. An examination of the records of the offenses covered by the Cambridge survey reveals that 8 per cent of the men convicted of sexual offenses against children had previous convictions for both heterosexual and homosexual offenses.

the treatment of adult homosexual behavior in private as a criminal offense, and suggests that it would be more likely that such a change in the law would protect boys rather than endanger them.

In addition, an argument of a more general character in favor of retaining the present law has been put to us by some of our witnesses. It is that to change the law in such a way that homosexual acts between consenting adults in private ceased to be criminal offenses must suggest to the average citizen a degree of toleration by the legislature of homosexual behavior, and that such a change would "open the floodgates" and result in unbridled license. It is true that a change of this sort would amount to a limited degree of such toleration, but we do not share the fears of our witnesses that the change would have the effect they expect. This expectation seems to us to exaggerate the effect of the law on human behavior. It may well be true that the present law deters from homosexual acts some who would otherwise commit them, and to that extent an increase in homosexual behavior can be expected. But it is no less true that if the amount of homosexual behavior has, in fact, increased in recent years, then the law has failed to act as an effective deterrent. It seems to us that the law itself probably makes little difference to the amount of homosexual behavior which actually occurs; whatever the law may be, there will always be strong social forces opposed to homosexual behavior. It is highly improbable that the man to whom homosexual behavior is repugnant would find it any less repugnant because the law permitted it in certain circumstances; so that even if, as has been suggested to us, homosexuals tend to proselytize, there is no valid reason for supposing that any considerable number of conversions would follow the change in the law.

We recognize that a proposal to change a law which has operated for many years, so as to make legally permissible acts which were formerly unlawful, is open to criticisms which might not be made in relation to a proposal to omit from a code of laws being formulated de novo any provision making these acts illegal. To reverse a long-standing tradition is a serious matter and not to be suggested lightly. But the task entrusted to us, as we conceive it, is to state what we regard as a just and equitable law. We therefore do not think it appropriate that consideration of this question should be unduly influenced by a regard for the present law, much of which derives from traditions whose origins are obscure.

There remains one additional counter-argument which we believe to be decisive, namely, the importance which society and the law ought to give to individual freedom of choice and action in matters of private morality. Unless a deliberate attempt is to be made by society, acting through the agency of the law, to equate the sphere of crime with that of sin, there must remain a realm of private morality and immorality which is, in brief and crude terms, not the law's business. To say this is not to condone or encourage private immorality. On the contrary, to emphasize the personal and private nature of moral or immoral conduct is to emphasize the personal and private responsibility of the individual for his own actions, and that is a responsibility which a mature agent can properly be expected to carry for himself without the threat of punishment from the law.

We accordingly recommend that homosexual behavior between consenting adults in private should no longer be a criminal offense.

This proposal immediately raises three questions: What is meant by "consenting"? What is meant by "in private"? What is meant by "adult"?

So far as concerns the first of these, we should expect that the question whether or not there has been "consent" in a particular case would be decided by the same criteria as apply to heterosexual acts between adults. We should expect, for example, that a "consent" which had been obtained by fraud or threats of violence would be no defense to a criminal charge; and that a criminal charge would also lie where drugs had been used to render the partner incapable of giving or withholding consent, or where the partner was incapable for some other reason (for example, mental defect) of giving a valid consent.

We are aware that the quality of the consent may vary; consent may amount to anything from an eager response to a grudging submission. We are aware, too, that money, gifts, or hospitality are sometimes used to induce consent. But these considerations apply equally to heterosexual relationships, and we find in them no ground for differentiating, so far as the behavior of adults is concerned, between homosexual and heterosexual relationships.

Our words "in private" are not intended to provide a legal definition. Many heterosexual acts are not criminal if committed in private but are punishable if committed in circumstances which outrage public decency, and we should expect the same criteria to apply to homosexual acts. It is our intention that the law should continue to regard as criminal any indecent act committed in a place where members of the public may be likely to see and be offended by it, but where there is no possibility of public offense of this nature it becomes a matter of the private responsibility of the persons concerned and as such, in our opinion, is outside the proper purview of the criminal law. It will be for the courts to decide, in cases of doubt, whether or not public decency has been outraged, and we cannot see that there would be any greater difficulty about establishing this in the case of homosexual acts than there is at present in the case of heterosexual acts.

The question of the age at which a man is to be regarded as "adult" is much more difficult. A wide range of ages has been covered by proposals made in the evidence which has been offered to us by our witnesses. On the analogy of heterosexual behavior there is a case for making the age sixteen, for heterosexual acts committed by consenting partners over that age in private are not criminal. At the other end of the scale an age as high as thirty was suggested. Within these two extremes, the ages most frequently suggested to us have been eighteen and twenty-one.

It seems to us that there are four sets of considerations which should govern the decision on this point. The first is connected with the need to protect young and immature persons; the second is connected with the age at which the pattern of a man's sexual development can be said to be fixed; the third is connected with the meaning of the word "adult" in the sense of "responsible for his own actions"; and the fourth is connected with the consequences which would follow from the fixing of any particular age. Unfortunately, these various considerations may not all lead to the same answer.

There must obviously be an element of arbitrariness in any decision on this point; but, all things considered, the legal age of contractual responsibility seems to us to afford the best criterion for the definition of adulthood in this respect. We have encountered several cases in which young men have been induced by means of gifts of money or hospitality to indulge in homosexual behavior with older men, and we have felt obliged to have regard to the large numbers of young men who leave their homes at or about the age of eighteen and, either for their employment or their education or to fulfill their national-service obligations, are then for the first time launched into the world in circumstances which render them particularly vulnerable to advances of this sort. It is arguable that such men should be expected, as one of the conditions of their being considered sufficiently grown-up to leave home, to be able to look after themselves in this respect also, the more so if they are being trained for responsibility in the services or in civil life. Some of us feel, on various grounds, that the age of adulthood should be fixed at eighteen. Nevertheless, most of us would prefer to see the age fixed at twenty-one, not because we think that to fix the age at eighteen would result in any greater readiness on the part of young men between eighteen and twenty-one to lend themselves to homosexual practices than exists at present, but because to fix it at eighteen would lay them open to attentions and pressures of an undesirable kind, from which the adoption of the later age would help to protect them, and from which they ought, in view of their special vulnerability, to be protected. We therefore recommend that for the purpose of the amendment of the law which we have proposed, the age at which a man is deemed to be an adult should be twenty-one.

RESERVATION BY MR. ADAIR

It is with regret that I find it necessary to dissociate myself from the other members of the Committee on what is undoubtedly the most important recommendation in Part Two of the report—to take homosexual acts committed in private by consenting male adults out of the realm of the criminal law.

As I look at the matter, we are investigating in this part of our inquiry a course of conduct which is contrary to the best interests of the community, and one which can have very serious effects on the whole moral fabric of social life. The influence of example in forming the views and developing the characters of young people can scarcely be overestimated. The presence in a district of, for example, adult male lovers living openly and notoriously under the approval of the law is bound to have a regrettable and pernicious effect on the young people of the community. No one interested in the moral, physical, or spiritual welfare of public life wishes to see homosexuality extending its scope, but rather reduced in extent, or at least kept effectively in check.

Existing homosexual trends and tendencies are currently the cause of much public concern and disgust, and the case for relaxing legal restrictions does not appear to me to be a compelling one. The more serious phases of such conduct have been recognized by our law as criminal for a continuous period of not less than four hundred years, and a very heavy onus therefore rests on the advocates of the change now proposed to demonstrate by cogent evidence that the withdrawal of hitherto criminous conduct from the realm of criminal law is clearly justified.

I have studied carefully the evidence led before us, and find that it came in the main from four sources—official, medical, legal, and sociological; and on the threshold I feel compelled to say that in each group there is in varying degrees a diversity of opinion on the proposal. Nor is it without significance that in those instances where it might be said that the majority of the group favored the change now proposed, that majority was proportionately markedly smaller than that in the Committee now making this recommendation.

In much of the evidence we heard, particularly in the fourth group, I detect a marked degree of sentimentalism—a deep-rooted sympathy with and for the individual who is by nature homosexual and, therefore, considered of necessity a subject for medical and not legal attention. These considerations have been allowed to obscure the other type, who, in the absence of any innate tendency, whether from monetary or other reasons, takes up this type of behavior, and have tended, too, to obscure also the interests of the public in general and the decent self-disciplined citizen in particular. It seems to me significant that in the deliberations of a large proportion of organizations which made representations—including the two churches—psychiatrist members or advisers played a prominent part.

While I have acquired over a long period of years the utmost confidence in the ability and opinions of many mental specialists, I have frequently found the views of others, as expressed on occasions, quite inexplicable and in not a few cases manifestly indefensible. When it is clear from evidence given before the Committee that many psychiatrists hold the view that the vast majority of criminal offenders, whatever the nature of their criminal acts, should be medically treated rather than be dealt with by the law, I may be excused if I look critically at such evidence and require corroboration from convincing sources before accepting a view which, though not without idealistic content, is scarcely compatible with the realities of communal life as now constituted.

Furthermore, it appears clear to me that many of those who considered the matter and were parties to the representations made to us were under the belief that if the individuals involved in homosexual practices were handed over to the medical profession this would be an adequate answer to the problem. They were apparently unacquainted with the very limited powers of the medical profession in bringing about a change in either outlook or behavior.

I feel obliged to make the following observations on some aspects of the course proposed by my colleagues:

(i) If the sanctions of the criminal law are removed, there is also removed one, if not the main, motive which at the present time influences homosexuals to consult medical advisers. The proportion of homosexuals who today consult medical advisers with regard to either their state or their behavior is admittedly small. Of those who do, there is a considerable proportion who do so either because they have already found themselves in the hands of the police and have been sent for examination by the court, or because they desire expert evidence that may influence the court's outlook, or because circumstances have arisen that cause them to anticipate police attention. It appears, therefore, that even the small number who attend for medical examination will be reduced considerably if the proposed change be carried out.

(ii) If the sanctions of the criminal law are removed, there are also removed from the police opportunities to carry out important preventive work of social benefit to the community. It may be that my training and experience as a Procurator-Fiscal in Scotland, acting in close association with the police in the detection and investigation of crimes of all kinds, has colored my view on the importance of such sanctions. I have found on many occasions that in the knowledge that unlawful conduct was in contemplation a police officer could prevent it by a word in season or by making his presence known; this has been particularly so in the case of sexual offenders. To accept the recommendation here made is to take away from the police the only justification they have for operating in this practical and preventive fashion.

(iii) If the recommendation be adopted, the moral force of the law will be weakened. I am convinced that the main body of the community recognizes clearly the moral force of the criminal law of the land. Many citizens, it must be admitted, regard the prohibitions expressly imposed by law as the utmost limits set to their activities and are prepared to take full advantage of any omission or relaxation. It would be surprising if there are not considerable numbers with this philosophy among those with whom we are concerned in this inquiry, and the removal of the present prohibition from the criminal code will be regarded as condoning or licensing licentiousness, and will open up for such people a new field of permitted conduct with unwholesome and distasteful implications.

What this may mean by way of increase in the behavior can only be matter for speculation, but one thing seems to stand out—homosexual, like most practices, propagate themselves. To my mind inquiries as to what has occurred following a similar or other change in other countries give but very slender ground for comparison and deduction. Not only have we differences of background, social philosophy, tradition, etc., but if the behavior is made lawful the police authorities are freed from responsibility for investigating and assessing the volume of the conduct and, indeed, as has been pointed out, have largely lost their rights to inquire. In the result, the very nature of such conduct would tend to conceal itself from police notice, and might readily occur to an increasing extent without official recognition.

(iv) If the recommendation be adopted, it will deprive young adult employees in those professions and occupations where the practices are particularly rife from a strong defense against corrupt approach by superiors and elders. Although it was not possible to assess from the evidence available the extent of homosexual practices in the theatrical profession and in some other occupations, it was clearly established that in certain of these quarters there were decided dangers of advances and influences having to be met and overcome. So long as the individual so approached knows that any compliance is a criminal offense, there are those who on this account will not only decline but who will feel in a stronger defensive position by having this answer.

(v) The present state of medical and mental science, and the limited knowledge and powers of the medical profession under existing circumstances to deal with homosexual patients, make the change recommended by the Committee premature and inopportune. I respectfully refer to the observations in the report on the limitations of present-day treatment and the need for enlightened research as adopted by medical and other members.

(vi) The current relaxed attitude toward moral conduct and relationships, so prevalent everywhere, makes the present an inopportune time for loosening bonds and removing restrictions. A period so soon after two world wars, with the varied and abnormal conditions that are generally agreed as having contributed to the present state of affairs, not only in this but in other moral standards, is not a time when any suggestion which in the eyes of many signifies an approval of homosexual conduct should be introduced. So, too, when we see a definite and general increase in the number of offenses being prosecuted and there is a general acceptance of the fact that this is but one of various evidences of a marked growth of homosexual practices, the time cannot be regarded as opportune for removing restrictions as recommended.

(vii) The fact that activities inherently hurtful to community life are carried out clandestinely and in privacy does not adequately justify the removal of such conduct from the criminal code. It is indisputable that many acts committed in private may be contrary to the public good and as such fall under the criminal law. In my view, homosexual acts are of this class, and the mere fact that the discrimination made by the majority of the Committee, by which freedom from control is not recommended for persons between eighteen and twenty-one years of age, is a definite recognition of this principle.

It is of the essence of most crimes that they are committed in privacy and secrecy, if for no other purpose than to avoid detection. In this connection, it is difficult to think of an act committed with more regard for privacy than the crime of incest.

The fact that the proportionate number of homosexual acts committed brought to the knowledge of the courts or the police is small is not an adequate reason for making the acts lawful. I would quote Blackstone: "What though the forfeit of the law is not exacted in every instance? It no wise follows that it is, therefore, a useless law or without salutary influence on the masses of the people."

THE HOMOSEXUAL'S
TEMPTATIONS AND OPPORTUNITIES

Hervey Cleckley

A tendency to carry out acts that may endanger the normal development and adjustment of others is characteristic of homosexuality. I do not
say that this tendency is universal. It could be argued theoretically that
most people with inverted inclinations are as capable of refraining from
any act that may harm the vulnerable as are people whose sexual desires
are ordinary. No reliable statistical evidence is available to prove or dis-
prove such an argument. All opinions must therefore be based on personal
observation and study of what is necessarily a very small fraction of the
total material; this and similar studies by other observers should prove of
value. All opinions must therefore be tentative, for none can accurately or
honestly claim the support of science.

If science could really demonstrate as fact that the homosexual, under
similar circumstances and temptations, is no more prone than the heterosexual to carry out erotic acts undesirable to others and to society and that
his acts are no more deleterious, physicians could happily and confidently
reassure the community about many situations that arise in connection with
homosexuality. But even if this most unlikely supposition were proved by
evidence, some problems would still remain. Could we even then tell the
parents of an adolescent boy that there is no reason why they should not
let him be taken on a two weeks' camping trip by a homosexual scoutmaster
or camp counselor?

Let us approach the matter in another way. Would anyone with good
sense advise an unchaperoned camping trip for a teen-age girl with a
young heterosexual male? I do not attempt to deny that there may be men
sufficiently conscientious to resist the considerable temptations that might
arise while bathing naked in the creek with a beautiful young girl, while
sleeping with her alone night after night, or at any other moment during
such an expedition. Any man who deliberately chose such a strenuous
form of exercise of his self-control would, it seems to me, be better fitted
for life in a monastery than as a counselor for adolescents. It may be
granted that a few who conscientiously made such a choice might prove
themselves suitable candidates for a monk's vocation. I am afraid that
most would find a more appropriate environment in some psychiatric
institution.

No remarkable imagination is required to see that the homosexual is
inevitably subjected to temptations and opportunities that might prove too
much for St. Anthony. How many normal men—schoolteachers, physicians, taxicab drivers, or even clergymen—would be able to dress and

Abridged from Hervey Cleckley, *The Caricature of Love* (New York: Ronald
Press, 1957), ch. 4, 15, 17. Copyright 1957 The Ronald Press Company. Reprinted
by permission of the author and the publisher. Hervey Cleckley, a professor of neurol-
ogy and psychiatry at the University of Georgia, is the author of a number of books
on the ethical framework of psychiatric disorders.

undress daily with chorus girls, live in a dormitory at some women's college, sleep with a great number of women, some of surpassing voluptuousness, and refrain from all erotic activity? After a few months of this, how much tranquility and peace of mind would be left to those who did refrain? Those able to refrain longest might find support for their endurance in loyalty to a wife. But homosexuals lack such incentive in their efforts to curb their sexual impulses.

Another fact to be considered is that those who arouse the homosexual's desires are not automatically aware of the possibilities in the situation, as in even the simplest relations between man and woman. No woman is likely to undress in ignorance of what is likely to follow when she is alone with a man. Few girls, even at age ten, would get into bed with a boy or with a strange man. No stenographer would ride out to a lonely spot in the woods with her employer to spend several hours in the moonlight without thinking that he might at least try to kiss her. However, a twelve-year-old boy invited by his schoolteacher to go on a hike seldom has any prepared or familiar method for turning aside homosexual advances to which he may be exposed and which are likely to cause him deep bewilderment.

The girl child or adolescent, in addition to what she personally has learned about avoiding sexual exploitation by the male, can also find reasonable safeguards in customs, laws, and conventions that are basic in our social structure. Adolescent girls do not share locker rooms and showers with men. Parents, teachers, and others concerned with giving the very young a fair chance to develop judgment, mature attitudes, and sensible standards of behavior before being unduly influenced into traumatic sexual situations, have little means of offering such protection against the predatory homosexual. Like a wartime spy disguised in the uniform of the opposing side, he moves freely and undetected in the very areas from which he should be barred. He is accorded entirely unsupervised access to the immature of his own sex.

More fundamental still in accounting for the prevalence of socially unacceptable conduct in the homosexual are other characteristics that are, I believe, inherent in his erotic status. In my own clinical experience, evidence has been particularly impressive for the following features in homosexual erotic patterns:

First, homosexuals show a tendency to reject each other as worthy sexual partners, particularly as possible mates for a romantic and ideal union. Though able to give each other some sort of transient physical pleasure, and very prone to indulge in promiscuous activities, there is apparently a specific drive for what is intrinsically impossible, that is to say, for a normal heterosexual male partner. This discriminatory quality of impulse is, I believe, an important influence in the fact that homosexuals rarely find reasonable or lasting satisfaction in efforts at permanent union. Not being able to entice the really normal male into any sort of relationship, they are continually seeking new partners or victims among homosexuals who superficially appear somewhat virile, that is, among so-called "bisexuals" or psychiatrically confused men of questionable status who pass for normal. Often they are specifically driven to attempt the seduction of adolescents who, prior to the acts they hope to accomplish, perhaps represent for them an image of the male who is still heterosexual. If they succeed, he is not likely to remain an inspiring or an altogether acceptable object for what they call and think of as "love."

Second, the inability of the homosexual to conceive accurately of society's distaste for what to him seems desirable drives him to explain all negative feelings toward him as unwarranted prejudice. Unaware in his direct experience of what men and women can be to each other as mates, he has little means of contrasting his own sexual experiences and longings and concepts of love with heterosexual life. Homosexuality is the best and most attractive way of life that he is able to understand through his own feelings and imagination, the best that he is able to know at first hand, to evaluate emotionally. Despite the frustrations and sufferings his sexual career brings, he is likely to choose this as an alternative—to nothing at all. He may therefore be far from insincere when he seeks to indoctrinate either the adolescent, or the older shy and bookish youth whose ascetic ideals and puritanical upbringing may have made him spurn heterosexual desire as ignoble lust. He may feel entirely justified in quoting poets and philosophers (and, alas, also psychiatrists) in his efforts to bring to younger or more unsophisticated persons the enlightenment and emancipation that he feels will enable them to express their real natures. He may tell himself that he is working to free others from what he regards as the prejudices, vulgarities, and smugness of a philistine society. Thus he may believe that he will enable them to enjoy something far better, something more like the rare Hellenic joys said to have been prevalent long ago in Athenian splendor. He can (correctly) cite Plato as authority in his argument that the sexual relation of grown men with boys is a nobler and more spiritual relation than that of man and woman.[1]

Finally, the man or boy who desires a girl still too young for marriage may be restrained from immediate and rashly hedonistic sexual acts by his hopes for a full, happy, and lasting union with her in the future which might otherwise be jeopardized. For the aroused homosexual there is no such future goal. Much as he may tell himself that an ideal, real, and lasting sexual union between males is not only beautiful but possible, he will fail to find within himself a genuine foundation for this belief. He may even tell himself that if he delays in the enlightenment and initiation of this youth, the vulgarizing, conventional, and unesthetic influences in society may blight the lad's now-radiant potentialities or susceptibilities, and stupid social forces make of him a dull philistine unable to accept and appreciate the rare intellectual and spiritual fulfilments of Greek love.

As pointed out by Cory, homosexuals speak of themselves as leading the *gay* life. The same author, in a chapter entitled "Love Is a Wonderful Thing," maintains that homosexual relations are full of joy, romance, and fulfilment. Many of the incidents cited in his book do not, however, confirm such an estimate of the results when men attempt to make love with each other. Cory admits that promiscuity is prevalent in such relations.[2]

Edward Carpenter, whose favorable opinions on the subject have for decades been noted, is quoted by Wickham as follows:

[1] Plato, "Phaedrus," in *Dialogues of Plato*, trans. B. Jowett (London: Oxford University Press, 1892), 1, 431–489; "The Symposium," *ibid.*, 541–594.
[2] D. W. Cory, *The Homosexual in America* (New York: Greenberg, 1951).

The question is not whether the [inverted] instinct is capable of morbid and extravagant manifestation . . . but whether it is capable of a healthy and sane expression. And this it has abundantly shown itself to be.[3]

I agree that this is, indeed, the question. But what of the answer? On what evidence does Carpenter base his enthusiastic affirmation? Outstanding triumphs in literature, sculpture, painting, and other arts, it is often pointed out, have been achieved by people generally regarded as homosexual. These triumphs are not necessarily evidence that inverted sexual instincts find a healthy and sane expression in personal relations, that they bring love and fulfilment to mates of the same sex. The surrounding world has indeed been impressed by morbid manifestations of homosexuality, but few if any such relations can be found that command general respect. Is this distinctly negative attitude of the majority due merely to prejudice? Or is there something intrinsically pathologic about the invert's eroticism that prevents his establishing relations comparable with the accepted and respected love between man and woman?

All the homosexuals that I have ever observed do not seem able to confine themselves to each other as sexual partners. What they call "love" is apparently not a good translation of what this term means in heterosexual feeling. They often show a specific tendency to mock and deride each other for showing the very qualities that they share with each other. Often their choice for an ideal, or even a genuinely desirable, love-object, in contrast with a more or less scorned pickup, is directed paradoxically toward the unattainable—characteristically, in men, toward the normal male.

The opinion has been often expressed that ignorant or hostile attitudes on the part of society cause all or most of the homosexual's difficulty. In all cases that I have personally studied, the factors intrinsic in the erotic impulse and attitude impressed me as more fundamental in the maladjustment. A real source of the homosexual's unhappiness arises from his inability to find any mate that can be genuinely or consistently loved. It is this, far more than persecution by society, that accounts for the wretched unhappiness or the flip promiscuity so typical of the sexual life of inverts. Among the more serious of the group this often promotes cynical disillusionment, beliefs in a duplicity of nature or fate, a rejection of ordinary human goals and of the simple interests and enthusiasms that enrich ordinary human existence.

Not only in great cities but even in villages, these emotionally crippled and unfortunate people have ample opportunity to live with each other as mates. It is remarkable how little the community bestirs itself to interfere with them. And yet, hate, spite, pettiness, mockery, gross and casual infidelity to what would be basic in relations between man and woman, appear to be the rule in such attempts at abnormal union.

A typical example is furnished by a particularly intelligent Lesbian. Among other fine abilities and desirable human qualities, she has the appearance of a pretty and sexually attractive woman. She is in fact remarkably endowed physically, having such glamor that she invariably arouses attention in men, and sometimes hopes that are never to be realized. After study and treatment by me and later by a psychoanalyst to whom she had been referred many years ago, this woman established herself in one

[3]Harvey Wickham, *The Impuritans* (New York: Dial Press, 1929), p. 106.

of the nation's large cities. She has become financially successful and prominent. Paradoxically, she has achieved this status through her charm and her appeal for men as an entertainer in a high-class night club. As a talented dancer, a sultry singer, she is able to suggest subtly that she is as responsive to the male as most men are to her. She knows and uses like a virtuoso every gesture and tone in the vocabulary of flirtation, every catch of the voice, every erotic nuance of feminine motion or posture. Men often think they sense in her a smoldering passion of breathless intensity, and often suspect it is particularly directed toward them in person. It is thus not difficult to understand her success in her profession.

Despite her fame and fortune, she finds life not only petty and rather pointless, but at times bitter indeed. Totally without normal response to the male, she lives her real life among Bohemian groups where deviation is accepted as the standard of enlightenment. Time after time, during the course of casual and utterly promiscuous Lesbian activities, she has considered herself truly in love with another woman. On such occasions the two sometimes set up an establishment and attempt to live as mates. Experience has taught this patient to accept such projects as inevitably doomed. Disillusionment is usually swift. No positive and meaningful union can occur, no valid happiness can materialize. Carping, fantastic jealousies, absurd and childish demands, mistrust, small and large acts of bitterness make their appearance. There is much grim and gloomy talk about how passion fades, how lovers inevitably betray, how fate makes all dreams false.

In speaking of the experience that came nearer than any other to affording a temporary illusion of love and fulfilment, this girl described a brief relationship with an older and wealthier woman who had taken her on a sort of honeymoon trip to South America. She admitted that, even from the start, each had been jealously watching every reaction of the other in uneasy anticipation of derisive rejection. Each had vied with the other in petty demands for proof of utter and eternal devotion and each had fretted and carped at the other, no matter what either did. She herself remained, she reported, carefully on guard in order to be the first to break away into some plain and mocking infidelity with another woman. Thus she was able to avoid the role of being herself discarded and humiliated. She had apparently beaten the other woman to the punch, so to speak, and broken off the affair with what was to her as near an approximation to "romantic" memories as anything that she could ever attain. Having been the one who acted first seemed to leave a perversely sweet savor that she almost poetically cherished.

This remarkable woman is not spiteful and frivolous in any of her behavior except that concerning sex and what she, for the want of better knowledge, thinks of as "love." Except in this specific emotional area, she does not seem untrustworthy, superficial, or shallow. Never finding satisfaction that is personal or genuine, she is, one might say, driven, or at least continually prodded on, by an oddly virginal unfulfilment into new and ever unrewarding liaisons. I would not say that behind her longings, her seekings, there is none of the warm and real stuff of love. There is much to indicate that she has a sort of embryonic capacity for this, perhaps even in high degree. It cannot, however, embody itself sufficiently in the ambivalent Lesbian situations ever to be quite born, to become solidly real. Her potentialities for genuine love, nascent again in each new effort to mate, apparently bring suffering enough to set off adaptive and protective reactions that soon bleach them of warmth and seriousness.

Though this woman's sexual history strongly suggests general irresponsibility and the stunted emotional status of one intrinsically callous and petty, I think it is the pathologic restriction to a biologically inappropriate role in mating that curtails her erotic activity and fulfilment to such frustrating shallows. There is much more to her than can be given in relations not naturally designed for sexual love and happy mating. The psychiatric disorder that has tragically distorted this major human drive from its healthy goal has fixed it upon a course that leads inevitably into biologic mirage.

Edmund Bergler, a prominent psychoanalyst who has for years devoted his work especially to sexual problems, says:

Sometimes homosexuals assert that they are completely "happy," the only thing bothering them being the "unreasonable approach" of the environment. That is a conventional blind. There are no happy homosexuals, and there would not be, even if the outer world left them in peace. The reason is an internal one. . . .

A man who unconsciously runs after disappointment cannot be consciously happy. The amount of conflict, of jealousy for instance, between homosexuals surpasses anything known even in bad heterosexual relationships.[4]

Another example is afforded by the relations between two brilliant, technically trained men, men of almost thirty, who are both instructors in a metropolitan university. For months these two have engaged in abnormal sex practices together. They consider themselves lovers and each has avowed that only from the other has he been offered real understanding, or anything else that makes life worth living. Eloquently and articulately they protest their love for each other, quoting the poets of all times and nations, ascribing to each other physical charms more consistent with such mythological sirens as Helen of Troy or the pagan goddess Astarte than with the masculine actualities. They philosophize about the rare nature of their oneness, the pure honesty of their love, the spiritual development each has induced in the other.

Despite such avowals, however, in actuality they carp at and deride each other, fly into pouts of distrust and recrimination. Neither can refrain from hurting and frustrating his alleged mate. No issue is too trivial to serve as grounds or pretext for a quarrel. Each quarrel leads to petulant rages and vociferous accusations, eventually to silent and sulking despairs. Outlandish and even impossible pranks of infidelity, with bus-boys, bellhops, letter-carriers, and so on, are imagined by each one whenever the other is out of sight. Wrangles over alleged and real acts of unfaithfulness drive one or the other out into the night, whence he eventually returns, sometimes to open arms, sometimes to cold scorn, or to new sarcastic demands for proof of good behavior during the absence.

They abase themselves to each other as if to demigods but soon either may be railing at his idol as a "bitch," a "slut," or a whorish "queen." They boast pitifully of their union as a beautiful, clean relation and think of it

---

[4]Edmund Bergler, "The Myth of a New National Disease," *Psychiatric Quarterly*, 22 (January 1948), 66–88.

as rare if not unique. When separated, they write notes to each other, capriciously confessing sexual activity with others and driving one another into despairs and rages of impotent jealousy.

After a recent quarrel about sundry infidelities one of these intellectuals was beaten up in the streets and seriously injured by some man in a slum whom he accosted and sought to engage in perverse activities. The other of the enamored pair meanwhile was arrested in a tourist camp for attempting to carry out on a twelve-year-old boy, despite the child's refusal, what the legal charge described as "a detestable and abominable act against nature."

If persons of this type could really find sweethearts and mates and if meaningful love between them could be achieved, there is little reason to believe that they would be a serious problem to society. What they did would then be their own business and theirs only. Parents would not have to worry about the danger of their molesting children and would, it seems likely, leave them in peace and continue to treat them respectfully. Most homosexuals, however, apparently are unable to find satisfactory relations among themselves.

It is not difficult to see why, in their unhappiness, they rationalize their complex and profound problem into a belief that society is the chief cause of their troubles, that they are misunderstood and persecuted. Often the argument is that society does not appreciate the artist, the truly creative spirit, and that accordingly this intellectually and esthetically superior person must expatriate himself or withdraw into some cult of those with similar attitudes. Here he often icily bemoans the vulgarity or materialism of the herd, calls attention to his exalted standards, and voices his distaste, in verse or prose or conversation, for the normal attitudes and aims of those not sexually disordered.

Not all attempts at permanent union among homosexuals are so transient as those of the beautiful Lesbian, or so stormy as that of the two university instructors, mentioned above. A greater durability and a relative immunity from major and uproarious dissension between partners is, apparently, sometimes purchased at the price of wholeheartedness. When the two are content not to seek in each other very intense fulfilment or to demand a close approximation of personal mating, they may, it seems, enjoy for longer periods some measure of companionship plus some pleasure in their sexual activities.

An example of this is afforded by the benign, middle-aged man, often nearer neuter in his sexual status than vigorously homosexual, who supports and protects a younger companion more obviously effeminate than himself. Such relations follow many patterns but sometimes a sober and moderately affectionate atmosphere may prevail despite jealousies, little tiffs, and fusses about trifles that are not really womanly, or feminine, but effeminate. Often such a pair in their approximation of a marriage for security strain little at high passion for each other, avoid spending much time in *gay* bars, and partake sparingly, if at all, of extravagances at the *drag* or at other gatherings where inversion is flaunted.[5] Some promiscuity, particularly in the younger male, is perhaps inevitable. Jealousy and suspicion without grounds can

[5]See Cory, *op. cit.*

scarcely be avoided. Such unpleasantnesses in some partnerships of this sort may be sufficiently well tolerated to postpone separation for a considerable period. The hand of the older man which generally holds the purse strings seldom becomes careless or impetuous, but he is apt to allow his protégé some little indulgences. The protégé is often specifically averse to jobs that would make him self-supporting and usually dabbles at some sinecure where little more than appearance of employment is maintained.

Situations of this sort which I have had opportunity to observe, though they offer only limited rewards to the participants, often avoid the bitter and sometimes tragic farces and horrors that befall homosexuals who, in violent sincerity, try to force their union into greater depths, into more ambitious relations that become progressively more unnatural and painful and impossible. Those who settle for small stakes and content themselves with relatively trivial goals in each other do not, so far as I can observe, achieve anything comparable to happiness between man and woman. They do, I believe, achieve the best that is available in homosexual relations. In none of these affairs have I ever observed confirmation of the opinion quoted by Edward Carpenter: "Happy indeed is that man who has won a real Urning for his friend—he walks on roses, without having to fear the thorns."[6]

No simple explanation can adequately answer the fictional soldier who asked: "If you guys like being queer why don't you be queer with each other?"[7] For many years I wondered why this peculiarity, which emerged so often in my own patients, is not emphasized, why it is, in fact, never to my knowledge mentioned in psychiatric literature. I have elsewhere reported this observation and discussed some of the patients who revealed so vividly this particular predilection.[8] It seems to me that clinical evidence of this is impressive.

Psychiatrists have apparently ignored this feature of homosexuality, but it has been remarked upon by others. The homosexual's specific attraction toward the normal person of his own sex is carefully considered by the author of The Invert.[9] This little volume, written by a male homosexual who uses the pseudonym "Anomaly," is probably the most realistic presentation available of the personal reactions, the peculiar status, and the complicated problems of a serious person trying to make the best adjustment possible despite his grave disorder. No attempt is made to glorify homosexuality as a superior passion or as a natural human need. With courage and superb dignity, the distortion of basic impulse is recognized as a misfortune. "Anomaly" offers no glib solutions. He does not join the popular chorus and proclaim that antisexual prejudices in society and persecution constitute the chief cause of all the problems which those like himself must face. Instead, he offers a wise understanding, genuine and hard-earned, which should be helpful not only to those similarly deviated, but also to their perplexed and distressed families. The homosexual who can accept the insight offered by this book and live by it is likely, I believe, to find satisfaction

[6]Edward Carpenter, Love's Coming of Age (New York: Vanguard Press, 1928), p. 127.
[7]James Jones, From Here to Eternity (New York: Scribner, 1951), p. 390.
[8]Hervey Cleckley, The Mask of Sanity, 3rd ed. (St. Louis: Mosby, 1955), pp. 319–341.
[9]"Anomaly," The Invert (London: Bailliere, Tindall & Cox, 1948).

far more real than in what attracts him to the *gay* bars or to aloof, esthetic circles where pale nihilistic scorn for the ordinary is languidly whipped up. In this anonymous writer's viewpoint the healthy man, no matter how distasteful to him homoerotic characteristics may be, will find a charity and manliness that he cannot but respect and envy. Such respect as "Anomaly" deserves and commands will, I believe, do more to dispel unkind mockery and hostile generalizations in the heterosexual world than all efforts to prove "scientifically" that homosexual inclinations are natural and normal in all people.

This serious commentator reports:

> As I gained the confidence of individual inverts, they almost always told me that they had a particular friend or, at least, that they wanted someone as a friend. They usually assured me that this friend, or hoped-for friend, was "completely normal." Whatever the conditions, extent, or depth of these unusual friendships (they were as often as not quite innocent), it was evident that from the invert's point of view a prime condition for their existence was that the other party must be a hundred per cent MAN.[10]

In short, those who "know what they are talking about make it quite clear that in the most uninhibited circles *inverts do not pursue or desire their own kind.*"[11]

Perhaps this selectivity described by "Anomaly," and by Proust, is not universal in homosexual choices. I have encountered it so often, however, in my psychiatric practice that I cannot ignore it as a major factor in the inmost emotional difficulties of homosexuals. What appears to be, in erotic relations, a wilful perversity, a deliberate preference for rejection or destructiveness, may, instead, be the influence of such a specific inclination not well recognized by the person whom it nonetheless motivates.

If this is correct, it contributes a great deal toward explaining the frustration, ambivalence, and promiscuity already noted. It may also play an important part in the choice by so many inverts of young boys who are still normal.

[10]*Ibid.*, p. 179.
[11]*Ibid.*, p. 182.

GUIDES FOR READING AND DISCUSSION

1. What general criteria can a democratic society use to distinguish non-victimizing deviations that ought to be discouraged from those that ought to be permitted?

2. If homosexuality is socially harmless except in that it competes with the fundamental social unit of the family, is this a sufficient reason to apply sanctions against homosexuals? What kinds of sanctions? Is prohibition of homosexuality "protection of the public order," which is one legitimate function of law?

3. The sharpest issue concerning homosexuality is a factual one. Does such a relation between two consenting adults typically remain stable, or do homosexuals generally seek to recruit minors—to pervert them, in Dr. Cleckley's view? If he is right in this point, how does this affect the argument of the Wolfenden Commission? If homosexuals are not recruited, how is the practice perpetuated from one generation to the next?

4. One would expect any particular society to have consistent attitudes toward all deviations from traditional family behavior. Britain, however, has

an extremely conservative divorce law (defended, as we have seen, by a royal commission) but a much more liberal attitude toward homosexuality; on the other hand, in the United States as a whole, the attitudes are perhaps reversed. What factors might explain such differences? How much consistency is there actually in "conservative" or "liberal" positions on sexual behavior?

SUGGESTED ADDITIONAL READINGS

Donald W. Cory, *The Homosexual in America* (New York: Greenberg, 1951).

Clellan S. Ford and Frank A. Beach, *Patterns of Sexual Behavior* (New York: Harper, 1951).

Evelyn Hooker, "The Adjustment of the Male Overt Homosexual," *Journal of Projective Techniques,* 21 (1957), 18–31.

Gordon Westwood, *A Minority: A Report on the Life of the Male Homosexual in Great Britain* (London: Longmans, 1960); see also the review by Geoffrey Gorer in *Encounter,* May 1961.

3

ETHNIC MINORITIES

ARE STEREOTYPES BASED ON REALITY OR MISCONCEPTION?

In *An American Dilemma,* probably still the best work on ethnic relations, Gunnar Myrdal introduced what he termed the "principle of cumulation." There is, he wrote, a general interdependence among all the factors in Negro-white relations.

> White prejudice and discrimination keep the Negro low in standards of living, health, education, manners and morals. This, in turn, gives support to white prejudice. White prejudice and Negro standards thus mutually "cause" each other. . . . Such a static "accommodation" is, however, entirely accidental. If either of the factors changes, this will cause a change in the other factor, too, and start a process of interaction where the change in one factor will continuously be supported by the reaction of the other factor.

The "principle of cumulation" is less well known today than the "self-fulfilling prophecy," the term subsequently introduced by Robert Merton to indicate the relation between perception and reality.

Note, however, an important difference between the concepts. Myrdal emphasizes the *interaction* between perception and reality; Merton concentrates on the *effect* of perception on reality. Merton sees the stereotypes underlying anti-Semitism, for example, as prejudice. He shows how the ambiguities of language can maintain and reinforce stereotypes, which are thus protected against contrary evidence. The same act is described favorably or unfavorably depending on who the actor is: the "thrift" of the Gentile is the Jew's "miserliness."

It does not imply any moral justification of anti-Semitism to ask, as Becker does, what it is about the Jews' place in the social structure that has made them perennial victims of discrimination. They are not randomly chosen. For Becker, anti-Semitism is one instance of the general population's standard negative reaction to a "middleman trading people," and he cites other examples from around the world. In countries like Thailand, Burma, and Indonesia—where the Chinese immigrants were typically commercial intermediaries between the small Caucasian upper class and the mass of the natives—a whole range of anti-Semitic stereotypes and symbols were reproduced against the "Jews of Asia."

Is Merton or Becker right? In most cases, and surely in the case of the Jews, the correct answer is: both. Like every other national or religious group, Jews maintain institutions designed to perpetuate their distinctive traditions.[2] But secondary characteristics derive also from the Jews' place in the social structure (Becker) and from Gentiles' attitudes (Myrdal). All of these together are distorted and misconceived by Gentiles (Merton). Whether any particular stereotype is rooted mainly in fact or in fancy, that

[1]Gunnar Myrdal *et al., An American Dilemma: The Negro Problem and Modern Democracy* (New York: Harper, 1944), pp. 75–76.
[2]See Will Herberg, *Protestant-Catholic-Jew* (New York: Doubleday-Anchor, 1960).

is to say, is an *empirical* question; it requires independent investigation and separate assessment. It cannot be resolved by doctrinal fiat—whether racist or liberal. *Prejudice* means "prejudgment"—judgment before the facts are known.

We can range minorities along a continuum from those who, apart from the effects of prejudice, conform to the stereotype to those who do not. Negroes fall close to one end. They are not distinguished by specific, socially significant characteristics that they wish to maintain, but only by superficial features (skin color, hair type, etc.) and by the *effects* of discriminatory institutions (less education, lower wages, etc.).[3] At the other extreme, one might take such a group as nineteenth-century Mormons. The Gentile stereotype that they wanted to practice polygamy and thus break the law was in this case in accord with the fact. The Mormons, like the typical national minority in Europe, wanted to establish, maintain, and even extend their peculiar customs; the Negroes want mainly to eliminate their differences from white society—differences in occupation, in education, in the incidence of disease or illegitimacy, or by any other social index. A minority that accepts the general norms of society and wants to live by them is fundamentally different from one that is defined precisely by its insistence on different norms. It is not useful to pass over this distinction by labeling both groups "minorities" and by denouncing all negative attitudes toward either as "prejudice." If we agree that polygamy—to continue with the same example—is immoral, then opposition to polygamists may be ill advised, but it is not irrational.

[3] The differences, for instance, between the standards of whites and Negroes in the South described by Waring (pp. 175–183) are the effects of discriminatory institutions.

THE SELF-FULFILLING PROPHECY

Robert K. Merton

In a series of works seldom consulted outside the academic fraternity, W. I. Thomas, the dean of American sociologists, set forth a theorem basic to the social sciences: "If men define situations as real, they are real in their consequences." Were the Thomas theorem and its implications more widely known, more men would understand more of the workings of our society. Though it lacks the sweep and precision of a Newtonian theorem, it possesses the same gift of relevance, being instructively applicable to many, if indeed not most, social processes.

Abridged from Robert K. Merton, "The Self-Fulfilling Prophecy," *Antioch Review*, 8:2 (Summer 1948), 193–210. Reprinted by permission of the author and the Antioch Press. Robert Merton is a professor of sociology at Columbia University and the author of books and articles on social theory, social problems, and survey research.

"If men define situations as real, they are real in their consequences," wrote Professor Thomas. The suspicion that he was driving at a crucial point becomes all the more insistent when we note that essentially the same theorem had been repeatedly set forth by disciplined and observant minds long before Thomas.

When we find such otherwise discrepant minds as the redoubtable Bishop Bossuet in his passionate seventeenth-century defense of Catholic orthodoxy, the ironic Mandeville in his eighteenth-century allegory honeycombed with observations on the paradoxes of human society, the irascible genius Marx in his revision of Hegel's theory of historical change, the seminal Freud in works which have perhaps gone further than any others of his day toward modifying man's outlook on man, and the erudite, dogmatic, and occasionally sound Yale professor, William Graham Sumner, who lives on as the Karl Marx of the middle classes—when we find this mixed company (and I select from a longer if less distinguished list) agreeing on the truth and the pertinence of what is substantially the Thomas theorem, we may conclude that perhaps it is worth our attention as well.

To what, then, are Thomas and Bossuet, Mandeville, Marx, Freud, and Sumner directing our attention?

The first part of the theorem provides an unceasing reminder that men respond not only to the objective features of a situation, but also, and at times primarily, to the meaning this situation has for them. And once they have assigned some meaning to the situation, their consequent behavior and some of the consequences of that behavior are determined by the ascribed meaning. But this is still rather abstract, and abstractions have a way of becoming unintelligible if they are not occasionally tied to concrete data. What is a case in point?

It is the year 1932. The Last National Bank is a flourishing institution. A large part of its resources is liquid without being watered. Cartwright Millingville has ample reason to be proud of the banking institution over which he presides. Until Black Wednesday. As he enters his bank, he notices that business is unusually brisk. A little odd, that, since the men at the A.M.O.K. steel plant and the K.O.M.A. mattress factory are not usually paid until Saturday. Yet here are two dozen men, obviously from the factories, queued up in front of the tellers' cages. As he turns into his private office, the president muses rather compassionately: "Hope they haven't been laid off in midweek. They should be in the shop at this hour."

But speculations of this sort have never made for a thriving bank, and Millingville turns to the pile of documents upon his desk. His precise signature is affixed to fewer than a score of papers when he is disturbed by the absence of something familiar and the intrusion of something alien. The low discreet hum of bank business has given way to a strange and annoying stridency of many voices. A situation has been defined as real. And that is the beginning of what ends as Black Wednesday—the last Wednesday, it might be noted, of the Last National Bank.

Cartwright Millingville had never heard of the Thomas theorem. But he had no difficulty in recognizing its workings. He knew that, despite the comparative liquidity of the bank's assets, a rumor of insolvency, once believed by enough depositors, would result in the insolvency of the bank. And by the close of Black Wednesday—and Blacker Thursday—when the long lines of anxious depositors, each frantically seeking to salvage his own, grew to longer lines of even more anxious depositors, it turned out he was right.

The stable financial structure of the bank had depended upon one set of definitions of the situation: belief in the validity of the interlocking system of economic promises men live by. Once depositors had defined the situation otherwise, once they questioned the possibility of having these promises fulfilled, the consequences of this unreal definition were real enough.

A familiar type-case this, and one doesn't need the Thomas theorem to understand how it happened—not, at least, if one is old enough to have voted for Franklin Roosevelt in 1932. But with the aid of the theorem the tragic history of Millingville's bank can perhaps be converted into a sociological parable which may help us understand not only what happened to hundreds of banks in the 1930's but also what happens to the relations between Negro and white, between Protestant and Catholic and Jew in these days.

The parable tells us that public definitions of a situation (prophecies or predictions) become an integral part of the situation and thus affect subsequent developments. This is peculiar to human affairs. It is not found in the world of nature untouched by human hands. Predictions of the return of Halley's comet do not influence its orbit. But the rumored insolvency of Millingville's bank did affect the actual outcome. The prophecy of collapse led to its own fulfillment.

So common is the pattern of the self-fulfilling prophecy that each of us has his favored specimen. Consider the case of the examination neurosis. Convinced that he is destined to fail, the anxious student devotes more time to worry than to study and then turns in a poor examination. The initially fallacious anxiety is transformed into an entirely justified fear. Or it is believed that war between two nations is inevitable. Actuated by this conviction, representatives of the two nations become progressively alienated, apprehensively countering each "offensive" move of the other with a "defensive" move of their own. Stockpiles of armaments, raw materials, and armed men grow larger and eventually the anticipation of war helps create the actuality.

The self-fulfilling prophecy is, in the beginning, a *false* definition of the situation evoking a new behavior which makes the originally false conception come *true*. The specious validity of the self-fulfilling prophecy perpetuates a reign of error. For the prophet will cite the actual course of events as proof that he was right from the very beginning. (Yet we know that Millingville's bank was solvent, that it would have survived for many years had not the misleading rumor *created* the very condition of its own fulfillment.) Such are the perversities of social logic.

It is the self-fulfilling prophecy which goes far toward explaining the dynamics of ethnic and racial conflict in the America of today. That this is the case, at least for relations between Negroes and whites, may be gathered from the fifteen hundred pages which make up Gunnar Myrdal's *An American Dilemma*. That the self-fulfilling prophecy may have even more general bearing upon the relations between ethnic groups than Myrdal has indicated is the thesis of the considerably briefer discussion that follows.[1]

As a result of their failure to comprehend the operation of the self-fulfilling prophecy, many Americans of good will (sometimes reluctantly) retain enduring ethnic and racial prejudices. They experience these beliefs, not as prejudices, not as prejudgments, but as irresistible products of their own observation. "The facts of the case" permit them no other conclusion.

Thus our fair-minded white citizen strongly supports a policy of excluding Negroes from his labor union. His views are, of course, based not upon prejudice, but upon the cold hard facts. And the facts seem clear enough. Negroes, "lately from the nonindustrial South, are undisciplined in traditions of trade unionism and the art of collective bargaining." The Negro is a strikebreaker. The Negro, with his "low standard of living," rushes in to take jobs at less than prevailing wages. The Negro is, in short, "a traitor to the working class," and should manifestly be excluded from union organizations So run the facts of the case as seen by our tolerant but hard-headed union member, innocent of any understanding of the self-fulfilling prophecy as a basic process of society.

Our unionist fails to see, of course, that he and his kind have produced the very "facts" which he observes. For by defining the situation as one in which Negroes are held to be incorrigibly at odds with principles of unionism and by excluding Negroes from unions, he invited a series of consequences which indeed made it difficult if not impossible for many Negroes to avoid the role of scab. Out of work after World War I, and kept out of unions, thousands of Negroes could not resist strikebound employers who held a door invitingly open upon a world of jobs from which they were otherwise excluded.

History creates its own test of the theory of self-fulfilling prophecies. That Negroes were strikebreakers because they were excluded from unions (and from a wide range of jobs) rather than excluded because they were strikebreakers can be seen from the virtual disappearance of Negroes as scabs in industries where they have gained admission to unions in the last decades.

The application of the Thomas theorem also suggests how the tragic, often vicious, circle of self-fulfilling prophecies can be broken. The initial definition of the situation which has set the circle in motion must be abandoned. Only when the original assumption is questioned, and a new definition of the situation introduced, does the consequent flow of events give the lie to the assumption. Only then does the belief no longer father the reality.

But to question these deep-rooted definitions of the situation is no simple act of the will. The will, or for that matter, good will, cannot be turned on and off like a faucet. Social intelligence and good will are themselves *products* of distinct social forces. They are not brought into being by mass propaganda and mass education, in the usual sense of these terms so dear to the sociological panaceans. In the social realm, no more than in the

---

[1]Counterpart of the self-fulfilling prophecy is the "suicidal prophecy" which so alters human behavior from what would have been its course had the prophecy not been made, that it *fails* to be borne out. The prophecy destroys itself. This important type is not considered here. For examples of both types of social prophecy, see R. M. MacIver, *The More Perfect Union* (New York: Macmillan, 1948); for a general statement, see Robert K. Merton, "The Unanticipated Consequences of Purposive Social Action," *American Sociological Review*, 1 (1936), 894–904.

psychological realm, do false ideas quietly vanish when confronted with the truth. One does not expect a paranoiac to abandon his hard-won distortions and delusions upon being informed that they are altogether groundless. If psychic ills could be cured merely by the dissemination of truth, the psychiatrists of this country would be suffering from technological unemployment rather than from overwork. Nor will a continuing "educational campaign" itself destroy racial prejudice and discrimination.

This is not a particularly popular position. The appeal to education as a cure-all for the most varied social problems is rooted deep in the mores of America. Yet it is nonetheless illusory for all that. For how would this program of racial education proceed? Who is to do the educating? The teachers in our communities? But, in some measure, like many other Americans, the teachers share the same prejudices they are being urged to combat. And when they don't, aren't they being asked to serve as conscientious martyrs in the cause of educational utopianism? How long the tenure of an elementary school teacher in Alabama or Mississippi or Georgia who attempted meticulously to disabuse his young pupils of the racial beliefs they acquired at home? Education may serve as an operational adjunct but not as the chief basis for any but excruciatingly slow change in the prevailing patterns of race relations.

To understand further why educational campaigns cannot be counted on to eliminate prevailing ethnic hostilities, we must examine the operation of in-groups and out-groups in our society. Ethnic out-groups, to adopt Sumner's useful bit of sociological jargon, consist of all those who are believed to differ significantly from "ourselves" in terms of nationality, race, or religion. Counterpart of the ethnic out-group is of course the ethnic in-group, constituted by those who "belong." There is nothing fixed or eternal about the lines separating the in-group from out-groups. As situations change, the lines of separation change. For a large number of white Americans, Joe Louis is a member of an out-group—when the situation is defined in racial terms. On another occasion, when Louis defeated the nazified Schmeling, many of these same white Americans acclaimed him as a member of the (national) in-group. National loyalty took precedence over racial separatism. These abrupt shifts in group boundaries sometimes prove embarrassing. Thus, when Negro-Americans ran away with the honors in the Olympic games held in Berlin, the Nazis, pointing to the second-class citizenship assigned Negroes in various regions of this country, denied that the United States had really won the games, since the Negro athletes were by our own admission "not full-fledged" Americans. And what could Southern racists say to that?

Under the benevolent guidance of the dominant in-group, ethnic out-groups are continuously subjected to a lively process of prejudice which, I think, goes far toward vitiating mass education and mass propaganda for ethnic tolerance. This is the process whereby "in-group virtues become out-group vices," to paraphrase a remark by the sociologist Donald Young. Or, more colloquially and perhaps more instructively, it may be called the "damned-if-you-do and damned-if-you-don't" process in ethnic and racial relations.

To discover that ethnic out-groups are damned if they do embrace the values of white Protestant society and damned if they don't, we have first to turn to one of the in-group culture heroes, examine the qualities with which he is endowed by biographers and popular belief, and thus distill the qualities of mind and action and character which are generally regarded as altogether admirable.

Periodic public-opinion polls are not needed to justify the selection of Abe Lincoln as the culture hero who most fully embodies the cardinal American virtues. As the Lynds point out in *Middletown,* the people of that typical small city allow George Washington alone to join Lincoln as the greatest of Americans. He is claimed as their very own by almost as many well-to-do Republicans as by less well-to-do Democrats.

Even the inevitable schoolboy knows that Lincoln was thrifty, hardworking, eager for knowledge, ambitious, devoted to the rights of the average man, and eminently successful in climbing the ladder of opportunity from the lowermost rung of laborer to the respectable heights of merchant and lawyer. (We need follow his dizzying ascent no further.)

If one did not know that these attributes and achievements are numbered high among the values of middle-class America, one would soon discover it by glancing through the Lynds' account of "The Middletown Spirit." For there we find the image of the Great Emancipator fully reflected in the values in which Middletown believes. And since these are their values, it is not surprising to find the Middletowns of America condemning and disparaging those individuals and groups who fail, presumably, to exhibit these virtues. If it appears to the white in-group that Negroes are *not* educated in the same measure as themselves, that they have an "unduly" high proportion of unskilled workers and an "unduly" low proportion of successful business and professional men, that they are thriftless, and so on through the catalogue of middle-class virtue and sin, it is not difficult to understand the charge that the Negro is "inferior" to the white.

Sensitized to the workings of the self-fulfilling prophecy, we should be prepared to find that the anti-Negro charges which are not patently false are only speciously true. The allegations are true in the Pickwickian sense that we have found self-fulfilling prophecies in general to be true. Thus, if the dominant in-group believes that Negroes are inferior, and sees to it that funds for education are not "wasted on these incompetents" and then proclaims as final evidence of this inferiority that Negroes have proportionately "only" one-fifth as many college graduates as whites, one can scarcely be amazed by this transparent bit of social legerdemain. Having seen the rabbit carefully though not too adroitly placed in the hat, we can only look askance at the triumphant air with which it is finally produced. (In fact, it is a little embarrassing to note that a larger proportion of Negro than of white high school graduates have gone on to college; apparently, the Negroes who are hardy enough to scale the high walls of discrimination represent an even more highly selected group than the run-of-the-high-school white population.)

So, too, when the gentleman from Mississippi (a state which spends five times as much on the average white pupil as on the average Negro pupil) proclaims the essential inferiority of the Negro by pointing to the per capita ratio of physicians among Negroes as less than one-fourth that of whites, we are impressed more by his scrambled logic than by his profound prejudices. So plain is the mechanism of the self-fulfilling prophecy in these instances that only those forever devoted to the victory of sentiment over fact can take these specious evidences seriously. Yet the spurious evidence often creates a genuine belief. Self-hypnosis through one's own propaganda is a not infrequent phase of the self-fulfilling prophecy.

So much for out-groups being damned if they don't (apparently) manifest in-group virtues. It is a tasteless bit of ethnocentrism, seasoned with self-interest. But what of the second phase of this process? Can one seriously mean that out-groups are also damned if they *do* possess these virtues? One can.

Through a faultlessly bisymmetrical prejudice, ethnic and racial out-groups get it coming and going. The systematic condemnation of the out-grouper continues largely *irrespective of what he does.* More: through a freakish exercise of capricious judicial logic, the victim is punished for the crime. Superficial appearances notwithstanding, prejudice and discrimination aimed at the out-group are not a result of what the out-group does, but are rooted deep in the structure of our society and the social psychology of its members.

To understand how this happens, we must examine the moral alchemy through which the in-group readily transmutes virtue into vice and vice into virtue, as the occasion may demand. Our studies will proceed by the case-method.

We begin with the engagingly simple formula of moral alchemy: the same behavior must be differently evaluated according to the person who exhibits it. For example, the proficient alchemist will at once know that the word "firm" is properly declined as follows:

> I am firm,
> Thou art obstinate,
> He is pigheaded.

There are some, unversed in the skills of this science, who will tell you that one and the same term should be applied to all three instances of identical behavior. Such unalchemical nonsense should simply be ignored.

With this experiment in mind, we are prepared to observe how the very same behavior undergoes a complete change of evaluation in its transition from the in-group Abe Lincoln to the out-group Abe Cohen or Abe Kurokawa. We proceed systematically. Did Lincoln work far into the night? This testifies that he was industrious, resolute, perseverant, and eager to realize his capacities to the full. Do the out-group Jews or Japanese keep these same hours? This only bears witness to their sweatshop mentality, their ruthless undercutting of American standards, their unfair competitive practices. Is the in-group hero frugal, thrifty, and sparing? Then the out-group villain is stingy, miserly, and penny-pinching. All honor is due the in-group Abe for his having been smart, shrewd, and intelligent and, by the same token, all contempt is owing the out-group Abes for their being sharp, cunning, crafty, and too clever by far. Did the indomitable Lincoln refuse to remain content with a life of work with his hands? Did he prefer to make use of his brain? Then, all praise for his plucky climb up the shaky ladder of opportunity. But, of course, the eschewing of manual work for brain work among the merchants and lawyers of the out-group deserves nothing but censure for a parasitic way of life. Was Abe Lincoln eager to learn the accumulated wisdom of the ages by unending study? The trouble with the Jew is that he's a greasy grind, with his head always in a book, while decent people are going to a show or a ball game. Was the resolute Lincoln unwilling to limit his standards to those of his provincial community? That is what we should expect of a man of vision. And if the out-groupers criticize the vulnerable areas in our society, then send 'em back where they came from. Did Lincoln, rising high above his origins, never forget the rights of the common man and applaud the right of workers to strike? This testifies only that, like all real Americans, this greatest of Americans was deathlessly devoted to the cause of freedom. But, as you examine the statistics on strikes, remember that these un-American practices are the result of out-groupers pursuing their evil agitation among otherwise contented workers.

Once stated, the classical formula of moral alchemy is clear enough. Through the adroit use of these rich vocabularies of encomium and opprobrium, the in-group readily transmutes its own virtues into others' vices. But why do so many in-groupers qualify as moral alchemists? Why are so many in the dominant in-group so fully devoted to this continuing experiment in moral transmutation?

An explanation may be found by putting ourselves at some distance from this country and following the anthropologist Malinowski to the Trobriand Islands. For there we find an instructively similar pattern. Among the Trobrianders, to a degree which Americans, despite Hollywood and the confession magazines, have apparently not yet approximated, success with women confers honor and prestige on a man. Sexual prowess is a positive value, a moral virtue. But if a rank-and-file Trobriander has "too much" sexual success, if he achieves "too many" triumphs of the heart, an achievement which should of course be limited to the elite, the chiefs or men of power, then this glorious record becomes a scandal and an abomination. The chiefs are quick *to resent any personal achievement not warranted by social position.* The moral virtues remain virtues only so long as they are jealously confined to the proper in-group. The right activity by the wrong people becomes a thing of contempt, not of honor. For clearly, only in this way, by holding these virtues exclusively to themselves, can the men of power retain their distinction, their prestige, and their power. No wiser procedure could be devised to hold intact a system of social stratification and social power.

The Trobrianders could teach us more. For it seems clear that the chiefs have not calculatingly devised this program of entrenchment. Their behavior is spontaneous, unthinking, and immediate. Their resentment of "too much" ambition or "too much" success in the ordinary Trobriander is not contrived, it is genuine. It just happens that this prompt emotional response to the "misplaced" manifestation of in-group virtues also serves the useful expedient of reinforcing the chiefs' special claims to the good things of Trobriand life. Nothing could be more remote from the truth and more distorted a reading of the facts than to assume that this conversion of in-group virtues into out-group vices is part of a calculated deliberate plot of Trobriand chiefs to keep Trobriand commoners in their place. It is merely that the chiefs have been indoctrinated with an appreciation of the proper order of things, and see it as their heavy burden to enforce the mediocrity of others.

Nor, in quick revulsion from the culpabilities of the moral alchemists, need we succumb to the equivalent error of simply upending the moral status of the in-group and the out-groups. It is not that Jews and Negroes are one and all angelic while Gentiles and whites are one and all fiendish. It is not that individual virtue will now be found exclusively on the wrong side of the ethnic-racial tracks and individual viciousness on the right side. It is conceivable even that there are as many corrupt and vicious men and women among Negroes and Jews as among Gentile whites. It is only that the ugly fence which encloses the in-group happens to exclude the people who make up the out-groups from being treated with the decency ordinarily accorded human beings.

MIDDLEMAN TRADING PEOPLES

Howard Becker

When one surveys the long perspective of man's record, here and there some very interesting clusters of middleman trading conduct can be found—conduct most clearly exemplified by particular peoples.

If, for example, we were to pay a visit to one of the great Egyptian ports, Naucratis, at about the sixth or seventh century B.C., we should see, at this "Shanghai at the mouth of the Nile," Egyptian people bustling about, doing a great deal of business with all sorts of descriptions of other peoples—fair-skinned Libyans, reddish-hued Phoenicians, people from the wastelands of the Sinai peninsula, and a number of others. The people who would be doing most of the business at these stores or *emporia* (from which we get our term "emporium") would be speaking a tongue we should recognize, perhaps, as related to the tongue of modern Greece. To be sure, they wouldn't be saying *Kali mera* ("Good morning") or that sort of thing, but they would be using words and phrases that we could recognize.

If we questioned them a little more closely, we should discover that the greater number of these traders, who were driving very shrewd bargains with the natives and with the more "civilized" Egyptians, came from the trading center of Miletus, which lies eastward over abreast of Athens and can be reached without getting out of sight of land in crossing the Aegean. Moreover, we should find that another term for Naucratis, or parts of it, at least, would be "the town of the Milesians."

We should also discover that these Milesians were not, strictly speaking, at home even in their homeland; that is, in the town of Miletus and its little hinterland on the coast of Asia Minor. We should find that although they were busy scurrying about in the seventh century B.C., they had memories, deposited in folklore and the like, of having come originally, not from Asia

Abridged from Howard Becker, *Man in Reciprocity* (New York: Frederick A. Praeger, Inc., 1956), ch. 15. Copyright, 1956, by Frederick A. Praeger, Inc. Reprinted by permission of the publisher. Howard Becker was a professor of sociology who wrote widely on sociological theory and social history.

Minor, but from the mainland peninsula of Greece proper, perhaps from the eastern coast of the Peloponnesus, perhaps from Attica, perhaps from other eastward-lying portions of the Greek peninsula.

Indeed, we should discover there were folk memories going still further back, memories of a great migration down through the passes of Thrace on the eastern coast and perhaps others on the western that had led them from the Russian steppes or the Hungarian plains from a nomadic life as herdsmen to a southern life as tillers—as agriculturists. Eventually, it would become clear that under the pressure of peoples more ruthless and more powerful than themselves they had been expelled from mainland Greece proper, and, going across the little stepping-stone islands of the Cyclades and Sporades, they had finally clutched the irregular coastal fringe of Asia Minor and held it fast. There they rapidly established the trading center of Miletus, expanding, setting up *emporia* or subordinate trading centers (some ninety of them) all up and down the eastern coast of the Aegean, up into the Black Sea, at Olbia, near the site of present-day Odessa in Russia, and then finally at the port of Naucratis in Egypt.

We should soon learn, moreover, that these Milesian Greek traders had a very distinct reputation, among the Egyptians and among the other peoples among whom they came, as drivers of rather shrewd and hard bargains. "As honey attracts bees, so money attracts Milesians." They were thought to be in some respects the heirs of the *Phoinikes*—the red-skinned people, the Phoenicians—and even as Homer spoke of the Phoenicians as crafty, lying, but wonderfully clever traders, so we should likewise find that these Greeks (direct ancestors of the Greeks we know in many instances at the present day, although there has been some mixture since) were a middle-man trading people, not at home, precisely speaking, in the land to which they had come. Indeed, we should find them operating, oftentimes on a very slender footing, literally, having just a little standing room, so to speak, at the ports of Egypt—a little toe-ledge here and there along that irregular coastal fringe of the Aegean and Mediterranean where, as Plato said, the Greeks lived like frogs scattered around the edge of a pond.

Yet these people, living as middlemen even in the physical sense, if you will, were nevertheless among the most advanced peoples of their day. They represented the point at which cultures came into contact with each other, intermingled, cross-fertilized. The Milesians not only were familiar with the Greek culture of the mainland, but also were conversant with the Near Eastern cultures of Lydia, of Cappadocia, of Phrygia, of the Phoenician lands, of Egypt, of the whole Levantine world. Traders they were, wandering about, speaking with great facility this, that, or the other tongue that they found necessary to transact their business. Gradually, because there were so many of them, scattered so widely, they established their own language as a sort of *lingua graeca,* the *koiné,* as the general medium of commercial communication in that portion of the world.

Moving up closer to the present, to the time when the Mahdi was raising Cain in Egypt near the present Anglo-Egyptian Sudan, and when he was being confronted by various British generals, including the famous and ill-starred "Chinese Gordon," let us look up and down the fringes of the Nile. Here we are at a little trading depot near Aswan, now the site of the great dam of that name. Sizing up the man behind the counter, we'll discover that we are dealing with a Greek. This is in the time of the Mahdi, remember, so we are in the nineteenth century chatting with a Greek who has come, perhaps, from the little island of Cephalonia to seek his fortune in a foreign land. Living on the edge of the Nile, he is a middleman dealing with the Egyptian *fellahin* on the one hand, and the gliding *sambouks* and the puffing steamers that ply up and down the river on the other; and we might find that our trader bears the name—which perhaps is not literally accurate in this case, although he adopted it in later life—the name of Basil Zaharoff.

Basil Zaharoff was *the* munitions trafficker of World War I, a Greek who started his career as trader (and a marvellously shrewd trader he was) in little outposts in Egypt and in Abyssinia, in faraway lands, dealing with all sorts and conditions of people, acquiring the familiarity with the commercial world of the Levant and the Mediterranean, and eventually with the commercial world of Europe, that finally made him the munitions king of Europe, and perhaps a man who had a heavy share of responsibility for some of the more unsavory munitions deals of World War I.

Here we have a specimen picked from a middleman people, the modern Greeks who in the nineteenth century, and the twentieth as well, controlled most of the coastal trade of the Near East. Going on a Sunday to any port from, let us say, Odessa to Tripoli, you would see the flags of the various seafaring nations flying in the harbor, and as a steady and persisting background for all the others, even the Union Jack, you would find the blue-and-white flag of Greece. As far as the small coastal or river-bank shipping was concerned, the Greeks controlled that coastal shipping very effectively.

Not only that: you would find that these Greeks, when they went among the native *fellahin*—Muslem, Christian, or "pagan"—and among other Europeans as well, were, in some respects, if not markedly superior or inferior, at least different. For example, Greek Orthodox Christianity is strikingly at variance with Roman Catholicism and with Protestantism. The result is that when a Greek such as Basil Zaharoff, for instance, was operating among Coptic Christians in Egypt, he quite naturally thought that between himself and these other Christians—the Egyptian Christians—there was a great gulf fixed. Certainly, in the light of Greek theology, they were all heretics. He himself, as a possessor of the one true faith, consequently was not bound to be so strict, perhaps, in his dealings with them—not so strict, ethically speaking, as he might be if he were dealing with a fellow member of the Greek Orthodox Church.

The outsider is always fair game; the situation is one in which the world is cleft in two. In short, a dual ethic prevails. This means *one* set of ethical principles for oneself and for those who also speak Greek and owe allegiance to the patriarchs of the Greek Orthodox Church, and another set not quite so rigid, a little more elastic here and there. "Both ends can be played against the middle" on occasion when confronting "lesser breeds without the law," people not belonging to *the* good people. Here, then, is a conception of a people to some extent set apart, at least religiously select and exclusive ("chosen") and, as an accompaniment, possessing a dual ethic. So much, in our present framework, for the Greek trader in earlier times and the present.

Turn now from this picture to another, likewise in the Near East, but in some respects affording radical contrasts, in others amazingly similar. Suppose that in the time of Gladstone, in the 1870's, you had been reading a great deal about the terrible atrocities perpetrated by the Turks on the Armenians, that you wandered among the Armenian communities of Turkey in the effort to find out what Armenians were really like on their native heath.

You would discover that these Armenians in some cases were Greek Orthodox, but that a substantial contingent held allegiance to a specifically Armenian brand of Christianity. They were herded together by the Turks, forced to live in little quarters or ghettoes in the Turkish cities, where they carried on numerous handicrafts, a considerable amount of trade, and much business in money-lending, in mortgage loans, in money-changing and in foreign exchange. To be sure, you would also notice some Armenian peasants on the land, but in general you would find that a significant proportion of Armenian Christians, utterly distinct from the Turk in religion and many other ways, were urban dwellers with a definite range of occupations.

You would soon learn that these Armenians were frowned upon and generally despised by their Moslem overlords, and that they were barbarically persecuted from time to time. Lurid stories of massacres of Armenians by Turks used to be standard fare in any Women's Home Missionary Society in the United States, and they occasionally were all too true.

You would also find, however, that these Armenians, although persecuted, possessed wealth and influence to a considerable degree because they had succeeded, in the course of centuries, in making themselves indispensable to their overlords. The Turk, after all, was not familiar with the intricate web of seaborne traffic, with the many languages of the Near East, with commercial accounting even when elementary—in short, was not able to get along without his despised Christian semi-slave.

We should likewise find that the Armenian reciprocated the contempt visited upon him by his master, because after all the Turks were followers of a false prophet, Mohammed (hence were certain to be assigned to everlasting torment), and their manners and customs were like those mentioned by the missionary who, when asked about the peoples among whom he worked, said, "Manners, none; customs, beastly."

The feeling on both sides, then, was that here was a people set apart. On the Moslem side, the Armenians were obviously a people set apart because not Moslem, and also inferior in other respects. On the Armenian side, they felt themselves a chosen people because of a conviction of a special mission, because of the possession of an ancient and eternally valid faith to which they held in spite of all persecutions, and because of a considerable degree of success in weathering the storms of persecution and, as I have said, in making themselves virtually indispensable to their overlords.

Here, then, is another middleman trading people with, perhaps, distinct traces of a dual ethic. After all, when you're trafficking with a Turk who occasionally engages in massacres attended by very gruesome disemboweling scenes, you don't feel quite so rigidly bound by the requirements of commercial honesty as you do in dealing with a fellow Armenian. A dual ethic therefore developed here, likewise the notion of a chosen people, and likewise the middleman mentality of a people (in this instance a primarily urban people) engaged in a narrow range of despised artisan and commercial occupations.

Leaving the Near East, we now go a little farther afield, taking a ship down the Red Sea and around Arabia until near the opening of the Persian Gulf, then striking eastward along the coast, hugging the shore, until we finally turn southeast and wind up our voyage at Bombay. As we walk about the streets of this metropolis in India, we notice here and there people whose clothing is strikingly different from that of the ordinary Hindus, and who physically are in some respects of a slightly different type.

After we have made a few more or less discreet inquiries, we find that the people we have been noticing are Parsees. The Parsees compose a sect of sun-worshipping Persians, followers of Zoroaster, believers in a religion holding that the world is cleft in twain. There are the children of light on the one hand, the followers of Ahura Mazda, and on the other the children of darkness, followers of Ahriman. Ahura Mazda, the prince of the powers of the air, is the god of fire, of light (Mazda lamps!), whereas Ahriman is the prince of darkness.

The cosmic drama is a terrific struggle between Ahura Mazda and Ahriman and their respective followers. The children of light and their leader will eventually be the conquerors, but only after a battle to the death. Holy to Ahura Mazda and to the people he has set apart, as a peculiar people, from among all other peoples upon the face of the earth, are the four holy elements, earth, water, air, fire, which must under no circumstances be polluted. Fire, as the source of light, is especially holy. Thus, the Parsee dead are exposed, to be consumed by the scavenger birds, and thereby, in their mortal disappearance, to pollute neither the water, nor the air, nor the earth, nor the fire. Vultures and buzzards apparently share in none of the holy elements.

The Parsees are an urban folk settled in the Indian cities as well as here and there in Persia, and, because of their odd ways and their great desire not to engage in any polluting activity, they are limited to a small range of handicraft and commercial dealings of one sort or another that don't involve too much contact with animal life or the products of animal life. Moreover, the Parsees not only frequently figure as the money-changers but also are numerous among the bankers of western India. Vastly outnumbered by the Hindus, nevertheless they are functionally an important people.

Here again, then, we take note of a people set apart religiously, with a very specific set of beliefs that causes them to follow a small range of occupations, and living as virtual strangers in the midst of a much larger population whose ways are not their ways. Further, these Parsees, if the Hindus are to be believed, occasionally manifest traces of a dual ethic—they don't always deal in quite the same way with Hindus as they do with fellow Parsees. Indeed, if we were translating the milder Hindu epithets in as inoffensive a way as possible, we might call the Parsees clannish.

We might also learn, however, that the Parsees had competitors in Bombay, and pretty keen competitors at that. Looking about us to see who these competitors could be, we soon observe a man going along the street with a gauze bandage tied over his mouth and the lower part of his nose, and carrying with him a small, short-handled broom. He would shuffle along, in little hesitant steps at about one-third an ordinary walking pace.

He is a Jain, a member of a quasi-Hindu sect that, with the utmost literacy, preaches non-violence and the preservation of all life of whatever sort or description. Consequently, the Jain ties over his mouth and nose a gauze bandage in order that he may not breathe in small insects and thereby destroy them—because all life is holy. When he walks along the street he carries with him a little broom with which he brushes the path in front of him in order that he may not unwittingly step on an ant or beetle and in thereby killing it commit a grievous sin.

These are not fairy tales; such "goings-on" are amply documented for the sect of the Jains in Anno Domini 1956. Naturally, the Jains are pretty much cramped in their style, as it were, by the peculiar belief they practice. To wit: they can't possibly be tillers of the soil because after all, no matter how kindly the agriculturist is, he does occasionally cut earthworms in two.

It is plain, isn't it, that a people straining air and sweeping sidewalks in the effort to avoid the destruction of any life, however lowly, after all is a special sort of people following a special set of customs? Our Jains, because they had to earn a living in some way, worried along as artisans, as money-changers, as takers of mortgages in land—and, by the way, even now are cordially despised by the orthodox Hindus among whom they do business.

Suppose, further, that we're travelling in pre-World War II days, and that we get as far as Java. In Batavia and in other cities in Java we might perhaps investigate a bit—and while we're supposing, let's be interested in the wholesale rice business and in dealings in pepper and coffee and other such things.

Arriving in Batavia, you think, "Well, after all I can do my business here because I know Dutch, and Java is a Dutch dependency; I'll be able to carry on intelligible conversation with these Dutch businessmen." Then you wander into a wholesale rice warehouse, and to your chagrin you discover that your Dutch does you no particular good because you're forced to resort to Pidgin English in talking to a Chinese who's a long way from home, but who "knows his way around" in business. You tell him that you're a big rice man, and he promptly shuttles back and forth with his little abacus, his Chinese computing machine. It's quite a mystery to you, but it demonstrably works much better than the comptometer might in your hands. In less time than you can get out pencil and notebook, he tells you what the rates for rice on the various markets are, and what you will have to offer if you want to do business with him. His prices are too high, and you don't trust the "heathen Chinee" anyway. You therefore go to another wholesale rice dealer, and behold! he's another Chinese.

To make a long story short, you find that a very large part of the wholesale rice business of Java is controlled not by the Dutch, not by the Javanese, but by the Chinese. Moreover, you discover that these Chinese live to themselves in little Chinatowns, that oftentimes their coffins are returned for burial to China, that they import "picture brides" from China, and that relations with the Javanese among whom they live are not always of the most cordial. In other words, the Chinese in Java are also a people set apart.

Let's go back now, assuming that we're in a period before the ruthless, gruesome Nazi exterminations, to little towns such as Seibersbach or Gmünd in the Hunsrück, i.e., near the left bank of the Rhine in that small triangle between the Moselle and the Nahe, with Coblenz a little farther north, Frankfurt a little farther south, and Wiesbaden over there in the southwest.

In Seibersbach, and likewise in Gmünd, you run across a very small building with a six-pointed star above the doorway, and you notice that ceremonials are carried out there on Saturday. You also observe that the people who come to those ceremonials, closing up their businesses to do so, have a peculiar sort of dinner on Friday night. Looking through various windows of their homes, you see the father of the family wearing a skull-cap and you also notice, if you watch very closely, that the mother of the family in cooking her food is very careful to have one set of dishes for milk and another for meat. "Thou shalt not seethe the kid in its mother's milk."

Suddenly it dawns on you that you're looking at Orthodox Jews who are doing hide and grain trading, petty banking, and in several other ways acting as leaven in the lump of these loutish little Rhineland towns. When you ask about the Seibersbach synagogue, you are told that the roll of its members goes back, back, back to the fourteenth century. Further, you learn that many of the families listed in the synagogue rolls have sent off shoots that have taken root in the United States, in Britain, in South Africa, in Australia, and that the clan of the Rosensteins, for example, has branches over almost the whole world.

Interesting also is the fact that the members of the synagogue still think of themselves as some day destined to receive a Messiah who is to come and relieve them, the chosen people of Jehovah, of their heavy yoke of scorn and persecution. Then the Jews will no longer be the suffering servants of mankind, but will share in the general redemption.

Manifestly, Jews like those just described have a very special conception of their mission in life, and it is also plain that they are a people set apart as far as their family and community lives are concerned. (I'm speaking as heretofore of the German Orthodox Jew.) As a consequence of such sociological circumstances, it can occasion small wonder that they are charged by the Seibersbach peasants with the practice of a dual ethic, that they are called clannish, and that, when a demagogue such as Hitler or any one of his numerous predecessors wants to make capital out of a general depression or other crisis, they and thousands of other Jews in little villages throughout Germany or Poland or Russia are picked as scapegoats—another middleman trading people.

Let's go north for a change—to Britain north of the Tweed. Moreover, let's not stop at the Border, but travel as far as, say, the Clyde, or perhaps even to the Highlands-skirting Tay. In the middle of the eighteenth century we might find near the Tay, on the outskirts of Dundee, a young Scot who was the youngest son of a very large family living on a little plot of ground that yielded only a niggardly livelihood. Tiring of the "noble prospect" to be seen by gazing northward toward the Grampians, our young Scot, without ever having heard of Dr. Johnson, coined for himself the axiom "The noblest 'prospect' that a Scotsman ever sees is the high-road that leads him to England." Going south to seek his fortune, he came into contact with a company of "merchant adventurers" who were setting up trading stations throughout the world—perhaps the East India Company, perhaps the Hudson's Bay Company, perhaps some other farflung commercial enterprise. This belated Quentin Durward, we find, took a job with the Hudson's Bay Company, travelled from post to post throughout the frozen area of Great Slave Lake and Great Bear Lake, getting as far north as Dawson City, long before the Klondike Rush. Look at the map of Canada, and see the Mackays and Maclures and Mackintocks and Mackenzies stamped all over its hardest, most dangerous frontiers.

You might also find that these Scots, or their descendants, were said by the French-Canadian *voyageurs,* and by the Indians who came to trade furs for whiskey and flour, to be hard people with whom to drive a bargain—as unduly canny, perhaps. They refrained from intermarrying with the Indians as the French *voyageurs* so freely did, holding themselves to some degree aloof. Indeed, on occasion these Scots manifested an overweening spiritual pride, a number of them being Presbyterians of the strictest persuasion—that is, orthodox Calvinists, believing themselves of that small handful of the elect set apart from before the foundation of the world to be saved, whereas the rest of mankind was irrevocably damned.

The person possessing the assurance of salvation frequently exhibits a slight degree of spiritual overconfidence, and also a tendency to deal in one way with a fellow member of the chosen few, and in another with the worldly reprobate who is going to hell anyway. Since there are no pockets in a shroud, there is no reason why the righteous should not relieve the wicked of some of his unnecessary cash before he departs—observing, to be sure, the canons of fair dealing. If these are observed, can the righteous man be blamed if the reprobate insists on wasting his substance?

Roving, hard-headed Scots did business in the Old World as well as in the New. We should certainly find them as mercenary soldiers as far back as Louis XI; the Scots Guard of the French king occupied for a long time much the same position as does the Swiss Guard of the papacy. When a young Scotsman wished to seek his fortune in Quentin Durward's day he thought of the Scots Guard or of mercenary service in Flanders or in Germany, where there might be a little looting occasionally, and where one might go home with saddlebags comfortably lined to buy a little plot of land in Midlothian or Angus and there settle down as a respectable burgher and tacksman for the rest of one's life.

We should also discover that these Scots travelled up into Sweden with packs on their backs. Most of the pack peddlers of the sixteenth century, as far as the Scandinavians were concerned, were neither Jews nor Armenians, but Scots. When Gustavus Adolphus, the Lion of the North, swept over Europe, he had thousands of Scottish troopers in his pay. In Poland, likewise, the Scots were so thick both as mercenary soldiers and traders that a little town called New Scotland was established in Poland, from which to this day a great many people bearing curious Polish versions of MacLean, Fraser, Ross, and other clannish folk still come.

These tall, long-headed, primarily Nordic and Atlantic Mediterranean people, then, manifested on occasion—not always, to be sure—many of the traits of what I have termed middleman traders.

Note that a wide range of races has here been reviewed. Attention has been called to the Greeks, who are not wholly Nordic by any manner of means and never were, but who have a large proportion of so-called Mediterranean blood, some Dinaric blood, and some Alpine blood. They also have some "Armenoid" blood, as far as that's concerned, but at least the Greeks are a people different in many respects from the Armenians. As we go farther afield, we find that the Parsees, coming originally from Persia, are much more clearly of so-called "Aryan" racial stock ("Aryan" is, of course, a linguistic term, but we can use it in this sense to indicate race in the very rough and large sense). The Jains, however, are not as clearly "Aryan" as the Parsees; here again we have another racial stock. The Chinese, of course, are utterly different, racially speaking; and so likewise are the Jews. The Scot, Highlander or Lowlander, Borderer or Islander, is again distinct in racial type from other peoples we have surveyed.

Yet, under the appropriate circumstances, given the proper situation, you find the traits of middleman traders, who manifest their shrewdness, their dual ethic, their conception of being a race set apart, in outwardly varying but essentially similar ways. An Armenian is not a Scotsman, nor a Scotsman a Chinese, but still certain phases of the social conduct in which representatives of these peoples engage, in spite of their tremendous ethnic diversities, are recognizably the same. The middleman trader acquires his traits through a special kind of reciprocity in social situations, not through the germ plasm.

GUIDES FOR READING AND DISCUSSION

1. Assume that the United States has been consistently committed to reducing prejudice and discrimination. What differences would have been necessary in programs set up for this purpose with respect, for example, to nineteenth-century Mormons and present-day Negroes? How about such other minorities as, say, American Indians, homosexuals, Communists or Nazis, Roman Catholics?

2. How would a social researcher go about determining the extent to which stereotypes are based on reality or misconception? Is there any consistent relation between stereotypes and the groups to which they are applied?

3. Can a person be a "liberal" and at the same time maintain that some stereotypes confirm rather than distort reality?

SUGGESTED ADDITIONAL READINGS

Gordon Allport, *The Nature of Prejudice* (New York: Doubleday-Anchor, 1954.

Morton Deutsch and Mary E. Collins, *Interracial Housing: A Psychological Evaluation of a Social Experiment* (Minneapolis: University of Minnesota Press, 1951); summarized in William Petersen, ed., *American Social Patterns* (New York: Doubleday-Anchor, 1956).

John Harding et al., "Prejudice and Ethnic Relations," in Gardner Lindzey, ed., *Handbook of Social Psychology* (Cambridge: Addison-Wesley, 1954), 2, 1021–1061.

Harold R. Isaacs, "Back to Africa," *New Yorker*, May 13, 1961.

Gunnar Myrdal, *An American Dilemma: The Negro Problem and Modern Democracy* (New York: Harper, 1944), ch. 3, Appendix 3, and *passim*.

Robert E. Park, *Race and Culture* (Glencoe, Ill.: Free Press, 1950).

William Petersen, "Prejudice in American Society," *Commentary*, October 1958; together with a criticism by Herbert C. Kelman and Thomas F. Pettigrew and a rejoinder, *ibid.*, November 1959.

William G. Sumner, *Folkways* (Boston: Ginn, 1906).

On May 17, 1954, the Supreme Court handed down its historic decision on school segregation. Speaking for the unanimous court, Chief Justice Warren declared:

To separate [Negro children] from others of similar age and qualifications solely because of their race generates a feeling of inferiority as to their status in the community that may affect their hearts and minds in a way unlikely ever to be undone. . . . In the field of public education the doctrine of "separate but equal" has no place. Separate educational facilities are inherently unequal.

This decision continued the postwar trend, effected in part through other court decisions, toward removing the bars to full citizenship for Negroes.

It was also a reversal of a previous Supreme Court decision, handed down in 1896 in the case of *Plessy* v. *Ferguson*. Plessy, a man of one-eighth Negro descent, challenged a Louisiana law segregating railroad passengers; the Court declared that the state's police power clearly included the right to separate one race from the other, that accommodation in "separate but equal" facilities did not imply the inferiority of either race and thus did not violate constitutional rights. Schools for Negroes were, however, almost universally separate and inferior. And by the Court's 1954 decision, "separate but equal" was declared to be a contradiction in terms.

The Court ordered that desegregation should proceed "with all deliberate speed." It would be difficult to maintain that the whole country has complied even with this intentionally vague formulation. In the border region, at least token integration has been completed, and often—as in Baltimore and Washington, D.C., for instance—with remarkably little fuss. In Little Rock and Mississippi, on the other hand, the acts of public officials sworn to uphold the law have become an international scandal. In the Deep South the question has never been whether or when to comply with the law, but only how to find effective tactics of delay, evasion, and contempt.

Opposition to integration has ranged from insurrectionary and terroristic tactics to reasonable and moderate attempts to explain white Southerners' fears. The article by Mr. Waring, one of the best statements of a Southern white to appear in the national press, exemplifies the more moderate position. Waring bases his case for segregation on the vast differences between white and Negro standards of life in the South, and thus on the fear that integration will debase the white community. In a brief addendum, the editors have responded to some of his arguments. The article by Professor Hook defends school integration by placing it in the general context of democratic morals.

THE SOUTHERN CASE
AGAINST DESEGREGATION

Thomas R. Waring

Although the Supreme Court has declared that separation of the races in public schools is unconstitutional, few white Southerners are able to accept the prospect of mingling white and Negro pupils. Resistance to the court decree is stiffening throughout the region.

Many white Northerners are unable to understand the depth of feeling in the Southern states, whose area is about a sixth of the nation and whose population is roughly a fourth of the total. The purpose of this article is to try to put before open-minded readers the point of view of the Southerner— whom the rest of the United States apparently cannot believe to be open-minded at all on the subject of race.

At the outset it is only fair to warn the Northern reader that he may be infuriated long before he reaches the end. This, I suspect, is just as inevitable as the outraged feelings of the Southerner when he reads the Northern press with its own interpretation of the American dilemma. Both sides have been shouting at each other so loudly that it is difficult any longer to hear facts through the din of name-calling. If, in the course of speaking for the South, I should raise blood pressure among some Northerners, I apologize for causing pain—with the hope that I may be able to reach Northern minds that are truly open so that some good may come along with the discomfort.

The reader outside the South may, unfortunately, react in still another way. He may find it difficult, if not impossible, to believe much of what I say. To this I can only reply that as editor of a South Carolina newspaper with a circulation of 56,000, with twenty-eight years of journalistic experience in both the North and the South, I have had to be in possession of accurate information on this as on any other subject covered in my work. Across an editor's desk pass, day by day and year after year, reports, letters, statistics—in other words, facts. By means of these facts, plus personal conversations with people from all over the world, an editor manages to keep in touch with public opinion.

It is the public opinion of the South that I am about to report. That opinion is a fact. It exists, and can be demonstrated. What I am saying is documented by facts and statistics. If these should seem to the reader to add up merely to bias, bigotry, and even untruth, I shall regret it. Facts, however, remain facts.

One of the reasons these facts may be unfamiliar—and therefore incredible—is the almost unanimous attitude of the national press, daily and weekly, toward the subject of race. I read many newspapers and news magazines, and people send me clippings from others that I do not see regularly. From my observation, the testimony these publications print is almost entirely one-sided. While less violent than the Negro press—which

Reprinted from Thomas R. Waring, "The Southern Case Against Desegregation," *Harper's Magazine* (January 1956), pp. 39–45, by permission of the author and the publisher. Mr. Waring is editor of the *Charleston News and Courier*.

understandably presents only the militant anti-segregation case—the metropolitan press almost without exception has abandoned fair and objective reporting of the race story. For facts it frequently substitutes propaganda.

Furthermore, with the exception of a small coterie of Southern writers whom Northern editors regard as "enlightened," spokesmen for the Southern view cannot gain access to Northern ears. This article will be one of the few of its kind published in a magazine of national circulation. The South, alas, lacks a magazine or other organ with nationwide distribution.

Perhaps my first assertion of a seldom realized truth will be the most difficult to believe. This statement is that white Southerners of good will—and the percentage of decency runs about the same in the South as anywhere else—favor uplift of the Negro, and that these white Southerners are in the vast majority. If it is impossible to prove the percentage of decency among Southerners, it is equally impossible to show that people in the North—or any other region—have a monopoly of it. But the South fears, and with reason, that the uplift is being forced at too fast a pace. The vagaries of custom and race taboos have many inconsistencies. The rules of segregation, both written and unwritten, change with conditions. And the sudden rewriting by the Supreme Court of regional laws and state constitutions has stirred as much resentment in Southern breasts as would be aroused among Northerners if suddenly their own freedom from race restrictions were denied by federal fiat. (Do I hear a muffled cheer from one or two Northerners who may take a dim view of mingling the races?)

Interference with sovereignty usually produces rage. In matters of education, the states long have been sovereign—until suddenly nine men have held otherwise.

Is it any wonder that the Southerner is bitter over what he believes to be a flouting of the Constitution for political reasons?

Aside from legal questions—and they are deep and broad—the Southerner believes that, as a practical matter, he is better equipped by experience to cope with race problems than people from other regions, no matter what their intellectual or political attainments. One of the proofs that this belief is founded not merely on pride or emotional prejudice lies in the fact that Northerners who spend some time in the South—not tourists or weekend visitors, but people who make their homes here—come rather sooner than later to agree that this is so. These transplanted Northerners come to see that there are far more bonds of friendship and active, productive good will between the white Southerner and his Negro neighbor than they had believed—or could believe until they became eye-witnesses and partakers of this relationship.

Although the South is both willing and eager to have the Negro earn greater acceptance on many levels—especially economic—it does not consider, for reasons that I shall submit, that mixed education is the way to achieve this acceptance—certainly not at this stage of affairs.

What may lie in the distant future is more than any of us can predict with accuracy. Southerners know that race problems are as old as history. While views and philosophies may change through the ages, some basic truths stand out like the Ten Commandments. Southerners are not yet ready to accept an eleventh, "Thou shalt not protect the purity of thy race."

Before going into the actual reasons for the Southerner's objections to mixed education—before asking the burning question, how can the races best live together—let us examine for a moment the pattern of separation. It is a pattern that Thomas Jefferson, Abraham Lincoln, and at one time Dwight D. Eisenhower have favored as best for both races. In 1888, Henry W. Grady, Atlanta editor—described by Don Shoemaker of the Southern Education Reporting Service as a Southern "liberal" of his time—summed up the situation as follows:

Neither "provincialism" nor "sectionalism" holds the South together but something deeper than these and essential to our system. The problem is how to carry within her body politic two separate races, and nearly equal in numbers. [Since Grady spoke, the whites in the South have come to outnumber the Negroes four to one, but the proportions vary greatly by neighborhoods.] She must carry these races in peace—for discord means ruin. She must carry them separately—for assimilation means debasement. She must carry them in equal justice—for to this she is pledged in honor and gratitude. She must carry them to the end, for in human probability she will never be quit of either.

While Grady's statements were made nearly seventy years ago and therefore are subject to the criticism that they do not reflect "modern conditions," to many Southerners they are true both now and for the future.

The presence of large numbers of Negroes—especially in the tidewater regions of Virginia, the Carolinas, and Georgia, and the plantation country of Alabama and Louisiana, Mississippi and East Texas—means that the races necessarily live in intimate daily association. Why, then, should not the children of people who live in the same community—sometimes as close neighbors—attend the same schools?

Southerners believe they have valid reasons, aside from "prejudice" about the color of skin, for their insistence on sending white children to exclusively white schools. Without debating superiority of either race, they are keenly aware of cultural differences. In some ways the standards of white people are none too high. The same economic conditions that have held back Negroes have worked against the whites. The increasing prosperity of the South is removing some of these disadvantages for both races, though not necessarily in precisely the same way.

Whether all the differences will eventually be removed, or enough of them to make mixed education acceptable to a substantial number of white people, the differences are too great *at present* to encourage white parents to permit their children to mingle freely in school. This has nothing to do with the frequent practice of children of both races of playing together when young, or with cordial relationships in many other contacts of ordinary life.

Volumes could be written on racial differences from many angles, including anthropology and sociology. I shall merely try to summarize five of the differences that most immediately come to the minds of white parents in the South. These are health; home environment; marital standards; crime; and a wide disparity in average intellectual development.

(1) *Health.* Negro parents as a whole—for reasons that white people may sympathetically deplore but which nevertheless exist—are not so careful on the average as their white neighbors in looking after the health and cleanliness of their children. The incidence of venereal disease, for instance, is much greater among Negroes than among whites.

Statistics to document this statement are difficult to come by, though the statement itself would be generally accepted in the South. The U.S. Public Health Service some years ago quietly stopped identifying statistics by races. South Carolina figures, available for 1952–53, give a clue to the situation in that state; it probably is much the same elsewhere in the South. Out of a population 60 per cent white and 40 per cent Negro, 6,315 cases of syphilis were reported, of which 89 per cent were among Negroes. Infection with gonorrhea was found in six Negroes to one white person, but some physicians report that many cases of gonorrhea among Negroes go unrecorded.

During the same period—1952–53—a campaign against venereal disease was carried on, county by county. A spot check of four representative counties in different parts of South Carolina showed that cases of syphilis were found among 1.3 per cent of the white persons examined. This was a fairly constant percentage. The percentage of infection among Negroes ranged in the same counties from 8.5 to 10.8 per cent, averaging more than 9 per cent.

Fastidious parents do not favor joint use of school washrooms when they would not permit it at home—and there's no use to tell them that it is unlikely that anyone will catch venereal disease from a toilet seat. They just don't want to take risks of any kind with their children.

(2) *Home environment.* For most colored children in the South the cultural background is different in many ways from that of their white neighbors—and while these differences may have various explanations, they add up in the public's mind as racial. Slavery is so long in the past that nobody thinks about it any more, but the master and servant, or boss and laborer, relationship between whites and Negroes is still the rule rather than the exception. The emergence of a middle class among the Negroes has been extremely slow—again, the reasons count for less in the minds of white parents than the fact itself. Indeed, the professional and commercial class among Negroes is so small that its members are in perhaps the most unenviable position of all. They have progressed beyond the cultural level of the vast bulk of their own people, but are not accepted among the whites, who fear to let down any dikes lest they be engulfed in a black flood.

Someone may suggest that here is an opening wedge for integration in the schools, by admitting a few well-scrubbed and polished colored children of cultivated parents. In reply, let me say that this would be no more acceptable to the colored people than to the whites. The solution, perhaps—as it is among upper-bracket white people who do not send their children to public schools—might be private schools for prosperous Negroes as for prosperous whites. In any case, white people feel that cultural gaps on other levels should be filled in before discussing integrated schools.

(3) *Marital habits.* Among many Southern Negroes they are, to state it mildly, casual—even more so, in fact, than among the often-divorced personalities of Northern café society. Many Negro couples—the statistics are not readily available, for obvious reasons—do not bother with divorce because there was no actual marriage in the first place. Statistics on the results of such casual unions, however, are available. On the average one Southern Negro child in five is illegitimate. It is possible the figure may be even higher, since illegitimate births are more likely to go unrecorded. Even

among Negroes who observe marriage conventions, illegitimacy has little if any stigma.

Many white persons believe that morals among their own race are lax enough as it is, without exposing their children to an even more primitive view of sex habits. Moreover, while these parents do not believe there is any surge of desire among their offspring to mate with colored people, they abhor any steps that might encourage intermarriage. They believe that lifting the racial school barriers would be such a step. Miscegenation has been on the wane of recent years. Whatever mixing of blood may have occurred —and admittedly that was due largely to lustful white men seeking out acquiescent Negro women—has been without benefit of either law or custom. On some levels of society, breaking the racial barriers might lead to mixed marriages. The mixture of races which white Southerners have observed in Latin American countries gives them a dim view of legalizing cohabitation with Negroes.

(4) *Crime.* For many years, crime in the South has been more prevalent among Negroes than among white people. Though the Northern press no longer identifies criminals by race, white Southerners have reason to believe that much of the outbreak of crime and juvenile delinquency in Northern cities is due to the influx of Negro population. They believe the North now is getting a taste of the same race troubles that the South fears would grow out of mixed schooling, on a much bigger scale. They want no "Blackboard Jungles" in the South.

Maintaining order is a first concern of Southerners. What they have heard about the fruits of integration in the North does not encourage them to adopt the Northern race pattern. In Chicago, three hundred policemen have been assigned for a year or more to guard a nonsegregated housing project, with no bigger population than a Southern village where a single constable keeps the peace. In the County of Charleston, South Carolina—with 190,000 population, nearly half Negro—the total law-enforcement manpower of combined city and county forces is 175.

While the homicide rate in the South is high, it is due in large measure to knifings and shootings among the colored people. Interracial homicide is relatively rare. (One of the reasons why the ghastly killing of Emmett Till in Mississippi made hot news—and some of that news was superheated and garnished with prejudice in the Northern press—was the very fact that it *was* unusual. No lynching, as even most Northerners now realize, has occurred in years.)

With racial bars down and rowdies of both races daring one another to make something of the vast increase in daily contacts, opportunities for interracial strife are frightening. Conservative, law-abiding people—and, believe it or not, they constitute the bulk of Southern whites—are deeply fearful that hatred and bloodshed would increase without separation of the races.

And they know that, in the long run, if there is riotous bloodshed it will be for the most part Negroes' blood. The thin tolerance of the ruffian and lower elements of the white people could erupt into animosity and brutality if race pressure became unbearable. Schools would be a focal point for such disturbance, first among pupils themselves and later by enraged parents. Instead of learning out of books, the younger generation would be schooled in survival—as several Northern sources have told me already is happening in some areas of New York, Philadelphia, and Washington, D.C.

(5) *Intellectual development.* Again for whatever the reasons may be, Southern Negroes usually are below the intellectual level of their white counterparts. *U.S. News and World Report*—the fairest nationally circulated publication I am acquainted with in its treatment of the race issue—has reported that in Washington colored children are about two grades behind the whites in attainment. This discrepancy, I believe, is about par for other communities. In Washington it was found that there were even language difficulties to surmount. The children used different terms for some things.

Some advocates of integration say the way to cure these differences is to let the children mingle so that the Negroes will learn from the whites. The trouble with this theory is that, even if it works, a single generation of white children will bear the brunt of the load. While they are rubbing off white civilization onto the colored children, Negro culture will also rub off onto the whites.

Few Southern parents are willing to sacrifice their own offspring in order to level off intellectual differences in this fashion. They reason that their children will get along better in later life if they have, as youngsters, the best available cultural contacts. Such an attitude is not, I understand, altogether unknown in the North. Many parents in New York City, for example, make considerable financial sacrifices to send their children to private schools, to spare them the undesirable associations and the low-geared teaching standards of most public schools.

If this sounds snobbish to a Northern reader, let me ask you to examine your own conscience. Can you honestly say that you are eager to send your own child to a classroom where the majority of other pupils will be considerably more backward in their studies, and extremely different in social background and cultural attainment? Which would you *really* put first: your theory of racial justice, or justice to your own child?

In reply to objections to integration by white Southerners, someone may ask: What about the Negroes? What do they think?

At the outset, let me say—as a person who has spent most of his life in the South, has known Negroes from earliest childhood, and as a newspaperman who has been dealing with race matters every day for many years —that I cannot say just what goes on in the minds of the Negroes. Nor do I believe that a white man can put himself in the place of a colored man any more than he can, by taking thought, add a cubit to his stature. Until the school question became agitated in recent years, however, race relations on the whole were good. Since the agitation, relations are not yet bad in a broad sense—but they are not improving by reason of the crusade for integration.

The leadership in that crusade comes from outside the South. It is sparked by the National Association for the Advancement of Colored People. Southerners have reason to believe that this organization has a very large measure of white influence among its leaders. They recognize that both major political parties are courting the Negro vote, which holds the balance of power in key cities of populous Northern states. They are bewildered by the array of power aligned on the side of the NAACP in press, pulpit, and politics. The NAACP and its allies seem well supplied with money. They have won legal victories and they are not disposed to compromise on any front. In fact, the NAACP seems—to white Southerners—more interested in forcing the Negro into the white man's company than in equipping the Negro to qualify fully for such association.

A small but pointed illustration occurred in Charleston when a white community-theater group tried to produce *Porgy* (the original play, not the opera) with a Negro cast in the city where the story is laid. There was a grave question about how the community, in a time when racial agitation was so bitter, would accept a play performed almost exclusively by Negroes. Many difficulties had to be surmounted in casting and production. But the sponsoring group, in consultation with NAACP and other Negro spokesmen, decided to proceed, and spent a sizable amount of money getting the production under way.

One of the key questions was the seating of the audience. Under South Carolina law separate seating for the races is required. The chairman of the local NAACP chapter agreed in writing, I have been informed, to an arrangement for separate seating by means of a vertical line down the center aisle, whites on one side and Negroes on the other. At the last moment, with the play already in rehearsal, the NAACP repudiated the agreement.

The Negro cast pleaded with the white sponsors to go through with the production in spite of the NAACP. By this time, however, it became obvious that the delicate circumstances had become too explosive and the production was canceled. A possible good-will gesture, opening a new line of communication, thus was halted because the NAACP would accept nothing less than complete integration—regardless of both state law and local custom.

Whether the NAACP really speaks for the rank and file of Negroes is debatable. Public expressions of opinion from Negroes in the South, other than the NAACP, are relatively few. Some white people feel that a Negro is so accustomed to telling a white man what he thinks the white man wants to hear, that they put little stock in whatever the Negro says on race. It would not be hard to believe that, given a choice, a Negro naturally would prefer all restrictions to be removed. That does not mean, however, that all Negroes want to associate with white people. Far from it; many Negroes prefer their own churches and, it stands to reason, should be equally satisfied with their own schools, so long as an equal allotment of public money is given them.

While the allotment has not always been equal—Negroes pay only a small fraction of taxes—the sums of money spent on Negro schooling have increased by leaps and bounds. On the average the South spends a greater percentage of its per capita income on schools than other regions, and nowadays the Negroes are getting their share in most areas. One thing is certain: if the schools were integrated, many a Negro school teacher would lose his or her job. Even if the white people would accept mixed pupils— and few apparently would do so—they would insist on white teachers.

Whenever a Southern Negro does object to the drive for integration, he is subject to pressure from his own people. Two Negro clergymen—what are known as "local preachers"—recently wrote letters to newspapers in lower South Carolina opposing the mixing of schools. Both were disciplined by their church superiors. Many white people on friendly terms with Negroes are convinced that, as a rule, the Negroes are not eager for mixed schools so long as the schools for Negroes are adequate.

This conviction leads them to hope that a voluntary approach eventually may help to solve the problem within the Supreme Court ruling. Judge John J. Parker of Charlotte, North Carolina, senior judge of the Fourth Circuit Court of Appeals, has said:

> It is important that we point out exactly what the Supreme Court has decided and what it has not decided in this [the Clarendon County] case. . . . It has not decided that the states must mix persons of different races in the schools. . . . Nothing in the Constitution or in the decision of the Supreme Court takes away from the people freedom to choose the schools they attend. The Constitution, in other words, does not require integration. It does not forbid such segregation as occurs as the result of voluntary action. It merely forbids the use of governmental power to enforce segregation. The Fourteenth Amendment is a limitation upon the exercise of power by the state or state agencies, not a limitation upon the freedom of individuals.

The Alabama state legislature has set up a new basis for assignment of pupils which does not mention race, though its provisions might tend to keep white and Negro pupils apart. In South Carolina, a committee of fifty-two representative citizens is circulating a resolution—already signed by many thousands—asking the State Legislature to interpose its authority between the federal government and local school boards to maintain segregation. Such a move would be based on the Tenth Amendment to the U.S. Constitution, reserving to the states and the people all powers not specifically granted to the federal government.

These are only two of many tentative plans to get around the Supreme Courts decision by methods of law. Another proposal is revival of the principle of nullification, which states both in the North and South have used in years gone by. A recent example was the public disregard of Prohibition. Segregation, perhaps, may be bootlegged in some regions. How that can be done is not immediately apparent—but the resourcefulness of the rum-runners and speakeasies was not foreseen by sponsors of the Volstead Act.

As in Prohibition, there is danger that white hoodlums may enter the picture. Sporadic outbreaks of the Ku Klux Klan have been reported. To combat the lawless element, law-abiding white men—who are determined not to yield to pressures they still regard as contrary to the guarantees of the Constitution—have been forming protective organizations. These go under many names. In Mississippi, South Carolina, and some of the other states they are called Citizens Councils.

Much has been said about the adoption of "economic pressure" as a weapon by these white groups. In some instances Negroes have reported that their sharecropper contracts have not been renewed because they signed petitions to integrate schools. Other forms of pressure have been reported, and in some localities Negroes have retaliated with boycotts against white merchants who were active in the Councils. White leaders of the resistance movements repeatedly have said they were not organizing boycotts and pressures against the Negroes and that they are determined there shall be no reign of terror as predicted by some Negro spokesmen.

Hodding Carter—one of a handful of Southern writers granted access to the national magazines—has predicted that attempts to enforce integration in the public schools of Mississippi would be likely to create violence. White leaders are exploring many other avenues in hopes of preventing strong-arm methods from being tried. They fear also that the very existence of the public schools is in peril. Rather than accept mixed public schools, some white Southerners may seek other means of educating their children.

Even if the schools are not abandoned, it seems unlikely that the white people will submit to heavy taxation to operate schools that many of them refuse to patronize. If they are not throttled outright, the public school systems in some areas may be starved to death. The spread of resistance organizations, far from being the product of demagogues, is at the local level among ordinary people, without "big-name" leadership. School trustees and other officials are getting the message from the grass roots.

Acceptance of the Supreme Court's order in border states and lip service in some other quarters have encouraged some advocates to believe that many Southern communities soon will yield to integration. While the borders of the old Confederacy may narrow, the determination of white people in areas with heavy Negro population is not relaxing. Not only regions where Negroes predominate by ten to one are rejecting the prospect of mixed schools. Pickens County in Piedmont, South Carolina, has the smallest number of Negroes (about one in ten) of any county in the state; its grand jury—most fundamental of all bodies safeguarding the people's liberty—has gone on record against mixed schools. On Edisto Island, at the opposite side of the state, where a white face looks out of place, insistence on mingling would be almost academic. If any attempt were made to force white children into Negro schools, the white people would move off the island, or find other means of educating their children.

Talk about segregation may promote migration of Negroes from the South. Already thousands have left the cotton fields and villages to seek jobs in Northern cities. On the farms, machines have replaced them. With the minimum wage advancing to $1 an hour, Southern employers will demand production from their laborers that not all Negroes will be able or willing to supply. These employers also may seek ways to mechanize or to employ white labor. As industries move South, more attractive opportunities for white people are opening.

If the North continues to appeal to Negroes as a land of integration and the South continues to attract white settlers, the racial proportions may grow more nearly equal. Then the North may become more tolerant of the Southerners' view of race problems, and the South better able to handle its dwindling Negro problem. Southerners will gladly share the load.

Meanwhile, stripped of emotions, the race problem for both Southern whites and Negroes is a practical matter of daily living. The problem has been recognized by thoughtful Americans from the early days of the Republic. It would be foolish to deny that any Negro pupils ever will enter Southern white schools. (Some already have.) But it would be equally foolhardy to predict that their numbers will be significant at an early date.

SEGREGATION OF WHOM?

The Editors

One of the most tragic features of the South's reaction to the Supreme Court's decision has been the behavior of Southern white liberals. These men have had an important historic role to play. If legally sanctioned mass discrimination is to be removed from the South without outside force, it is they who must carry on from Washington's initiative. Their usual role, however, has rather been to condone the South and to appeal for sympathy with their own moral dilemma.

Segregation may be illegal and even unjust, Mr. Waring suggests; but to right this wrong will only make matters worse. The very fact that Negroes have been kept in a subordinate position for generations means that, as a group, they are less well educated, more afflicted with communicable diseases, and in other respects unattractive. Mr. Waring asks us to consider the predicament of a white middle-class parent whose children have to go to school with dirty, ignorant Negroes from across the tracks. And, indeed, none would deny that there are significant over-all differences between Negroes and whites, particularly in the South. But this is only one of several such dichotomies in American society. The statistical differentiations between native-born and immigrants, between the middle class and the working class, between—for that matter—Southern whites and whites in the rest of the country, are also significant.

Suppose we in the North were to sit down and compile good, solid facts to validate the position that Southern whites are an inferior group. It would be an easy task.

Take the problem of health—specifically, infant mortality, which public-health administrators often use as an index of hereditary deficiencies, community-health services, and family care. For 1959 the rate for the *white* population of the whole of the United States was 23.2 infant deaths per 1,000 live births. In almost every Southern and border state, the rate for the *white* population was higher[1]—in spite of the notoriously incomplete reporting in the rural regions in the South.

Or take crime. Few have sensed the Southern bent toward lawlessness so acutely as has W. J. Cash, a Southerner. According to Cash, all of the elements of the Southern character structure contributed toward "the perpetuation and acceleration of the tendency to violence."[2] The homicide rate of the South is the highest of any region, about eight times that of New England. In 1959, the number of cases of murder and non-negligent manslaughter per 100,000 population was 4.8 for the nation as a whole. Statistics on the various states show the rate as 10.4 in Arkansas, 12.9 in Alabama, 13.4 in Georgia; or—at the other extreme—0.5 in Vermont, 1.0 in Minnesota and Utah.[3] Southern apologists typically explain these figures by pointing to the large Negro population in the Southern states;

[1] U. S. Bureau of the Census, *Statistical Abstract of the United States, 1961*, p. 63.
[2] W. J. Cash, *The Mind of the South* (New York: Doubleday-Anchor, 1954), p. 55.
[3] *Statistical Abstract*, p. 141.

but this explanation is altogether too simple. "The death rate by homicide for white persons in the South is approximately five times as high as in New England, and the Negro homicide rate in New England is slightly lower than the white homicide rate in the same area."[4] Moreover, the high crime rate among Southern Negroes is based at least in part on the fact that Negro neighborhoods are largely deprived of police protection, as of other municipal facilities. As long as the Negroes rob and kill each other, they disturb no one of importance, and only serve to verify the Southern dictum that they are by nature animalic.

Or take intellectual development. In 1958, the average expenditure on public schools for the whole of the United States was only $341 per pupil— an extremely low average, resulting primarily from the fact that virtually every one of the Southern states fell below this figure: Texas, for instance, had an average expenditure of $323; Mississippi, only $174 (as contrasted, at the other extreme, with $524 in Alaska or $507 in New York).[5] Undoubtedly one reason for this poor showing among Southern states is that Negro schools in the South are allotted extremely low sums of money for their operation; however, the funds allotted to schools for white children are, by and large, not very much higher.

Following Mr. Waring's logic, it would be reasonable to bar the migration of this "inferior" group to the rest of the country. Indeed, during the 1930's such a law was enacted by California, which wanted to protect its citizens from what it regarded as an invasion of "Okies." The law was struck down by the Supreme Court, and in our opinion correctly so. For, by the very first principle of the American credo, each person has the right to be judged on the basis of his own virtues and faults, not those ascribed to the various social groups of which he may be a member.

[4]Edwin H. Sutherland and Donald R. Cressey, *Principles of Criminology,* 5th ed. (New York: Lippincott, 1955), p. 154.
[5]*Statistical Abstract,* p. 104.

DEMOCRACY AND DESEGREGATION

Sidney Hook

It is commonly agreed that the United States Supreme Court's decision on integration in education is one of the most important rulings in its long and controversial history. For years now, the decision has been subjected to a steadily mounting barrage of criticism on all sorts of grounds and from almost all points of the ideological compass. What has been most surprising is the absence of a principled defense of desegregation and the program of school integration from the point of view of the ethics of democracy. Most defenses of the decision, particularly since Little Rock, have

Abridged from Sidney Hook, *Democracy and Desegregation* (New York: The New Leader, April 21, 1958). Reprinted by permission of the author and the publisher. Sidney Hook is Chairman of the Department of Philosophy at New York University, and the author of numerous books on philosophical, educational, and political subjects.

consisted in shifting the issue by insisting that the supreme law of the land, whatever we may think of its wisdom, should be obeyed. Although this is a justifiable position with respect to the laws of a democracy, which, if unwise and unjust, are modifiable and reversible, it evades the basic moral issues that in the last analysis underlie every fundamental conflict of values and social policy.

The opposition to desegregation comes from various groups. The old-line Southerners, who represent the majority of the opposition, hardly deign to offer reasons for their opposition except that laws against desegregation destroy their traditional "way of life." They are more convinced of the validity of their way of life than of the abstract rights of man and of citizens in whose name such ways of life may be condemned. That their way of life has a history; that it involves the use and abuse of other human beings who are bitterly opposed to this way of life; and that, unless they have some other justification for the status quo than that it is a status quo, a new status quo may be imposed upon them with the same warrant—all this they are content to ignore. For they hope to reverse the decision or transform it into a dead letter not by argument or reason but by delaying tactics and sporadic outbursts of recalcitrance.

A second group opposes desegregation on constitutional grounds. Some regard this area of human relations as one in which the Supreme Court is really legislating and therefore usurping the functions of Congress and state legislatures. Others believe that education is exclusively a matter for state jurisdiction and no concern of the federal government. A third group protests against the clear violation of previous controlling precedents—especially *Plessy* v. *Ferguson*—which established the "separate but equal" doctrine. These constitutional questions are not really germane to the basic argument. It is true that the Supreme Court "legislates." It always has. The ultimate question is the character, grounds, and wisdom of its legislation. Education may be exclusively a matter for state jurisdiction. Yet the effects of some state actions may have consequences affecting the rights and privileges of citizens. Aside from this, the moral issue of segregation in education still remains, whether it is a question for the states or the federal government. That the Supreme Court decision overturns earlier precedents is true. This is not unusual. The real question is: Should the precedents be retained or overturned? I shall, therefore, avoid the strictly legalistic aspects of the question.

Finally, I come to the criticism made by some conservative liberals and liberal conservatives who see in the legal prohibition of segregation in educational facilities (as in employment and in housing) a violation of one's personal freedom or private right to choose one's associations, companions, neighbors, and fellow workers. There is some written criticism of desegregation along these lines, but the volume of spoken criticism is much greater. Even before the Supreme Court decision, some exponents of discrimination as a personal right related it to the defense of free enterprise. Natural law as well as Judeo-Christian ideals have been invoked to prove that man is essentially a discriminatory creature because he is capable of choice. The greater his knowledge, the greater his range of discrimination. According to this argument, many of our difficulties arise from attempts to curb by law the exercise of a discrimination which is ours by natural right and which is justified in addition by the greater power it gives us to advance the arts of civilization.

Since the desegregation decision, this note has been struck with increasing frequency by critics who believe that discrimination in education lies in the field of private morals and is thus beyond the reach of law. They are prepared to defend the human rights, they tell us, of all minorities, but they insist that the right to discriminate in education, even if this results in segregated schools, is one of the basic human rights. The more liberal among these critics make a distinction between the public and private domain according to which it would be wrong to *permit* segregation on buses and railroads because these lie in the public domain but wrong to *prevent* segregation, on the ground of personal freedom, in private life. Education, they say, is one of those areas of personal life that are by their very nature outside the purview of law in a democratic society.

The case against Negro segregation in any area of public life, whether enforced by law or by custom, rests upon simple ethical principles which are implicit in the Declaration of Independence and which later guided the adoption of the Thirteenth and Fourteenth Amendments. These principles of equality and freedom are expressed in the language of natural rights, but they are best defended in terms of their empirical consequences: The Negroes are part of the human race and as such should enjoy the same human rights of freedom and the same protection of our laws as any other group of human beings in the United States. The Thirteenth Amendment abolished their slavery and involuntary servitude generally. In so doing, we sought to redress a crime—one perhaps even greater than those committed in some settlements against the Indians. If slavery is abolished, then all the institutional restraints and indignities which constituted servitude must be abolished, too. There can be no justification for first- and second-class citizens derivative from a previous condition of servitude. Morally, Negroes are entitled to life, liberty, property, and equal protection of laws on the same terms as the rest of us. This is independent of vicissitudes in the Supreme Court's interpretations of these rights we enjoy as citizens of our individual states or as citizens of the Federal Republic.

Atoning in part for the long history of moral evasion by previous Courts, the Supreme Court in *Brown* v. *Board of Education of Topeka* declared that segregated public educational facilities are "inherently unequal." Despite the obscurity of the Court's language, this was not based on a discovery of a new fact or a rediscovery of an old law, but on the reaffirmation of a moral principle that led to a new law in the land. The moral principle is the same one which justified the abolition of slavery. In the light of the *historical* situation which has developed since the abolition of slavery, segregated educational facilities are "inherently unequal," not because of the actual differences in facilities, great as they are, but because they are inherently cruel, unjust, and degrading to the group discriminated against. They are degrading in the same way that the yellow patch or badge of inferiority, the mark of the pariah, the stigma of the outcast, are degrading. Even if the physical facilities of Negro schools (or buses) were physically better than those set aside for the whites, segregation would still be degrading for the same reason that we regard a well-fed slave as still a slave.

Has the individual ever a right to discriminate, and, if so, where?

More than a decade ago I pointed to the necessity of establishing a principle which would guide us in drawing a line between "justifiable" and "unjustifiable" discrimination: "The presence of a justifying principle with respect to legitimate and illegitimate discrimination is necessary in order to allay fears that, under the cover of social welfare, individual freedom and the rights of privacy may be abridged."[1] I no longer believe that the principle I then too briefly formulated in terms of the needs of *personal growth* is adequate. But it seemed to me that it enabled us to condemn all types of community segregation and at the same time permit a man to choose his friends and control the pattern of his personal and family life. I mention this merely to indicate that critics of laws against segregation are not alone in their concern for personal freedom and the right to privacy. But the unfortunate thing is that their argument so interprets the right of privacy that it embraces the entire realm of the social or public, if not the narrowly political. The fact is that extreme Southern segregationists have defined *their* right of privacy, their right to live according to customs and folkways they call the Southern way of life, so as to deny the equal protection of laws to all but native whites.

Opponents of integration do not contest the right of every child, Negro or white, to receive an education in the public schools. They know that the public schools are supported by tax money levied directly or indirectly upon all citizens irrespective of race. They contend, however, that it is wrong to force parents to send their children to an integrated school. For this deprives them of rights which clearly belong to them in all free societies—the private right over their children and the social right to free association. At most, these spokesmen hold, the state may prescribe some of the content of education but not the context of association and social life which invariably develops out of attendance at school.

It is instructive to explore some of the implications of this position and observe to what it commits anyone holding it. If it is wrong to force white parents to send their children to an integrated school because of *their* private right over their children, it is wrong to force Negro parents to send *their* children to segregated schools, and wrong to force white parents who do not object to *their* children associating with Negro children to do the same. The same principle obviously obtains with respect to the feelings of parents toward the children of *any* minority. It is wrong to force parents to send their children to legally unsegregated public schools if they do not wish *their* children to associate with the children of religious, racial, or ethnic minorities. Since most of these critics do not propose to abolish our compulsory education laws, and rule out private education as economically unfeasible, they must require the state or community to build separate schools for any group of parents who wish to safeguard their children from any kind of context and association they regard as seriously undesirable.

Educational context and associations, however, extend far beyond the classroom into school buses, lunchrooms, playgrounds, pools, gymnasiums. If desegregated schools violate the personal and social rights of parents to

[1]Review of *To Secure These Rights, The New Leader,* March 13, 1947.

discriminate against undesirable associates and contexts for their children, so do desegregated buses and all other public educational facilities where context and association are prolonged for hours. Since these are normally incidental to public education, special facilities would have to be provided for the entire gamut of parental fastidiousness. What holds for public education must by these principles also hold for public health and medical facilities. Parents may object to having Negro physicians or nurses treat their children in public hospitals to which Negro children are admitted. And it is surely obvious that public housing projects which legally bar segregation also violate the private rights of white parents not to have their children associate with undesirables.

Actually, parents are *not* forced to send their children to an integrated school. Parents may choose to send their children to private schools which are not integrated. Or, in most states, they may provide education at home. This the law permits *(Pierce* v. *Society of Sisters).* To be sure, they have to pay a certain economic price for it, even though in its tradition of tolerance the community subsidizes these private schools by giving them remission from taxes and allowing those who contribute to their support to deduct contributions from their taxable income. One would think this was a generous, even overgenerous, attitude toward individuals whose prejudice against permitting their children to associate with Negroes was so overwhelming. But—the objection runs—it will not do to tell parents they can educate their children at home or send them to private schools. This involves another kind of discrimination. Since private education requires the possession of means, it would make the safeguarding of certain private rights dependent upon economic status and consequently underprivilege those who are forced to send their children to public school.

In other words, unless we can guarantee the equal economic status of the prejudiced, segregation would be a privilege of the rich! But why should we be concerned with economic equality here? Why not make the segregationists pay the costs of their prejudices? If the cost is sufficiently high, they may give up their opposition to integration if not their prejudices. In time even their prejudices may wither.

What a strange state of affairs! These opponents of school integration tell us they really are not opposed to equality. But equality can be legislated only in the political sphere; all we can enforce is the right to vote, *political* equality. The numerous ways in which economic inequalities affect the political realm, especially in the winning of consent, bother this school of thought not at all. But with respect to the exercise of the private right of sending children to segregated schools, they become economic equalitarians. Is it not more humane to fortify the principle of political equality by equality of educational opportunity, which is negated by segregated schools, than by invoking the principle of economic equality to justify perpetuating such schools?

One of the main premises of the segregationist argument is contained in the explicit acceptance of William Faulkner's declaration that "enforced integration is no better than enforced segregation." This is a very curious statement. Leaving aside the strictly legal questions created by the most recent interpretations of Section I of the Fourteenth Amendment, particularly the provision extending the equal protection of laws to all citizens, this equation in condemnation seems to me completely inadmissible morally. It assumes either that integration and segregation are, morally, on all fours, or that the evils of enforcement *always* outweigh any alternative good to be derived therefrom. This is not necessarily true and in the case in hand—the historical situation of the Negro in the United States—patently false. To deny children equal public educational opportunities and possibilities of proper vocational fulfilment merely because of the color of their skin or their religion or national origin, whether enforced by law or by social custom, is manifestly unjust. On the other hand, to require students, if they wish a public school education supported by tax monies levied upon all alike, to attend unsegregated schools is not unjust.

There are situations in which legally to compel certain practices is as bad as legally to prohibit them. This is so when the practices in question are equally evil, or when they are morally indifferent. Legally to compel us to consume bananas is as bad as legally to prohibit us from doing so. But what is true for bananas would not be true for habit-forming drugs, or for smoking in a powder plant. To enforce vaccination or the medical segregation of children with contagious diseases is certainly not as bad as preventing it even if we admit it is always deplorable to compel parents to comply with school and health laws.

Some anti-integrationists make a distinction between segregation as a "social custom" and segregation as "discrimination enforced by law." They oppose the latter—but then, just as resolutely, oppose the legal prohibition of such discrimination as a social custom. They do so on the ground that this violates the personal freedom of those who discriminate to act as they please "within the four walls" of their own home.

There are social customs and social customs. A social custom which violates human rights, and imposes unfair and cruel penalties upon individuals, hurts no less even if it is not enforced by law. It is enough that it is enforced by habit, custom, use, and wont. Suttee was a social custom, too—as was child marriage, infanticide, dueling, and quite a number of other quaint practices described in anthropological texts. If there is any relation between morality and law, the existence of certain evil social practices *may* (not must) justify us in taking legal action to prevent them. And if this is of necessity an abridgment of some human freedom, as is true of every law, it is taken in behalf of other human freedoms. The human freedoms we safeguard by legal action against segregation and unfair discrimination are more important than those we restrict. Some Southern moderates see this in the case of certain public facilities, such as transportation. But surely the social discrimination which prevents a Negro student from attending a medical or engineering school, which bars him from certain vocations even after he has spent years of his adult life in preparing himself for it, which denies him housing in restricted communities without even providing him with the separate and equal facilities of the segregated bus, is a much crasser violation of his rights as a human being. The classification which puts transportation in the field of the political, and education and employment in the field of the personal, is completely arbitrary as well as irrelevant. For the moral question is primary and it cuts across all categories.

It is on moral grounds that we are justified in adopting a Fair Education

Practices Act prohibiting certain discriminatory practices not only in public schools but sometimes even in private schools which are dependent upon the public largesse in various ways. It is on moral grounds that we are justified in adopting a Fair Employment Practices Act. Finally, it is on moral grounds that we are justified in adopting a Fair Housing Law, the exact provisions of which we need not specify here. I believe I am as much concerned with preserving the rights of privacy as any segregationist, but I cannot see how the right of every person to do as he pleases within the four walls of his own house is undermined by legislation designed to make it possible for our colored neighbor to live within *his* four walls.

Many inconsistencies and confusions in this position flow from vague distinctions between the political, the public, the social, and the personal or private. According to this view, only the political sphere is the sphere of equality. Focal to it is the right to vote. The social sphere is the sphere in which discrimination is legitimate even if unwise. The public sphere includes both. The private sphere is one of exclusion. But to what sphere, then, belong the inalienable human rights "to life, liberty, and the pursuit of happiness"?

A moment's reflection will show that they have mixed everything up. Equality "exists" *first* in the field of human rights. It is the premise from which we derive the most powerful argument against slavery. Political equality, especially equality in voting, is only one form of equality. Negroes desire political equality in order to enforce recognition of their human rights, which they believe they have even when they lack political equality. They were liberated and admitted to citizenship even before the Fifteenth Amendment specifically forbade abridgment of the right to vote on account of race, color, or previous condition of servitude. Under certain historical conditions, restrictions on the right to vote—age, literacy, residence—provided they are *equitably* applied to all, may actually lead to inequality in the exercise of the vote. It is manifestly improper to confuse the political realm with one very special form of political life—a democracy of universal suffrage. It is clear that sometimes we may wonder whether a people is ready for universal suffrage but never whether they have human or social rights, no matter how primitive they are.

The social realm, the locus of most of our associations with other human beings, is the sphere in which the questions of justice arise in their most complex as well as most acute form. The social realm is emphatically not in the first instance the realm of discrimination and inequality, although they are found there. That would automatically and necessarily make it one of injustice. It is precisely here that, as moral creatures, reflecting upon the consequences of our actions on others, we are called upon to apply appropriate rules of equality and, where differences are relevant, rules of equitable inequality in the light of some shared ideal, even if it be no more than the ideal of peace or mutual sufferance. The nub of many an error here is the confusion, where social relationships and membership in social groups are involved, between "discriminating *against*" and "discriminating *between*" and treating them as synonymous expressions. In identifying the social world with discriminating *against,* one is describing it as it appears to the eyes of the snob with vestigial cultural longings for feudal hierarchy.

Finally, there is an ambiguity in the category of the private. In one sense, the opposite of the "private" is the "public," as when we contrast private societies with public ones; in another, the opposite of the "private" is the "social." In the second sense, the "private" means the "personal." The personal realm is not merely the solitary: It involves our friends and families. Because our associations here have no consequences that extend beyond those who are engaged in them, we owe no one an accounting for our choices, however arbitrary, biased, prejudiced, or unwise. We may walk, dance, drink, talk philosophy, quarrel, or pray with whomever we please. And we *must* not prevent others from doing the same except where, as sometimes is the case in private quarrels, the consequences affect the lives of others. It is evident that since many kinds of private associations, in the first sense of private, have their locus in social space and not in the space within one's four walls, situations may arise which require some kind of public regulation. By arbitrarily extending the realm of the personal and delimiting the realm of the public, the segregationists would give those in possession of power justification to impose their way of life, subtly if possible, brutally if necessary, on any minority and (crowning irony) to do it in the name of personal freedom. Morally, no set of principles will be sufficient to determine by themselves in which cases the law should intervene when private prejudices result in public discrimination. The consequences in each situation must be considered. But we are not without knowledge about the kind of consequences that some types of action have. And at some point, after consultation and negotiation have run their course, the law must be applied.

It is a hateful thing to enforce laws in education, where ideally there should be no coercion except the inescapable cogencies encountered in the quest for truth and beauty. But ideal societies exist only in heaven. It is commonly acknowledged that the state may not only enforce compulsory attendance but prescribe the content or subject matter of instruction in order to insure an education appropriate for the exercise of citizenship. The content of education has some fixed elements, but its variables depend on the *kind* of society in which instruction is given and on its history. The mode of association within a school may have a definite bearing on the content and values of the education it gives. This has always been true of the American public school, which has played a great and unique role in the creation of the modern American nation. It not only provided a ladder of opportunity on which millions climbed out of poverty, but by virtue of its integrated classrooms, in which students studied and played in common, unified the most diverse ethnic groups that elsewhere lived together in snarling hostility. It never even tried to do this in the South, because the pattern of segregation prevailed from the beginning in the schools, which were late in getting founded. The requirements of citizenship in a *democratic* community require the integration of the public classrooms even more than integration in the armed services. Unassailable evidence shows that Negro students, especially in high schools, smart under the restrictions of the segregated school. The more willingly they accept the promised heritage of American ideals, the more they resent their educational conditions. A typical study among Negro high school students in Dade County, Florida, shows that, when asked to state the changes they most desired in their way of life, they named most frequently changes in the area of education. Can the democratic state be indifferent to this?

Some assert that the desegregation decision would probably have caused no great furor if it had not been followed by enforced integration. This is really saying that there would have been no trouble at Little Rock if nothing had been done about the matter, if the nine Negro children had not sought to go to the high school. True, there never is any trouble if a law is not enforced, except to those who suffer from its lack of enforcement. One might argue that a more gradual approach might have met with less opposition. This is beside the point to those for whom the issue is not the time and manner of enforcement but the *fact* of enforcement. No matter how gradual, sooner or later the moment comes when the readiness of the community to accept the law of the land is tested by the exercise of the Negro child's right to attend the public high school of his district. Once tested, the law cannot abdicate before the interference of mob violence without making a mockery of the Negro child's constitutional right to the equal protection of the laws.

Is it any different from the situation in which the Negro's right to vote is protected? The state does not actually compel him to vote, any more than it compels parents, black or white, to send their children to a public school. But if he chooses to exercise his right to vote and is prevented from doing so by others, the state would be enforcing his *right* to vote, not actually compelling him to vote against his will.

In reflecting on Little Rock, we must not lose sight of the fact that the people of Little Rock, although opposed to the desegregation decision, voted in effect twice to accept the gradual integration plan—once in election for the city officials, once for a local school board. They were not hard-core segregationists resolved to defy government by force rather than yield to an unpopular court decision. We must note also the willingness of the local officials from the mayor down to comply, as well as the peaceful illustrations of compliance in neighboring states where the governors did not predict and thereby invite violence. Something else again is the deafening silence of the two Arkansas senators. No one asked them to fight, but only to open their mouths in safety as widely as they did on vote-risky occasions of lesser moment. Nonetheless, it is false to gauge the true sentiment of a community by the behavior of a hate-crazed minority. One can easily misread the significance of the picture of white students—also a small minority—jeering at Negro children. These children are a product of segregated schools. They reflect the unreasoning authority and hysterical feeling of their homes and parents, which they may come to challenge if only they stay long enough in desegregated schools to test their prejudices against their experiences.

What happened at Little Rock is a national disgrace, but it does not tell the whole story. It does not tell the story of successful integration on a much larger scale in many other communities of the South. It does not tell the story of the great strides that have been made in reducing discrimination all over the country since 1940. It does not tell the story revealed in the most recent and most intensive poll conducted by Professor Tumin and his Princeton associates in Guilford County, North Carolina.[2] This shows that there is considerable variation in the attitude toward segregation among

[2]Melvin M. Tumin, "Readiness and Resistance to Desegregation: A Social Portrait of the Hard Core," *Social Forces,* 36:3 (March 1958), 256–265.

Southern whites. Those who, although opposed to integration, were prepared to live with the Court decision and eschew all violence numbered more than 75 per cent. The hard-core segregationists are found mainly among the poor whites, not among the individuals who have high status and vested interest in a stable community. Together with the better-educated and always less prejudiced elements, the latter are more likely to be the opinion-makers in the long haul than the hard-core intransigents. It remains to be seen how representative polls of this character are for the South as a whole, even when their reliability has been tested in local areas. But, together with the record of integration to date, it presents impressive evidence for the belief that a fairly large spread exists in the attitude of Southerners toward desegregation.

Although gradualness and patience are a sine qua non of peaceful enforcement, once the law is openly flouted it must be enforced. Worse in such situations than the risks of a firm and rapid enforcement would be the abandonment of the legal position already won or the indefinite postponement of further integration until such time as God softens the hearts of the hard-core segregationists. Beyond a certain point, the longer the delay, the more costly in tears and suffering will be the process of desegregation for everyone concerned, but especially for those who have so far endured the greatest indignities. For a basic human right is violated wherever segregation is practiced, no less in public education than in public transportation, and the denial of this right to Negroes in education seriously affects the expression of their basic political rights as well.

I conclude as I began. The same argument which opposes slavery opposes the perpetuation of the discrimination that continues in another form some of the practices of slavery. If slavery was a crime, segregation is the still open and unhealed wound it left on the body of the Negro. It bleeds afresh every time the pattern is imposed upon him. Freedom opened the doors not only to citizenship for Negroes but to personhood and brought them into the kingdom of moral ends. In a way, those who oppose legal desegregation in the name of personal freedom were answered a long time ago by Mr. Justice Harlan, grandfather of the present Justice, in his famous dissent in the civil rights cases, with which the present Court is only now catching up. Their argument, were it accepted widely, would help pin the badge of servitude upon our Negro fellow citizens in their vocations, their education, their housing, and even their use of public accommodations. Generalized, it is an argument against razing by legal measures the walls of the ghettos by which a local majority arbitrarily and unfairly keeps any minority—racial, religious, or ethnic—fenced in and deprived of the benefits of their rights as American citizens and as members of a democratic community.

The history of America has been not only a history of promises made but of promises redeemed. For a long time, American Negroes were excluded from even the promise of American life. After the Civil War, they were cruelly denied the fulfilment of the promise implied in their liberation. For the greater part of the near-century since the Emancipation Proclamation, progress was slow, uncertain, and gained through bitter struggle. Since the war against Nazism and its racial ideology, however, enormous gains have been made in integrating Negro citizens into the pattern of democratic life. Little Rock is a severe defeat in a long war which the American people are winning—a war which must be won if we are to survive as a free culture the assaults of Communist totalitarianism. The processes of education work gradually but effectively in eroding the bigotry of fanaticism. That is why the lawful spread of integrated education in South and North is our best hope for making the promises of American life come true. The tide of its advance measures the authentic growth of the democratic idea.

GUIDES FOR READING AND DISCUSSION

1. Can integration of the schools be attained through legal coercion? If the Supreme Court had not intervened, would the Southern white community have acquiesced eventually in the dominant national pattern? How much substance is there to the complaint that the Court has intervened illegitimately in a purely local custom?

2. Assume that Waring is correct in his allegations concerning the differences between Negro and white standards in the South. According to democratic principles, is it proper for the state to help maintain these differences? How could one decide the moral question of whether whites or Negroes ought to carry the main burden of effecting a change?

3. Southern whites often point out that school segregation is increasing in the North, and in some respects this is so. How does de facto segregation in the North and West differ from legally imposed segregation in the South?

SUGGESTED ADDITIONAL READINGS

Albert P. Blaustein and Clarence C. Ferguson, Jr., *Desegregation and the Law* (New Brunswick, N.J.: Rutgers University Press, 1957).

Patrick McCauley and Edward W. Ball, eds., *Southern Schools: Progress and Problems* (Nashville, Tenn.: Southern Education Reporting Service, 1959).

Hoke Norris, ed., *We Dissent* (New York: St. Martin's Press, 1962).

Melvin M. Tumin, *Segregation and Desegregation: A Digest of Current Research* (New York: Anti-Defamation League, 1957).

WHAT SHOULD AMERICA'S
IMMIGRATION POLICY BE?

The mass emigration from Europe during the nineteenth century was on a scale new in human history. Of the estimated 67 million persons who crossed an ocean from 1800 to 1950, some 60 million were Europeans, and two thirds of these went to the United States. It is reasonable to assume that—with the growth of the world's population, and with the increasing disparity between American living standards and those even of European countries, not to mention those of underdeveloped areas—this migration would have increased, had it not been blocked by immigration restrictions. No responsible voice in the United States today holds that there should be no limitation to numbers; the dispute is over how those permitted to immigrate are to be chosen.

The restrictions set up in the laws of the 1920's were imposed mainly on the basis of the aspirant immigrants' native country. Each nation was given a quota, relatively large for the countries of northwest Europe, small for those of southern and eastern Europe, and miniscule or zero for the rest of the world outside the Western Hemisphere.[1] The present basic law, the McCarran-Walter Act of 1952, retained the principle of national quotas; and this is the main reason it is opposed.

Drawn up in an attempt to codify and align all the laws pertaining to these matters, the McCarran-Walter Act was passed by Congress, vetoed by President Truman with a strong negative statement, and then passed again over his veto. Truman then appointed a commission, headed by Philip B. Perlman, to survey and evaluate immigration and naturalization policies, and to recommend changes. Its report, *Whom We Shall Welcome,* is an all-out attack on present policy; and at almost every session of Congress new bills are introduced embodying some of the Perlman Commission's recommendations. Immigration law, thus, is in flux, for the present compromise is a poor one from everyone's point of view. Those who oppose the national-quota system were dismayed by its retention in the new law, while those who support the McCarran-Walter Act have seen its fundamental principles contradicted in a number of postwar laws granting special admission to refugees from Nazi or Communist countries.

Is the national-quota system based on racist principles, and thus discriminatory? The first two selections, by Petersen and Alexander, offer opposed views on this crucial question. In the third article, Professor Jaffe suggests a rationale for a new law.

[1]For a fuller discussion, see William Petersen, *Population* (New York: Macmillan, 1960), ch. 5.

THE "SCIENTIFIC" BASIS OF
OUR IMMIGRATION POLICY

William Petersen

According to the arguments of many of its opponents, the Mc-Carran-Walter Immigration Act of 1952 is not merely bad policy but a kind of freakish accident. The late Pat McCarran, the son of a poor Irish immigrant, somehow did not develop into the champion of the people one might have expected from his background. Elected to the Senate by the smallest constituency in the United States, he became a permanent fixture there and chairman of several of its key committees. When he sponsored an immigration bill in conflict with American ideals, two thirds of the Senate passed it over President Truman's veto out of fear of the retaliation that lay in McCarran's power through his control over appropriations.

So at least one standard liberal argument runs. In another version of this devil theory, the culprit was not a single individual but the small minority of the electorate that espouses racism. Somehow, according to this view, the democratic credo has been frustrated by the activities of certain nativist and proto-fascist groups on the periphery of our society.

But the amorphous prejudice that the mass of native Americans feel, or felt, against immigrants was not sufficient in itself, even in its extremist versions, to effect the basic change in American policy that the "national-quota" system represents, and that made this latest offense to democratic ideals possible. The responsibility must be sought elsewhere. What social group made racist sentiment respectable, and thus an appropriate basis for American legislation? Who legitimized the national-quota system?

The process by which a policy becomes legitimate ordinarily begins with its explicit justification in terms of logic, science, or religion—in terms, that is, of universally accepted values. By its very nature, such a transformation can be undertaken only by those whose intellectual authority the society respects—in this case, America's leading social scientists. Before the immigration laws of the 1920's could be passed, a generation of anthropologists, economists, sociologists, and historians had labored to give the principle of the national-origins quota an underpinning that would square with the dominant American value system. By the writings of these scholars during the half century before 1920, a new, alternative system of values was established in sufficient strength to sway the thinking of the mass and, eventually, to set national policy. But if this analysis is correct, proponents of a more liberal immigration policy will not be able to get their ideas written into law until they recognize that this new, divergent value system has achieved a certain legitimation, which can be shaken only by fundamental opposition.

One of the principles established by the American and French revolutions was that—as the French constitution of 1791 put it—"the liberty

Abridged from William Petersen, "The 'Scientific' Basis of Our Immigration Policy," *Commentary* (July 1955), pp. 77–86. Copyright 1955 by the American Jewish Committee. Reprinted by permission of the publisher.

of all to move about, to remain, or to leave" is a "natural and civil right." In the United States, this doctrine was reinforced by another: This country was ordained as a haven for "the wretched refuse of your teeming shores"— to quote Emma Lazarus' words inscribed on the base of the Statue of Liberty. Against this background, the xenophobia implicit in the present immigration policy could not be established as a general norm. The Alien and Sedition Acts were repealed under Jefferson, and in the aftermath were an important reason for the eclipse of the Federalist party that had enacted them. The nativist movement of the 1830's, the Know-Nothing party of the 1850's, the American Protective Association of the early 1890's, the Ku Klux Klan reborn in 1915—all these movements, while indicating the persistence of anti-foreigner sentiment in America, also reflect the fact that it was, and is, usually limited to noisy groups of merely local importance. In the face of America's dominant value system, as exemplified in such fundamental documents as the Declaration of Independence, even the government's power to deny entry to various categories of people universally agreed to be undesirable—prostitutes, "lunatics," "idiots," "anarchists," criminals, polygamists—was established only gradually, after the Supreme Court had denied the constitutionality of a series of state laws. The first attempts at a broader restriction of immigration were formally an extension of this type of regulation. Thus, a number of states tried to check the influx of the poor by imposing a head tax on immigrants, but these attempts were frustrated by several Supreme Court decisions. Similarly, successive bills in Congress barring the admission of illiterates were vetoed by Presidents Cleveland, Taft, and Wilson. As Wilson put it, illiteracy is a measure not of a man's small innate ability but of his limited opportunities; and in Wilson's day these were not considered a legitimate reason for denying anyone his "natural" right to immigrate here.

Even the laws barring Chinese immigration were enacted without obliterating the distinction between police *regulation* (e.g., exclusion of criminals) and *restriction* based on a broader criterion (e.g., exclusion of illiterates). The argument of white Californians that the Chinese were unassimilable to American life was valid—because, as Milton Konvitz has put it, they were denied citizenship through naturalization, held ineligible to testify in any case in a court of law for or against a white person, subject to special heavy taxes, unable to vote, excluded from schools. The Chinese were made "the scapegoat for mining and real estate booms and slumps; for crime waves requiring vigilance committees; for corruption, extravagances, and profligacy in state and city government; and for the land and railway monopoly."[1]

But even though the rest of the country had almost no reliable knowledge on which to judge the question, white California could not get its way immediately. American law and institutions were based on principles that could not be used to sanction the exclusion of any ethnic group. Twice the Supreme Court threw out Chinese exclusion laws as unconstitutional; it finally accepted them because one member of that court, Justice Stephen J. Field—a native of California—was able to persuade his colleagues of

---

[1]Milton R. Konvitz, *The Alien and the Asiatic in American Law* (Ithaca, N.Y.: Cornell University Press, 1946), p. 10.

the correctness of his arguments. The Chinese were thus the first to be excluded as an ethnic group, rather than as individuals with specifically objectionable personal characteristics. So gross a violation of the national ethos, accepted finally only because it affected what was regarded as a peripheral case, set a precedent, and the interpretation of cultural differences in racial terms eventually became the keystone of American immigration policy.

Whom We Shall Welcome, the report of the Perlman Commission that President Truman appointed to review and criticize the McCarran Act, pointed out—correctly—that the national-quota system was based on anthropological theories that no reputable social scientist would now defend. America's immigration policy runs counter to the basic credo of the country, and the policy gets no support from present-day science. How then was it established? Let us retrace the steps by which a man's place of birth became the main legal criterion for judging his application to enter the United States.

At the beginning of the nineteenth century one Elkanah Watson noticed that without immigration—which had been interrupted by the wars in Europe—the population of the United States had increased by about one third during each of the two decades following the 1790 census. His calculation as to how the population of the country would continue to increase up to 1900, if that same extraordinary rate of growth were maintained, was widely accepted as a significant contribution to demography.

In 1873, Francis A. Walker, the Superintendent of the Census, wrote an article gently deriding Watson's thesis and those who took it seriously.[2] In the first place, Walker wrote, "Geometrical progression is rarely attained, and never long maintained, in human affairs. Whenever it is found, the most improbable supposition which could be formed respecting it is that it will continue." That is, the fact that the population of the United States had twice increased by about a third within ten years warranted no prediction concerning the future. That Watson's forecast had been confirmed for a while was simply a matter of luck: "Mr. Watson simply bet nine times upon the red. Five times the red won—a wonderful run of luck, certainly." The rate of population growth would have declined much earlier had not immigration happened to compensate for the decline in the birth rate:

The change [in the birth rate] came; came later even than it had been reasonable to expect. It began when the people of the United States began to leave agricultural for manufacturing pursuits; to turn from the country to the town; to live in up-and-down houses, and to follow closely the fashion of foreign life. The first effects of it were covered from the common sight by a flood of immigration unprecedented in history.

All this Walker wrote in 1873, when the number of immigrants from southern and eastern Europe totaled only 12,703.

Twenty years later, when the new immigration was approaching its peak of more than half a million a year, Walker wrote three articles in an entirely different vein.[3] Immigration, he now found, "instead of constituting

[2]Francis A. Walker, "Our Population in 1900," *Atlantic Monthly*, October 1873.
[3]Francis A. Walker, "Immigration and Degradation," *Forum*, August 1891; "Immigration," *Yale Review*, August 1892; "Restriction of Immigration," *Atlantic Monthly*, June 1896.

a net reinforcement to the population, simply resulted in a replacement of native by foreign elements." He proved this by using Watson's projection of American population growth, but now in the contrary sense. In 1840 and 1850, he pointed out, in spite of the large immigration during this period, the census count differed from Watson's projection by only a few percentage points. The threefold increase in immigration from one decade to the next, Walker asserted, had merely caused the native birth rate to decline proportionately; for the American "was unwilling himself to engage in the lowest kind of day labor with these new elements of population . . . [and] even more unwilling to bring sons and daughters into the world to enter into that competition."

The typical immigrant, in Walker's view, had changed from "the most enterprising, thrifty, alert, adventurous, and courageous of the community from which he came" to "the least thrifty and prosperous . . . [from] every foul and stagnant pool of population in Europe, which no breath of intellectual or industrial life has stirred for ages." He therefore proposed a new policy—the exclusion not only of criminals, paupers, etc., but also of hundreds of thousands of people, "the great majority of whom would be subject to no individual objections" but who came from the wrong sort of country. For Walker, the question was how to protect "the quality of American citizenship from degradation through the tumultuous access of vast throngs of ignorant and brutalized peasantry from the countries of eastern and southern Europe."

In spite of Walker's high standing as a social scientist, it is rather easy to show that his later articles were ad hoc concoctions designed to lend scientific flavor to certain ethnocentric prejudices without foundation in empirical data. The most significant fact to be noted about the three articles in which he advanced his vehement objections to immigration is their dates: 1891, 1892, and 1896—the decade after the main source of American immigration had shifted to southern and eastern Europe. His emotional reaction to the foreignness of "tumultuous" hordes of "brutalized" peasants led him to conclude that immigration had to be curbed; then, and only then, did he look for a scientific theory that would support this conclusion. Nor did he even attempt to refute his own earlier article; he simply ignored it.

In the meantime, American historians had been fashioning evidence to show that a fundamental affinity existed between the Germanic peoples and the American way of life. Edward N. Saveth has given us the story of this episode of historiography in a fascinating work, *American Historians and European Immigrants, 1875–1925* (Columbia University Press, 1948). Historians like John Fiske, John W. Burgess, and Henry Cabot Lodge, Sr. (until he became a candidate for political office) held that American institutions were derived from the ancient Teutons, either directly or through the Anglo-Saxons; and they supported this hypothesis by finding analogies, say, between the structure of the Teutonic and the New England village. Accordingly, an infusion of such "alien" and "inferior races" as the Latins or the Slavs would weaken the foundations of American society.

A revolt against this "Teutonic hypothesis" was led by Frederick Jackson Turner, who emphasized the original elements, without European precedent, of America's frontier society. But he, too, considered immigrants from southern Italy to be "of doubtful value judged from the ethical point of view," and the Jews a "people of exceptionally stunted growth and of deficient lung capacity." He wrote:

Italians, Slovaks, Poles, and other immigrants of eastern Europe, together with the Russian Jews, have struck hard blows since 1880 at the standard of comfort of the American workmen. They have made New York City a great reservoir for the pipe lines that run to the misery pools of Europe.

Though the eminent John Bach McMaster, for instance, sounded a contrary note, this was the dominant tone of American historians up to the 1920's, when the national-quota act was passed. And their theories provided a good part of that act's scholarly underpinning.

The only important counterweight to the pro-Nordic tendency of the professional historians was the ancestor veneration (what Dr. Saveth calls "filiopietism") of the amateurs with non-Anglo-Saxon names. However, "because their insecurity was greater," writes Dr. Saveth, "the jingoism of the historians of recent immigrant ancestry far exceeded the chauvinism of historians derived from the older American stock." The patent exaggerations of the writings sponsored by the Huguenot Society of America, the Scotch-Irish Society of America, the American Irish Historical Society, the American Jewish Historical Society, and the rest, probably served only to reinforce by contrast the Teutonic and frontier myths, which were at least offered with the proper professional credentials and the appropriate academic apparatus.

More important, however, in clearing the way for the national-quota act of 1924 than either Walker's or the historians' theories was the *Report* of the Senate Immigration Commission of 1907–11, headed by Senator William P. Dillingham of Vermont. The sheer mass of data contained in this document, much of it based on first-hand investigation, tended to overwhelm opposing views: no one person or organization could stand up against four years of investigation and forty-two volumes of evidence and interpretation. Even the one member of the Commission who disagreed with some of its important recommendations, Congressman William S. Bennet of New York, did no more than say so in a half-page statement: "As the report of the Commission is finally adopted within a half hour of the time when, under the law, it must be filed, there is no time for the preparation of an elaborate dissent." The Commission presented its views in abridged form in two volumes; and a more popular version by Jenks (one of the Commission's members) and Lauck long remained a standard text on immigration.[4]

One of the forty-two volumes prepared by the Senate Immigration Commission was a *Dictionary of Races or Peoples,* which—in accordance with the practice of the Bureau of Immigration—classified immigrants to the United States into forty-five ethnic groups. These groups were defined in different ways: by physical differences (for example, Negroes); by language (Germans, including German-speaking Swiss, Austrians, etc.); by nationality, even when not associated with a state (Ruthenians); by

[4]Jeremiah W. Jenks and W. Jett Lauck, *The Immigration Problem: A Study of American Immigration Conditions and Needs,* 3rd rev. ed. (New York: Funk and Wagnalls, 1913).

geography (Scandinavians, West Indians). Though the practice of the Bureau of Immigration had included Jews among the Slavs, the more "scientific" *Dictionary* pointed out that the "Hebrews" were in the Chaldaic "group" of the Semitic "stock" of the Caucasian race.

Almost all the data that the Commission collected on the different peoples of the world were broken down according to "race." Sometimes conclusions about a specific group in a specific situation were based on a very small sample, but this fact was disguised by presenting the data as percentages; thus, of the Greeks employed in the packing industry who had been in the United States for over ten years, "60 per cent" had visited abroad—or three out of a total of five persons.

The main body of the Commission's *Report* traced in great detail the immigration from southern and eastern Europe, and declared it to have a causal connection with the economic dislocations and troubles in the United States over the same period—which was marked by rapid industrialization and urbanization. In the only significant contemporary rejoinder to the *Report*, Isaac Hourwich's *Immigration and Labor* (Putnam, 1912), a wealth of data was presented to show that this causal relation was specious. Dr. Hourwich pointed out that the correlation between immigration and unemployment was negative, not positive; that the "displacement" of native American girls from the mills was motivated by their own desire for the new office jobs then opening up; and that, similarly, miners and those in other low-status jobs were "displaced" not by unemployment but by the attraction of better-paying, higher-status jobs.

Strangely enough, Dr. Hourwich was accused by the other side of having *too much* documentation behind him. In an important review of the book, Henry Pratt Fairchild (for many years a professor emeritus at New York University) criticized the documentation as "dangerous":

> It is a safe assumption that the impressive mass of material—statistical tables, charts, diagrams, and footnotes—will seem to the ordinary reader a sufficient proof of any conclusions which the author wishes to draw from them. It is because this assumption is grounded in human nature that the book is dangerous.

This was a peculiar criticism altogether, and especially when applied to a book written in answer to forty-two volumes crammed tight with tables, charts, diagrams, and footnotes, and stamped with official authority to boot.

The most direct connection between racist doctrine and American immigration policy was established by the influence of Dr. Harry H. Laughlin of the Eugenics Record Office of the Carnegie Institution of Washington. Well known as an advocate of sterilization of inmates of institutions, Laughlin became "expert eugenics agent" to the House Committee on Immigration and Naturalization. A report he submitted to it in 1922, *Expert Analysis of the Metal and the Dross in America's Melting Pot*,[5] so impressed Congress that, according to one authority, "it is often considered the principal basis of the Act of 1924."[6]

---

[5] U.S. House of Representatives, *Hearings before the Committee on Immigration and Naturalization*, November 21, 1922, 67th Congress, 3rd Session, Serial 7-C (Washington: U.S. Government Printing Office, 1923).

[6] Roy L. Garis, *Immigration Restriction: A Study of the Opposition to and Regulation of Immigration into the United States* (New York: Macmillan, 1927), pp. 239–240.

Laughlin used a so-called contingency analysis, in order to show that the distribution of social ills was not random. He compared the proportion of persons from each ethnic group in prisons, asylums, and similar institutions with the proportion of the country's total population that this ethnic group constituted. For example: in 1910, persons of Italian birth made up 1.46 per cent of the total population; if proportionally represented in the 93 insane asylums that Laughlin surveyed, they would have constituted 1.46 per cent of the total number of inmates, or 1,228. Since there were actually 1,938 Italian-born persons in these institutions, the incidence of insanity among Italians was concluded to be more than one and a half times higher than that of the general population. For social inadequacies of all types, Laughlin found that the various groups into which he divided the population were represented as follows in relation to their "expected figure" of 100:

Total native white	91.89
Of native parents	84.33
Of mixed parents	116.65
Of foreign parents	109.40
Total foreign-born white	145.75
Northwest Europe	130.42
Southern and eastern Europe	143.24

Laughlin concluded from these statistics that all foreigners are inferior, and especially those from southern and eastern Europe. He also asserted that the "first and primary factor" that had caused the different proportions of ethnic representation in institutions was "differences in constitutional susceptibility of specific races and nativity groups to certain definite types of social inadequacy." That is to say, such "degeneracies" as "criminality" are "inherited in the blood." The implications of such an analysis for policy were clear:

There has, thus far, been no suggestion in our laws of any requirement except personal value in our sorting of would-be immigrants. [However,] the surest biological principle . . . to direct the future of America along safe and sound racial channels is to control the hereditary quality of the immigration stream.

The flaws in this "expert analysis" were numerous and fundamental. The notion that "criminality" and most other social inadequacies are hereditary was no longer generally accepted even in the 1920's, so unfounded had it been shown to be. Today only crackpots dare repeat it.

Strangely enough, Laughlin's own data on feeble-mindedness (one of the few such inadequacies that *may* be inherited) refute his general conclusion. Only two foreign groups showed a ratio of feeble-mindedness higher than 100—Serbians, with *two* cases, and Australians, with *three* cases. The foreign-born as a group showed a ratio for feeble-mindedness of only 31.6; and those from southern and eastern Europe, one of 33. In contrast, native whites as a group were above 100, as also the subgroup formed by those with native parents.

Moreover, even if one should grant that "criminality" is inherited, it does not follow that its heredity can be traced through such vague and ambiguous groups as Laughlin's "races." In general, he used the classification of "races" recommended in the Senate Commission's *Report,* but he went beyond even its grossly unscientific methods—breaking down, for example, native white Americans into four subgroups: "Mountain White,"

"American Yankee," "American Southerner," and "Middle-West American." That these classifications should have been accepted as "races or nativity groups," rather than as the cultural groups they patently were, indicates an extraordinary will on the part of the Congressmen to accept Laughlin's main point.

His data were in any case incomplete and statistically biased. He had returns from only 445 of the 657 state and federal institutions that were relevant to his analysis, and he made no allowance for the bias that this incomplete sample introduced. He did not correct for the differences in age structure and sex ratio of the several groups, although immigrants tended to be concentrated in the middle male age-group, which in every society has the highest incidence of many social ills.

Finally, Laughlin ignored the differences in the availability of institutional care in the various sections of the country. Institutions were relatively scarce in the immigrant-free South, for instance, while immigrants were concentrated in Northern cities, where social care was much more adequate. As Antonio Stella has demonstrated, by Laughlin's method of analysis Negroes prove to be far less afflicted with "social inadequacies" than do whites.[7] Feeble-mindedness is eight times more prevalent among native whites than among Negroes; epilepsy, nearly ten times; blindness, twenty-four times; tuberculosis, two and a half times; insanity, one and a half times; deafness, one and a half times; physical deformity, eight times; dependency, four times. In only one social ill, crime, is the quota fulfillment of Negroes higher than that of native whites, for the one institution with which the Southern Negro is adequately supplied is—prisons.

Laughlin submitted his report in 1922, and two years later the policy he recommended was enacted into permanent law. It is true, as many have pointed out, that the immigration laws of the 1920's were passed during the period of xenophobia and labor unrest following World War I. But it is not true—as this observation is meant to imply—that these laws, like the Palmer raids, were merely another manifestation of temporary hysteria. Their enactment came as the culmination of decades of effort, and on the basis of principles that had thus become legitimized.

Why was it that American social scientists of the pre-1914 period generally supported a national-quota system and the anthropological theories implicit in it? Without attempting a definitive answer to so large a question, one can suggest three probably relevant factors.

(1) The main source of immigration to the United States shifted from northwest Europe to southern and eastern Europe at about the same time that the American economy underwent a fundamental transformation. The German or Swedish peasant who immigrated during the years right after the Civil War took advantage of the Homestead Act and became an American farmer; but when the Italian or Polish peasant arrived this frontier was closed, and burgeoning American industry had begun to call for more and more unskilled labor. The new immigrants, therefore, had simultaneously to undergo two processes of adjustment: from their native cultures to the American one, and from a rural to an urban way of life—the second

---

[7]Antonio Stella, *Some Aspects of Italian Immigration to the United States* (New York: Putnam, 1924), pp. 108–109.

adaptation being much the more difficult one. The social ills attributed to the innate inadequacies of the new immigrants were the result basically of the extremely rapid development of an industrial society, but it was the new immigrants who became the most conspicuous casualties of the process. Not only did city slums (for example) develop much faster after large numbers of Poles (for example) began to arrive, but it was the Poles who lived in the slums and thus developed the characteristics typical of slum residents. Given the level of their scientific disciplines at that time, social scientists drew the "obvious" conclusion that Poles had caused slums.

(2) Such a conclusion, moreover, was in line with the general climate of opinion of the period. The Darwinian theory, having conquered biology, was advancing into the social sciences: this was the heyday of Social Darwinism and physical anthropology. Man had finally come to be viewed as part of nature, and his physical group characteristics—such as pigmentation and cerebral index—acquired a new significance by analogy with the characteristics differentiating other animal and plant species and varieties. While a racist analysis at that time often had the same nastiness that it has today, as in the writings of Madison Grant and Lothrop Stoddard, sometimes it also became, by its link with evolutionary theory and the dispassionate application of the latter to human origins, the expression of a kind of naive, science-oriented progressivism. We contemporaries of Adolf Hitler have been taught that false anthropological theories can have horrible consequences, but it would be anachronistic to expect people living before 1914 to have either our greater knowledge on this matter or our far greater sensitivity to the implications.

(3) Finally, virtually all the men who legitimized the national-origins system were themselves of Anglo-Saxon background. The new immigrants, just because they had come to this country only recently, had not yet produced their share of professors or statesmen. The men who wrote the important works on immigration and race were named Walker, Fiske, Burgess, Lodge, Turner, Dillingham, Fairchild, Hall, Commons, Ross, Garis, and so on; while the few who answered their arguments were named, for example, Hourwich and Stella—and, as an exception to the rule, Willcox. With respect to any one individual, such a distinction would be invidious, but the predominantly Anglo-Saxon family background and German intellectual tradition of the American scholarly community as a whole in that period certainly had some influence on the theories it evolved.

None of these three points holds today. We now know that the scholarly basis on which the national-origins quotas rest was itself compounded out of ignorance and prejudice. Why, then, though aware that racist theory is both false and gravely dangerous to our democratic system, do we retain a law deriving from that theory? In broadest terms, it is because the national-quotas system has acquired an independent legitimation: during the thirty years that it has been part of the law of the land it has established a certain tradition, so that the burden of proof now lies with those who advocate a different immigration policy. The opponents of the national-quota system have two enormously powerful weapons—our present knowledge concerning group differences and the continued pertinence of the basic American credo; but very often these weapons have not been used effectively.

A DEFENSE OF THE
McCARRAN-WALTER ACT

Robert C. Alexander

There are two fundamental principles of basic policy from which to choose in controlling immigration into any country. The first is that every alien shall be admitted unless there is some law or other authority which, in an individual case, requires that he be excluded. The second is that no alien shall be admitted unless there is some law or other authority which permits such entry. As these two basic concepts are almost diametrically opposed, it follows that a nation may adopt either, but not both, in determining its immigration policy and formulating its system of control.

The United States has always followed the first principle, while most of the other countries of the world have predicated their control of immigration on the second. This, of course, does not mean that aliens have an inherent or abstract legal right to enter the United States, as immigration into any country is only a privilege. But, once an alien is found by our administrative authorities to be without disqualification for admission, a definite legal right to enter is acquired, and he cannot be excluded by whim or caprice. Thus, under the due-process clause in the Fifth Amendment to the Constitution, our courts are available, through the writ of habeas corpus, to aliens who are detained at a port of entry; foreign countries, on the other hand, generally deny such access to their courts, there being no analogous legal right to be adjudicated.

The immigration laws of the United States were enacted by Congress over a period of many years without any appreciable over-all planning, particularly concerning the ethnic composition of our population. In fact, it may be said that our immigration laws "just grew," like Topsy or the streets of Boston. Our early history shows that we welcomed all immigrants from all sources. Only in later years were restrictions—first, qualitative in nature, and finally, quantitative in limitation and procedural in character— imposed upon immigration. The sum total of all restrictions to date, however, has not changed the fundamental policy of the United States, which still permits any alien to come to this country from any part of the world at any time, unless some provision of our law, in his individual case, precludes migration. If the restriction is qualitative, it may bar the alien indefinitely; but if it is merely quantitative or procedural, it will only delay his migration.

Our immigration laws today are incorporated, with very few exceptions, in the Immigration and Nationality Act of 1952, which is also known as the McCarran-Walter Act. This statute was not hastily drawn. Nearly five

Abridged from Robert C. Alexander, "A Defense of the McCarran-Walter Act," reprinted from a symposium, *Immigration* (*Law and Contemporary Problems*, 21:2 [Spring 1956], 382–400), by permission from *Law and Contemporary Problems*, published by the Duke University School of Law, Durham, N.C. Copyright, 1956, by Duke University. Mr. Alexander has had a number of government-service positions, and serves as a government consultant on immigration matters.

years of comprehensive study[1] and painstaking drafting were required to produce it. Public hearings were held on the early drafts of the bills while the legislation was pending in Congress, and the bills were redrafted and reintroduced several times before Congress enacted H. R. 5678, Congressman Walter's second draft bill, with amendments agreeable to the Senate and the House of Representatives. President Truman returned the bill to the House of Representatives on June 25, 1952, with a veto message; but on June 26, 1952, the House of Representatives voted, 278 to 113, to sustain the bill, which became a law on June 27, 1952, when the Senate voted, 57 to 26, to override the veto. The act became fully effective on December 24, 1952.

The act is primarily a compilation and codification of our previous laws on immigration, deportation, nationality, and naturalization, and is only secondarily a very limited revision of these laws. Some of its severest critics privately concede that it is a vast improvement over the old laws because of its codification features alone, and they concur in many of its revisionary clauses. Their principal objection to it seems only to be that it does not go quite as far as they would wish in substantively revising some of the old laws. Nevertheless, these critics are notably silent today regarding the act's admittedly desirable features, preferring to concentrate their attention and attacks on the few provisions that they consider unsatisfactory. This may tend to create in the public mind the erroneous impression that they are opposed to the entire act; but the fact is that they have incorporated many of its improvements and prescient provisions in the multitude of "dream" bills, many of them identical, with which they have flooded Congress. A defense of the act, accordingly, does not require a comprehensive and exhaustive review of its numerous provisions, many of which are acceptable to even its most uncompromising critics. Instead, a discussion of the few provisions under attack and the merit, or lack of it, in the complaints would appear to be sufficient.

Most of the criticism of the McCarran-Walter Act seems to be directed at the national-origins system it employs for the allocation of annual immigration quotas. A myth has been propagated by some critics that this system is based upon a super-race theory and that it was intended to discriminate against peoples who were considered to be racially or otherwise inferior—more specifically, the southern European, southeastern European, and Asian countries, to which only small quotas have been allocated. If, however, the fact that some countries have smaller quotas than others constitutes discrimination, then any quota system would be discriminatory, unless all countries were allocated equal quotas—an expedient that no one has yet advocated.

The national-origins quota system was originally authorized in the Act of May 6, 1924. It was perpetuated with only a slight revision in the new act, having established its basic merit through its many years of operation. Under the system as originally enacted, the quota countries of the world were allocated portions of a theoretical annual world quota of 150,000, subject to a minimum-quota limitation of 100, below which the quota of no country could fall. This minimum-quota provision raised the actual total of the world's quotas to approximately 154,000. Each quota country,

[1]See S. Rep. No. 1515, 81st Cong., 1st Sess. (1951).

therefore, received a minimum quota of 100 or a larger portion of the theoretical world quota in precise proportion to its contribution of immigrants and their descendants to the United States.

The McCarran-Walter Act made a minor, but perhaps significant, change in the method of computing quotas. It abandoned the theoretical world quota and substituted a uniform ratio of one sixth of one per cent of the number of people in each of our foreign national-origins groups as the new mathematical basis for computing each national-origins quota. This has resulted in a slight reduction of some quotas, but the addition of several new quotas for the Asian peoples, whom the McCarran-Walter Act made eligible, for the first time, for quota immigration and naturalization in the United States, has brought the total of the world's quotas back to approximately 154,000.

The national-origins quota system is like a mirror held up before the American people. As our various foreign origins are determined upon a basis of nationality and reflected in the mirror, the quotas of the countries of our origin are proportioned. The basic policy of the system is to grant to each group its fair share—no more and no less—of the permissible volume of annual quota immigration. Any other distribution of the quotas would, indeed, be discriminatory. One who objects to such an equitable distribution of immigration quotas must object to the ethnic composition of our population and must wish to alter it in favor of some particular group or groups. Thus, for example, in demanding a proportionately larger quota for Italy, one would be advocating that we become proportionately more Italian than we are. Italians would quite naturally favor this, but do the people in all of our other national-origins groups, which constitute the majority, also favor it? Without necessarily entertaining the slightest disregard or lack of friendship and admiration for the Italian people, the majority would naturally favor immigrants of their own national origins.

In a democracy like the United States, the majority prevails, without oppression of minorities. Those who believe in minority rule, or in the tail-wagging-the-dog policies of such a system, must have little faith in our institutions or in our American way of life. Perhaps this explains one of the reasons why the Communist Party in the United States has organized a drive to arouse opposition to the McCarran-Walter Act. In a recent article,[2] Mr. J. B. Matthews, a recognized authority on Communist subversive activity, refers to the questioning of a witness by the Senate Subcommittee on Internal Security, on June 23, 1954, regarding the Communist origin of the now-exposed National Committee to Repeal the McCarran Acts. He states that the witness, who invoked the Fifth Amendment of our Constitution in refusing to answer questions concerning the Communist origin of the NCRMA, was the Communist Party's top commissar in the field of immigration. This does not mean, of course, that all who criticize the McCarran-Walter Act are Communists, or even Communist sympathizers, but it should cause patriotic Americans who have no political axe to grind to ponder before they join any movement to attack the law.

[2] *American Mercury*, October 1955, p. 51.

Some foreign countries, notably those with large quotas, are not filling their annual allotments. On the other hand, some of the smaller quotas of other countries are not only filled annually, but are oversubscribed for many years to come by thousands of prospective immigrants registered on quota waiting lists at American consular offices abroad. These prospective immigrants and their agents, advocates, or sympathizers in the United States look covetously upon the unfilled portions of the quotas of other countries and contend that the national-origins quota system has failed, has not accomplished its purpose, and is out of balance because we are not actually receiving immigrants annually in the precise proportions envisaged under it. What they really object to is the fact that the McCarran-Walter Act has not changed the provisions of the old laws requiring a strict compartmentalization of the quotas.

An immigration quota is not, of course, a guarantee that the United States will actually receive any specific number of immigrants in any year from any quota country. A quota is a ceiling—not a floor—on the annual volume of immigrants chargeable to a quota country. If the overflow of immigrants from oversubscribed quotas were permitted to utilize the unfilled portions of undersubscribed quotas, this would not bring the national-origins system into proportionate balance, but, on the contrary, would further unbalance it. However, the advocates of such use of the unused portions of quotas are probably not really interested in matters of balance anyway.

The fact is that the national-origins system has not failed. Congress did not attempt to freeze or stabilize the ethnic composition of our people at the 1920 census level. Such an attempt would have required permanent fixation not only of permissible immigration, but also of actual immigration each year, as well as a similar control over the emigration and the birth and mortality rates of each national-origins group—a ridiculous undertaking for anyone to attribute to the national legislature. If, indeed, it had been the intention of Congress even to guarantee that we would actually receive annual immigration in a certain proportionate volume, the largest quota would have been designated as the "key quota," and all other quotas would have been usable only concurrently and at the same proportionate rate of utilization as the "key quota."

The use of the unfilled portions of quotas which some critics advocate would necessitate the creation of a "jackpot" into which the unfilled portions of all quotas would be deposited, to be withdrawn by immigrants chargeable to oversubscribed quotas. "Jackpot bills" have been introduced in Congress year after year, but substantial support has never been mustered for such a diversion of unused quota numbers. Even the proponents do not agree among themselves on a method of dividing the "jackpot." And the executive branch of the government historically has taken the position that if Congress should desire to make use of the unfilled portions of quotas under a "jackpot" plan, a statutory method of dividing the "jackpot" should be enacted, as it would be an invidious task, indeed, for any administrative officer to attempt such distribution.

On the question of administrative feasibility, it should be noted that the extent to which any quota is unfilled cannot be determined until the end of the quota year, when it would obviously be too late to use the unfilled portion in that year. Consequently, if any of the unused portions of quotas are to be utilized, it would seem to be administratively necessary that this be done in a subsequent year or years. If, during such year or years, any portion of the accumulated "jackpot" were unused, this might be added to the currently unfilled portions of the quotas for use in a subsequent year or years, and the snow-balling process that would develop could create an administrative monstrosity that no rational executive officer would be willing to attempt to manage. The budgetary and personnel planning for such a program alone would require a crystal ball of omniscient prophetic vision to determine when and where the shifting and fluctuating demand for operating funds and personnel would be required from month to month, to say nothing of day to day.

These are some of the reasons why every Congress has frowned upon the unused-quota "jackpot bills" and has favored the enactment of special legislation from time to time, along the lines of the Displaced Persons Act of 1948, as amended, and the Refugee Relief Act of 1953.

Some critics advocate the complete abandonment of the national-origins quota system and the institution of an entirely new system. As charges have been made that the small-quota countries are objects of discrimination, it seems obvious that if such charges are to be obviated, no country should be given a quota smaller than that of any other country—but no one seems to advocate such a system of numerically equal quotas for all countries of the world. Perhaps the critics desire only to discriminate against other countries, on the theory that the national-origins system discriminates against the wrong ones. In any event, they are stuck with their own label of discrimination and can only remove it by advocating a system of numerically equal quotas for all countries.

It would, of course, be possible to fix each country's quota in proportion to its population among all other foreign countries, and, thus, the countries with the larger populations would be allocated the larger quotas. Aside from a possible recurrence of the charges of discrimination heard today, however, such a system would mean that the United States had relinquished its control over the quotas and surrendered them to the shifting tides and vicissitudes of foreign populations. It would also mean that the United States had, at last, been inveigled into undertaking, unwisely, the Herculean task of draining off the excess populations of some foreign countries without having within its power any means of preventing a continuous state of overpopulation in those countries. While the United States may bear some share of responsibility for the dislocation of populations resulting from conditions growing out of World War II, in which we were involved, in no sense can it be held responsible for the overpopulation of foreign countries resulting from high birth rates; and no foreseeable Congress is likely to enact any laws predicated upon the assumption of such responsibility.

It would also be possible to apportion each country's quota in accordance with the proportionate demand in that country to the world demand for the privilege of immigrating into the United States. Here again, however, the United States would be surrendering its control over the quotas in favor of foreign migratory pressures and perhaps a sky-rocketing demand, real or fictitious, in each foreign country. Even if we could develop means of verifying the demand in each country, the basic defects of such a system would remain.

Some critics also urge that we play the role of the Good Samaritan and use our immigration quotas to relieve the excess-population problems of foreign countries. Notwithstanding the fact that we are spending billions of dollars to provide aid and relief in such countries, they would have us bring the objects of our charity to this country. But what did the Good Samaritan do? According to the Biblical story, as told by Jesus to St. Luke, a man had gone from Jerusalem to Jericho, where he fell among thieves, who stripped him of his raiment, wounded him, and departed, leaving him half-dead on a roadside. A priest and a Levite saw him there, but they passed him by, on the other side of the road. Then came the Good Samaritan. But let St. Luke finish the story in his own words:

But a certain Samaritan, as he journeyed, came where he was; and when he saw him, he had compassion on him,
And went to him, and bound up his wounds, pouring in oil and wine, and set him on his beast, and brought him to an inn, and took care of him.
And on the morrow when he departed, he took out two pence, and gave them to the host, and said unto him; and whatsoever thou spendest more, when I come again, I will repay thee [10:33–35].

It should be noted that St. Luke does not say the Good Samaritan took the poor man home with him, but rather "brought him to an inn." With respect to the aid and relief rendered by the Good Samaritan, the taxpayers of the United States are matching it, dollar for dollar, in foreign aid today. Moreover, we have welcomed to this country 237,790 immigrants, quota and nonquota, in the year 1955, and some countries did not use one third of their quotas.

On September 4, 1952, President Truman created, by an Executive Order, a Commission on Immigration and Naturalization, which purported to make, in less than four months, a study of our immigration, deportation, nationality, and naturalization laws and policies, filing its report on January 1, 1953.[3] As the Commission consumed the first two months of its life in becoming organized and holding hearings of testimony of witnesses largely comprising persons who were opposed to our immigration laws, and as most of the fourth (last) month was used in writing its report, it had scarcely more than the intervening third month left for devotion to its primary task, which was to make a study of the laws and policies developed during our entire history.

In utter disregard of the current polls of public opinion, reflected in Congress by the recent enactment of the McCarran-Walter Act over the veto of President Truman, this Commission filed a report which, with some amplification, followed the pattern of his veto message. It recommended that the national-origins quota system, which had just won a notable victory over the same arguments advanced in Congress, be abolished in its entirety. However, the Commission was unable to devise a substitute system and contented itself with a recommendation that another commission, of permanent character, be created to supersede the Secretary of State and the

[3]President's Commission on Immigration and Naturalization, *Whom We Shall Welcome* (Washington, D.C.: U.S. Government Printing Office, 1953).

Attorney General in the administration of our immigration laws and to make a triennial distribution of the authorized annual volume of quota immigration, which would be called a blanket quota. Such distribution, the Commission said, should be made without regard to national origin, race, creed, or color, but bearing in mind such factors as asylum, reunion of families, needs in the United States, general immigration, and "needs in the free world."[4]

While the precise meaning of some of the terms suggested is not clear, such as the distinction between race and color in an ethnological or anthropological sense, and whether needs in the United States would be embraced within the term "needs in the free world" or whether the United States was not regarded by the Commission as a part of the free world, the Commission apparently believed that such ambiguities could be resolved by the proposed new commission. The Commission, however, succeeded in arousing less public sentiment against the McCarran-Walter Act than against its own report.

It seems fairly certain that unless every foreign country's quota is computed upon the basis of a public, definite, and identical mathematical formula, so that all countries may know in advance what their quotas, as well as the quotas of other countries, will be from year to year, the government of the United States may be deluged with both foreign and domestic complaints and charges of graft, corruption, undue influence, national bias or prejudice, special favoritism, and perhaps even national animosity. The flood of diplomatic protests alone could seriously interfere with the normal conduct of our foreign relations. Moreover, the internal strife which could be created by some justifiably dissatisfied foreign national-origins groups in the United States could well disrupt our national unity, and, thus, one of the prime objectives of the Kremlin for many years would, at last, be accomplished.

The McCarran-Walter Act established a limitation upon the use by colonial possessions of the quotas of their governing countries. No colony may now use more than 100 quota numbers annually from the quota of its governing country. Under the old law, there was no limitation, for example, upon the use of the British quota of 65,361 annually by eligible immigrants from the British colonial possessions, which include the Bahamas, Barbados, British Guiana, British Honduras, Cyprus, Hong Kong, Jamaica, the Leeward Islands, Malta, Trinidad, and the Windward Islands, each of which now has a subquota of 100 annually. The self-governing countries of the British Commonwealth of Nations, such as Australia, India, and New Zealand, and such independent countries as Egypt, Iran, Israel, and the Philippines were already limited by the old law to minimum quotas of 100 annually. Under the McCarran-Walter Act, no colonial possession has access to a larger quota than that of any independent country of the world. The mere statement of this fact indicates the inherent equities in it, although it has been subjected to considerable attack.

Critics contend that the establishment of subquotas constituted an act of racial discrimination against the people of the British Crown Colony of Jamaica, which no longer has unlimited access to the annual British quota

[4]*Ibid.*, pp. 263–264.

of 65,361. However, a similar charge has not been made with respect to the other British colonies, such as Cyprus and Malta, to which the sub-quota system also applies. Furthermore, the facts are that the British national-origins group among our people reflected in the national-origins mirror in 1920 was not substantially of British colonial origin, but rather consisted largely of people who originated in the British Isles. The sub-quotas now available to the British colonies total 1,100 annually and are not inequitable when viewed in the proper light of the proportionate reflection of British colonials in our national-origins mirror. The fact is that Congress has dealt generously with the colonial possessions of all countries. If they had been allotted subquotas in true proportion to their actual reflection in the national-origins mirror, they would not have been entitled to a quota of even 100 immigrants annually.

The McCarran-Walter Act established quotas for the peoples of all Asian countries and, for the first time in our history, authorized quota immigration and naturalization in the United States for *all* aliens of Asian birth or Asian ancestry. The act abolished the Asiatic barred zone specified in the Act of February 5, 1917, which barred from immigration into the United States the indigenous natives thereof, with few exceptions. The act created a new Asia-Pacific triangle of eligibility for quota immigrants born therein or belonging to races indigenous thereto. The Asia-Pacific triangle itself was allotted a quota of 100 annually, which is now available to quota immigrants of Asian ancestry not properly chargeable to the quota of any of the twenty-one countries within the triangle, each of which has a quota of at least 100.

Under the national-origins system, the countries of Asia were in a position similar to that of many colonies of European countries with respect to the computation of their quotas. If they had been allocated quotas in true proportion to their reflection in our national-origins mirror, some of them might not have been entitled to a quota of even one full number annually and, thus, could have sent us only one immigrant at intervals of several years. However, Congress was again generous in dealing with Asians under the McCarran-Walter Act by taking into consideration the fact that most of the peoples of Asia had been denied the privilege of quota immigration and naturalization in the United States throughout our previous history and, consequently, could not be expected to make a large reflection in our national-origins mirror. They were, therefore, exempted from the necessity of making any reflection at all.

As a counterbalance to a possibly disproportionate volume of Asian immigration, however, Congress provided that *quota* immigrants attributable by birth or *ancestry* to one or more countries in the triangle should generally be charged to the quota of a country within the triangle, or to the quota of the triangle. The act has been criticized, accordingly, because it did not grant to individuals of Asian ancestry the privilege of migrating under the quotas of European countries if they were born in such countries, or grant them nonquota status if they were natives of the independent countries of the western hemisphere. However, it was considered that if the thousands of people of Asian ancestry born in the quota countries of Europe were given access to such quotas, and if the 600,000 people of Asian ancestry born in the nonquota countries of the western hemisphere were granted the privilege of immigrating into the United States without numerical limitation, too drastic a change could result in the ethnic composition of the population of the United States, because the peoples of Asia would be deriving immigration privileges not only in great disproportion to their largest possible reflection in the national-origins mirror, but in even greater disproportion to the privileges granted any other of our foreign national-origins groups.

Perhaps there will always be two schools of extremist thought in the United States on the subject of immigration. However, between the extremely restrictionist view, which would bar all aliens, and the opposite, but equally extreme, anti-restrictionist philosophy, which would abolish all restrictions, there must be a large middle ground upon which unprejudiced and patriotic citizens may stand. In keeping our doors ajar to worthy aliens and preventing the unworthy from approaching them, we are not only holding aloft the beacon light of liberty and refuge for the unjustly oppressed, but, by the God-given right of our fathers who came here before us and built a nation with freedom and justice for all, we shall preserve it.

THE PHILOSOPHY OF A
NEW IMMIGRATION LAW

Louis L. Jaffe

The battle over immigration policy has been waged in terms which conceal the true nature of the difficulty. To the opponents of the McCarran-Walter Act, that law is the child of iniquitous prejudice and hysterical fear. It is defended as a bulwark against racial deterioration and political subversion. The writer takes his stand with those who denounce the law. Its quota provisions were born in racial prejudice. They give needless offense to many of our citizens and to the people of other countries; they bedevil the conduct of our foreign relations and add nothing to our public welfare. The provisions dealing with the qualifications of particular immigrants and with the deportation of aliens already here are likewise marred by cruelties which reflect a combination of elements: hysterical responses to current dangers, xenophobia, and the downright callousness of the unimaginative. But the writer is inclined to believe that the difficulty lies even deeper than these conflicts of attitude and mood. It is the basic difficulty of defining a positive role for immigration sufficiently persuasive to win popular support. Without a positive philosophy, without a clearly held view of the function of immigration, the ever present impulses of fear and hate rush into the vacuum.

Abridged from Louis L. Jaffe, "The Philosophy of a New Immigration Law," reprinted from a symposium, *Immigration* (*Law and Contemporary Problems*, 21:2 [Spring 1956], 358–375), by permission from *Law and Contemporary Problems*, published by the Duke University School of Law, Durham, N.C. Copyright, 1956, by Duke University; Louis Jaffe, Byrne Professor of Administrative Law at Harvard University, is the author of books and articles on administrative law.

The economic functions of immigration are today marginal and relatively unimportant, and almost any conceivable immigration policy likely to be adopted must be justified in non-economic terms. This would appear to represent a complete reversal of the earlier policy, the purpose of which was almost entirely economic, the other alleged functions being essentially by-products. It is this radical reversal that creates the dilemma.

We must, then, explore and evaluate potential functions of a non-economic character. The most immediate and obvious, because already expressed in the law, is family reunification. This satisfies a need of persons already in the country, some of them citizens, some of them resident aliens. Since the free admission of spouses and children of citizens is not restricted, an American citizen may without impediment marry a noncitizen abroad. These nonquota provisions should be extended to adopted children and parents of citizens. Such persons today receive a preference within quotas, but where the quota is small or oversubscribed, the entry may be too long delayed. Somewhat related to family reunification is the motif of racial reunification. Racial groups whose ties with the homeland are still fresh may, for one reason or another, desire new immigration. This may proceed from a sympathy for those who are impoverished or frustrated, or from the closely related emotion of guilt: guilt of being well situated while one's brethren are in want or distress. It may be supposed that, as time passes, this identification will diminish, particularly if the new infusions are relatively small. But racial consciousness has been somewhat more persistent than might have been expected.

Then, there is the much broader conception: that it is the destiny of America to be a haven for all strains of the human race. This is a sentiment which is woven from many strands. First is the idea that our own specific character depends on it; our genius, conceived as the product of racial amalgam, must be kept fresh. It is doubtful that this particular version is deeply felt by many people. And as immigration now stands, the totals involved are too small to be racially significant. A closely related and more valid idea is that if our culture is to remain vital and progressive it will do well to attract new and varied intelligence. This effect can be achieved by relatively small numbers well within present limitations, provided, of course, that space is left open for genius. This must be achieved by administrative discretion, though administrative discretion is not notably receptive to genius, which is apt to be queer and radical. The present law allows the Attorney General to give preference to skills which are "urgently needed" and which will be "substantially beneficial" to our "cultural interests." This, undoubtedly, gives very broad discretion, but the Attorney General should not be required, at least in connection with cultural interest, to certify urgent need.

This notion of the destiny of America is also linked to the Christian concept of brotherhood. There are those—they must be very few—who believe that the Christian ethic condemns all barriers. A larger number, which, however, probably falls far short of a majority, though it does not accept the standard as absolute, does admit the claim of brotherhood. In its view, a nation, to be a significant and valuable organism and to perform its function, must maintain its coherence. This group would, thus, not deny that a nation may protect itself from unlimited immigration. It would be argued that, in the end, the world would be no better off and, indeed, perhaps worse. The vast forces working toward overpopulation would be in no way alleviated or mitigated by wholesale migration to the less heavily settled areas; indeed, they would be given further encouragement. America might then become just one more overpopulated area and robbed of her capacity to make any special or significant contribution. But America, it would be argued, should, at the same time, proclaim its adherence to the concept of brotherhood by admitting some members of every race on a nondiscriminatory basis. This would serve as a symbolic recognition of the ideal.

This concept calls for a standing law under which, each year, there is admitted some given number of immigrants. Obviously, this function points to no particular number. It should not be ridiculously small. Should it be divided into national-origin quotas? There are those who feel that any quota based on national origin is invidious, since it recognizes the fact of race, or at the least must be based on some arbitrary ratio. It would appear, however, that, abstractly considered, a national-origins system would not, ipso facto, give offense if the scheme were not based on a concept or intention to discriminate. But it seems fairly certain that any scheme that would be accepted by Congress would discriminate at least against the Orientals. It is also arguable that race should be recognized in the sense that the people of each nation should receive a "fair" opportunity to come here. This might be based on their relative populations. The fact is, however, that "overpopulation" with its consequent distress is much more severe in some countries, and it might be thought that a "fair" formula should recognize it. One suggestion is first-come-first-served, with a provision that no nation should have more than a certain percentage of the whole.[1] This would appear to give everyone an equal opportunity and to avoid the difficulties of formulating a national-quota system.

The refugee, particularly from political and religious persecution, and, in a lesser degree, from national calamity, makes the most intense appeal to the emotions of brotherhood; and the most significant relaxations of our standing policy have been the two acts designed to provide a haven for European refugees. The first of these acts, the Displaced Persons Act of 1948, provided for the admission of 400,000 persons displaced by war and revolution. As a result, in the years 1950, 1951, and 1952, for example, the total immigration from quota countries was 197,460, 156,547, and 194,247 respectively. The act represented a substantial departure from the existing national-origins quota provisions. Thus, under it, there have been admitted, in the four years in which it operated (1948–52), for example, 132,000 Poles (regular quota 6,400) and 33,000 Yugoslavs (regular quota 933). The statute required that one half of the regular annual quota be "mortgaged" until the overage should be discharged,[2] but despite this un-

---

[1] This is the proposal of the Lehman bill, which set a limit of 10 per cent of the annual total on immigration from any country. This bill is the most carefully developed and thought-through substitute for the present quota provisions. The writer of this article was a member of the drafting group which developed the bill. He generally concurs with its proposals, but with possible differences in emphasis and commitment on certain points. What he says in this article does not necessarily represent the consensus of the group or the thought of any other member of the group. The bill was last introduced in the 84th Congress, First Session, as S.1206.

[2] This provision was abandoned and the existent mortgages were canceled in 1957 [Eds.].

fortunate device, the immediate operation of the act worked a substantial variation from the particular quotas involved.

The Refugee Relief Act of 1953 included a quota for Italians, Greeks, and Dutch (irrespective of their "refugee" character) who were within the family-preference quotas of the standing act, and the 1954 amendment provided that the "refugee" and family preference quotas are to be interchangeable. This would permit, for example, 60,000 Italians to enter within the two and one half years of the act as compared with the regular annual quota of 5,600, though there may be a question whether there are 60,000 Italians who are within the preference class. The act, thus, goes a little way toward recognizing the special population problems of these three countries. Indeed, it is doubtful that the "refugee" concept was relevant to the Italian, Dutch, and Greek situation in the first place. There is evidence that those responsible for the legislation did not intend it to be workable, but were making a rather empty gesture in the direction of these three countries which had specific overpopulation problems and, in the case of at least one or two of them, important lobbies in this country. Is it, then, a function of immigration to relieve world overpopulation? Clearly, it cannot be in any general sense. That would be to return to the policy of unlimited immigration. But it is argued that in Italy, for example, a net decline in the birth rate is in sight, and temporary relief may ease its immediate problems. Is it the theory, then, that an immediate problem of this sort is comparable to the refugee problem and makes a special appeal to the claims of brotherhood? Perhaps; but it would be more frank to recognize that we have now arrived at one more and perhaps one of the most important functions of immigration policy, namely as an instrument of foreign policy.

The greatest failure of the McCarran-Walter Act was its failure to recognize the foreign-policy function of immigration. It is true that, in its broad outlines, the act merely codified the policy of 1924. But it is the first fact of our national life that our world position has, since then, changed radically. Even the 1924 Act, by offending the Japanese, made its contribution to the deterioration of our foreign relations. There is a consensus that, for our national welfare and security, we need the friendship and cooperation of other nations. Since we seek to lead under the banner of Democracy and Christian Brotherhood, our immigration policy should manifest a belief in those ideals. Therefore, even the many who do not believe in them or who do not, on balance, see their necessary application to immigration (and this is, perhaps, a substantial majority) can be led, perhaps, to see their expediency. It is true that Canada and Australia have, in the past, pursued discriminatory policies and may not have, thus, suffered in world estimation. But we are more vulnerable, perhaps because our professions of virtue are more strident, perhaps because our power is greater, perhaps because we demand more insistently that others follow our leadership. In any case, our present quota system only serves to irritate. Indeed, as the refugee-relief bills show, it does not even represent our actual policy.

The Italian, Greek, and Dutch clauses of the Refugee Relief Act are a somewhat special expression, however, of our foreign policy. These are, in a sense, discriminatory. There are other overpopulated areas (all of Asia, for example) to which we would not, I think, extend such relief. It is said—

and with much truth—that the overpopulation problem in these European countries may be within view of solution so that our aid may hasten it, whereas this is not true of Asia. But this is not, I would suppose, the whole truth: these statutes would seem to be part of our policy of strengthening western Europe and cementing our alliances. It probably also reflects a realization that these stocks are no longer alien in American eyes. Finally, Congress may have preferred this solution to a major revision of the Mc-Carran-Walter Act and hoped to mollify two of the strongest pressure groups behind immigration reform.

The policy of allowing free immigration from the Americas probably is intended to express a notion of American continental solidarity. It is a feature of the good-neighbor policy, and of our bid for hemisphere leadership. It, thus, may be thought of as another example of immigration policy as a function of foreign policy. Viewed in the light of a rather narrow logic, it is discriminatory,[3] but (in form at least) it is not racially discriminatory. In any case, since it is probably felt abroad that the Americas have a special community of interest, it is doubtful that it gives rise to resentment.

If special treatment is to be given to the population problems of particular countries, ad hoc legislation rather than general reform may be the likely method. That is unavoidable if (1) immigration policy is to be used as an instrument of foreign policy, and (2) the bolstering of Europe and our influence there is to take precedence in our foreign policy. This discrimination may cost some losses in Asia, but that is, perhaps, but a minor aspect of a general policy which chooses to prefer Europe to Asia. It is, therefore, in a sense, inconsistent with an immigration policy expressing a more universal concept of brotherhood.

The present predicament is the need to develop a positive philosophy for immigration that will be persuasive enough to win popular support. Everyone can agree on immigration to meet our need for special skills; somewhat more problematic is its use to fill shortages in common and semiskilled jobs. And, perhaps, everyone can agree on family reunification more or less in its present form. These two functions, however, account for only a very limited number of immigrants. Beyond this, the possible functions of immigration are more debatable, at least in their appeal to public opinion. Among them are these: to maintain our racial variety and energy; to keep our culture fresh and progressive; to attest our belief in universal brotherhood; to testify to our sympathy for those in any way in need. Each of these has its supporters, each its violent opponents, and each, a large number, perhaps a majority, of indifferents. If, however, the favoring minorities are important and insistent enough, their support may suffice to enact a law that gives some recognition to these functions.

At the present moment, it would appear to be most feasible to unite the largest number of persons (it could even be a majority) on immigration as an instrument in foreign affairs. Under this guise, some of the same functions would be given recognition. If America be, in fact, a haven, even on a token basis, of oppressed or hopeless peoples, its claim to lead the world in the name of brotherhood is more persuasive.

[3]S.1206, 84th Cong., 1st Sess. (1955), would bring the western hemisphere under the quota system. See Charles P. Schwartz, "American Immigration Policy," *Columbia Law Review,* 55 (1955), 311 ff., for the arguments pro and con.

GUIDES FOR READING AND DISCUSSION

1. It has often been charged that America's stance as the main defender of democracy is weakened by discriminatory immigration laws, so that the country's effort to build a strong anti-totalitarian alliance is less successful than it might otherwise be. Is this point well based? What evidence could be adduced for and against it?

2. Although a minority of the public and of Congress keep the issue alive, immigration policy is much less an element of the typical liberal amalgam than are other instances of discrimination. Why should this be so? Even first- and second-generation Americans, often with relatives overseas, usually have less interest in this than in other public issues. Why is this the case?

3. If one grants that a restriction in numbers of immigrants is necessary, and that a restriction by national origin is unwarranted, what would be a reasonable policy for the United States today? Are Jaffe's recommendations the best possible compromise?

SUGGESTED ADDITIONAL READINGS

William S. Bernard *et al.*, eds., *American Immigration Policy: A Reappraisal* (New York: Harper, 1950).

"Immigration," *Law and Contemporary Problems*, vol. 21, no. 2, Spring 1956, entire issue.

Jeremiah W. Jenks and W. Jett Lauck, *The Immigration Problem: A Study of Immigration Conditions and Needs*, 3rd rev. ed. (New York: Funk and Wagnalls, 1913).

Harry H. Laughlin, "Expert Analysis of the Metal and the Dross in America's Modern Melting Pot," in U.S. House of Representatives, *Hearings before the Committee on Immigration and Naturalization*, November 21, 1922; 67th Congress, 3rd Session, serial 7-C (Washington: U.S. Government Printing Office, 1923).

President's Commission on Immigration and Naturalization, *Whom We Shall Welcome* (Washington: U.S. Government Printing Office, 1953).

Benjamin Munn Ziegler, ed., *Immigration: An American Dilemma* (Boston: Heath, 1953).

According to the ideology of the trade-union movement, it has been "at the vanguard of the struggle" not merely for its own economic advantages but also for greater social justice and equality. And it is true that the liberal-labor coalition in the Democratic party has actually been a potent force in realizing the important advances in social democracy during this century. With respect to some liberal measures, however, trade unions have been at best an unwilling partner in this coalition. In particular, union policy on Negroes, however much it has improved since the organization of the CIO, has never been one of labor's best features. In the trade-union movement—as also in the Democratic party, whose political fate depends on keeping peace with the Southern sector—the improvement of Negro welfare has too often been advocated in programs but ignored in fact.

According to another element of the labor movement's ideology, it has grown strong by the efforts of its own organizers; and this is true in part. But a necessary precondition to the rise of the industrial unions was facilitative federal legislation, sponsored and passed by representatives of the liberal middle class. Liberals favor trade unions in the name of social justice, as organizations of the underdog; and the AFL-CIO, today something of a counterpart of big business, still retains the stance of an organization fighting for the men at the bottom of the social ladder. It may be living off its capital of good will, and in some respects squandering it. If the "right to work," now a slogan of the radical right, should be reinterpreted in the context of union policy toward Negroes and other minorities, the labor movement might undergo a disastrous decline.

For most working-class occupations, decisions on hiring policy, the grading of jobs, promotion, and the like, are now made jointly by the employer and a trade union. Indeed, in many instances the union exercises something like the monopolistic control that management once enjoyed. Union policy toward Negroes, most of whom are manual laborers, has thus become an increasingly important determinant of Negroes' welfare. Liberals who support both Negroes' civil rights and trade unions cannot easily evade the dilemma that anti-Negro unions pose.

In the dialogue between Herbert Hill, labor secretary of the National Association for the Advancement of Colored People, and Harry Fleischman, director of the National Labor Service, there is obviously a broad base of agreement. Both men deplore discrimination by unions; and though their emphasis is not the same, both agree that it is less prevalent than it used to be. But it is the differences between them that are important, since they reflect divergencies in the liberal-labor coalition.

The dispute between Hill and Fleischman, seemingly merely empirical, is not only that. More fundamentally, it is one current expression of a persistent controversy in Western civilization over the moral and spiritual consequence of material well-being. That poverty is bad, that a good government tries to abolish it and to alleviate its consequences, are axioms in the American credo. Slum neighborhoods breed crime and disease; poor people are more likely to be deficient in morals, in physical and mental health. This straightforward denunciation of poverty, however, is countered by some of the most important value systems that shape Western man's beliefs. According to these faiths, economic debasement frees, purifies, immunizes. The Christian knows that "Blessed are ye poor, for yours is the kingdom of God"; the socialist knows that "the workers are the saviors of society, the redeemers of the race" (Eugene V. Debs); the bohemian knows that true artistic creativity flourishes in garrets, and dies in the fleshpots of Hollywood. Moreover, one who believes that the poor are morally and mentally superior ordinarily implies that they are superior *because* they are poor, rather than in spite of their being poor. Nevertheless, this view of the Noble Poor is contradicted in every demand for slum clearance, for minimum-wage laws, for social security, for every program to remove the poor from their presumably ennobling environment.

The automatic approbation of the working classes, and thus of such working-class organizations as the trade unions, is one version of the doctrine of the Noble Poor. It has been challenged in Professor Lipset's interesting and provocative paper. This offers a wealth of evidence for two main points: (1) Because of their social situation, members of the working class are more likely to hold authoritarian views. (2) As a consequence, workers can be expected to oppose liberal programs except when these coincide with their own economic interests. In short, the provinciality and poverty of working-class existence constitute important sources of anti-democratic sentiment. The paper has stimulated a good deal of controversy, particularly from left-liberal critics in such magazines as the *New Statesman and Nation;* see also the cited article in the *British Journal of Sociology.* In part this angry reaction is to Lipset's specific thesis; in part it continues the long controversy over the social effects of poverty.

LABOR UNIONS AND THE NEGRO

Herbert Hill

The removal of the sanction of law from racial segregation has sharply posed the issue of the Negro's status in virtually every area of American life. As much as the public schools, religious organizations, and business firms, the labor movement is on trial today. For labor's democratic ideals are in serious conflict with a tradition of racial discrimination in the unions that is currently very much alive.

Reprinted from Herbert Hill, "Labor Unions and the Negro," *Commentary* (December 1959), pp. 479–488. Copyright 1959 by the American Jewish Committee. Reprinted by permission of the author and the publisher. Herbert Hill is National Labor Secretary of the National Association for the Advancement of Colored People.

To some degree, union discrimination simply reflects the racial and religious prejudices among union members—prejudices that many unionists share with other prejudiced persons. Thus recently in the North, groups of white workers participated in violence against Negroes at Trumbull Park in Chicago and at Levittown, Pennsylvania. And in the South, workers have given considerable support to the White Citizens Councils and other groups seeking to perpetuate segregated institutions.

But trade-union discrimination against the Negro is something more than the simple result of rank-and-file prejudices. To understand this, one must make a distinction, in the history of the American labor movement, between economic and non-economic liberalism. Organized labor's struggle for the right to bargain collectively, unemployment insurance, and minimum-wage laws was a central part of the liberal program. But in non-economic matters —in such areas as civil liberties for political dissidents, and equality of opportunity for racial minorities—the practices of many important labor unions can hardly be described as liberal. Many unions have a long history of racial discrimination—and it is this tradition of discrimination which is responsible, at least in part, for the marginal status that Negro wage earners have today in key sectors of the American economy.

Today, as in the past, there is a profound disparity between the public image presented by the national AFL-CIO, with its professed devotion to racial equality, and the day-to-day experience of many Negro workers, in the North as well as the South, with individual unions. To be sure, there are important exceptions, particularly in the mass-production industries, where a large concentration of Negro workers actually preceded unionization. Such unions as the United Automobile Workers, the United Packinghouse Workers, and the Rubber Workers Union have conscientiously worked to eradicate institutionalized job bias. Nevertheless, the Negro is discriminated against by unions in major areas of the economy—such as the building and construction trades (International Brotherhood of Electrical Workers, Plumbers Union, Carpenters Union, Operating Engineers, etc.), the railroad industry (the four "operating" railroad brotherhoods, and the Brotherhood of Railway and Steamship Clerks), the metal crafts (the Boilermakers, Iron Ship Builders Union, etc.), and pulp and paper manufacturing (Pulp, Sulphite, and Paper Mill Workers Union, United Papermakers and Paperworkers Union). In these and other industries, trade unions practice either total exclusion of the Negro, segregation (in the form of "Jim Crow" locals, or "auxiliaries"), or enforce separate, racial seniority lines which limit Negro employment to menial and unskilled classifications.

The Negro worker's historical experience with organized labor has not been a happy one. In the South, unions frequently acted to force Negroes out of jobs that had formerly been considered theirs. Before the Civil War, Negroes had been carpenters, bricklayers, painters, blacksmiths, harnessmakers, tailors, and shoemakers. However, in urban centers like New Orleans, "the Negro who in ante-bellum days performed all types of labor, skilled and unskilled, found himself gradually almost eliminated from the various trades."[1] Unionization in the South often led to the redesignating of

<hr/>

[1]Charles B. Rousseve, *The Negro in Louisiana* (New Orleans: Xavier University Press, 1937), pp. 135–136.

"Negro jobs" as "white man's work," and even to excluding Negroes from entire industries.

In the North, unions were stronger at an earlier period, especially among the craft occupations. But, as Gunnar Myrdal stated:

Most of the time they effectively kept Negroes out of skilled work. [The fact] that the American Federation of Labor as such is officially against racial discrimination does not mean much. The Federation has never done anything to check racial discrimination exercised by its member organizations.[2]

The AFL's failure to organize the Negro worker and to accord him full brotherhood within the union ranks was not a policy born of necessity. The old Knights of Labor, the International Workers of the World, and (much later) industrial unions in the Congress of Industrial Organizations were able to organize Negro and white workers together, in the North and in the South; whereas the early AFL attacked the organizing activities of the Knights of Labor among unskilled and Negro workers.

To be sure, the AFL executive council stated, shortly after the organization's founding, that a union that draws the color line "cannot be admitted into affiliation to this body." But soon afterward, in 1899, the AFL admitted the International Association of Machinists, then a rigid "lily-white" organization. And the traditional hostility of the AFL leaders to immigration —particularly Asian immigration—fostered a veritable racist ideology. At the 1901 convention of the AFL, the Resolutions Committee denounced the Chinese as "people of vice and sexual immorality" who were of "inferior social standards." Samuel Gompers, president of the AFL, observed that the "Negro slaves of the South were as a race kind and faithful," but the "Chinese as a race are cruel and treacherous." Gompers later expressed his belief in "the principle that maintenance of the nation depended upon maintenance of racial purity." He also recalled his vigorous support for Mayor E. Z. Schmitz of San Francisco, "a labor candidate and elected on a labor platform [who] began the work of segregating Japanese children from white children in the public schools."[3]

Throughout the Gompers period, the AFL continued to uphold a racist position. In 1914, it demanded that "all races native to Asia" be excluded permanently from the United States, declaring that "the racial incompatibility as between the peoples of the Orient and the United States presents a problem of race preservation which . . . can only be effectively solved by a policy of exclusion." The AFL under Gompers worked to halt immigration from eastern Europe as well. It believed that the flood of immigrants (among whom were those fleeing the tyranny of the Russian tsar and the anti-Jewish pogroms) threatened both labor standards and "racial purity."

Gompers also criticized American Negroes for allowing themselves to be used by employers as "cheap men." He urged Negroes to "form colored workers' unions"; the AFL, he wrote, "does not necessarily proclaim that the social barriers which exist between the whites and the blacks could be or should be obliterated. . . ." And he warned that "if the colored man continues to lend himself to the work of tearing down what the white man has built

[2]Gunnar Myrdal, *An American Dilemma* (New York: Harper, 1944), p. 402.
[3]Samuel Gompers, *Seventy Years of Life and Labor* (New York: Dutton, 1925), 2, 160.

up, a race hatred far worse than any ever known will result. Caucasian civilization will serve notice that its uplifting process is not to be interfered with in any way." Professor Karson has summarized the results of Gompers' attitudes:

There was no evidence that the Federation leadership in the first half of the twentieth century gave more than occasional lip-service opposition to racial discrimination within the union movement. After 1900, in cases where Negro workers were refused admission to an affiliated AFL union, the Federation adopted a policy of organizing them into separate locals or directly affiliated "federal" labor unions.[4]

This policy was sanctioned by Article XI, Section VI, of the AFL Constitution, which read: "Separate charters will be issued to central labor unions, local unions, federal labor unions, composed exclusively of colored members, where in the judgment of the Executive Council it appears advisable and to the best interests of the trade-union movement to do so."

In the early years of this century, the hostile feeling toward Negroes in American trade unions often led to racial and ethnic violence. In the tragic East St. Louis race riots of July 1917, trade-union provocation was a major factor.

When workers at the Aluminum Ore Company went on strike, the firm brought up a small number of Negroes from the Deep South to be used as strikebreakers. In response, the local AFL leaders provoked a veritable hysteria of race hatred. Finally, raging fires on July 2, 1917, engulfed the entire Negro residential district of East St. Louis, destroying $7,000,000 worth of property, driving 10,000 colored persons from their homes, and ending in the death of more than two hundred Negroes and eight whites.

About a month before the riots, Edward F. Mason, secretary of the East St. Louis AFL Central Trades & Labor Union, called on union members to march to City Hall on May 28, 1917, to demand a halt to "the importation" of Negroes:

The immigration of the Southern Negro into our city for the past eight months has reached a point where drastic action must be taken. . . . On next Monday evening the entire body of delegates to the Central Trades and Labor Union will call upon the Mayor and the City Council and demand that they take some action to retard this growing menace and . . . get rid of a certain portion of those who are already here.

Richard L. Stokes, in the St. Louis *Globe-Democrat* (July 8, 1917), reported that on the night of the march on City Hall, "some of the [union] leaders made speeches advising that in case the authorities took no action, they should resort to mob law." And immediately after the May 28 meeting, there began a series of sporadic violent attacks against Negroes, which culminated in the holocaust a few weeks later. John T. Stewart reported the fires and riots in the St. Louis *Star* for July 3:

Negroes were "flushed" from the burning houses, and ran for their lives, screaming and begging for mercy. . . . Rioters formed in gangs and trooped through the streets, chasing Negroes. They stood around in groups, laughing and jeering while they witnessed the final writhings of the terror and pain-racked

---

[1]Marc Karson, *American Labor Unions in Politics, 1900–18* (Carbondale, Ill.: Southern Illinois University Press, 1958), p. 139.

wretches who crawled to the streets to die after their flesh had been cooked in their own homes. . . .

Shortly after the riots, the St. Louis *Post-Dispatch* quoted the opinion of City Clerk Whelan, president of the Central Trades & Labor Union of East St. Louis. "Before the tenseness of this situation is relieved," said Whelan, "these employers must convince the laboring whites that they will be given preference over imported blacks in applying for work. . . ."

Special investigators for the National Association for the Advancement of Colored People later reported that "by all accounts of eye-witnesses, both white and black, the East St. Louis outrage was deliberately planned and executed." As for the excuse offered by the unions, William English Walling, a highly respected liberal journalist and reformer, noted in a telegram to President Wilson: "The pretext of labor invasion from the South is invalid."

AFL President Gompers, however, attempted to defend the rioters, in response to a sharp attack on them by former President Theodore Roosevelt. At a meeting held at Carnegie Hall in New York City, welcoming envoys from the new Russian Provisional government, Roosevelt (according to the New York *Herald*) heatedly condemned the riot, "for which, so far as we can see, there was no justification and no provocation, and which was waged with such appalling fatality as to leave an indelible stigma upon the American name." Gompers rose to excuse the rioters, on the grounds that the capitalists of East St. Louis had been "luring colored men into that city to supplant white labor." Roosevelt would not be put off. "Justice with me is not a mere form of words," he shouted. "In the past I have had to listen too often to the same kind of apologies for the murders committed against the Armenians and the Jews. . . . I say to you, sir, that there can be no justification, no apology for such gross atrocities. . . ."

Few union officials today would dare speak out as bluntly as Gompers did half a century ago. The new era of public relations in the AFL began in the 1920's under the leadership of benign William Green, who occasionally spoke against racism but did nothing to curb it in the AFL. The Negro had established his first beachheads in industry during World War I, but most AFL unions still practiced a rigorous exclusionist policy throughout the 1920's. In some instances still, Negroes were able to enter industry only when employers hired them as strikebreakers.[5] In other industries, predominantly those employing mass-production methods, the Negro was able to gain a modest foothold because the craft-proud AFL would not organize them. But the limited gains of the Negroes in the 1920's were destroyed during the depression, largely because the AFL had not extended union protection to the Negro in the earlier period. As late as 1933, the Brotherhood of Sleeping Car Porters, with 35,000 members, had almost half the total number of Negro members in the AFL.

[5]According to the Inter-Church Commission of Inquiry into the 1919 steel strike: "It is evident that the great numbers of Negroes who flowed into the Chicago and Pittsburgh plants were conscious of strikebreaking. For this attitude, the steel strikers rightly blamed American organized labor. . . . Through many an experience Negroes came to believe that the only way they could break into a unionized industry was through strikebreaking." This was also a factor in the terrible Chicago race riots of 1919 and in other racial disturbances of that period.

As a result of pressure by the NAACP, the AFL's 1934 convention passed a resolution authorizing a "Committee of Five to Investigate the Conditions of Negro Workers." Green called a meeting of the committee in Washington in 1935, at which the NAACP was represented by its Chief Counsel, Charles H. Houston. The latter reported that signed statements of specific acts of racial discrimination by AFL affiliates were being collected by NAACP branches throughout the country for presentation at subsequent hearings. But Green soon afterward notified the NAACP that no more hearings would be held, since the first Washington hearing had gathered "sufficient information."

John Brophy, of the Mine Workers Union, who was secretary of the Committee of Five, resigned in protest. "The maneuvering," said Brophy, "on the part of the Executive Council plainly indicated that you wanted the 'Committee of Five to Investigate Conditions of Negro Workers' to be merely a face-saving device for the AFL rather than an honest attempt to find a solution to the Negro problem in the American labor movement."

"Internal autonomy" was the excuse Green offered in a later case involving the New York local of the Motion Pictures Operators Union, which restricted colored workers to a small number of Harlem theaters and forced them to accept low-paying jobs. Green, in response to an appeal from the NAACP, said it was impossible for the AFL to interfere in the internal affairs of affiliated unions. This plea of autonomy is often invoked even today.

In 1939, the AFL organized shipyard workers in the Tampa (Florida) shipbuilding industry. Prior to unionization, some 600 semiskilled and skilled Negroes had worked in the Tampa yards. As soon as the International Brotherhood of Boilermakers was recognized as the bargaining agent, however, the Negro workers were forced out of their jobs by the union's exclusionist policy. Green made an ineffectual gesture toward an investigation, but the 600 Negro workers were still kept out of their old jobs. The same thing happened soon afterward at the New Orleans shipyards and at the Boeing Aircraft Plant in Seattle, where the International Association of Machinists was empowered to bargain collectively. Nevertheless, in 1940, before the Brotherhood of Sleeping Car Porters' convention, Green asserted —without a blush—that "so long as I can express myself, I shall fight against racial intolerance and hatred in America."

In 1941, the Federation rejected resolutions, introduced by A. Philip Randolph and Milton P. Webster of the Brotherhood of Sleeping Car Porters, condemning auxiliary "Jim Crow" locals, exclusion of Negroes, and other discriminatory practices of AFL affiliates. At the 1944 convention, when twenty-two international unions still barred Negroes from membership by constitutional provision, John P. Frey, secretary of the Resolutions Committee, defended the AFL's policies in these terms:

I am familiar with the South. I spent many years there as an organizer and otherwise, and I know that in some of the denominations the whites go to their church, and the colored go to their church buildings of the same denominations. They get along as Christians should. In fact, the colored members prefer to have the privilege of employing and discharging their own pastors.

This basic AFL attitude continued after the end of World War II. The 1946 AFL convention defeated resolutions aimed at ending the system of

"Jim Crow" auxiliary locals. In 1949, a resolution endorsing federal Fair Employment Practices legislation passed only after delegates deleted the words "and labor unions" from a motion calling for the "elimination of discrimination in industry and labor unions based upon race, color, religion, national origin or ancestry. . . ."

Discrimination has traditionally been most severe in the AFL building-trades unions and the powerful railroad brotherhoods. The result of this today is that when the colored worker is forced out of the railroad industry, where employment is diminishing, he is prevented from finding employment in the construction industry, where the job market has been rapidly expanding.

Fifty years ago Negro firemen, brakemen, and switchmen worked on all the Southern and Southwestern railroads. As late as 1920, there were 6,595 Negro firemen, and a total of 8,275 Negro brakemen, switchmen, flagmen, and yardmen. In 1940, the number of firemen had dwindled to 2,263 and the other job categories to 2,739. Today's Negro employment figures in these highly skilled, well-paid railroad jobs are much lower, for there has been virtually no hiring of Negro replacements as the older workers have retired or died.

The efforts of the four railway brotherhoods to keep Negroes out date back to the 1890's at least. In 1909, the Firemen's Brotherhood staged a violent strike against Negro firemen on the Georgia railroad, demanding their replacement by white men. In 1890, the Trainmen and the Conductors negotiated what is called the "Washington Agreement" with most of the Southeastern railroads; this provided that Negroes were not to be employed as baggagemen, flagmen, or yard foremen. A similar agreement was concluded with the Mississippi Valley railroads in 1911.

During World War II, the federal Fair Employment Practices Commission was able to crack discriminatory patterns in several major industries, but it could not budge the railroad brotherhoods. The FEPC formally charged that the unions had clauses in their constitutions excluding Negroes from membership, and also cited hostile acts by the unions against the remaining Negro train and engine service workers. The brotherhoods simply ignored the charges. The FEPC held a four-day hearing in Washington in September 1943, charging the railroad unions with impeding the war effort; the unions simply refused to attend. The FEPC ordered the carriers and the unions to cease and desist their discriminatory practices; neither obeyed the order. Instead, both preferred charges against the FEPC before the Smith Committee of the House of Representatives and hinted at a work stoppage (in wartime) if the government insisted on an end to discrimination.

Where they do work on the rail lines today, Negro employees are denied proper job classifications, seniority rights, and wages. During World War II, the FEPC tried to determine the difference between a steward and a waiter-in-charge in dining cars; it finally concluded that the only difference was that the (white) steward wore a black coat, while the (Negro) waiter-in-charge wore a white coat and was paid half the steward's wages. Today, when the Pullman company places a Negro in charge of a sleeping car, it calls him a "porter-in-charge" instead of a Pullman conductor, thereby saving a substantial amount on his wages.

Because of these discriminatory practices, Negro railway workers formed their own union organizations and turned to the courts for protection. In 1948, seven all-Negro rail unions banded together into the Negro Railway Labor Executive Committee, which brought many cases to the federal courts on behalf of colored railway workers. In the Steele and Tunstall cases, the U.S. Supreme Court decided that a majority union cannot, under the Railway Labor Act, make contracts and discriminate against nonmember minority groups. The principle established by this decision is all that stands in the way of total extinction for the Negro railroad worker.

But the American Federation of Labor and the railroad brotherhoods were never able to hold the fate of America's working people, white or colored, in their unchallenged control. The phenomenal success of union organization in major manufacturing centers across the country in 1937 and 1938 was not limited to white industrial workers. In the early Congress of Industrial Organizations, tens of thousands of American Negroes became union members.

In the great sit-down strikes involving entire industries, Negroes were placed on organizing committees, appointed as picket captains, and participated in the local union leadership. Even in the South, though organizers were kidnapped, clubbed, tarred and feathered, and a few lost their lives, the CIO was able to organize important numbers of white and Negro workers in the same unions.

The CIO record in race relations toward the end of its years as a separate organization did not always fulfill the bright promise of its early days. In some Southern plants, rigid patterns of job discrimination were established based on separate racial lines of advancement, limiting all Negroes, however well qualified, to menial job classifications, and denying them equal seniority rights. Nevertheless, the rise of the CIO was a great step forward for tens of thousands of colored and white workers alike.

At the merger convention of AFL and CIO in 1955, a constitutional provision was adopted declaring that "all workers without regard to race, creed, color, national origin or ancestry shall share equally in the full benefits of union organization." In both North and South, however, racial discrimination and segregation have continued in the merged labor movement.

In addition to the Brotherhood of Firemen and Enginemen, the Brotherhood of Railroad Trainmen, and the Airline Pilots Association, which still exclude Negroes by constitutional provision, a number of important international unions continue to exclude them by tacit consent. Many other AFL-CIO unions limit Negro membership to segregated or "auxiliary" locals. Others negotiate contracts which contain separate lines of promotion and seniority for whites and Negroes, thus barring Negroes from skilled and supervisory jobs.

The Brotherhood of Railway and Steamship Clerks, which maintains many segregated local lodges in Northern cities as well as in the South, is a good illustration of the current pattern of discrimination. In this union, as in others, the existence of segregated locals and separate seniority rosters frequently limits job mobility and violates the seniority rights of Negro union members. The union has persisted in its racist practices despite repeated protests. On April 30, 1957, the New York State Commission

Against Discrimination ordered the merger of the "lily-white" George M. Harrison Lodge (Lodge 783) and the all-Negro Friendship Lodge (Lodge 6118). The white union refused to comply; the locals remain segregated to this day. Similar situations exist in Chicago, where the Negro workers are in segregated local Lodge 6132; in Tulsa, Oklahoma, in Lodge 6257;[6] and in East St. Louis and St. Louis, where there are fourteen all-colored local lodges and fourteen all-white lodges together with segregated joint councils. The practice of segregation is so well institutionalized in this union that the designation of the Negro lodges begins with the numeral "6." In Minneapolis, Lodge 364 of the Railway Clerks refused for a year to accept a single Negro into membership; it finally did so only after the Minnesota Fair Employment Practices Commission had threatened to use its full penal powers. Ironically, the president of the Railway Clerks, George M. Harrison, is a member of the Civil Rights Committee of the AFL-CIO and a Federation vice-president.

Discrimination also exists in some important mass-production industries, organized by industrial unions. For example, the United Brotherhood of Papermakers and Paperworkers Union and the International Brotherhood of Pulp, Sulphite and Paper Mill Workers operate segregated locals in more than forty major pulp and paper mills. Negro employment is limited to menial and unskilled classifications by separate, racial seniority lines of progression in virtually all unionized pulp and paper mills. These are "necessary," the union representative will hasten to explain, to prevent a Negro from "supervising white men."

The building trades, as always, remain the citadel of anti-Negro discrimination. Addressing a conference of Negro trade unionists in Detroit on February 7, 1959, A. Philip Randolph declared that "racial discrimination is practiced by building-trades unions in practically every community of the country, varying in intensity from community to community and local to local. . . ." This charge was substantiated by an extensive survey made by the National Urban League of the racial practices of building-trades unions in thirty-two cities, which revealed a broad pattern of anti-Negro practices. In many instances, Negroes are totally excluded from membership in building-trades unions in Northern communities. In some, they are admitted on a segregated basis, as in New York City, where the Carpenters Union operates Local 1088 as an all-Negro local.

Since unions in the building trades control the hiring process, their refusal to admit colored persons to membership effectively prevents qualified Negro craftsmen from securing employment. For example, the International Brotherhood of Electrical Workers (not to be confused with the International Union of Electrical Workers, whose president is James B. Carey) largely excludes Negroes from membership in the key local unions having jurisdiction in new construction, installation, and wiring. Thus, because IBEW Local 26 in Washington, D.C., refuses membership to nonwhite per-

[6]On March 3, 1957, the president of the Negro local in Tulsa, in a letter to the general chairman of the Union's "Frisco System Board," requested the elimination of segregated locals and stated: "At a meeting held February 15, members of this organization decided that it would be to our best interests to merge with [white] Lodge 777 and surrender our charter. Since the schools of our city and state have integrated without incidents, we are sure the same would happen between our Lodges." The Brotherhood of Railway Clerks refused the request.

sons, Negroes were prevented from working on the construction of the national AFL-CIO headquarters, the new House of Representatives office building, and other public and private construction in the nation's capital. Although the Taft-Hartley law forbids the "closed shop," as does so-called "right to work" legislation now adopted by twenty states, the building-trades unions continue to exercise almost complete control of all hiring on construction projects over the United States. A recent study in Texas by the Fund for the Republic concludes:

A review of actual labor-management practices in the traditional "closed shop" trades in Texas confirms the fact that "right to work" has not brought about any basic change over the past eleven years. In the building construction industry, the statute is almost universally violated. . . .[7]

Significantly, the Fund for the Republic study reported how

. . . an unlawful closed shop operated to deprive certain Negro employees of work they had performed in the past, despite their continued membership in a Negro local of the union whose white-local members were engaging in this job imperialism. . . .

With but two exceptions,[8] no significant departure from the national pattern of racial exclusion has occurred in the major building-trades unions since the end of World War II.

Quite as injurious to Negroes as the closed shop is union control of admissions into apprenticeship training programs. In the building trades, union power is used to limit the supply of skilled workers, and Negroes and members of other minority groups are the most frequent victims of such exclusionist practices. In the printing trades, too, union control of apprenticeship programs has operated to bar Negroes from skilled jobs.

As of January 1, 1959, complaints of discrimination were pending with the President's Committee on Government Contracts against many of America's leading international unions.[9] In addition, many other complaints against local unions were pending with state and municipal Fair Employment Practices Commissions.

The record seems clear: in the four years since the merger of the AFL and the CIO, the national labor organization has failed to eliminate even the most obvious instances of racism within affiliated unions. As for the Federation's Civil Rights Department, its performance would seem to indicate that its major function is to create a "liberal" public-relations image.

[7]Frederic Meyers, *Right to Work in Practice* (New York: Fund for the Republic, 1959), p. 34.

[8]Local 38 of the International Brotherhood of Electrical Workers in Cleveland and Local 8 of the Bricklayers, Masons, and Plasterers Union in Milwaukee, Wisconsin, originally defied the orders of Fair Employment Practices commissions, but admitted a token number of Negro mechanics when confronted by widespread public denunciation and the threat of litigation. In the IBEW case, the union still refuses to admit Theodore Pinkston, the plaintiff before the Cleveland Community Relations Commission, and other qualified Negro workers. *Ibid.*, p. 34.

[9]Among them were the International Brotherhood of Electrical Workers, the International Association of Machinists, the International Union of Operating Engineers, the Communications Workers of America, the United Brotherhood of Carpenters and Joiners of America, the Bricklayers, Masons and Plasterers International Union, the International Brotherhood of Boilermakers, the Iron Ship Builders Union, the International Union of Elevator Constructors, the Order of Railroad Telegraphers, the Brotherhood of Locomotive Firemen and Enginemen, and the Brotherhood of Railroad Trainmen.

The 1959 AFL-CIO convention in San Francisco differed little from the pattern of AFL conventions under Gompers and Green. Even as the delegates were meeting, the local Fair Employment Practices Commission was investigating the complaint of Ray Bass, a Negro who for over a year has been denied membership in the Bartenders Union solely because of his color and therefore denied employment. Meanwhile, the convention again rejected proposals to compel the railroad brotherhoods and other unions to end discrimination in the near future. It also prepared to re-admit (provisionally) the International Longshoremens Association to the Federation, despite Randolph's charge that the ILA discriminated against Negro and Puerto Rican workers.[10] (Since the merger, the AFL-CIO had also admitted the Railroad Trainmen, and the Locomotive Firemen and Enginemen— both with racial-exclusion clauses in their constitutions. In November 1958, the Locomotive Firemen and Enginemen successfully defended these clauses in the Federal Court of Appeals in Cincinnati, Ohio; and the continued silence of the national AFL-CIO in this case is instructive, indeed.)

Negro wage earners, perhaps more than any other group among American workers, need the protection and benefits that derive from full membership in a trade union. And international unions can, if they are prepared to invoke authority, eliminate discriminatory employment practices. In 1958, for example, the United Automobile Workers eliminated the traditional discriminatory seniority provisions which limited Negro seniority and promotion at the General Motors Fisher Body plant in St. Louis. At the large Magnolia Oil Refinery in Beaumont, Texas, thirty-two Negro workers were recently promoted for the first time into the hitherto all-white "process mechanical division," and several other Negroes were employed in production departments previously barred to them. The Oil, Chemical and Atomic Workers International Union helped, rather than resisted, their efforts. A new union policy formally prohibited separate lines of promotion in collective-bargaining agreements; and the union called on its members to eliminate discriminatory practices and segregated locals. The International Association of Machinists, which until a decade ago had an all-white clause in its constitution, has also cautiously begun to curb discrimination within its ranks. In too many trades and crafts, however, union power today remains a major obstacle to securing equal employment opportunities for the Negro.

This is not the only obstacle the Negro worker faces, of course. Because there is a disproportionate concentration of Negro workers in the ranks of the unskilled and semiskilled, there has already been a high rate of Negro displacement and unemployment as the result of automation and other technological innovations. Periodic recessions, too, have had a devastating effect on the Negro community; during several months in 1958, nonwhite unemployment was more than two and a half times as great as unemploy-

[10]AFL-CIO President George Meany claimed ignorance of such discrimination. He said: "Now, in regard to Phil Randolph . . . I never knew of discrimination in the ILA . . . and to come at this late date where he has an audience, a convention of the AFL-CIO, and come up with this material, I just don't think is playing the game." However, the Urban League had, a week before the convention, sent a lengthy report on water-front discrimination to Meany, members of the AFL-CIO Executive Council, and members of its special subcommittee on the ILA. Several of these members—including Meany—had formally acknowledged receipt of the report.

ment among white workers. Inevitably, then, in the face of these developments, and the continued inability of the AFL-CIO to curb discrimination in its ranks, the Negro worker has turned to governmental agencies, and to the courts, for protection.

In several cases, discriminatory unions have invoked the legal doctrine of "voluntary association" to justify their exclusion of Negroes. In the Wisconsin Supreme Court, for example, the Bricklayers Union in 1956 challenged the Wisconsin Industrial Commission's recommendation that it admit two Negroes to membership. The court upheld the union; it declared:

> Membership in a voluntary association is a privilege which may be accorded or withheld, and not a right which can be gained and then enforced. The courts cannot compel the admission of an individual into such an association, and if his application is refused, he is entirely without legal remedy, no matter how arbitrary or unjust may be his exclusion. . . .

Nevertheless, the body of law that has been evolving over the last two decades has tended to forge new protections for the Negro worker. In these cases,[11] the principle of "voluntary association" has been no defense to the charge of racial discrimination. In the 1958 case of *Sam H. Clark* v. *Norfolk and Western Railway Company and Brotherhood of Locomotive Trainmen,* a Federal District Court granted a permanent injunction preventing the union from halting promotion of Negroes into certain job classifications; the Negro plaintiffs were also awarded compensatory damages. In a 1959 case, *Oliphant* v. *Brotherhood of Locomotive Firemen and Enginemen,* the Supreme Court refused to review a ruling of the Circuit Court in Cincinnati, which upheld the union's refusal to admit Negroes; but the Supreme Court clearly hinted that it would welcome reviewing, in some other case, the basic constitutional question: whether a union has a right to restrict membership because of race.

Negro workers have placed so many of their hopes in the courts, and in state and local Fair Employment Practices Commissions, because organized labor seems incapable of overcoming its habitual discriminatory practices. On the level of the small shop and local union, the traditions of discrimination have often been institutionalized. A form of caste psychology impels many workers to regard their own positions as "white men's jobs," to which no Negro should aspire. These workers and, often, their union leaders regard jobs in their industries as a kind of private privilege, to be accorded and denied by them as they see fit. Often, Negroes are not alone in being barred from such unions, which attempt to maintain an artificial labor shortage. This is especially true in the building and printing trades, which have much of the character of the medieval guild. On the local level, the inertia which sustains discrimination is to be found among skilled workers in big industry as well as among craftsmen, and in the North almost as commonly as in the South.

The national labor leadership, for its part, indignantly explains that it is besieged at this time by too many enemies to risk internal conflict over discrimination. The Congressional exposures of union corruption, as well

---

[11]Among them: *Joseph James* v. *Marinship Corporation and International Brotherhood of Boilermakers, Tunstall* v. *Brotherhood of Locomotive Firemen & Enginemen, Steele* v. *Louisville & Nashville Railroad Company,* and *Betts* v. *Easely* and *Syres* v. *Oil Workers International Union.*

as industry's more aggressive attitude, have caused labor's leadership to adopt a defensive posture. Within the large unions, automation and technological progress have stimulated new tensions between skilled and unskilled workers; the struggles between unions in various jurisdictions, and in various parts of the country, continue unabated. Because of these pressures, the very AFL-CIO leaders who oppose bias in other institutions have been reluctant to combat it within the labor movement. "We don't want to be torn apart," is their argument. They fear that any militant decision to ban discrimination, no matter how gradually it was applied, would split the AFL-CIO wide open, and thus weaken the liberal cause.

However, for the Negro seeking employment, union discrimination is a cruel fact which these other considerations can hardly be expected to make easier. Given union control of the hiring process and of apprenticeship programs in the building trades, the printing trades, on the waterfront, on the railways, and in so many other industries, labor bias is no longer the private matter of a "voluntary association"—or of a "quasi-sovereignty," as Robert M. Hutchins describes American labor today. Such discrimination is a fundamental social barrier to the Negro, hardly less serious than segregation in the public schools. The intervention of the larger community may, it seems, be necessary to remove that barrier.

EQUALITY AND THE UNIONS

Harry Fleischman

A Rip Van Winkle who went to sleep before World War II and woke today would find the civil-rights changes in the nation unbelievable. Put yourself in his place and think back to the situation at that time. Then the federal government itself employed very few Negroes, and those primarily in menial tasks. Negroes in the armed forces were totally segregated. Twenty-one states either required or permitted public school segregation. Fewer than 100,000 Negroes in the South were estimated to have voted in the 1940 general election. And in the only Southern elections that really counted—the Democratic primaries—Negroes were barred entirely.

What was the status of Negroes in the nation's capital, its showplace of democracy? As late as 1947, the President's Committee on Civil Rights noted that a Negro in Washington

is refused service at downtown restaurants. He may not attend a downtown movie or play, and he has to go into the poorer section of the city to find a night's lodging. The Negro who decides to settle in the District must often find a home in an overcrowded, substandard area. He must often take a job below

Abridged from Harry Fleischman, "Equality and the Unions," *Religion and Labor* (February 1961), pp. 1–8, by permission of the publisher and the author. Mr. Fleischman is Director of the National Labor Service of the Jewish Labor Committee and author of numerous articles and pamphlets on labor, civil liberties, and race relations. This article was originally presented as an address at a National Urban League conference in September 1960.

the level of his ability. He must send his children to the inferior public schools set aside for Negroes and entrust his family's health to medical agencies which give inferior service.

What's more, the crazy-quilt pattern of segregation made it possible for Negro performers to appear on the stage in legitimate theaters, but barred Negroes from the audience. In Constitution Hall, run by the Daughters of the American Revolution, the reverse was the case. Concert audiences were admitted without distinction of color, but no Negro performers—not even Marian Anderson—were allowed to appear on the stage.

Today a major social revolution has taken place in Washington. Negro and white youngsters now attend the same public schools, Negroes and whites go to the same movie houses and theaters and to Constitution Hall —on the stage as well as in the audience. Recreation facilities, including playgrounds, swimming pools, and bowling alleys, are unsegregated. Whites and Negroes eat in the same restaurants. Negroes are employed as motor-men and bus drivers, as secretaries and account clerks in public utilities, in desegregated police and fire departments, and as sales people in department stores. Negro doctors, nurses, and lawyers have been admitted into their respective professional societies. A number of churches are integrated. Negroes are accepted as guests in first-class downtown hotels.

In the nation as a whole, we find that the white primary was eliminated by the Supreme Court. In 1960, more than 1,200,000 Negro voters were on the South's registration rolls. And, in many Southern cities, their votes are wooed (discreetly) by white politicians.

Desegregation of the armed forces is virtually complete, and most public schools on army posts in the South are integrated. Segregation, both in inter-state transportation and now within a single state, has been prohibited by the Supreme Court.

The Supreme Court decisions of 1954 and 1955 have wiped out the legal basis for school segregation, and Negroes attend some formerly all-white schools in most of the Southern states. Only the Deep South strongholds of Alabama, Georgia, Louisiana, Mississippi, and South Carolina have lily-white school systems. And even Louisiana has Negro students in some of its formerly all-white colleges and universities.

In 1941, the Fair Employment Practices Commission was established by an executive order of Franklin D. Roosevelt, wrested from him by A. Philip Randolph, president of the Brotherhood of Sleeping Car Porters. The National Urban League and the NAACP began the breakthrough for Negroes in defense and government jobs. That order, plus the need for full production in World War II's manpower crisis, gave additional stimulus to making increased use of Negro workers and eased their entrance into unions as well as defense factories.

When the war ended, Congress refused to appropriate funds to keep the federal FEPC going. To help fill the gap, unions joined with Negro and other civic groups to campaign for state and local FEP laws, which now protect workers in sixteen states covering more than half the nation's popu-lation. In addition, four Presidential executive orders, which, it must be pointed out, have met with very inadequate enforcement, nevertheless ban discrimination throughout the nation in federal agencies and plants with government contracts. Negro secretaries and professional employees are commonplace in many government offices today.

The total number of nonwhite workers in federal, state, and local government rose from 214,000 in 1940 to 845,000 in 1959. This almost fourfold increase compares with an increase of 43 per cent in total nonwhite employment during the same period.

Closing the wage gap has been much less dramatic. In 1939, the Negro worker earned an average of $364 a year, while the average white worker earned $956—two and a half times as much. In 1960, the gap narrowed to less than twice as much—$2,652 for the median Negro worker, $4,569 for the white.

And since Negro workers have traditionally been the last hired and the first fired, it should occasion no surprise to note that their unemployment rate has averaged about twice that of white workers. The difference has gradually narrowed in good times and widened in hard times. For example, in December 1952, when white unemployment was only 2.1 per cent, nonwhite unemployment was 3 per cent. But in March 1958, when a recession was at its height, whites out of work totaled 6.9 per cent, while Negro joblessness zoomed to 14.4 per cent.

And what is the picture in the labor movement?

Ever since the AFL was founded in 1866, racial equality has been official *policy* at the top level of organized labor. But the AFL, launched on the basis of craft unionism, sought high dues and job control to strengthen the unions and keep them alive in periods of depression. This exclusionism, to maintain job control, frequently led to the practice of discrimination against Negroes by individual unions and by rank-and-file union members.

As late as 1940, the AFL included twenty-six international unions with color bans written into their constitutions. In the NAACP Labor Manual, Herbert Hill, the Association's labor secretary, put Negro membership in the AFL at less than 6,000 as late as 1933. National Urban League figures for Negro union membership up to 1928 were 86,000. But no matter which statistics were accurate, it is obvious that Negro membership in unions was pitifully low.

While the prejudice that prevailed in many skilled-craft unions spilled over into the mass-production industries, the insatiable demand of these industries for more and more labor at the cheapest possible price led them to open the gates, first for immigrant groups and then for Negro workers. Unions organizing industries on an industrial basis soon recognized the need to win these workers in order to create effective collective-bargaining muscle. Thus, when the CIO was formed in 1935 to stimulate industrial unionism, it welcomed into membership workers of every creed, color, and nationality on the nation's assembly lines. Sons of Negro steel men who had been strikebreakers in 1918 became volunteer union organizers in 1936. Many AFL unions, witnessing the victorious surge of industrial unionism and interracial cooperation, adopted the same techniques. Negro membership in the unions zoomed.

At the AFL-CIO merger convention in 1955, the delegates unanimously adopted a resolution for "equal rights for all, regardless of race, color, creed, or national origin." A Civil Rights Committee was set up by the constitution to implement this policy—a stronger one than had previously applied to either the AFL or CIO. Affiliated unions were urged to include anti-discrimination clauses in every collective-bargaining agreement, safe-guarding workers against discrimination in hiring, upgrading, layoffs, pro-motions, training, apprenticeship, and transfers.

But official policies of top bodies are not necessarily transformed into action on the local level. Democratic and Republican national conventions in 1960—as in the past—went on record for some form of federal fair-employment legislation, yet no such bill has ever been passed by Congress. Unlike the labor movement, not a single national manufacturers' or trade association in the United States has a civil-rights policy, a civil-rights program, or any staff to advance fair-employment opportunities in industry. Individual employers and the Association of Commerce and Industry in New York State have been helpful in this regard, but they constitute the exceptions that prove the rule. All the major religious denominations inveigh strongly against segregation, but many a minister ruefully concedes that 11 o'clock Sunday morning is the nation's most segregated hour of the week. Unions, too, are faced with the problem of closing the gap between official policies and actual practices.

Twenty years ago, twenty-six AFL affiliates had bars to Negro member-ship in their constitutions; today only one union in the AFL-CIO—the Brotherhood of Locomotive Firemen and Enginemen—still has a constitu-tional color ban, and AFL-CIO President George Meany has said that either the ban goes at the BLFE's next convention, or the union will have to leave the AFL-CIO. In January 1960, the convention of the Brother-hood of Railroad Trainmen not only lifted its color ban by better than a four-to-one vote, but this action was introduced by a Southerner, B. Grady Byington of Macon, Georgia, the union's general chairman for the Central of Georgia Railway. The Brotherhood gleefully predicted that elimination of the clause would aid organizing efforts among railroad workers in the South, where many employees are Negro.

One and a half million Negro members of the AFL-CIO are increasingly awakening to both their rights and their powers. AFL-CIO unions with Negro top officers or executive board members include: the Allied Indus-trial Workers; the Hotel and Restaurant Employees; the United Rubber Workers; the Amalgamated Meat Cutters and Butcher Workmen; the Na-tional Agricultural Workers Union; the United Packinghouse Workers of America; the Tobacco Workers; the Oil, Chemical and Atomic Workers; the Hod Carriers and Common Laborers; the Brotherhood of Sleeping Car Porters; the United Transport Service Employees; and the National Mari-time Union.

Unfortunately, the positive guarantees of racial equality that appear in many union constitutions and by-laws do not tell the whole story. Although their parent bodies have dropped constitutional color bars, many locals, particularly in the building trades, still employ the following restrictive practices:

1. Refusal to accept Negroes as full-fledged members.
2. Reluctance to accept transfer cards of Negro unionists from other locals.
3. Restricting Negroes to membership in segregated locals.
4. Limiting job assignments for Negro workers.

5. Denying or severely restricting apprenticeship training opportunities for Negro youth.
6. Maintaining dual lines of promotion, one for whites and a more limited one for Negroes, in union contracts or actual plant practices.

Complaints received either by the National Urban League or the NAACP from Negro workers in the North as well as the South name the following unions as principal offenders: the International Brotherhood of Electrical Workers, Plumbers, Carpenters, Sheet Metal Workers, Plasterers, Lathers, Roofers, Painters, Operating Engineers, Bricklayers, Locomotive Firemen and Enginemen, Railway Clerks, Hod Carriers, Boilermakers, Railway Carmen, Maintenance of Way Employees, Railroad Telegraphers, Communications Workers, Papermakers and Paperworkers, and Pulp and Sulphite Workers.

In many cases, the international unions are unwilling to correct, or are inept in attempting to correct, these situations. The failure of the International Brotherhood of Electrical Workers to force its Local 26 in Washington, D.C., to end discrimination led Meany to offer to recruit personally Negro electricians if the President's Committee on Government Contracts would crack down on the government contractor to make him hire Negroes. Certainly this was an unprecedented offer from a top labor leader.

But while the refusal of some unions to accept Negroes as members or apprentices still receives the major spotlight in national publicity, actually the whole level of the debate on union racial practices has shifted considerably.

Professor Ray Marshall, who is conducting a survey for the Fund for the Republic on union racial practices and policies, recently noted that in 1940 discrimination was defined largely in terms of unions which would not admit Negroes. Today, he noted, debate covers the whole range of questions involving the participation of Negroes in union affairs. The main concern of Negro unionists today is election of Negroes to executive boards, appointment to union staff jobs, and upgrading of Negroes to more highly skilled positions. Fifteen years ago, Dr. Marshall added, two major problems were auxiliary locals and racial wage differentials; today both of these problems are almost nonexistent.[1]

A major problem that still remains is one of convincing Negroes that they should not be in segregated unions. For, while many Southern locals are segregated because of the insistence of white unionists, the American Federation of Musicians has 40-odd Negro locals, many of which have resisted merger efforts by the parent union. Officials of such locals are concerned about their fate in merged unions where the white membership is much larger; members are worried about representation at union conventions. Certainly this is one area where Urban Leagues and the Negro American Labor Council could do an effective job of effectuating mergers. Recognizing the legitimate concerns of Negro unionists who prefer segregated locals, A. Philip Randolph has insisted that "it does not follow that a merger of a racially segregated union with a white union will always result in a complete elimination of colored officials."[2] As if to underscore this point,

[1]Ray Marshall, speech at the Fisk University Race Relations Institute, July 1960.
[2]A. Philip Randolph, speech at the founding convention of the Negro American Labor Council, Detroit, May 27, 1960.

the first Negro president of an integrated lodge in the Brotherhood of Railway Clerks was elected in January 1960 in West New York, New Jersey. He won by a margin of two to one over a white opponent, although two thirds of the lodge's almost 1,000 members are white. The Railway Clerks, incidentally, have 18,000 lodges, 1,000 of which are integrated, while 150 are restricted to Negroes. Here, too, Secretary-Treasurer G. M. Gibbons claims that many of the Negro lodges resist integration for fear of being in a minority in integrated lodges.

The AFL-CIO, of course, is not itself a union, but a federation of more or less autonomous international unions. Its work is primarily political, legislative, and educational. The AFL-CIO Executive Council is hampered by a lack of punitive power to remove discriminatory practices—except to recommend expulsion of a discriminatory international union, a step which it is understandably reluctant to take. Its reluctance stems also from the fact that expulsion does not end discrimination; it only removes the discriminatory union from the house of labor, where the AFL-CIO's powers of persuasion can no longer be fruitful. (The International Brotherhood of Teamsters, expelled from the AFL-CIO for corruption, still flourishes with a larger membership than ever before.) Persuasion, unfortunately, takes a lot of time, especially when deep-rooted customs are involved. And the moral power the AFL-CIO can exercise is less effective than it should be upon the affiliates whose racial practices it would most like to change; economic and political pressure would be more effective in the short run.

What are the legal and political pressures that can help labor bring about compliance by recalcitrant unions with its goal of racial equality? Here are illustrations of a number of them:

Where state Fair Employment Practices laws are vigorously enforced, they can lead to prompt action. In Connecticut, Local 35 of the International Brotherhood of Electrical Workers refused to obey the mandate of its international union to abandon its discriminatory practices. But when the Connecticut Civil Rights Commission ordered the local to grant membership to two Negro applicants, and when the local was fined $2,000 by the state court—with the fine to go up $500 for every day discrimination continued—the local acted immediately.

When an international union joins an outside organization in a suit against one of its own local unions, that's news. And that is just what the Oil, Chemical and Atomic Workers Union did. In cooperation with the NAACP, the union sued its Local 434 and the Lion Oil Company for contracting that any new Negro employee should be hired as a yard laborer, ineligible for promotion, in defiance of the Presidential Executive Order forbidding racial or religious discrimination by any firm holding government contracts. The suit sought to have the federal government void its contracts with four of the largest oil companies in the South for violating this order. The NAACP-OCAW victory in this case was due largely to the cooperation of the union president, O. A. Knight, who has insisted that all locals eliminate discriminatory collective-bargaining provisions in any local contracts and abolish dual lines of promotion.

In July 1960, nine Negro workers at the Julius Kessler Distillery in Louisville, Kentucky, brought a $250,000 damage suit against the company and

Local 16 of the Distillery Workers Union because of alleged racial discrimination. The suit was dismissed when the company and the union local signed a supplemental agreement abolishing separate seniority lists for Negro and white workers.

In Baltimore, July 1960, the Negro American Labor Council and the NAACP supported Negro firemen who complained to the city's FEPC and the national AFL-CIO Civil Rights Committee that they had been excluded from Firefighters Union Local 734. Faced with a public hearing of the FEP body, the local opened its membership rolls to Negro firemen.

When Local 8 of the Bricklayers in Milwaukee refused to admit two qualified Negroes, the Wisconsin Industrial Commission went into court to force the local to open its doors to Negroes. The court held that unions are voluntary associations, that the Commission's rulings were unenforceable under existing law, and upheld the local's right to exclude Negroes. Nevertheless, the AFL-CIO Civil Rights Committee, in cooperation with international officials of the Bricklayers Union, persuaded Local 8 to reverse its policy and admit the Negroes. Trade-union moral pressure proved more effective than civil law.

In August 1960, the U.S. Labor Department issued an important ruling which may well set an excellent precedent for future cases. In Memphis, Tennessee, Local 988 of the United Auto Workers has 1,800 members, 500 of whom are Negroes. Some of the latter made repeated complaints to the international office that Negroes were excluded from serving on committees and that the rest rooms in the union hall were segregated. The UAW, in compliance with its constitution, put the local under the administration of a trustee to end the discrimination. Segregationist members of the local then attempted to use the Landrum-Griffin Act to remove the trusteeship. But after an investigation, the Labor Department ruled the trusteeship was established to carry out the legitimate objectives of the international union and therefore fulfilled the requirements of the Landrum-Griffin Act. This provides a valuable new tool to be used by bold international unions to end discrimination in labor's ranks.

And how has the Negro community responded to labor? As long ago as 1919, the National Urban League took a firm stand for the principle of collective bargaining, thereby becoming the first social agency to endorse organized labor. It urged Negro workers not to scab where a legitimate strike existed. Twenty-five years ago, when union programs were unknown to most social agencies, the League initiated a program of workers' education aimed at bringing Negroes widely into union membership. When industrial unionism began to attract Negroes by the hundreds of thousands, and major international unions assumed the responsibility of trade-union education, the League discontinued that program. The Leagues, fairly well staffed with professionals, have been better able than the NAACP to build factual cases against discriminating unions, but have been reluctant to use publicity or legal suits in attempting to change union racial practices. The Urban League has preferred to use persuasion and education based upon solid research to open the doors to unions for Negro workers.

Roy Wilkins, NAACP executive secretary, has noted that a "tremendous change in the image of the labor movement has taken place in the minds of

Negroes. Where, forty years ago, most Negroes viewed the labor movement as an instrument to discriminate against Negroes, Negroes now overwhelmingly see labor as a natural—if too hesitant—ally in the fight for civil rights."[3] Nevertheless, while the NAACP at its 1960 convention voted to continue to back unions and to oppose so-called "right-to-work" laws, and urged NAACP branches to prevent the use of Negroes for strikebreaking purposes during labor disputes, it added that the NAACP "as a last resort" will call on the NLRB to enforce anti-union shop provisions of the Taft-Hartley Act against any unions which bar Negro members. This approach has already created a strain on the civil-rights alliance between progressive labor leaders and the NAACP. As Dr. Ray Marshall has pointed out, it must be obvious to the NAACP that it "cannot easily move from informal cooperation with labor unions to open criticism of them and back again."[4]

While some AFL-CIO leaders have resented the pressure the NAACP has exerted, they are mindful of the cooperation the NAACP and the Urban Leagues gave in defeating "right-to-work" proposals in California, Ohio, and other states. Moreover, labor leaders, skilled in the strains and stresses of collective bargaining, are not unmindful of the fact that group pressures make it easier for unions to live up to their equalitarian ideals. When influential groups—Negro unionists organized in the Negro American Labor Council, the National Urban League, the NAACP, state FEP bodies, the President's Committee on Government Contracts, or other outside agencies —push the unions for action, some union leaders will tell their members, "We've got to go along with this anti-discrimination policy. It's the law, and besides failure to do so will hurt us with the public." While labor leaders, as a group, are far more committed to equality than their rank-and-file members, it is understandable that some leaders (who need rank-and-file support to win re-election) should seek compliance with civil-rights policies as fellow victims rather than as strong advocates.

When, on Memorial Day of 1960, a thousand Negro unionists from scores of international unions came together in Detroit to found the Negro American Labor Council under the leadership of A. Philip Randolph, a vice-president of the AFL-CIO, they forged a new tool to strengthen the drive for racial equality within the labor movement. Randolph emphasized that the NALC supports the AFL-CIO and its leadership, that it opposes a black labor federation, and that it would not engage in collective bargaining or usurp or duplicate the functions of established unions. In addition to calling for the removal of all union color bars to membership, job advancement, and apprenticeship training, as well as elimination of all racially segregated unions, the convention also called for greater representation for Negroes in union staffs at all levels from clerical workers to top union officials.

Randolph warned recently that a "gulf of misunderstanding seems to be widening between the Negro community and the labor community." This is particularly unfortunate, he added, "because the Negro community and organized labor need each other." Much of the success of the Negro community in the fight for civil rights in the federal, state, and city governments,

[3]Conversation with Roy Wilkins, September 1959.
[4]Marshall, *op. cit.*

he noted, "is due to the consistent cooperation and support of the AFL-CIO and the leadership of President Meany."

"But," Randolph added, "although George Meany is personally free from racial prejudice, this is no reason why, as president of the AFL-CIO, he should be free from pressure to stimulate and help him step up the fight against bias in labor."[5]

Some Negro groups have urged an amendment to the National Labor Relations Act which would forbid the recognition or certification as exclusive bargaining representative of any union that discriminates in the admission or representation of minority groups. This would affect only unions and still leave employers free to discriminate. Yet membership composition of unions is determined primarily by the hiring policy of the employer.

Would it not be much wiser, and prove just as easy to accomplish, for Negro and labor groups to join with other civic bodies in a massive campaign for a federal Fair Employment Practices Act which could effectively ban bias by *both* employers and unions?

In addition, it seems to me, we need:

1. Regular surveys of the civil-rights practices of all unions.
2. Self-starting compliance machinery for labor. Just as labor has campaigned to grant state FEP bodies power to investigate discrimination in an industry or union (even where no formal complaint exists), so where discrimination exists in any union, the AFL-CIO should have power to take positive action to bring about full compliance with its anti-discrimination policies.
3. Cooperation with intergroup-relations agencies to smooth and speed transition from segregated to integrated locals.
4. Coordination of the presently scattered civil-rights activities of international unions, state and city councils and locals, and intergroup-relations organizations.
5. Involving union educational directors and editors in conferences and workshops with civil-rights specialists to insure greater emphasis on civil-rights problems in the education and publication programs of unions.
6. Above all, placing civil rights—in the shop and the nation—higher on labor's action agenda. It must be a passion, not a part-time process.

Accomplishing this program requires the utmost cooperation and understanding. I was at Niagara Falls one winter day when the inexorable pressure of the ice-packed Niagara River crushed, twisted, and broke a bridge that joined the USA and Canada. I should hate to see frozen attitudes of fear, suspicion, and misunderstanding on the part of Negro and labor groups crush the attempts to bridge the current gaps between them. Winning civil rights demands Negro and labor unity.

[5]Randolph, *op. cit.*

WORKING-CLASS
AUTHORITARIANISM

Seymour Martin Lipset

The gradual realization that extremist and intolerant movements in modern society are more likely to be based on the lower classes than on the middle and upper classes has posed a tragic dilemma for those intellectuals of the democratic left who once believed the proletariat necessarily to be a force for liberty, racial equality, and social progress. The socialist Italian novelist Ignazio Silone asserted:

> The myth of the liberating power of the proletariat has dissolved with the myth of progress. The recent examples of the Nazi labor unions, like those of Salazar and Perón . . . have at last convinced even those who were reluctant to admit it on the sole grounds of the totalitarian degeneration of Communism.[1]

Dramatic demonstrations of this point have been given recently by the Southern workers' support of White Citizens Councils and segregation in the United States and by the active participation of many British workers in the 1958 race riots in England. A "Short Talk with a Fascist Beast" (an eighteen-year-old casual laborer who took part in the beating of Negroes in London), which appeared in the left-socialist *New Statesman,* portrays graphically the ideological syndrome which sometimes culminates in such behavior. "Len's" perspective is offered in detail as a prelude to an analytical survey of the authoritarian elements of the lower-class situation in modern society.

"That's why I'm with the fascists," he says. "They're against the blacks. That Salmon, he's a Communist. The Labour Party is Communist too. Like the unions." His mother and father, he says, are strict Labour supporters. Is he against the Labour Party? "Nah, I'm for them. They're for y'know—us. I'm for the unions too." Even though they were dominated by Communists? "Sure," he says. "I like the Communist Party. It's powerful, like." How can he be for the Communists when the fascists hate them?

Len says, "Well, y'know, I'm for the fascists when they're against the nigs. But the fascists is really for the rich people y'know, like the Tories. All for the guv'nors, people like that. But the Communists are very powerful." I told him the Communist Party of Britain was quite small.

"But," he says, "they got Russia behind them." His voice was full of marvel. "I admire Russia. Y'know, the people. They're peaceful. They're strong. When they say they'll do a thing, they do it. Not like us. Makes you think: they got a weapon over there can wipe us all out, with one wave of a general's arm. Destroy

Abridged from Seymour Martin Lipset, *Political Man: The Social Bases of Politics* (Garden City, N.Y.: Doubleday, 1960), ch. 4. Reprinted by permission of the author and publisher. Seymour Lipset is a professor of sociology at the University of California, Berkeley, and the author of many books and articles on political sociology and social stratification. In 1962, *Political Man,* from which this article is reprinted, received the MacIver Award from the American Sociological Association.

[1]"The Choice of Comrades," *Encounter,* 3 (December 1954), 25. Arnold A. Rogow, writing in the socialist magazine *Dissent,* even suggests that "the liberal and radical approach has always lacked a popular base, that in essence, the liberal tradition has been a confined minority, perhaps elitist, tradition." "The Revolt Against Social Equality," *Dissent,* 4 (1957), 370.

us completely and totally. Honest, those Russians. When they say they'll do a thing, they do it. Like in Hungary. I pity those people, the Hungarians. But did you see the Russians went in and stopped them. Tanks. Not like us in Cyprus. Our soldiers get shot in the back and what do we do? The Communists is for the small man."[2]

Such strikingly visible demonstrations of working-class ethnic prejudice and support for totalitarian political movements have been paralleled in studies of public opinion, religion, family patterns, and personality structure. Many of these studies suggest that the lower-class way of life produces individuals with rigid and intolerant approaches to politics.

At first glance the facts of political history may seem to contradict this. Since their beginnings in the nineteenth century, workers' organizations and parties have been a major force in extending political democracy, and in waging progressive political and economic battles. Before 1914, the classic division between the working-class left parties and the economically privileged right was not based solely upon such issues as redistribution of income, status, and educational opportunities, but also rested upon civil liberties and international policy. The workers, judged by the policies of their parties, were often the backbone of the fight for greater political democracy, religious freedom, minority rights, and international peace, while the parties backed by the conservative middle and upper classes in much of Europe tended to favor more extremist political forms, to resist the extension of the suffrage, to back the established church, and to support jingoistic foreign policies.

Events since 1914 have gradually eroded these patterns. In some nations working-class groups have proved to be the most nationalistic sector of the population. In some they have been in the forefront of the struggle against equal rights for minority groups, and have sought to limit immigration or to impose racial standards in countries with open immigration. The conclusion of the anti-fascist era and the emergence of the cold war have shown that the struggle for freedom is not a simple variant of the economic class struggle. The threat to freedom posed by the Communist movement is as great as that once posed by Fascism and Nazism; and Communism, in all countries where it is strong, is supported mainly by the lower levels of the working class, or the rural population. No other party has been as thoroughly and completely the party of the working class and the poor. Socialist parties, past and present, secured much more support from the middle classes than the Communists have.

Some socialists and liberals have suggested that this proves nothing about authoritarian tendencies in the working class, since the Communist party often masquerades as a party seeking to fulfill the classic Western democratic ideals of liberty, equality, and fraternity. They argue that most Communist supporters, particularly the less educated, are deceived into thinking that the Communists are simply more militant and efficient socialists. I would suggest, however, the alternative hypothesis that, rather than being a source of strain, the intransigent and intolerant aspects of Communist ideology attract members from that large stratum with low incomes, low-status occupations, and low education, which in modern industrial societies has meant largely, though not exclusively, the working class.

[2]Clancy Sigel in the *New Statesman*, October 4, 1958, p. 440.

The social situation of the lower strata, particularly in poorer countries with low levels of education, predisposes them to view politics as black and white, good and evil. Consequently, other things being equal, they should be more likely than other strata to prefer extremist movements which suggest easy and quick solutions to social problems and have a rigid outlook.

The poorer strata everywhere are more liberal or leftist on economic issues; they favor more welfare-state measures, higher wages, graduated income taxes, support of trade unions, and so forth. But when liberalism is defined in non-economic terms—as support of civil liberties, internationalism, etc.—the correlation is reversed. The well-to-do are more liberal, the poorer are more intolerant.[3]

Public-opinion data from a number of countries indicate that the lower classes are much less committed to democracy as a political system than are the urban middle and upper classes. In Germany, for example, a study conducted by the UNESCO Institute at Cologne in 1953 asked a systematic sample of 3,000 Germans: "Do you think that it would be better if there were one party, several parties, or no party?" The results analyzed according to occupational group indicate that the lower strata of the working class and the rural population were less likely to support a multiparty system (a reasonable index of democratic attitudes in Westernized countries) than the middle and upper strata. (See Table 1.)

TABLE 1

Preferred Party System of German Males, by Occupational Group, 1953

Occupational Group	Several Parties	One Party	No Party	No Opinion	Total Number of Persons
Civil servants	88%	6%	3%	3%	111
Upper white-collar	77	13	2	8	58
Free professionals	69	13	8	10	38
Skilled workers	65	22	5	8	277
Artisans	64	16	9	11	124
Lower white-collar	62	19	7	12	221
Small businessmen	60	15	12	13	156
Farmers	56	22	6	16	241
Semiskilled workers	49	28	7	16	301
Unskilled workers	40	27	11	22	172

Computed from IBM cards supplied to author by the UNESCO Institute at Cologne.

Comparable results were obtained in 1958 when a similar question was asked of national or regional samples in Austria, Japan, Brazil, Canada, Mexico, West Germany, the Netherlands, Belgium, Italy, and France. Although the proportion favoring a multiparty system varied from country to country, the lower classes within each nation were least likely to favor it.

Surveys in Japan, Great Britain, and the United States designed to secure general reactions to problems of civil liberties, or the rights of various minorities, have produced similar results. In Japan, the workers and the

[3]See two articles by G. H. Smith, "Liberalism and Level of Information," *Journal of Educational Psychology*, 39 (1948), 65–82; and "The Relation of 'Enlightenment' to Liberal-Conservative Opinion," *Journal of Social Psychology*, 28 (1948), 3–17.

rural population were more authoritarian and less concerned with civil liberties than the middle and upper classes.[4]

In England, the psychologist H. J. Eysenck found comparable differences between people who were "tough-minded" and those who were "tender-minded" in their general social outlook. The first group tended to be intolerant of deviations from the standard moral or religious codes, to be anti-Negro, anti-Semitic, and xenophobic, while the "tender-minded" were tolerant of deviation, unprejudiced, and internationalist.[5] Summing up his findings, based on attitude scales given to supporters of different British parties, Eysenck reported:

Middle-class Conservatives are more tender-minded than working-class Conservatives; middle-class Liberals are more tender-minded than working-class Liberals; middle-class Socialists are more tender-minded than working-class Socialists; and even middle-class Communists are more tender-minded than working-class Communists.[6]

The evidence from various American studies is also clear and consistent —the lower strata are the least tolerant.[7] In the most systematic of these, based on a national sample of nearly 5,000 Americans, Samuel A. Stouffer divided his respondents into three categories, "less tolerant, in-between, and more tolerant," by using a scale based on responses to questions about such civil liberties as the right of free speech for Communists, critics of religion, advocates of nationalization of industry, and the like. As the data presented in Table 2 demonstrate, tolerance increases with moves up the social ladder.

The findings of public-opinion surveys in thirteen different countries that the lower strata are less committed to democratic norms than the middle classes are reaffirmed by the research of more psychologically oriented investigators, who have studied the social correlates of the "authoritarian personality."[8] Many studies in this area, summarized recently, show a consistent

[4]See Kotaro Kido and Masataka Sugi, "A Report of Research on Social Stratification and Mobility in Tokyo" (III), *Japanese Sociological Review*, 4 (1954), 74–100; National Public Opinion Institute of Japan, Report No. 26, *A Survey Concerning the Protection of Civil Liberties* (Tokyo, 1951).

[5]See H. J. Eysenck, *The Psychology of Politics* (London: Routledge and Kegan Paul, 1954), p. 127.

[6]*Ibid.*, p. 137. For a critique of the methods used in this study, which raises serious questions about its procedures, see Richard Christie, "Eysenck's Treatment of the Personality of Communists," *Psychological Bulletin*, 53 (1956), 411–430.

[7]See Arnold W. Rose, *Studies in Reduction of Prejudice* (Chicago: American Council on Race Relations, 1948), for a review of the literature bearing on this point prior to 1948. Several studies have shown the key importance of education and the independent effect of economic status, both basic components of low status. See Daniel J. Levinson and R. Nevitt Sanford, "A Scale for the Measurement of Anti-Semitism," *Journal of Psychology*, 17 (1944), 339–370; H. H. Harlan, "Some Factors Affecting Attitudes toward Jews," *American Sociological Review*, 7 (1942), 816–827, for data on attitudes toward one ethnic group. See also James G. Martin and Frank R. Westie, "The Tolerant Personality," *American Sociological Review*, 24 (1959), 521–528. For a digest of recent research in the field of race relations in the United States, see Melvin M. Tumin, *Segregation and Desegregation* (New York: Anti-Defamation League of B'nai B'rith, 1957).

[8]See Theodore Adorno *et al.*, *The Authoritarian Personality* (New York: Harper & Bros., 1950). This, the original study, has less consistent results on this point than the many follow-up studies. The authors themselves (p. 178) point to the inadequacy of their sample.

association between authoritarianism and lower-class status.[9] One survey of 460 Los Angeles adults reported that "the working class contains a higher proportion of authoritarians than either the middle or the upper class," and that among workers, those who explicitly identified themselves as "working class" rather than "middle class" were more authoritarian.[10] Recent research further suggests that people may be well adjusted *and* authoritarian.[11] And the fact that this is often the case in lower-class groups fits the hypothesis that authoritarian attitudes are "normal" and expected in such groups.[12]

TABLE 2
Proportion of American Males Who Are "Most Tolerant" on Civil-Liberties Issues

Professional and semiprofessional	66%	(159)
Proprietors, managers, and officials	51	(223)
Clerical and sales	49	(200)
Manual workers	30	(685)
Farmers or farm workers	20	(202)

Samuel A. Stouffer, *Communism, Conformity and Civil Liberties* (New York: Doubleday, 1955), p. 139. The figures for manual and farm workers were calculated from IBM cards kindly supplied by Professor Stouffer.

Many observers have called attention to a connection between low social status and fundamentalist or chiliastic religion. This suggests that extremist religion is a product of the same social forces that sustain authoritarian political attitudes. The liberal Protestant churches, on the other hand, have been predominantly middle class in membership. In the United States, this has created a dilemma for the liberal Protestant clergy, who have tended to be liberal in their politics as well as their religion and, hence, have often wanted to spread their social and religious gospel among the lower strata. But they have found that these classes want ministers who will preach of hell-fire and salvation rather than modern Protestant theology.[13]

Jehovah's Witnesses, whose membership in the United States runs into the hundreds of thousands, is an excellent example of a rapidly growing sect which "continues to attract, as in the past, the underprivileged strata." The Witnesses' principal teaching is that the Kingdom of Heaven is at hand: "The end of the age is near. Armageddon is just around the corner, when the wicked will be destroyed, and the theocracy, or rule of God, will be set up upon the earth." And like the Communists, their organization is "hier-

[9]Richard Christie and Peggy Cook, "A Guide to Published Literature Relating to the Authoritarian Personality," *Journal of Psychology*, 45 (1958), 171–199.
[10]W. J. McKinnon and R. Centers, "Authoritarianism and Urban Stratification," *American Journal of Sociology*, 61 (1956), 618.
[11]Anthony Davids and Charles W. Eriksen, "Some Social and Cultural Factors Determining Relations Between Authoritarianism and Measures of Neuroticism," *Journal of Consulting Psychology*, 21 (1957), 155–159. This article contains many references to the relevant literature.
[12]The greater compatibility of the demands of Communist party membership and working-class background, as indicated by Almond's finding that twice as many of the middle-class party members as of the working-class group in his sample of Communists had neurotic problems, hints again at the normality and congruence of extremist politics with a working-class background. Gabriel Almond, *The Appeals of Communism* (Princeton: Princeton University Press, 1954), pp. 245–246.
[13]See Liston Pope, *Millhands and Preachers* (New Haven: Yale University Press, 1942), pp. 105–116.

archical and highly authoritarian. There is little democratic participation in the management or in the formation of policies of the movement as a whole."[14]

Direct connections between the social roots of political and of religious extremism have been observed in a number of countries. In tsarist Russia, the young Trotsky recognized the relationship and successfully recruited the first working-class members of the South Russian Workers' Union (a revolutionary Marxist organization of the late 1890s) from adherents to religious sects.[15] In Holland and Sweden, recent studies show that the Communists are strongest in regions which were once centers of fundamentalist religious revivalism. In Finland, Communism and revivalist Christianity often are strong in the same areas. In the poor eastern parts of Finland, the Communists have been very careful not to offend people's religious feelings. It is reported that many Communist meetings actually begin with religious hymns.[16]

Religious sects supported by lower-class elements do not necessarily or usually become centers of political protest. In fact, such sects often drain off the discontent and frustration which would otherwise flow into channels of political extremism. The point here is that rigid fundamentalism and dogmatism are linked to the same underlying characteristics, attitudes, and predispositions, which find another outlet in allegiance to extremist political movements.

In his excellent study of the sources of Swedish Communism, Sven Rydenfelt analyzed the differences between two socially and economically comparable northern counties of Sweden—Vasterbotten and Norrbotten—in an attempt to explain the relatively low Communist vote in the former (2 per cent) and the much larger one in the latter (21 per cent). The Liberal party, which in Sweden gives much more support than any other party to religious extremism, was strong in Vasterbotten (30 per cent) and weak in Norrbotten (9 per cent). Since the total extremist vote in both was almost identical—30 and 32 per cent—he concluded that a general predisposition toward radicalism existed in both counties, containing some of the poorest, most socially isolated, and rootless groups in Sweden, but that its expression differed, taking a religious form in one county, and a Communist in the other: "The Communists and the religious radicals, as for instance, the Pentecostal sects, seem to be competing for the allegiance of the same groups."[17]

[14]See Charles S. Braden, *These Also Believe: A Study of Modern American Cults and Minority Religious Movements* (New York: Macmillan, 1949), pp. 384, 370, 363. It may be suggested that, as in authoritarian political movements, the intolerant character of most of the sects is an attractive feature and not a source of strain for their lower-class members. Although no systematic evidence is available, this assumption would help account for the lack of tolerance for factionalism within these sects, and for the endless schisms, with the new groups as intolerant as the old, since the splits usually occur over the issue of *whose* intolerant views and methods shall prevail.

[15]See Isaac Deutscher, *The Prophet Armed, Trotsky; 1879–1921* (London: Oxford University Press, 1954), pp. 30–31.

[16]See Sven Rydenfelt, *Kommunismen i Sverige: En samhällsvetenskaplig studie* (Lund: Gleerupska Universitetsbokhandeln, 1954), pp. 296, 336–337; Wiardi Beckman Institute, "Verkiezingen in Nederland" (Amsterdam, 1951, mimeographed), pp. 15, 93–94; Jaakko Nousiainen, *Kommunismi Kuopion läänissä* (Helsinki: Joensuu, 1956).

[17]See W. Phillips Davison's extensive review of Rydenfelt, *op. cit.*, in *Public Opinion Quarterly*, 18 (1954–55), 375–388.

A number of elements contribute to authoritarian predisposition in lower-class individuals. Low education, low participation in political or voluntary organizations of any type, little reading, isolated occupations, economic insecurity, and authoritarian family patterns are some of the most important. These elements are interrelated, but they are by no means identical.

There is consistent evidence that degree of formal education, itself closely correlated with social and economic status, is also highly correlated with democratic attitudes. Data from Stouffer's study and from the UNESCO Research Institute's survey support this contention.[18] Inferior education and low occupational position are of course connected, and both are part of the complex making up low status, which is associated with a lack of tolerance.

Low-status groups are also less apt to participate in formal organizations, read fewer magazines and books regularly, possess less information on public affairs, vote less, and, in general, take less interest in politics. The available evidence suggests that each of these attributes is related to attitudes toward democracy. The 1953 UNESCO analysis of German data found that, at every occupational level, those who belonged to voluntary associations were more likely to favor a multiparty than a single-party system. American findings, too, indicate that authoritarians "do not join many community groups" as compared with non-authoritarians.[19] And it has been discovered that people poorly informed on public issues are more likely to be both *more liberal* on economic issues and *less liberal* on non-economic ones.[20] Nonvoters and those less interested in political matters are much more intolerant and xenophobic than those who vote and have political interests.[21]

The "hard core" of "chronic know-nothings" comes disproportionately from the less literate, lower socio-economic groups. These people are not only uninformed, but "harder to reach, no matter what the level or nature of the information." Here is another hint of the complex character of the relationship between education, liberalism, and status. Non-economic liberalism is not a simple matter of acquiring education and information; it is at least in part a basic attitude which is actively discouraged by the social situation of lower-status persons.[22]

---

[18] A study based on a national sample of Americans reported that education made no difference in the extent of authoritarian responses on an "authoritarian-personality" scale among workers, but that higher educational attainment reduced such responses among the middle class. The well-educated upper-middle class were least "authoritarian." Morris Janowitz and Dwaine Marvick, "Authoritarianism and Political Behavior," *Political Opinion Quarterly,* 17 (1953), 195–196. The independent effect of education even when other social factors are least favorable has special long-range significance in view of the rising educational level of the population. Kornhauser and his associates found that auto workers with an eighth-grade education were more authoritarian than those with more education. See A. Kornhauser, A. L. Sheppard, and A. J. Mayer, *When Labor Votes* (New York: University Books, 1956), for further data on variations in authoritarianism *within* a working-class sample.

[19] F. H. Sanford, *Authoritarianism and Leadership* (Philadelphia: Stevenson Brothers, 1950), p. 168. See also Mirra Komarovsky, "The Voluntary Associations of Urban Dwellers," *American Sociological Review,* 11 (1946), 688.

[20] Smith, "Liberalism and Level of Information," *op. cit.,* p. 71.

[21] G. M. Connelly and H. H. Field, "The Non-Voter, Who He Is, and What He Thinks," *Public Opinion Quarterly,* 8 (1944), 179; Stouffer, *op. cit., passim*; Janowitz and Marvick, *op. cit.,* p. 200.

[22] See Herbert Hyman and Paul B. Sheatsley, "Some Reasons Why Information Campaigns Fail," *Public Opinion Quarterly,* 11 (1947), 413.

Economic underprivilege is psychological underprivilege: habits of submission, little access to sources of information, lack of verbal facility . . . appear to produce a lack of self-confidence which increases the unwillingness of the low-status person to participate in many phases of our predominantly middle-class culture . . .[23]

These characteristics also reflect the extent to which the lower strata are *isolated* from the activities, controversies, and organizations of democratic society—an isolation which prevents them from acquiring the sophisticated and complex view of the political structure which makes understandable and necessary the norms of tolerance. It is instructive to examine those occupations which are most isolated, in every sense, from contact with the world outside their own group. Manual workers in "isolated occupations" which require them to live in one-industry towns or areas—miners, maritime workers, forestry workers, fishermen, and sheepshearers—exhibit high rates of Communist support in most countries.[24] ·

Similarly, as all public-opinion surveys show, the rural population, both farmers and laborers, tends to oppose civil liberties and multiparty systems more than any other occupational group. Election surveys indicate that farm owners have been among the strongest supporters of fascist parties, while farm workers, poor farmers, and sharecroppers have given even stronger backing to the Communists than has the rest of labor in countries like Italy, France, and India.[25]

A second and no less important factor predisposing the lower classes toward authoritarianism is a relative lack of economic and psychological security. The lower one goes on the socio-economic ladder, the greater economic uncertainty one finds. White-collar workers, even those who are not paid more than skilled manual workers, are less likely to suffer the tensions created by fear of loss of income. Such insecurity will of course affect the individual's politics and attitudes. High states of tension require immediate alleviation, and this is frequently found in the venting of hostility against a scapegoat and the search for a short-term solution by support of extremist groups. Research indicates that the unemployed are less tolerant toward minorities than the employed, and more likely to be Communists if

[23]Genevieve Knupfer, "Portrait of the Underdog," *Public Opinion Quarterly*, 11 (1947), 114.
[24]The greatest amount of comparative material is available on the miners. For Britain, see Herbert G. Nicholas, *British General Election of 1950* (London: Macmillan, 1951), pp. 318, 342, 361. For the United States, see Paul F. Brissenden, *The IWW: A Study of American Syndicalism* (New York: Columbia University Press, 1920), p. 74; Harold F. Gosnell, *Grass Roots Politics* (Washington: American Council on Public Affairs, 1942), pp. 31–32. For France, see François Goguel, "Géographie des élections sociales de 1950–51," *Revue Française de Science Politique*, 3 (1953), 246–271. For Germany, see Ossip K. Flechtheim, *Die Kommunistische Partei Deutschlands in der Weimarer Republik* (Offenbach am Main: Bollwerk-Verlag Karl Drott, 1948), p. 211. Data are also available for Australia, Scandinavia, Spain, and Chile.
[25]According to Carl Friedrich, agricultural groups are more emotionally nationalistic and potentially authoritarian politically because of the fact that they are more isolated than are urban dwellers from meeting people who are different. See "The Agricultural Basis of Emotional Nationalism," *Public Opinion Quarterly*, 1 (1937) 50–51. See also Rudolf Heberle, *From Democracy to Nazism: A Regional Case Study on Political Parties in Germany* (Baton Rouge: Louisiana State University Press, 1945), pp. 32 ff., for a discussion of the appeal of Nazism to the German rural population; and Kido and Sugi, *op. cit.*, for similar survey findings in Japan.

they are workers, or fascists if they are middle class. Industries which have a high rate of Communists in their ranks also have high economic instability.

The lower classes' insecurities and tensions which flow from economic instability are reinforced by their particular patterns of family life. There is a great deal of direct frustration and aggression in the day-to-day lives of members of the lower classes, both children and adults. A comprehensive review of the many studies of child-rearing patterns in the United States completed in the past twenty-five years reports as their "most consistent finding"

the more frequent use of physical punishment by working-class parents. The middle class, in contrast, resorts to reasoning, isolation, and . . . "love-oriented" techniques of discipline. . . . Such parents are more likely to overlook offenses, and when they do punish they are less likely to ridicule or inflict physical pain.[26]

A further link between such child-rearing practices and adult hostility and authoritarianism is suggested by the finding that physical punishments for aggression, characteristic of the working class, tend to increase aggressive behavior.[27]

Acceptance of the norms of democracy requires a high level of sophistication and ego security. The less sophisticated and stable an individual, the more likely he is to favor a simplified view of politics, to fail to understand the rationale underlying tolerance of those with whom he disagrees, and to find difficulty in grasping or tolerating a gradualist image of political change.

Several studies focusing on various aspects of working-class life and culture have emphasized different components of an unsophisticated perspective. Greater suggestibility, absence of a sense of past and future (lack of a prolonged time perspective), inability to take a complex view, greater difficulty in abstracting from concrete experience, and lack of imagination (inner "reworking" of experience)—each has been singled out by numerous students of quite different problems as characteristic of low status. All of these qualities are part of the complex psychological basis of authoritarianism.

Cantril considered suggestibility to be a major psychological explanation for participation in extremist movements.[28] The two conditions for suggesti-

[26]See Urie Bronfenbrenner, "Socialization and Social Class through Time and Space," in E. E. Maccoby, T. M. Newcomb, and E. L. Hartley, eds., *Readings in Social Psychology* (New York: Holt, 1958), p. 419. The sociologist Allison Davis has summarized in a similar vein research findings relating to intrafamily relations in different classes: "The lower classes not uncommonly teach their children and adolescents to strike out with fists or knife and to be certain to hit first. Both girls and boys at adolescence may curse their father to his face or even attack him with fists, sticks, or axes in free-for-all family encounters. Husbands and wives sometimes stage pitched battles in the home; wives have their husbands arrested, and husbands try to break in or burn down their own homes when locked out. Such fights with fists or weapons, and the whipping of wives, occur sooner or later in many lower-class families. They may not appear today, nor tomorrow, but they *will* appear if the observer remains long enough to see them." Allison Davis, "Socialization and Adolescent Personality," in Guy E. Swanson *et al.*, eds. *Readings in Social Psychology* (New York: Holt, 1954), p. 528.

[27]Some hint of the complex of psychological factors underlying lower-class authoritarianism is given in Saul M. Siegel, "The Relationship of Hostility to Authoritarianism," *Journal of Abnormal and Social Psychology*, 52 (1956), 368–372.

[28]Hadley Cantril, *The Psychology of Social Movements* (New York: Wiley, 1941), p. 65.

bility are both typical of low-status persons: either the lack of an adequate frame of reference or general perspective, or a fixed, rigid one. A poorly developed frame of reference reflects a limited education, a paucity of the rich associations on a general level which provide a basis for evaluating experience. A fixed or rigid one—in a sense, the opposite side of the same coin—reflects the tendency to elevate whatever general principles are learned to absolutes which even experience may fail to qualify and correct.

The stimulating book by the British journalist Richard Hoggart, *The Uses of Literacy,* makes the same point in another way. Low-status persons without rich and flexible perspectives are likely to lack a developed sense of the past *and* the future.

Their education is unlikely to have left them with any historical panorama or with any idea of a continuing tradition. . . . A great many people, though they may possess a considerable amount of disconnected information, have little idea of an historical or ideological pattern or process. . . . With little intellectual or cultural furniture, with little training in the testing of opposing views against reason and existing judgments, judgments are usually made according to the promptings of those group apothegms which come first to mind. . . . Similarly, there can be little real sense of the future. . . . Such a mind is, I think, particularly accessible to the temptation to live in a constant present.[29]

Working-class life as a whole emphasizes the concrete and immediate. As Hoggart puts it:

If we want to capture something of the essence of working-class life . . . we must say that it is the "dense and concrete" life, a life whose main stress is on the intimate, the sensory, the detailed and the personal. This would no doubt be true of working-class groups anywhere in the world.[30]

This emphasis on the immediately perceivable and concern with the personal and concrete is part and parcel of the short-time perspective and the inability to perceive the complex possibilities and consequences of actions which often result in a general readiness to support extremist political and religious movements, and a generally lower level of liberalism on non-economic questions.

Even within extremist movements these differences in the perceptions and perspectives of working-class as against middle-class persons affect their experiences, readiness to join a "cause," and reasons for defecting. Gabriel Almond's study of 221 ex-Communists in four countries provides data on this point. He distinguishes between the "exoteric" (simple, for mass consumption) and "esoteric" (complex, for the inner circle) doctrines of the party. In contrast to middle-class members:

Relatively few working-class respondents had been exposed to the esoteric doctrine of the party before joining, and . . . they tended to remain unindoctrinated while in the party. [The middle-class recruits] tended to come to the party with more complex value patterns and expectations which were more likely to obstruct assimilation into the party. . . . The working-class member, on the other hand, is relatively untroubled by doctrinal apparatus, less exposed to the media of communication, and his imagination and logical powers are relatively undeveloped.[31]

[29]Hoggart, *op. cit.,* pp. 158–159.
[30]*Ibid.,* p. 88.
[31]Almond, *op. cit.,* pp. 244, 177.

One aspect of the lower classes' lack of sophistication and education is their anti-intellectualism (a phenomenon Engels long ago noted as a problem faced by working-class movements). While the complex esoteric ideology of Communism may have been one of the principal features attracting middle-class people to it, the fundamental anti-intellectualism which it shares with other extremist movements has been a source of strain for the "genuine" intellectuals within it. Thus it has been the working-class rank and file which has been least disturbed by Communism's ideological shifts, and least likely to defect.[32] Their commitment, once established, cannot usually be shaken by a sudden realization that the party, after all, does not conform to liberal and humanistic values.

This helps to explain why socialist parties have been led by a high proportion of intellectuals, in spite of an original ideological emphasis on maintaining a working-class orientation, while the Communists have alienated their intellectual leaders and are led preponderantly by those with working-class occupations.[33] Almond's study concluded:

While the party is open to all comers, working-class party members have better prospects of success in the party than middle-class recruits. This is probably due both to party policy, which has always manifested greater confidence in the reliability of working-class recruits, and to the difficulties of assimilation into the party generally experienced by middle-class party members.[34]

Despite the profoundly anti-democratic tendencies in lower-class groups, workers' political organizations and movements in the more industrialized democratic countries have supported *both* economic and political liberalism.[35] Workers' organizations, trade unions, and political parties played a

[32]*Ibid.*, pp. 313 ff., 392.

[33]For French data from 1936 to 1956, see Mattei Dogan, "Les candidats et les élus," in L'Association Française de Science Politique, *Les elections du 2 janvier* (Paris: Librairie Armand Colin, 1956), p. 462; and "L'origine sociale du personnel parlementaire français," in Maurice Duverger, ed., *Partis politiques et classes sociales en France* (Paris: Librairie Armand Colin, 1955), pp. 291–329. For a comparison of German Social Democratic and Communist parliamentary leadership before Hitler, see Viktor Engelhardt, "Die Zusammensetzung des Reichstags nach Alter, Beruf, und Religionsbekenntnis," *Die Arbeit*, 8 (1931), 34.

[34]Almond, *op. cit.,* p. 190.

[35]There have been many exceptions to this. The Australian Labor party has been the foremost supporter of a "white Australia." Similarly, in the United States until the advent of the ideological New Deal in the 1930s, the lower-class-based Democratic party has always been the more anti-Negro of the two parties. The American labor movement has opposed nonwhite immigration, and much of it maintains barriers against Negro members.

When the American Socialist party was a mass movement before World War I, its largest circulation newspapers, such as the Milwaukee *Social Democratic Herald* and the *Appeal to Reason,* opposed racial integration. The latter stated explicitly, "Socialism will separate the races." See David A. Shannon, *The Socialist Party of America* (New York: Macmillan, 1955), pp. 49–52. Even the Marxist Socialist movement of Western Europe was not immune to the virus of anti-Semitism. Thus, before World War I there were a number of anti-Semitic incidents in which Socialists were involved, some avowedly anti-Semitic leaders connected with different socialist parties, and strong resistance to committing the socialist organizations to opposition to anti-Semitism. See E. Silberner, "The Anti-Semitic Tradition in Modern Socialism," *Scripta Hierosolymitana,* 3 (1956), 378–396. In an article on the recent British race riots, Michael Rumney points out the working-class base of the anti-Negro sentiment and goes so far as to predict that "the Labour party will become the enemy of the Negro as time goes on." He reports that "while the Conservative party has been able to stand behind the police and take any means it feels necessary to preserve the peace, the Labour party has been strangely silent. If it speaks it will either antagonize the

major role in extending political democracy in the nineteenth and early twentieth centuries. However, these struggles for political freedom by the workers, like those of the middle class before them, took place in the context of a fight for economic rights.[36] Freedom of organization and of speech, together with universal suffrage, were necessary weapons in the battle for a better standard of living, social security, shorter hours, and the like. The upper classes resisted the extension of political freedom as part of their defense of economic and social privilege.

Few groups in history have ever voluntarily espoused civil liberties and freedom for those who advocate measures they consider despicable or dangerous. Religious freedom emerged in the Western world only because the contending powers each found themselves unable to destroy the other without destroying the entire society, and because in the course of the struggle itself many men lost faith and interest in religion, and consequently the desire to suppress dissent. Similarly, universal suffrage and freedom of organization and opposition developed in many countries either as concessions to the established strength of the lower classes, or as means of controlling them—a device advocated and used by such sophisticated conservatives as Disraeli and Bismarck.

Once in existence, however, and although originating in a conflict of interests, democratic norms became part of the institutional system. Thus the Western labor and socialist movement has incorporated these values into its general ideology. But the fact that the movement's ideology is democratic does not mean that its supporters actually understand the implications. The evidence seems to indicate that understanding of and adherence to these norms are highest among leaders and lowest among followers. The general opinions or predispositions of the rank and file are relatively unimportant in predicting behavior as long as the organization to which they are loyal continues to act democratically. In spite of the

men who riot against West Indians, or forfeit its claim to being the party of equal rights." See "Left Mythology and British Race Riots," *New Leader* (September 22, 1958), pp. 10–11.

British Gallup Poll surveys document these judgments. Thus, in a survey completed in July 1959, the poll asked whether Jews "have more or less power than they should really have," and found, when respondents were compared according to party choice, that the anti-Semitic response of "more power" was given by 38 per cent of the Labor voters, 30 per cent of the Tories, and 27 per cent of the Liberals. But in all fairness it must also be noted that almost every Jew in the House of Commons represents the Labor party, and that almost all of the approximately two dozen Jews represent overwhelmingly non-Jewish constituencies.

[36]Actually there are some striking similarities between the behavior of various middle-class strata when they constituted the lower strata within a predominantly aristocratic and feudal society, and the working class in newly industrialized societies who have not yet won a place in society. The affinities of both for religious and economic "radicalism," in the same sense, are striking. Calvin's doctrine of predestination, as Tawney points out, performed the same function for the eighteenth-century bourgeoisie as did Marx's theory of the inevitability of socialism for the proletariat in the nineteenth. Both "set their virtue at their best in sharp antithesis with the vices of the established order at its worst, taught them to feel that they were a chosen people, made them conscious of their great destiny in the Providential and resolute to realize it." The Communist party, as did the Puritans, insists on "personal responsibility, discipline, and asceticism," and although the historical contents differ, they may have the same sociological roots: in isolated, status-deprived occupational groups. See R. H. Tawney, *Religion and the Rise of Capitalism* (New York: Penguin Books, 1947), pp. 9, 99. For a similar point, see Donald G. MacRae, "The Bolshevik Ideology," *Cambridge Journal*, 3 (1950), 164–177.

workers' greater authoritarian propensity, their anti-Communist organizations still typically function as better defenders and carriers of democratic values than parties based on the middle class. In Germany, the United States, Great Britain, and Japan, individuals who support the democratic left party are more likely to support civil liberties and democratic values than people *within* each occupational stratum who back the conservative parties. Organized social democracy not only defends civil liberties but influences its supporters in the same direction.[37]

Conservatism is especially vulnerable in a political democracy, since, as Abraham Lincoln said, there are always more poor people than well-to-do ones; and promises to redistribute wealth are difficult to rebut. Consequently, conservatives have traditionally feared a thoroughgoing political democracy and have endeavored in most countries—by restricting the franchise or by manipulating the governmental structure through second chambers or overrepresentation of rural districts and small towns (traditional conservative strongholds)—to prevent a popular majority from controlling the government. The ideology of conservatism has frequently been based on elitist values which reject the idea that there is wisdom in the voice of the electorate. Other values often defended by conservatives, like militarism or nationalism, probably also have an attraction for individuals with authoritarian predispositions.[38]

It would be a mistake to conclude from the data presented here that the authoritarian predispositions of the lower classes necessarily constitute a threat to a democratic social system; nor should similar conclusions be drawn about the anti-democratic aspects of conservatism. Whether or not a given class supports restrictions on freedom depends on a wide constellation of factors, of which those discussed here are only a part.

The instability of the democratic process in general and the strength of the Communists in particular are closely related to national levels of economic development, including national levels of educational attainment. The Communists represent a mass movement in the poorer countries of Europe and elsewhere, but are weak where economic development and educational attainment are high. The lower classes of the less developed countries are poorer, more insecure, and less educated than are the lower

[37]A striking case in point occurred in Australia in 1950. During a period of much agitation about the dangers of the Communist party, a Gallup Poll survey reported that 80 per cent of the electorate favored outlawing the Communists. Shortly after this survey, the Conservative government submitted a proposal to outlaw the party to referendum. During the referendum electoral campaign, the Labor party and the trade unions came out vigorously against the proposal. Considerable shifting took place after this, to the point that the measure to outlaw the Communists was actually defeated by a small majority, and Catholic workers who had overwhelmingly favored the outlaw measure when first questioned by the Gallup Poll eventually followed the advice of their party and unions and voted against it. See Leicester Webb, *Communism and Democracy in Australia: A Survey of the 1951 Referendum* (New York: Praeger, 1955).

[38]A study of the 1952 elections in the United States revealed that at every educational level (grammar school, high school, and college) individuals who scored high on an "authoritarian-personality" scale were much more likely to vote for Eisenhower than for Stevenson. See Robert Lane, "Political Personality and Electoral Choice," *American Political Science Review*, 49 (1955), 173–190. In Britain, a study of working-class anti-Semitism found that the small group of Conservatives in the sample were much more anti-Semitic than the Liberals and the Laborites. See James H. Robb, *Working-Class Anti-Semite* (London: Tavistock, 1954), pp. 93–94.

strata of the well-to-do nations. In the more developed, stable democracies of Western Europe, North America, and Australasia the lower classes are "in the society" as well as "of it"—that is, their isolation from the rest of the culture is much less than the social isolation of the poorer groups in other countries, who are cut off by abysmally low incomes and very low educational levels, if not by widespread illiteracy. This incorporation of the workers into the body politic in the industrialized Western world has reduced their authoritarian tendencies greatly, although in the United States, for example, McCarthy demonstrated that an irresponsible demagogue who combines a nationalist and anti-elitist appeal can still secure considerable support from the less educated.[39]

While the evidence as to the effects of rising national standards of living and education permits us to be hopeful about working-class politics and behavior in those countries in which extremism is weak, it does suggest pessimistic conclusions with regard to the less economically developed, unstable democracies. Where an extremist party has secured the support of the lower classes—often by stressing equality and economic security at the expense of liberty—it is problematic whether this support can be taken away from it by democratic methods. The Communists, in particular, combine the two types of a chiliastic view of the world. Whether democratic working-class parties, able to demonstrate convincingly their ability to defend economic and class interests, can be built up in the less stable democracies is a moot question.

[39]"The history of the masses, however, has been a history of the most consistently anti-intellectual force in society. . . . It was the American lower classes, not the upper, who gave their overwhelming support to the attacks in recent years on civil liberties. It is among the working people that one finds dominant those sects and churches most hostile to the free spirit." Lewis S. Feuer, Introduction to *Marx and Engels, Basic Writings on Politics and Philosophy* (New York: Doubleday-Anchor, 1959), pp. xv–xvi. And in another wealthy country, white South Africa, Herbert Tingsten points out that "industrialization and commercialization . . . have formed that social class now constituting the stronghold of Boer nationalism: workers, shop assistants, clerks, lower grades of civil servants. Here, as in the United States, these 'poor whites'—more correctly, whites threatened by poverty—are the leading guardians of prejudice and white supremacy." *The Problem of South Africa* (London: Gollancz, 1955), p. 23.

GUIDES FOR READING AND DISCUSSION

1. According to Lipset, how do rank-and-file workers differ from trade-union leaders in their commitment to the principle of equal job opportunities? Might this explain the frequent contrast between unions' statements favoring equal rights and their actual practices?

2. Assuming that Hill is correct in his statement that many unions discriminate flagrantly against Negroes, what avenues of redress are open to a Negro who wants to combat such practices? If he is not permitted to join a union controlling a particular job market, for example, should the courts permit him to sue?

3. What evidence is there, pro or con, concerning the notion of the Happy Poor? Does the "progressive" ideology typically include the idea that in some senses poverty is ennobling?

SUGGESTED ADDITIONAL READINGS

AFL-CIO, *Policy Resolutions on Civil Rights and Civil Liberties,* Publication 8-B, 1960.

Tom Brooks, "Negro Militants, Jewish Liberals, and the Unions," *Commentary,* September 1961.

Commission on Civil Rights, *Report, 1961;* Book 3, *Employment* (Washington, D.C.: U.S. Government Printing Office, 1961).

John Dollard, *Caste and Class in a Southern Town* (New York: Harper, 1937).

August B. Hollingshead and Fredrick C. Redlich, *Social Class and Mental Illness: A Community Study* (New York: Wiley, 1958).

Genevieve Knupfer, "Portrait of the Underdog," *Public Opinion Quarterly,* 11 (Spring 1957), 103–114.

S. M. Miller and Frank Riessman, " 'Working-Class Authoritarianism': A Critique of Lipset," with "Reply," *British Journal of Sociology,* 12:3 (September 1961), 263–281.

Gunnar Myrdal, *An American Dilemma: The Negro Problem and Modern Democracy* (New York: Harper, 1944), ch. 18–19 and *passim.*

NAACP, *Racism within Organized Labor: A Report of Five Years of the AFL-CIO, 1955-1960* (New York, 1961).

————, *The Negro Wage-Earner and Apprenticeship Training Programs* (New York, 1960).

U.S. Department of Labor, *The Economic Situation of Negroes in the United States,* Bulletin S-3, 1960.

4

THE QUALITY OF
AMERICAN LIFE

McCARTHYISM: HOW IRRATIONAL, AND HOW REPRESSIVE?

The support of civil liberties and their denial, both part of the American tradition, are ordinarily analyzed from opposed points of view. In a standard history of the United States, the theme is likely to be the American democratic creed and its realization in New World institutions. Against the background of such accurate but one-sided history, the contrast is all the sharper when we read more specialized studies about the American Protective Association, the Ku Klux Klan, or what has come to be known as McCarthyism. This latest version of the anti-libertarian tradition was dormant for a period after the death of Senator McCarthy, but some of the same spirit is evident again in a revivified radical right. As long as Communist aggression remains a problem for the West, McCarthyism is likely to recur as one type of response to it.

McCarthyism represents a mood more than a political movement, and it is thus even more difficult to assess than most political issues. Was Senator McCarthy sincerely anti-Communist or only a demagogue who used the general opposition to Communism as a weapon with which to attack as Communist, or pro-Communist, or soft on Communism, so variegated a list of targets as the State Department, the U.S. Army, Harvard intellectuals, anti-Communist organizations like Americans for Democratic Action, anti-Communist individuals like James Wechsler, and in effect anyone else who disagreed with Senator McCarthy? Was his influence as great as the noisy headlines made it seem; or did some of his power depend on the fact that he was seen as newsworthy? Could his many supporters have been organized, under any conceivable circumstances, into a totalitarian party capable of taking power?

The three articles that follow all discuss the dilemma posed by the dual task of maintaining individual freedoms and protecting democratic institutions against totalitarian infiltration. However great their differences, all three authors are agreed in rejecting both McCarthy and the view that he was "witch-hunting" or opposing purely imaginary enemies. In Mr. Barth's view, the McCarthyist suppression of civil liberties was an irrational and unwarranted response to real but tremendously exaggerated problems. To his charge that McCarthyism was deeply repressive, Professor Roche replies—in an article written during its height—that "we've never had more freedom." Liberals, Roche suggests, were immobilized by their own rhetoric, by their exaggeration of a repression that *comparatively* was mild in all respects. And to Barth's contention that the Communist problem was too trivial to warrant extraordinary attention, Mr. Kristol responds: McCarthyism—however false, ineffective, and dangerous—was a response to the real threat of external aggression and internal subversion, which was largely ignored by liberals. McCarthyism was possible, in other words, because liberals as a group failed to face up to the great danger to democracy that international Communism represents.

THE CULT OF LOYALTY

Alan Barth

The relation of the individual to the State—or of individual liberty to national security—is the crucial issue of our time. The emphasis in this relation marks the essential distinction between a totalitarian society and a free society. A totalitarian society emphasizes the supremacy of the State, seeking national security through rigid governmental control of individual activity and expression. A free society emphasizes the supremacy of the individual, relying for its national security upon a democratic adjustment of diverse views and interests and upon the freely accorded devotion of its constituents.

The function of national security in a totalitarian society is to preserve the State, while the function of national security in a free society is to preserve freedom. Those who established the American Republic counted freedom among man's "unalienable" or "natural" rights and believed that it was in order to secure these rights that governments are instituted among men. But there is a looseness about freedom that makes it seem hazardous to security. It involves an inescapable element of risk. There have always been men everywhere who viewed it skeptically as a luxury to be enjoyed only within prescribed limits and when the nation is not subject to any external threat. It is commonly in the name of national security that individual liberty is lost.

Our purpose here is to show: (1) that we have accepted, without full awareness of their meaning, piecemeal encroachments on personal freedom that threaten to corrupt our richest inheritance; (2) that these encroachments have been accepted as the result of what are in large part groundless and neurotic fears; (3) that, although accepted in the name of national security, they operate, in fact, to impair the security they are intended to protect; and (4) that whether or not individual liberty is, as the founders of the United States believed it to be, an "unalienable" or "natural" right, it serves vital practical purposes and is an affirmative source of national strength.

This is by no means to suggest that national security can be neglected. The institutions of liberty are under attack. They are threatened by an aggressive totalitarianism abroad, and they need the protection of a strong and resolute government. If that government should fall, the institutions of liberty would fall with it. In some measure, too, the institutions are threatened in novel ways by agents of that totalitarianism at home. They are threatened most of all, however, by well-meaning and patriotic but frightened Americans, who have come to think of liberty as a liability rather than an asset.

The error of these men is that they confuse loyalty with orthodoxy. Acting upon this confusion, they tend to suppress diversity and to insist upon a

Reprinted from Alan Barth, *The Loyalty of Free Men* (New York: Viking, 1951), ch. 1. Copyright 1951 by Alan Barth. Reprinted by permission of the author and The Viking Press, Inc. Mr. Barth is an editorial writer for the *Washington Post*.

rigid conformity. But loyalty may take as many forms as religious worship. This much about it seems indisputable: like love, it must be freely given. It can be evoked but it cannot be commanded or coerced. Members of a family are loyal to one another, not through any oath or compulsion, but as a result of shared experiences, community of interest, and long mutual dependence. A great aggregation of individuals and families becomes and remains a nation, not through geographical propinquity alone, but rather through much this same process of shared experiences—which is to say, a common history—and, above all, through common acceptance of certain fundamental values. The national loyalty of free men is not so much to their government as to the purposes for which their government was created.

The United States, which is the supreme example of national union by voluntary compact, is peculiarly illustrative of the point. Founded by men committed to the idea that the just powers of government are derived from the consent of the governed, it began as an experiment. The vast American wilderness was populated by men and women who came to it voluntarily from a more settled world, desiring to participate in the experiment. Thus, a pledge of allegiance to the United States was essentially a pledge of allegiance to a political ideal. This ideal is, to be sure, very difficult of expression and susceptible of varying interpretations. But its kernel may fairly be said to lie in the concept of a society affording the widest possible scope for the realization of individual potentialities.

"The American compact," Walt Whitman wrote, "is altogether with individuals." Certainly respect for the individual personality is among the most settled and generally extolled of American principles. This is a respect necessarily rooted in the recognition, tolerance, and even encouragement of diversity. This country has grown to greatness on the premise that wide diversity of interest and opinion is not only consistent with loyalty but essential to the generation of it. The only genuine loyalty is the loyalty of free men.

The United States was established as a nation by men whose national loyalty was rooted elsewhere. Most of them had been born and bred in allegiance to the English crown. They were divorced from this allegiance and from divisive sectional loyalties only by common adherence to certain overriding ideas and values. There were no national traditions, no national heroes, no national history to unite them. When they dissolved the political bands that connected them with the British people and affixed their names to the Declaration of Independence, there was no nation to which they could pledge devotion; for the support of this Declaration, they said, "we mutually pledge *to each other* our Lives, our Fortunes, and our sacred Honor."

The new nation they created became an embodiment of the ideas they shared. It drew devotion not because of its past but because of its promise. The Constitution which made it a Federal Union guaranteed freedom of expression and of conscience. The constitutions of its constituent states had already provided similar guarantees. Freedom and opportunity were its dynamic elements. They were the elements that evoked loyalty and cemented union and afforded the matrix of growth.

The tolerance on which freedom and opportunity must rest was a necessity of early life in America. Conquest of a continental wilderness fostered a tradition of individualism. The opening of successive frontiers widely different in physical conditions and in the problems of settlement encouraged a variety of political forms. Differences of religion, of social background, of economic interest among the settlers required tolerance of diversity. Out of this necessity the early Americans made a virtue. The idea that they had raised a standard to which the lovers of liberty could repair became a source of tremendous pride to them. "This new world," Thomas Paine boasted in *Common Sense,* "hath been the asylum for the persecuted lovers of civil and religious liberty from *every part* of Europe."[1]

It was tolerance of diversity that made possible the union of thirteen disparate colonies. It was tolerance of wide differences in religious faith and cultural background that enabled America to absorb and gain enrichment from the great variety of immigrants seeking opportunity and freedom here. Opportunity and freedom were sufficient to make loyal Americans of the newcomers. There was never, until very recently, much fear that those who came to this country, let alone those who were its native sons, could grow up in American homes, attend American schools, play American games, join in the robust rivalry of American life, and turn out disloyal to America. "It is nothing to us," Congressman Page of Virginia contended in 1790 in support of a liberal naturalization policy:

> Whether Jews or Roman Catholics settle among us; whether subjects of Kings, or citizens of free States wish to reside in the United States, they will find it in their interest to be good citizens, and neither their religious nor political opinion can injure us, if we have good laws, well executed.[2]

Whatever may have been the vices and weaknesses of this country in the past, want of confidence in itself was not among them. The nation knew that the American dream would inspire all who had a chance to dream it.

But that sublime self-confidence has now disappeared. Aliens are suspect; there is no longer the old certainty that they will be swept into the mainstream of American life. Prospective immigrants must prove that they are not the bearers of contagious opinions, and even transient visitors are feared. In 1950 the State Department denied visas to the Dean of Canterbury and later to twelve members of the Communist-sponsored World Congress of Partisans for Peace, Pablo Picasso among them, because of their political and economic views. The faith of Americans in their own institutions is apparently no longer considered strong enough to withstand Communist propaganda. Eminent artists have been barred merely because their political sympathies were suspect. The German conductor Wilhelm Furtwängler was kept out because he had collaborated with the Nazis. Later Josef Krips, the conductor of the Vienna State Opera, was forbidden to fill a summer engagement with the Chicago Symphony Orchestra because he had previously conducted performances at Moscow and Leningrad.

[1]Quoted by Merle Curti, *The Roots of American Loyalty* (New York: Columbia University Press, 1946), p. 69.
[2]*Ibid.,* p. 73.

Tolerance of diversity and faith in the democratic process are giving way to reliance on the quarantine of hostile doctrines.

Indeed, even those born into the American heritage are now only tentatively trusted; they are obliged to affirm and reaffirm their allegiance. And beyond this ritual of affirmation, in the potency of which there is no longer any confidence, they are commonly required before entering upon any post affecting the national interest to deny disloyalty. Anyone who goes to work for the government of the United States today must swear that he does not advocate its overthrow. In point of fact, Congress thought it necessary in 1940 to make it a penal offense for any citizen to teach or advocate the duty or necessity of overthrowing "any government in the United States by force or violence."

A terrible distrust lies behind this shift to negativism. The country's doubts about the loyalty of its citizens are not unlike the doubts of a husband about the fidelity of his wife. The protestations that answer his doubts are never convincing and are likely to dissipate the mutual confidence that is the essence of a marriage. When men lose faith in one another, they lose the substance of what constitutes a community among them. Thus, to a national community, there is nothing that so dangerously corrupts its integrity as such a loss of faith. As in the case of the suspicious husband, this distrust is the expression of a neurotic insecurity.

Such insecurity is perhaps the most pervasive characteristic of our time. The fear of freedom and the difficulties of realizing its potentialities have been illuminatingly treated by the psychiatrists and the social psychologists. They have contributed invaluable insights, of which political theorists have as yet made too little use. The forces that have led great numbers of Europeans and Asiatics to seek the fellowship of disciplined submission to authority as an escape from the responsibilities and isolation of freedom are at work here too. They exhibit themselves in the exertion of powerful pressures, cultural as well as political, toward conformity and in an attitude novel among Americans that they can neither comprehend nor change the awful tides in which they feel themselves engulfed. The consequence is a stultifying tendency to seek unity through uniformity.

"Loyalty" has become a cult, an obsession, in the United States. But even loyalty itself is now defined negatively. It is thought of not so much in terms of an affirmative faith in the great purposes for which the American nation was created as in terms of stereotypes the mere questioning of which is deemed "disloyal." The whole postwar accent is on something called "un-Americanism"—a hyphenated synonym for unorthodoxy. Deviations to the Left are regarded as more suspicious or criminal than deviations to the Right; but the tendency is to question all deviations. "Loyalty" consists today in not being un-American, which is to say, in not being different or individualistic. The very diversity which was the wellspring of loyalty in the past is now distrusted.

The term "disloyalty" as it is commonly used today is nothing more or less than a circumlocution for treason. The authors of the Constitution went to a great deal of trouble in dealing with the subject of treason because they knew from experience how readily the term can be twisted to make discontent or dissent, or mere criticism of the government, a major crime.

They took care, therefore, to define treason in the narrowest terms. "Treason against the United States," they declared in Article III, Section 3, of the Constitution, "shall consist only in levying war against them or in adhering to their enemies, giving them aid and comfort." No acts other than those specified in the Constitution can be made treasonable by legislation. Congress can neither extend, nor restrict, nor define the crime. Its power over the subject is limited to prescribing the punishment.

The Constitution is no less exacting as to the means by which conviction of treason may be obtained. "No person shall be convicted of treason," Section 3 continues, "unless on the testimony of two witnesses to the same overt act, or on confession in open court."

James Madison explained in Number 43 of *The Federalist*—that brilliant exegesis of the Constitution characterized by Thomas Jefferson as "the best commentary on the principles of government which ever was written"— the reasons that prompted the Constitutional Convention to define treason so narrowly and to make conviction of it so difficult:

As treason may be committed against the United States, the authority of the United States ought to be enabled to punish it. But as new-fangled and artificial treasons have been the great engines by which violent factions, the natural offspring of free government, have usually wreaked their alternate malignity on each other, the convention have, with great judgment, opposed a barrier to this peculiar danger, by inserting a constitutional definition of the crime, fixing the proof necessary for conviction of it, and restraining the Congress, even in punishing it, from extending the consequences of guilt beyond the person of its author.

There is a whole lesson in political science in this paragraph—a lesson peculiarly applicable today. The use of "disloyalty" as a "new-fangled and artificial" form of treason has indeed promoted the rise of violent factions and led to a wreaking of "their alternate malignity on each other." There is no way to measure the impairment of national security that has resulted from this disruption of the sense of national community.

Disloyalty, to be sure, has not officially been held to constitute treason. But when a congressional committee or a quasi-judicial government board says that an individual is disloyal—or that he is un-American, or subversive, or a security risk, or ineligible for employment by the United States, or any of the other circumlocutions of the circumlocution—it is saying in not very euphemistic terms, or at least is encouraging the public to believe, that he is a traitor. The difference is that disloyalty is nowhere to be found detailed as a crime upon the statute books, that nowhere has it been defined, that nowhere has a punishment been prescribed for it by law. This ambiguity merely makes the charge more difficult to avoid and a condemnation less difficult to obtain.

Real disloyalty presents a threat to national security. It might find expression in betrayal of the nation—even in espionage or sabotage. Of course these are statutory crimes, clearly defined and punishable through the normal processes of indictment and trial by jury. The law can easily be used to punish any actual spy or saboteur. But the law can no more be used to punish a potential spy or a potential saboteur than it can be used to punish a potential pickpocket or a potential embezzler. The law punishes specifically prohibited antisocial acts. It does not prohibit and cannot punish antisocial ideas or intentions. The distinction has always been considered basic to a free society.

In a period of international tension, however, a potential spy or saboteur is likely to seem very dangerous—so dangerous that there is enormous temptation to deal with him outside the law. The United States, engaged in a worldwide struggle that has led to armed conflict in Asia, has yielded to this temptation to an alarming degree. It has devised an elaborate system and ritual for punishing men—and punishing them most cruelly—for crimes they have not committed but are suspected of desiring to commit. It punishes them by stigmatizing them as disloyal.

Anyone so stigmatized becomes to some degree an outcast. If he retains any friends, he knows himself to be a menace to them. Any association with them may result in their stigmatization too. Wherever he goes he is marked as a man who would be willing to betray his country. He remains at large but is regarded as a menace to society. He is expatriated without being exiled and denied the opportunity to gain a livelihood without the compensation of being maintained in prison at the community's expense. He and his fellows might come, in time, to constitute something new in American life—a caste of untouchables.

The punishment in such cases is something like that in the old story about the Quaker and his dog Tray. " 'Go to,' said the Quaker to poor Tray, 'I will not kill thee, but I will give thee a bad name,' as he turned him into the streets with the cry of 'mad dog,' and somebody else did kill Tray."

Perhaps the punishments meted out on the ground of disloyalty are not too severe for anyone who clearly and demonstrably intends to serve the interest of a foreign government to the detriment of his own countrymen. The fact is, however, that these penalties are meted out without any of the safeguards embodied in the Anglo-American system of justice for the protection of innocent persons against unjust conviction. They are inflicted on the loyal and the disloyal almost without discrimination.

By the simple stratagem of charging a man with disloyalty, instead of with treason or espionage or sabotage, it is possible to evade the constitutional requirements that he be indicted by a grand jury, that he enjoy a speedy and public trial by an impartial petit jury, that he be informed of the nature and cause of the accusation and confronted with the witnesses against him, that he be accorded the benefit of compulsory process to obtain witnesses in his favor. He is indicted and tried and sentenced by congressional committee or administrative tribunal, with the same men acting as prosecutors, judges, and jury. The presumption of innocence supposed to surround him is ignored. The mere charge of disloyalty is treated as evidence of guilt.

The part played by the press in this process of extra-legal punishment falls, because of its complexity, outside the scope of this discussion. It can only be noted here that it is the press which executes, so to speak, the sentences passed by congressional committees or by mere individuals speaking under the immunity from suits for slander or libel afforded by Congress. Newspapers especially tend to make headlines out of accusations and to treat denials less prominently. This stems in large measure from the concept of news as sensation and is scarcely less true of those newspapers that strive for objectivity than of those that deliberately use their news pages to serve editorial biases.

The tradition of objectivity, which is the great virtue of the American press, has operated in this context to make the press an instrument of those seeking to inflict punishment by publicity. Allegations which would otherwise be ignored because they would be recognized as groundless and libelous are blown up on front pages and given a significance out of all relation to their intrinsic merit after they have been made before a committee of Congress. Thus, what is one day properly regarded as unpublishable gossip is treated the next day as news of great moment because it has been uttered under official auspices. Refutation, no matter how compelling, never catches up with charges of disloyalty and never erases their imprint. In addition, of course, many newspapers welcome such charges and inflate them for political reasons or for their commercial value in stimulating street sales.

The cost of this system of punishment by publicity is worth reckoning. It entails sacrifices not only for the individuals who become involved in it, but also, on a wider scale, for the society as a whole. If all the elements of due process can be thus evaded, the personal security of individuals in the United States from arbitrary and summary punishment becomes a fiction. One result is to heighten the general insecurity of which this evasion of constitutional safeguards is a symptom.

The short-cut to punishment has an effect on society in other ways as well. The knowledge that men may be accused and found guilty of disloyalty in so summary a manner becomes a restraint on the exercise of constitutional rights. It is no longer safe to talk recklessly or foolishly. If the effect of this were no more than to silence recklessness and folly, perhaps the loss would not be great. But the discouragement of reckless and foolish talk tends inescapably to suppress sound and sensible dissent which may seem unpatriotic because it happens to be unpopular.

The trouble with putting any halter upon individual freedom to talk nonsense—even subversive or seditious nonsense—is that it tends to frustrate the democratic process. That process is one in which nonsense cannot be silenced by authority; it can be silenced, or overcome, only by sense. Since it is often not altogether easy to distinguish between the two, silencing of the one cannot help but result in silencing of the other. What happens, of course, is that unorthodox ideas, whether sensible or not, are suppressed in favor of orthodoxy. And consequently the attention of the society is diverted from its real problems, which call for adaptation and change, and focused instead upon a preservation of things as they are.[3]

[3]"The imagined insecurity of the strongest democracy in the world in the face of the cold war with Communism has created an atmosphere in which fear makes the maintenance of civil liberties precarious. Not only the liberties of real or suspected Communists are at stake. Far beyond them, the measures to protect our institutions from Communist infiltration have set up an unprecedented array of barriers to free association, of forced declarations of loyalty, of blacklists and purges, and, most menacing to the spirit of liberty, of taboos on those progressive programs and principles which are the heart of any expanding democracy."—"In the Shadow of Fear," Report of the American Civil Liberties Union, 1948–49.

The situation should not be overstated. There has been, as yet, no formal or statutory suppression of speech in the United States beyond the prohibition of advocacy of violent overthrow of the government and the punitive restrictions of the McCarran Act. Men may, and fortunately a number of them still do, express nonconformist views liable to be termed treasonable. But, as Senator Margaret Chase Smith observed in a speech expressing her revulsion against the name-calling tactics of Senator Joseph McCarthy, "Freedom of speech is not what it used to be in America. It has been so abused by some that it is not exercised by others." Freedom of speech does not mean, to be sure, that a man who says what is unpopular should be protected from the penalties of unpopularity. Heretics and reformers must expect denunciation. The alarming characteristic about what is happening today lies partly in the official source of the denunciation, partly in the easy identification of dissent with disloyalty, partly in the punishment of it by the government itself through extra-legal mechanisms.

The cult of loyalty, and its attendant hunt for heresy as a symptom of disloyalty, has generated an intellectually shackled feeling for which terror is too strong a term, but which is marked nevertheless by widespread anxiety. The feeling is most acute, naturally, in Washington, and among government employees. But outside the capital, the pressures for conformity are mounting to a degree never before experienced by the American people. The Committee on Un-American Activities in the national House of Representatives has spawned imitators in state legislatures; some of them, such as the Tenney Committee in California, the Canwell Committee in Washington, the Broyles Commission in Illinois, have rivaled the tactics of the congressional body. In their role of investigators and with the stated object of protecting national security, they have had the effect of penalizing Americans for exercising the fundamental rights of advocacy and association.

Similarly, the Federal Employee-Loyalty Program has been aped and embellished in states and municipalities—where there is far less warrant for such restrictions. Protective measures designed to keep disloyal persons out of jobs that directly affect the national security become merely punitive when applied indiscriminately to all forms of public employment. In many states extremely repressive legislation, of doubtful constitutionality, has been adopted. These laws are aimed at Communists, but their result is to penalize all forms of heterodoxy. Some of the laws deny a place on the ballot to Communists, thereby revealing a distrust of the democratic process. Some, like the Ober Law in Maryland, drastically restrict the right of citizens to join in voluntary associations if the purpose of these associations is officially regarded as subversive. A number of municipalities, especially in the South, have adopted ordinances banning Communists and Communist *sympathizers* from the city limits. Birmingham, Alabama, for instance, announced that it would jail anyone found guilty of "voluntary association" with a Communist. Other cities have undertaken to require the registration of all Communists. The patent invalidity of such edicts from a constitutional point of view has given no apparent pause to local legislative and law-enforcement bodies. In a number of places, police chiefs have intimated that they mean to apply virtual lynch law to political undesirables. Behind all these measures is a fear of freedom and a panicky willingness to disregard the great procedural safeguards that distinguish a free from a totalitarian society.

The hounding of heterodoxy in the name of loyalty takes an especially ugly and mischievous form in connection with schools and universities. The proliferation of loyalty tests and oaths required of teachers inhibits discussion precisely where it should be most free. But perhaps the gravest consequence of the official cult of loyalty is the inflammation of public opinion to a sometimes hysterical pitch. When political disagreement is branded as disloyalty, when neighbor is invited to look with suspicion on neighbor, the bonds of national unity are strained in a way that is directly injurious to national security. Tragic incidents such as the Peekskill riots in the summer of 1949—when war veterans expressed their devotion to American ideals by behaving like Nazi stormtroopers—flow inevitably from official stimulation of intolerance. No matter how wrong-headed Paul Robeson may be, nothing that he might have said or sung at Peekskill could have injured the credit and the peace of the United States as grievously as the silencing of his voice by violence.

The war in Korea gave a tremendous impetus to this intolerance. In the grip of its excitement, many normally rational and gentle people tended to look upon any association with Communism, no matter how remote or tenuous, as evidence of disloyalty and to regard a mere charge of such association as incontrovertible proof of guilt. A pathetic instance of this tendency occurred in connection with the cancellation of a talk scheduled to be given at a New Hampshire resort hotel by Professor Owen Lattimore in the summer of 1950. A woman who had been active in having Professor Lattimore's appearance cancelled gave this explanation of her attitude: "Just now with the critical condition of this country, anyone about whom there is any question should not be allowed to speak." This extraordinary patriotism came well after the Senate subcommittee appointed to investigate Senator McCarthy's charges had given Professor Lattimore the most complete exoneration of which it was capable and had called the charges "a fraud and a hoax" perpetrated on the United States Senate.

Apparently exoneration is impossible today for anyone who has ever expressed unorthodox opinions, unless he is willing to profess the most extreme anti-Communism and denounce everyone who shared his past beliefs. One is reminded a little bit of a letter written about 112 A.D. by the younger Pliny to the emperor Trajan:

I am also very uncertain . . . whether repentance should earn a pardon, or if, when a man has once been a Christian, he gains nothing by leaving the sect; whether nominal Christianity without crime deserves punishment or only when crime is coupled with it. In the meantime this is the procedure I have adopted when any so-called Christians have been brought before me. I asked them if they were Christians. If they admitted it, I asked them a second and again a third time, adding threats of death. If they still claimed to be Christians, I gave orders for their execution. . . . Soon in the usual way the investigation itself led to further accusations, covering several types of charge. An anonymous accusation appeared, containing many names. Some of those named denied that they were Christians or ever had been. As they joined with me in invocations to the gods and offered supplications with incense and wine to your Majesty's ikon, which I had brought in with the divine images for this purpose, and finally cursed Christ, I thought they could be discharged, as it is said that genuine Christians cannot be forced into these acts. Others whose names were quoted by the informer said they were Christians but soon withdrew their plea; to be sure, they had once been Christians but they had ceased, some three years before, some for a longer time and a few even for twenty-five years. All these worshipped your Majesty's ikon and the images of the gods; and cursed Christ.

The emperor commended Pliny's conduct but added this warning:

There should be no search made for Christians; though, if they are summoned and convicted, they must be punished. But the method should be that anyone who denies that he is a Christian and proves it by his actions, namely by worshipping our gods, whatever suspicion he may previously have incurred, should earn pardon by repentance. Public accusations by anonymous persons should have no place in criminal practice. Such a procedure would be thoroughly bad and out of keeping with the spirit of our age.[4]

Intolerance has taken its most extravagant form in relation to entertainment and the arts. Self-appointed censors have aimed, like Soviet commissars, to dictate the forms and observances of what they consider patriotism and to purge from the stage, screen, and radio any performer whose private associations or opinions cross the frontiers of conformity they have delineated. Paul Draper and Larry Adler were their most notable victims in 1949; their procedure has since been put on a mass-production basis. A formal index of their purge from radio and television was published in June 1950 under the title *Red Channels*; this interesting brochure, issued under the auspices of *Counterattack*, a newsletter founded in May 1947 by a group of former FBI men, contains the names of writers, actors, dancers, and directors, together with a listing of the committees and organizations with which they are alleged to have had some affiliation. The listing is based in most instances on statements made by or before the House Committee on Un-American Activities or its California counterpart, or on newspaper references, generally from the *Daily Worker*; in some cases it is based on nothing more than information contained in *Counterattack* itself, and often the alleged affiliation is so tenuous as to involve no more than an appearance as an entertainer before some group supposed to be subversive. *Red Channels* makes no charges; its technique is accusation by innuendo. It could perhaps be considered as negligible as Elizabeth Dilling's *Red Network* of a decade ago were it not for the fact that it has been made effective by an organized program of pressure and intimidation brought to bear upon the advertisers and broadcasters who employ the performers it blacklists.

Advertisers appealing to a mass market are obviously vulnerable to this kind of pressure. *Red Channels* scored its outstanding triumph shortly after its publication in the dismissal of Miss Jean Muir, a television actress, from the leading role in a network program. Her name appeared in the book, and a few telephone protests led the sponsor of the program to drop her from the program as a "controversial personality." It is clear that, if this sort of vigilantism is permitted to flourish, the American public will be able to see and hear only those entertainers who can pass the censorship of the vigilantes.

Censorship in the name of patriotism occurs on an unorganized basis too. Perhaps the most sensitive example of it was provided by a Hollywood

---

[4]Quoted in E. W. Barnes, *The Rise of Christianity* (New York: Longmans, Green, 1947), pp. 307–309.

motion-picture studio which, after six months of work, shelved plans to produce a film dealing with the life and exploits of Hiawatha, the Onondaga Indian chief immortalized by Longfellow. Hiawatha had succeeded in establishing peace among the warring Five Nations; and it was felt, according to a studio spokesman, that this might cause the film to be regarded as a message for peace and thus as Communist propaganda.[5]

Political discussion has been debased to a species of fishwivery by shrill and redundant accusations of disloyalty. The immunity from suit for slander afforded by the floor of Congress has been abused over and over again to launch extravagant attacks on the good faith of opponents in every issue of policy. Demagogic exploitation of popular anxiety, such as Senator McCarthy's blanket indictment of the State Department early in 1950, can have no other than a shattering effect on the confidence of the American people in their government. The prestige of the United States abroad suffers incalculably from such attacks. And the formulation of foreign policy is paralyzed at home by the fear that restraint and reason will be characterized as traitorous. In such an atmosphere only the most extreme chauvinism can pass for patriotism.

. . . mere anti-Communism has taken the place of a reasoned evaluation of American interests, allying this country with discredited regimes abroad. Those who dared to protest or dissent were liable to vilification as Communist sympathizers. . . . This is not an atmosphere conducive to national security. The men responsible for creating it may be credited with good intentions. But they are guilty nonetheless of the gravest and most dangerous form of disloyalty to the United States. They are disloyal to the principles and purposes that are the genius of the American society.

In the aftermath of World War I, when there was a similar fear that America might be subverted by enemies from within, the late Senator William E. Borah observed:

The safeguards of our liberty are not so much in danger from those who openly oppose them as from those who, professing to believe in them, are willing to ignore them when found inconvenient for their purposes; the former we can deal with, but the latter, professing loyalty, either by precept or example undermine the very first principles of our government and are far the more dangerous.

The disloyalty of the Americanists impairs national security more seriously than the comparable disloyalty of the Communists. It is more deeply subversive, strikes more injuriously at the real roots of loyalty and of American strength. It would, in fact, meet the threat of Communism by the substitution of Communist techniques for the techniques of freedom. If the relatively impotent Communists aim at overthrowing the government of the United States, the Americanists, whether they are aware of it or not, aim at overthrowing the essential values which that government was instituted to secure.

[5]*New York Times*, September 13, 1950.

WE'VE NEVER HAD
MORE FREEDOM

John P. Roche

My thesis is that American freedom has never been as firmly established or as broadly shared as is the case today. This thesis will seem overly
sanguine to some. And so I should make it clear at once that I am not
suggesting that the American Civil Liberties Union close up shop, nor am
I justifying for one minute the many abuses of civil liberty that do occur.
My optimism about the present, if optimism is the appropriate word, is
founded on a pessimistic estimate of the past rather than on any conviction
that we have achieved Nirvana. We still have a long way to go, and it will
take continued struggle by thousands of dedicated individuals to keep the
standard of freedom moving forward. Yet, there is no need to travel under
the illusion that we are moving downhill from a mystical, unfettered past;
on the contrary, it seems to me demonstrable that we are moving up the
road from the lynching and the tar-pot toward the aspiration of impartial
justice and the rule of law.

We are accustomed, when we consider our civil liberty, to extol the
"grass-roots" freedom of the early American scene—the New England town
meeting, the spontaneous democracy of the frontier. We bewail the fact that
the growth of the industrial state and the increasing bureaucratization of life
have created an impersonal civilization in which individualism and liberty
wither. Too often we forget that the other side of the direct democracy of
the town meeting was the direct democracy of the lynching. That brilliant
political sociologist Alexis de Tocqueville noted this ambivalence in his
penetrating treatment of "The Unlimited Power of the Majority and its
Consequences" in *Democracy in America*. Indeed, if one accepts majority
rule as the touchstone of democracy, he must accept the lynching as a
democratic institution, for in it we find the people's sovereignty in its
starkest form.

What has confused historians looking back at the intellectual and social
history of the United States is the fact that great diversity of opinion indu-
bitably existed in the nation. From this they have drawn the erroneous conclusion that there was toleration of divergent opinions among the populace
at large. It is my contention that the diversity of views was a consequence
not of tolerance and mutual respect, but of the existence of many communities within the society, each with its own rigid canons of orthodoxy.

In other words, if a man looked hard enough, he could probably find a
community within the United States that shared his own peculiar views,
and, joining it, he could help impose his eccentricities on all within reach.
The United States was the happy hunting ground of what David Riesman
has acutely termed "vested heresies." There was no monolithic centralized

Abridged from John P. Roche, "We've Never Had More Freedom," *The New Republic,* January 23, 1956, pp. 12–15; January 30, 1956, pp. 13–16; February 6, 1956,
pp. 13–15. Reprinted by permission of the author and the publisher. John P. Roche,
the chairman of the Department of Politics at Brandeis University, has written books
and articles on civil rights and the structure of democratic government.

state to fulfill the European model of authoritarianism, but there was decentralized authoritarianism aplenty. Of libertarianism, the respect for views considered fundamentally "wrong," there was little: the Populists, for example, were as ready to suppress economic orthodoxy as the economically orthodox were to expunge Populism.

Space does not permit extensive documentation of this hypothesis, but several examples can be quickly mentioned. First and foremost were the settlers of the Massachusetts Bay Colony, who came to this country from Britain—not to escape persecution but to establish the religious absolutism that the laws of England would not permit. Massachusetts Bay, the "Zion in the Wilderness," was the archetype for hundreds of subsequent religious communities that have been established on the twin principles of freedom for Truth, and suppression for Error. The internal authoritarianism of such groups as the Mormons, Amish, Mennonites, and Brethren—at least in the nineteenth century—is clear.

Some confusion is created by the fact that our forefathers certainly seem more tolerant than we are. In part that may be because they did not necessarily share our convictions as to what was important. Thus, from Jefferson's broad tolerance in religious matters is deduced a full belief in freedom of opinion. It would seem more accurate to say that Jefferson considered religion unimportant and was therefore willing to permit any nonsense to be spoken from the pulpit. However, in an area which Jefferson did consider important, he was prepared to excommunicate ideas. For example, in his capacity as *deus ex machina* of the University of Virginia, Jefferson insisted that the trustees (Board of Visitors, to be exact) should have the power to select textbooks in the field of Government. In a letter to Joseph Cabell, written a year before his death, the Sage of Monticello observed:

> There is one branch [of learning] in which we are the best judges, in which heresies may be taught of so interesting a character to our own State, and to the United States, as to make it a duty to lay down the principles which shall be taught. It is that of government. . . . It is our duty to guard against the dissemination of [Federalist-Nationalist] principles among our youth, and the diffusion of that poison, by a previous prescription of the texts to be followed in their discourses.

In short, freedom of ideas stopped when the insidious poisons of Marshall, Kent, and Story came into the picture; and it is not surprising that a year later we find Jefferson much concerned lest an unorthodox, i.e., Federalist-Nationalist, jurist be appointed to the chair of law at the University.

Some may object that this example has been taken from Jefferson's dotage; so another example taken from his political prime is apposite. It is seldom appreciated that Jefferson's fundamental objection to the Sedition Act of 1798 was based on his states-rights outlook. He was not necessarily opposed to sedition actions on principle; rather, he was opposed to Federalist-dominated courts enforcing the wrong orthodoxy on the press. In this spirit we find President Jefferson in 1803 writing to Governor McKean of Pennsylvania:

> The Federalists, having failed in destroying the freedom of the press with their gag-law, seem to have attacked it in an opposite direction; that is, by pushing its licentiousness and its lying to such a degree of prostitution as to deprive it of all

credit. . . . This is a dangerous state of things, and the press ought to be restored to its credibility if possible. The restraints provided by the laws of the States are sufficient for this, if applied. And I have therefore long thought that a few prosecutions of the most prominent offenders would have a wholesome effect in restoring the integrity of the presses. Not a general prosecution, for that would look like persecution; but a selected one.

I have quoted from Jefferson at some length not with the intention of defaming his character, but because he was a militant believer in freedom *as he defined it,* which makes the key point of this analysis.

Sincere obeisance has always been paid to the principles of freedom of speech, press, assembly, and opinion by the great majority of Americans. But few generations have looked with kindness upon those who challenged the established order. There have always been incisive differences of viewpoint as to what constituted speech and opinion, and what constituted subversive action. The general outcome of this conflict, which was seldom publicly articulated, was that each community established certain key symbols, to which it demanded unqualified allegiance of both idea and action. Outside of this myth-sector, broad differences of opinion were taken for granted. In the Old South, for example, there were few limitations on freedom of speech or press—provided the individual concerned accepted the validity of slavery; but the nonconformist was shown no mercy. It is often forgotten that the first Jew (Benjamin) and the second Catholic (Mallory) to hold Cabinet rank in this country took their seats around the table with Jefferson Davis in 1861!

Freedom of opinion in general has thus been recognized and honored; but woe unto the nonconformist who laid profane hands on the Ark of the Covenant, who rejected a key myth, for by his action he has transmuted his offense from permissible difference of opinion to forbidden conspiracy against the *lares* and *panates* of the community. The house gods may vary from community to community, as they often did in the era before the economic consolidation of the nation and the communications revolution, but the reaction was the same: tar and feathers, the knout, the club, the noose—the latter sometimes reinforced by the ritual of trial by jury. The Non-Partisan League organizer in Minnesota, the Wobbly in Colorado, the abolitionist in Georgia, the Socialist in Oklahoma, the Catholic in Know-Nothing territory, and other crusaders for now forgotten enthusiasms, all felt the scourge of the great god numbers. Indeed, a close reading of American social history leaves one with the ineradicable conviction that tar and feathers was standard armament for "grass-roots democracy."

Nor is the decentralized authoritarianism in our past limited to political and religious agitation. It is one of the ironies of history that the academic freedom of which the French and British are so proud is the consequence in the British instance of the virtually complete autonomy of the educational system from local pressures and, in the French instance, of the complete centralization of authority over the national educational system in an irresponsible bureaucracy. It is American "grass-roots democracy" that has put public educational institutions at the mercy of local pressure groups. Here as in all issues we pay our money and take our choice, for if local communities are restrained from doing evil, they can also be restrained from doing good.

In recent years, however, there has been a distinct let-up in the force of direct democracy in the United States, and with it an easing of pressure against nonconformity. The Negro, the trade-union organizer, the radical, even the Communist, have rights today that were nonexistent, or at best fragmentary, thirty years ago.

It is my contention that two major developments are responsible. The first is the increasing power and jurisdiction of the national government over national life, which has taken place as a concomitant, if not as a consequence, of the increasing industrialization and urbanization of the nation. The second is the rise of civil-liberty elites, leadership groups, in American society that have initiated unceasing legal and educational campaigns on behalf of the rights of nonconformists. Let us examine these two propositions in some detail.

The national government was insulated against "direct democracy"—and by design. The framers of the Constitution were superbly successful experimenters but they sought to bar mob rule. The instrument of government they created was contrived above all to exorcise passion from political decision-making, to make impossible the sudden seizure of power by any faction, however well motivated. It is not accidental then that the United States—a nation historically characterized by violent tides of political extremism—has never fallen into the hands of extremist politicians.

But an even more important factor is the social and economic consolidation that underlies this increase in national power. Here the outstanding characteristic is urbanization and the impersonalization that usually accompanies life in the metropolis and its suburbs. The growth of the city saw the disintegration of the rural system of social control, centered usually on that highly efficient intelligence service, the rural church. In the city it is quite possible to live differently, and believe differently, from one's neighbors without their even knowing, much less caring, about the deviation. While associations may be formed on a neighborhood basis, more frequently there are functional alignments: one's friends are the people one works with, who may be scattered all over town.

Moreover, except for the impersonal organ of the police, there are in the city no ready-made instruments of social control, of "direct democracy." Although such organizations as the American Legion may bid for the role with great vigor, they can seldom make a dent in the great wall of indifference. In sum, nonconformity, a psychological manifestation of strong individualism, is paradoxically sheltered by a blanket of urban anonymity.

Probably because most state legislatures are controlled firmly by nonurban forces, the city man has turned to the national government for his salvation. But he has not only turned over to Washington his economic destiny; he has also waived in favor of the federal government his ancestral right to take direct action against the desecrators of his house gods: *Enter*— the Smith Act.

To assert this is, of course, to oversimplify the background of the Smith Act, which was part and parcel of the national defense program; but I think it is interesting to compare the treatment of "subversives" in the 1940's and 1950's with that in 1917, 1863, or even 1776. Personally, I consider the Smith Act and its subsidiary legislation unwise and unnecessary—in my view, existing statutes were adequate to the danger—but in the long view

I have little sympathy for the imprisoned Communists. Compared with the treatment handed out to authentic radicals in 1918, they have merely attended a compulsory tea party. I wish no human being any hard luck, but I save my tears for those who suffered genuine martyrdom in the cause of human freedom. Few people have fallen under the arm of the Smith Act—probably about enough to fill Tom Mooney Hall. In fact, they are probably holding a protest meeting against the "police state" there this week, for most of those convicted are out on bail.

And yet if civil liberty has gained from this process of urbanization and nationalization of political decision-making, the gain has been accidental, a mere by-product of impersonal historical developments. In contrast, the second factor in my analysis, the growth of civil-liberty elites, involves human action and volition. Outstanding in this category of opinion leaders have been the lawyers, closely followed by ministers, teachers, editors, and businessmen. Perhaps most important of all have been the professors of law, for as the law has become more and more an educated profession—as distinct from the old system of informal "reading" in a lawyer's office—that rigorous emphasis on procedural regularity and due process which is the mark of the expert teacher has permeated the consciousness of generations of students. Moreover, law today is the access-way to careers in labor, business, and politics even more than was the case a century ago; so business elites, labor elites, and political elites have been influenced by this climate of opinion.

More important perhaps has been the infiltration of national government decision-making groups by the legal elite. The great legal migration to Washington that took place in the 1930's, as the consequence of the mushroom-like growth of the national administration, resulted in thousands of key jobs being held by firm advocates of due process of law and civil rights. The full impact of this legal colonization on the civil-rights climate of the national government can only be imagined; in practice it meant that the thousands of basic, mundane decisions in which human rights were involved were suffused with a new direction. In addition, to throw in a really intangible factor, the ablest law-school graduates become clerks to members of the judiciary, with all the potential influence that this anonymous function can imply. As De Tocqueville saw the legal profession of his day as a real check on the excesses of local democracy, so today we can see the lawyers as a force for regularized—even pettifogged—procedures of national governmental operation and for the maintenance of the myth of impartial justice, a myth never fully fleshed but nonetheless vital as a goal for collective aspirations.

But the improvement of the civil-liberties climate has also been due to the passionate efforts of crusading individuals and groups. It is almost true to say that the American Civil Liberties Union invented civil rights, for before this organization came on the scene after World War I, there was little articulated interest in or concern for the problem except among the oppressed. Much the ACLU did directly, but above all, it supplied a formula—a public-relations "package"—a body of civil-rights doctrine, around which could be mobilized the teachers, trade unionists, ministers, editors, and others who had previously lived in atomistic impotence. Roger Baldwin, a Madison Avenue advertising genius who somehow located on the wrong street, supplied the organization an impetus and a direction that gave the Union a nationwide reputation in an incredibly short space of time. For every dues-paying member, there were probably a hundred nonmembers, frequently in key opinion-forming positions in their communities, who followed the Union's leadership, rallied to its campaigns, and passed on its position to their opinion-constituents.

Although Americans pride themselves on their patriotism, and vigilant state legislatures have made it virtually impossible for the young to escape some exposure to the facts of the American past, the average American is nonetheless singularly deficient in historical sense. Born without an historical umbilical cord, *Homo Americanus* tramps from situation to situation through time, hardly concerning himself with the historical antecedents of his reactions, or with their probable historical consequences. His concern is with Hard Facts; he makes his judgments On The Merits; and his disregard, even scorn, for abstract thinking—and the intellectuals who engage in this peculiar avocation—is manifested in the public policy of the nation.

Recognizing the merits of this flexible technique, one must also note the defects that it contains. Each crisis is approached as though nothing like it had ever before occurred on this planet. McCarthy was treated by the liberal press as though Watson, Long, Coughlin, and other leading specimens of the genus demagogue had never trod the American stage; the conservative press perpetually screams about the imminent murder of American liberty, as though the business community had suffered at the hands of Roosevelt and Truman, instead of prospering and surviving to bellow *Tyranny!* another day. The Reign of Terror is always upon us; the Jacobins —or the men of Thermidor—are ever on the verge of power.

As today *The Daily Worker* and *Political Affairs* live in full expectation of suppression, so in the past the organs of the abolitionists, the Socialists, the IWW, the pacifists, the Non-Partisan League, the Anti-Masons, the Jeffersonians—and perhaps the Virginia Federalists!—and countless other embattled zealots published regular forecasts of the death of American liberty at the hands of their enemies. Moreover, the point of this article is that in an earlier period one could often speak accurately of a reign of terror, whereas today the terrorists are usually equipped with a papier-mâché guillotine.

In the nineteenth century, the dominant white, rural, Protestant subculture was constantly at war with other subcultures who rejected their key social symbols. Take, for instance, the nativist movement which in the 1840's and 1850's spawned a powerful political wing in the Know-Nothings, with a platform of virulent anti-Catholic sentiments. The nativists did not simply propagandize for their viewpoint; they organized murderous and destructive riots in the major eastern cities directed, interestingly enough, against the one immigrant Catholic group which demonstrated political talent, the Irish. The Protestant elements of the lumpenproletariat organized into street gangs with such names as the Plug Uglies, Black Snakes, Rough Skins, and Blood Tubs and carried on guerrilla street warfare with Irish home guards. Top standing in the league went to those successful enough to burn down a church or a nunnery.

At about the same time, the abolitionists were receiving brutal treatment from "Vigilance Committees" in various Southern communities. These committees of leading citizens actually offered rewards for delivery to the magistrates (that is, for kidnapping) of leading abolitionists. New Orleans, in fact, topped the list with an offer of $100,000 for Arthur Tappan and LaRoy Sunderland. William Lloyd Garrison estimated that 300 abolitionist agents were lynched, and recently a careful student of the period, Russel B. Nye, agreed that this was not an unreasonable figure. Most, though not all, of these anti-slavery advocates were unarmed fanatics who sought to exercise their freedom of speech in the South.

But for every lynching, there were hundreds of lesser penalties meted out. The tar-pot was constantly a-simmering, and the whip was kept limber. "Four Ohioans . . . whipped," "Rev. Aaron Kitchell . . . tarred and feathered," "Amos Dresser . . . 20 lashes in the marketplace and confiscation of belongings," "Rev. T. S. Kendall . . . tarred and ejected from town": so runs the gloomy catalogue of pain in Nye's book, and it goes on for page after page.[1]

Similarly, the organizer for the IWW, the Socialist party, or other economically unorthodox organizations was liable to encounter genuine repression from the communities in which he spread his gospel, and there is hardly a trade union in the country whose history is not spotted with the blood of its pioneers.

In another sector, Walter Metzger and Richard Hofstadter have recently demonstrated that academic freedom, as a viable proposition, cannot be found operating in American colleges and universities much before World War I. Although there were shining exceptions, the teacher was generally at the mercy of his administrators, and if there were comparatively few outright dismissals, great care was taken to see that the unorthodox did not get hired in the first place.[2] (In civil-liberties issues, the incidence of cases can be a deceptive guide. Far from necessarily indicating a high level of oppression, a high case rate *can* symbolize the opposite—that acts formerly taken for granted are being resisted.)

There is no need to continue such a detailed analysis. It is patent that real reigns of terror against deviant subcultures were the rule rather than the exception, with the ironic corollary that the persecuted were themselves often quite willing to persecute those more helpless than themselves—see the Irish attitude toward the Jews. But, as we have noted, what has tended to conceal this reality from later analysts of American social history is the fact that these persecutions were local rather than national in scope. The model Reign of Terror was built by the French Jacobins on a national scale, and, when applied to the heterogeneous United States, this model was clearly irrelevant.

Evidence suggests that only once have we approached a national reign of terror—in the era of Woodrow Wilson and his Grand Vizier, A. Mitchell Palmer. However, while Palmer and his assistants contributed manfully to

[1]Russel B. Nye, *Fettered Freedom: Civil Liberties and the Slavery Controversy, 1830–1860* (East Lansing: Michigan State College Press, 1949).
[2]Richard Hofstadter and Walter Metzger, *The Development of Academic Freedom in the United States* (New York: Columbia University Press, 1955).

the great Red Scare and the concomitant assaults on radicals of all shades, careful analysis of the period 1917–21 indicates that the great bulk of the actions taken against deviants were locally sponsored. In effect, the facilities of the Departments of Justice and Labor were put at the disposal of local extremists—American Legionnaires, American Protective Leagues, etc.—and the national government looked on benignly.

In this regard, the difference between World War I and World War II is immediately apparent. In the latter conflict, Attorney General Francis Biddle employed the Department of Justice as a buffer against local extremism, refusing, for example, to permit local United States Attorneys to prosecute alleged disloyal or subversive elements without prior permission from Washington. This should be compared with the policy of Wilson's two Attorneys General, who gave full discretion to the local United States officials to deal with these matters as they saw fit. Attorney General Gregory disapproved of the indictment of Eugene Debs, for instance, but allowed the United States Attorney for the Northern District of Ohio, E. S. Wertz, to follow his own tack in dealing with the Socialist leader.

Biddle's policy was extremely important for two main reasons: first, because willy-nilly the national government tends to establish institutional behavior patterns which other governments in the nation imitate; and, second, because United States prosecutors were withdrawn from bureaucratic competition with local officials. To be specific, if the United States Attorney for the Western District of Pennsylvania begins to hunt subversives, with all the publicity that such diversions receive, it becomes extremely difficult for analogous state officials not to join in and stage a safari of their own. Given the nature of the patronage system, local officials are always potential candidates for state office, so state officeholders must never permit them to get a unique hold on the public attention. This is true even when the same party controls both the state and national government, for then factional battles in primaries have to be reckoned with; it is more true when different parties control these two governments. Needless to add, once this institutional competition gets under way, there is no effective check on how extreme it will become except the danger of committing the mortal sin of American politics—boring the sovereign people.

Another factor to be considered is that the national government is far more responsive to the views of civil-liberty elites than are state and local governments. This is not necessarily due to superior enlightenment (although the high percentage of "enlightened" lawyers in key jobs in Washington, discussed earlier, fits into the picture here); superior vulnerability is probably a better explanation. When the *New York Times* thunders editorially against the Veterans Administration for depriving legless veteran James Kutcher of his disability pension, the VA quakes, but all the admonitory *Times* pronouncements in the world will hardly disturb the Board of Selectmen of East Siwash. There is *one* national government; there are thousands of local governments. Although it may seem that I am here contradicting my earlier assertion that the national government is more insulated from extremism than other governments, in fact the two propositions are supplementary rather than opposed. The various segments of the national government are highly vulnerable to pressure, the administration being the most poorly insulated; but it is virtually impossible for the same pressure complex to dominate *all* segments—the President, the Congress, and the courts.

It seems clear that today the old-fashioned American reign of terror is a disappearing phenomenon. Direct democracy—citizens taking the law into their own hands—is not completely dead; but, except in the South, it lives a fitful and anemic existence. A casualty that has been unreported, but which seems to me to have accompanied it, is the old-fashioned American radical. In place of the wild-eyed enthusiast, prepared to tell judge, jury, and community to go to hell, we have the Nonconformist in the Brooks Brothers suit. He prides himself on the Nonconformity, but, as the capital letters indicate, the deviant values which he holds are now an orthodoxy and he a bureaucrat. While the old-style radical stuck out his chin and took his licks, never expecting that the reward for apostasy would be good fellowship, our Nonconformist is hurt when society retaliates for his deviation, for he feels that he deserves a medal. He frequently lives well, probably in what Russell Lynes called "Upper Bohemia," has a Volkswagon and *no* television set, and meets his fellow sectarians at cocktail parties to discuss ominous portents of impending American totalitarianism. He may be identified by the opening notes of his song: "*Everyone* these days is afraid. . . ."

Let me give two examples. There are lawyers whom I know who work hard and well for unpopular causes (and I am *not* referring to legal defense of unpopular people, which is a different proposition) and yet are constantly disturbed because conservative businessmen refuse to purchase their services. Recently I had lunch with a group of these gentlemen. The first half of the conversation concerned the immoral character of the business community and the second half was a lamentation that these attorneys were being discriminated against for their opinions. When I gently suggested that businessmen were hardly violating their civil rights by refusing to purchase their services, there was stunned silence. I was a fake liberal!

The second example is that group of alleged radicals who, when officially queried on their political beliefs, plead the Fifth Amendment. I am not suggesting for a second that they are not within their legal rights in doing so; what I am suggesting is that by taking this way out they waive their moral status as radicals. "I refuse to testify on the ground that my testimony may incriminate me"—for a radical was there ever a starker summation of moral bankruptcy? Can one conceive of Gene Debs taking the Fifth? Debs, the Wobblies, and their radical brethren never lost an opportunity to tell the world exactly what they thought. There is a famous anecdote about a Socialist agitator who had been treated to tar and feathers by a town in Oklahoma and was being ridden out on a rail. Asked by one of his tormentors how he liked the ride, he replied: "If it wasn't for the honor of the thing, I'd just as soon walk."

The character of persecution has also changed. Typically the deviant in contemporary America faces restrictions of a bureaucratic nature: he is denied security clearance, he is discharged without honor from the army, and so on. It is surely no consolation to the employee discharged from government in a Kafkaesque proceeding to hear that in 1919 he might have been beaten to death with a tire-chain. And yet, compared with the segment of American society that lived in rightless limbo half a century ago, the segment that is today maltreated is minute, and this segment has a good chance of receiving at least the elements of due process of law.

But if the present position of the nonconformist has improved, his future situation is not necessarily so cheerful. As was suggested earlier, the decline of local democracy has ameliorated the condition of the individual deviant, but it has also contributed to an increasing concentration of power in the central government. It is now conceivable that we could have a nationwide reign of terror, whereas in the nineteenth century this was literally impossible. While no prophet of gloom, and certainly no advocate of such an anachronism as states' rights, I think we should notice carefully one instance of what the national government can do: the "unconstitutional" imprisonment in concentration camps of the West Coast American-Japanese in World War II. (I put unconstitutional in quotes because the Supreme Court, Justice Black speaking, found the Constitution flexible enough to permit this incarceration.) This was a case in which the fragmentation of power which normally operates in the national government went into hibernation, and President Roosevelt, the Congress *without dissent,* and the courts put the Nisei away for possessing not enemy beliefs, but enemy chromosomes.

A similar potential can be seen in the security program. During the Civil War, Northern "security risks" could flee to honor in the South, and vice versa, but today a man found to be a risk in New York is barred from broad categories of employment throughout the nation. He can no longer find security in a sympathetic subculture. The great power for good of the national government has as an inevitable concomitant a great power for evil. From my point of view there are no inexorable forces at work moving the United States toward authoritarianism, but the liberal community must realize that the instruments of national power it so casually bestowed upon the national government in the period 1935–52 are capable of employment against its interests. "The sword cares not who wields it, nor whose blood it sheds." It is perhaps at this point that an impartial sociological observer might regret the domestication of American nonconformists, alluded to above: so large a proportion of the American reform elite was taken into the firm in the 1930's and 1940's that few voices but those of the crackpot Right are disposed to criticize and attack.

Democratic government is by far the most difficult system to implement and operate yet conceived. The supreme danger that confronts it is a perpetual tendency to drift in the direction of majoritarianism. But majority rule is not democracy; to identify the two is to confuse the instrument with the premise. Once one identifies the two, he divorces himself from the democratic tradition and enters another, which either overtly or covertly asserts that power is its own justification. The essence of this approach to democracy is that the fists of the majority, like Frederick the Great's cannon, are inscribed *ultima ratio regnum*—the ultimate justification of the state.

To the democrat, power is not self-legitimatizing. On the contrary, power is legitimate only to the extent that it forwards certain ethical, philosophical, or religious ends. The basic purpose of power is to make possible a maximum development of human potentialities, and this purpose is in turn founded upon the unverifiable assumption that men are capable of rising to a level of unselfish dedication to each other and to the common weal.

Moreover, the democrat is denied the comforting crutch of certainty. While he holds his convictions *on the level of action* firmly enough to die for them on occasion, *on the level of thought* he is constantly engaged in questioning, in searching for better answers. It is his fate to be constantly battling for what he knows to be at best a half-truth, to be making a full action commitment on the basis of incomplete evidence.

To achieve working answers to everyday problems, the democrat accepts majority decisions as binding on the actions of the community. However, no decision is ever final. In the event that new evidence appears, a new trial is in order; and it is the dynamic function of the nonconformist to urge new trials, to submit new evidence, to demand a public hearing for a different view. Thus, in a healthy democracy the majority and the nonconformist depend upon each other, and each supplies a vital component to the whole. Stability is provided by the majority, while vitality flows from the nonconformist. Consequently, the democrat protects the rights of the nonconformist not merely as an act of decency, but more significantly as an imperative for himself and the whole society.

This is the idea, and if, as I have suggested, we in the United States have tarnished it somewhat, even tarnished it has a grandeur which no elitist theory can approach. It is toward this great dream of power as the ethical instrument of a self-governing community—not as the whim of a prince, a priest, or a proletariat, nor the passions of a majority—that I believe American public policy must be directed.

A major threat to the achievement of this goal seems to me to stem from the enlargement of the political sector. It is characteristic of totalitarian states that no sector of national life can exist free from political control. Everything from stamp clubs and bowling leagues to political parties and pressure groups must pay obeisance to political objectives; must, if demanded, purge themselves of Jews, kulaks, Trotskyites, or other deviants. The state becomes the only *real* organization, and all other groups are subservient to it. When this occurs, political criteria are injected into judgments where they have no rational meaning: chess players are evaluated in terms of their politics, not their chess; great physicists are condemned for their religion, while their scientific merit goes unevaluated.

The Soviet Union has pushed this tendency almost to its logical conclusion; and, faced with worldwide assault from Communism, free societies have been forced to review their own definition of "political." For example, it is patent that nineteenth-century clichés about freedom of organization cannot suffice to deal with a political party that is also a foreign intelligence service and a potential rebel army. Similarly, insurance companies, sport clubs, trade unions, children's camps have turned up which defy the classic definition of these organizations by having political rather than private objectives.

Faced with this strange and frightening phenomenon, the American people have moved in two directions to counteract the dangers they fear: first, they have rushed to set up a security program, or programs, based more on principles of vengeance than security; and, second, they have injected political criteria into areas where these principles have no meaning. In short, they have tended to defend themselves by imitating the tactics of the enemy, by enlarging the political sector.

Governments have the right to protect themselves from disloyal servants, and I heartily approve of rigid standards of loyalty for all persons in sensitive positions. But our national security programs proceed, by methods that vary from careful scrutiny to malevolent idiocy, to dismiss from governmental positions of every description persons of "doubtful" loyalty.

This is "Getting Commies" with a vengeance, but it does not necessarily add one iota to the security of the United States. The great bulk of government jobs are of a nonsensitive character, and it seems to me that a meaningful security program with respect to these posts would require only old-fashioned civil-service techniques with the burden of proof on the United States to demonstrate the malfeasance of the individual.

The second direction in which we have moved is toward applying political criteria in areas where they are senseless, if not pernicious. Many examples of this sort can be found on the American scene: harmonica players are denied a hall because of alleged subversive connections, boxers are required to take loyalty oaths before putting on the gloves, unemployed workers are refused compensation because of ties with Communist unions, etc. Most actions of this sort are merely silly and—as I have already suggested—there is certainly no reign of terror loose in the nation; but, silly or not, their cumulative effect is dangerous.

Consequently we should make all possible efforts to limit the political sector. In dealing, for example, with Communist public-school teachers, I feel the key level of examination is not that of Party membership, but that of teaching. It is my personal conviction that Communists make bad teachers because of the closed quality of their minds, to say nothing of their penchant for illegitimate extracurricular activities such as organizing secret student cells, but this proposition is a matter to be tested and adjudicated in individual instances.

Yet another broad tendency which seems to me to threaten our liberties is what I call the withering of decency. The assault against Communism has in the United States begun to resemble a campaign against rabid foxes —in word, if not in deed—and many seem to have forgotten a basic truth that can be overlooked only at great peril to an individual and a national soul: that Communists are human beings.

It has always been characteristic of public hysteria, reigns of terror, purges, and the like, that the enemy is dehumanized; he becomes a *thing.* The basic philosophical and theological case for human slavery from Aristotle down to our own times has rested on the premise that slaves are subhuman, and Hannah Arendt has pointed out the use to which modern totalitarianism has put this sophistry. How totalitarian regimes strip their opposition groups of humanity has also been recorded in such superb literary works as Koestler's *Darkness at Noon,* Orwell's *1984,* and Milosz's *Captive Mind.* Viewed from this perspective, the Moscow Trials were merely the disposal by the Stalinist state of some inadequate tools that had not fulfilled their tasks properly.

We all know from personal experience how easy it is to be carried away by frenzy and join the haters—the human capacity to hate is proof of a sort for the doctrine of Original Sin—and we all have regretted our dalliance. It is probably to prevent our hasty judgments from haunting us forever that we have built elaborate procedural labyrinths into our law, and it is to prevent such frenzied aberrations from poisoning the future that we have built delay into our political institutions.

However, we cannot expect our institutions alone to preserve our spiritual chastity; on the contrary, these institutions can in the long haul be no stronger than the morality that supports them. This is why it is so important that our political leaders *be* leaders, be willing to stick their necks out in the cause of decency. While I have never been a devotee of Dean Acheson's foreign policy, he stands at the top of my list for his courageous decency. Tactically it was a blunder to state that he would not "turn his back on Alger Hiss," but in a moral sense it was an affirmation of humanity against the blood cultists.

A final aspect of this withering of decency that deserves mention is the tendency that accompanies it to turn life into a conspiracy: No blunder is ever accidental, no policy maker is ever stupid. This approach to life supplies logical justification for exorcising decency from political relations, for if one assumes that individuals are mere instruments of alien forces, ideological automata, as it were, he is consistent when he treats his enemies as objects to be destroyed. A blunderer in the State Department loses his character as a fallible human being, perhaps deserving dismissal for incompetence, and becomes an enemy Knight on a cosmic chessboard, an object to be eliminated.

In evaluating errors in policy, we should always assume that the fault is bad judgment until the contrary can be conclusively demonstrated. In general, we should act upon the assumption that in politics, as in interpersonal relations, the simplest explanation is usually the best. If we abandon this common-sense rule, we enter a universe in which logic triumphs over life, and decency is a superfluous, if not a dangerous, quality.

DO WE DEFEND OUR RIGHTS
BY PROTECTING COMMUNISTS?

Irving Kristol

Heard ye not lately of a man
That went beside his witt,
And naked through the citty rann
Wrapt in a frantique fitt?

The above tantalizing bit of seventeenth-century verse was quoted recently in the London *Times Literary Supplement,* in the same issue in which there appeared, elsewhere in its pages, a review of the English edition of Alan Barth's *The Loyalty of Free Men.* This fortuitous juxtaposition was

Abridged from Irving Kristol, " 'Civil Liberties,' 1952—A Study in Confusion," *Commentary* (March 1952), pp. 228–236. Copyright 1952 by the American Jewish Committee. Reprinted by permission of the author and the publisher. Mr. Kristol, the senior editor of Basic Books, has written widely on political and philosophical subjects.

not without its ironic relevance, Mr. Barth's book having been provoked by the "frantique fitt" of McCarthyism, beneath which he saw a cool and calculating assault on the American democracy, and his defense being couched in a cool and calculating eloquence that turns out, upon close examination, to be not nearly the exercise in pure reason it seems.

A close examination, however, Mr. Barth's book and others of its kind have not received. It was hardly to be expected from Senator McCarthy and his friends, who are less famous for their habits of meticulous reading than for their preference for arguing in the large, while the more scholarly sections of American opinion have been so delighted to see the Senator get his, and so soothed by the cadences of a familiar tone, that they have not so much read these books as permitted themselves to be enchanted by them. This enchantment has had its political sequel, for as a result of it there has been drawn a line of battle. On the one side are the men of intellect and sensibility, fair-minded and generous-hearted and confessedly not infallible: the Alan Barths, the Henry Steele Commagers, the Zechariah Chafees, the Howard Mumford Joneses, the Ralph Barton Perrys, the William O. Douglases, and, rather more tentatively committed, the Francis Biddles. On the other side are the mindless men, the kind who get elected to office when the spirit of the age reverts to primitivism, and who wish, under cover of fighting Communism, to squeeze the nation into a Know-Nothing straitjacket.

The line is drawn—and those liberals who have rallied to their positions on the left of it find themselves ever more pressed against the outer walls of the city. The ready quotations from Jefferson about the trees of liberty and the blood of tyrants, the sonorous repetition of Justice Holmes's dissenting opinions, the schoolmaster's measured accents alternating with prophetic indignation—the whole battery has failed significantly to make an impression on the dominant American mood. Senator McCarthy remains blithely on the offensive and his critics give ground before him. It is a most exasperating and melancholy situation for liberals to be in; yet in proportion as they fail in strength, they gain in their sense of petulant righteousness.

Is it conceivable that the line was incorrectly drawn in the first place? The liberals are loath to weigh the possibility lest it give comfort to the enemy; Senator McCarthy for his part has no cause for dissatisfaction with things as they are; but those of us who are the displaced persons of this war might reflect on this question to our advantage. Perhaps it is a calamitous error to believe that because a vulgar demagogue lashes out at both Communism and liberalism as identical, it is necessary to protect Communism in order to defend liberalism. This way of putting the matter will surely shock liberals, who are convinced that it is only they who truly understand Communism and who thoughtfully oppose it. They are nonetheless mistaken, and it is a mistake on which McCarthyism waxes fat. For there is one thing that the American people know about Senator McCarthy: he, like them, is unequivocally anti-Communist. About the spokesmen for American liberalism, they feel they know no such thing. And with some justification.

With what justification, can be seen from an illustrative incident involving Professor Henry Steele Commager, a distinguished historian who never was a Communist and never will be. In the May 1947 issue of *Harper's*,

Professor Commager wrote a spirited article that began as follows:

> On May 6 a Russian-born girl, Mrs. Shura Lewis, gave a talk to the students of the Western High School of Washington, D.C. She talked about Russia—its school system, its public-health program, the position of women, of the aged, of the workers, the farmers, and the professional classes—and compared, superficially and uncritically, some American and Russian institutions. . . . Mrs. Lewis said nothing that had not been said a thousand times, in speeches, in newspapers, magazines and books. She said nothing that any normal person could find objectionable.

What greatly disturbed Professor Commager was that this inoffensive speech did give rise to a furor in Washington. Congressmen bellowed that our schools were being subverted, the principal of the school came forward with a humble apology, the superintendent of schools for the nation's capital swore it would never happen again, and the speech itself was reprinted (after some discussion of the wisdom of exposing the public to inflammation) in the *Congressional Record* as a horrible example. Professor Commager saw in this a reflection of an anti-Communist hysteria that threatened to engulf all civil liberties, and he pleaded earnestly that reason control the anti-Communist passion, lest we find ourselves saddled with an anti-Communist orthodoxy no less reprehensible than the Communist one. His article was hailed as a kind of liberal manifesto, and was reprinted—alongside John Stuart Mill and John Milton—in Howard Mumford Jones's *Primer of Intellectual Freedom* (1949). Evil won a transient victory in the seats of power and Good won a permanent niche in the anthologies—a familiar tale.

Familiar, that is, until one goes to the *Congressional Record* and reads through this speech that no "normal person could find objectionable." Mrs. Lewis's English was broken, but her sentiments were whole:

> They call it collective farm—the peasants farm and divide up products according to work put in by each individual during the years. As a result of planning, unemployment is completely wiped out. . . .
> In Russia right now people absolutely do not worry about today or tomorrow. They never think "All of a sudden I lose a job." That fear doesn't exist among Russian people. . . .
> No matter where you live you have to work. What the Russian people have, they are more secure about this. They work. They need not worry much about losing the job. They are free to travel from one place to another, and each person must work 25 years for after that he is able to get a pension. No matter where you work—in this plant or another, 25 years and then you get 50 per cent of your salary and live the rest of your life. . . .
> I never appreciated the life in Russia until I live here. Here you have to work hard in order to live, use all your courage not to die. . . .
> I read all the papers here and occasionally I go to the Library of Congress and read all papers printed in Moscow. It is very interesting, and when I read these papers always you can see here evidence of press where people talk all the time about having a war, to throw the atomic bomb on Russia, to destroy because they have a system which is very prideful. At the present time Russians are busy to restore all those houses, all those cities, all those towns. Russian people make streets, plants, produce new style of shoes, new fashion of dress, new production, and never they talk about having a war.

The echoes this awakened in Congress may have been exaggerated, but they were not factitious or beside the point. Obviously, Professor Commager can argue that it will not harm American school children to encounter an occasional Communist apologist in the flesh; one may even go further and say it would do them good. However, in the first place, Mrs. Lewis was not introduced as a Communist apologist but as an informed reporter, and, in the second place, everything she said should have been objectionable to every normal person, and especially to a historian like Professor Commager—for the good and sufficient reason that it was a tissue of lies. For Professor Commager to defend the rights of Communists to free speech is one thing; for him to assert that there is nothing objectionable in mendacious pleading in support of Communism is quite another. The conclusion "any normal person" will draw from such behavior is that, for whatever reason, his critical faculties are less alert when he looks out of the left corner of his eye.

Indeed, the heart of the matter is exactly that he looks at Communism out of the *left* corner of his eye. Professor Commager seems to be seduced by the insidious myth according to which Communism is a political trend continuous with liberalism and democratic socialism, only more impatient and inclined to the fanatical, only more "radical" than its companions who are not quite so "left." It is a myth that Senator McCarthy, for his own ends, is happy to accept, since it allows him to tag a New Dealer as being by nature an embryonic Communist. Neither the Professor nor the Senator is concerned to see that the antithesis of "left" and "right" no longer suits the political realities; that measured by the ideals of the French or even Russian revolution, Communism today is as counter-revolutionary as Louis XVI or Kolchak ever was; that if one wishes to defend the civil liberties of Communists (as the Senator does not), one must do so on the same grounds that one defends the civil liberties of Nazis and fascists—no more, no less.

Professor Commager might retort that he knows all this full well, and that he is for civil liberties for everyone, fascist, Communist, or what-have-you. But if a Nazi had, in 1938, addressed a high-school audience in this country, extolling the accomplishments of Hitler's regime, presenting a thoroughly fictitious account of life in Nazi Germany, never once mentioning the existence of concentration camps—would Professor Commager find in such a speech "nothing that any normal person could find objectionable"? It is doubtless an injustice to him even to conceive of the possibility.

This notion of Communism as "left" and therefore at an opposite pole from fascism, which is "right," appears to have become intrinsic to the liberal outlook. It is imbedded in the meretricious historical analogies, in the rolling phrases about "the forces of freedom and those of fear," beneath which there lies the gross metaphysics of the liberal Manichee, apportioning the universe to "forward-looking" and "backward-looking" demiurges. It helps explain how Professor Commager can permit himself to write: "After all, it is no accident that the nations dedicated to freedom won the two great wars of the twentieth century and those committed to totalitarianism went under"—when it is not only no accident, it is not even a fact. The same notion is evidenced in Zechariah Chafee's explanation (in his essay in the recent symposium *Civil Liberties under Attack*) of the origin of Communist fronts: "It is inevitable that the membership of organizations formed to bring about change should include some persons who want a great deal of change"—as if Professor Chafee and the Communists were agreed on the direction of the change, quarreling only over the measure. It is the presupposition from which Ralph Barton Perry (in his new book, *The Citizen Decides*) can deduce that Communism is "democratic" by virtue of being a revolt of the "masses" against the "classes," that the Soviet regime is a government "for the people with the consent of the people" though not by the people, and that the Chinese Communist leaders are "hostages" of a popular revolution.

Moreover, after staring out of the left corner of the eye for any length of time, there comes an irrepressible inclination to wink. How else explain, for instance, the attitude Alan Barth takes toward the Hiss-Chambers affair? He can begin a sentence: "Insofar as Chambers may be credited with having told the truth . . ."; or: "Whatever the guilt of Alger Hiss and whatever the utility of exposing it and punishing it a decade later . . ." About Whittaker Chambers and the Communist "informer" in general, he is no longer judiciously bland but is knowingly tart: "The ex-Communists, conscious of their betrayal of American values, wanted the comfort of company; they had to show that many others, even many who were highly respected, had been as recreant as they." In other words, Chambers in telling the truth is a man of malice, Hiss in denying it is his defenseless victim. Hiss's guilt is problematic and, in any case, not important; Chambers' wickedness is certain.

On Owen Lattimore, there is liberal unanimity: he got a raw deal. Professor Commager believes (in his contribution to *Civil Liberties under Attack*) that the attack on Lattimore was an attack on "independence and nonconformity." Professor Chafee laments: "Owen Lattimore did his own thinking and look how his services were appreciated." Alan Barth is casually positive: "Dr. Lattimore's ordeal was, of course, only the most spectacular instance of legislative punishment of teachers for expressing their opinions." About the worst that can be said for such arrant nonsense is that it is uttered in all sincerity. For the incontrovertible facts of the case are, "of course," that Owen Lattimore did *not* do his own thinking; that his "ordeal" was the public demonstration of this fact; that he was a faithful and enormously influential fellow-traveler who for more than a decade followed the Communist line as if magnetized by it, including a docile zig-zag during the Stalin-Hitler pact. Is it really no legitimate concern of Congress that such a man was appointed advisor to Chiang Kai-shek, that he accompanied Vice-President Wallace during his tour of Asia, that he was admired and listened to by important people in the State Department?

In his denunciation of Lattimore's pro-Communist record and in hurling unsubstantiated charges against him (chief of Soviet espionage, etc.), Senator McCarthy may well have been aiming a blow against independence of mind and nonconformity of spirit. For Messrs. Commager, Barth, and Chafee to defend Lattimore's pro-Communist record in order to defend such independence and nonconformity is for them to play the Senator's game, on the losing side.

It is equally futile for liberals to try to match Senator McCarthy's irresponsible declamations with a crafty rhetoric of their own, especially when his rhetoric, while not designedly pro-Communist, is compelled by the logic of disingenuousness and special pleading to become so in effect. The need for disingenuousness arises out of a refusal to see Communism for what it is:

a movement guided by conspiracy and aiming at totalitarianism, rather than merely another form of "dissent" or "nonconformity." Hence the liberal argument runs askew of reality and must clothe itself with neat obfuscation.

Once again, Professor Commager obliges with a superior specimen:

> The House Un-American Activities Committee has launched an attack on the Lawyers' Guild as a pro-Communist or "subversive" organization. The chief basis for this attack is, as far as we know, that the Guild has proffered its services to the defense of Communists under indictment for violation of the Smith Act. We need not inquire into the accuracy of this charge or into the degree of zeal displayed by the Lawyers' Guild. Let us ask rather what are the logical conclusions to be drawn by the position which the House Committee has adopted? They are two: that certain criminals are so despicable that they are not entitled to counsel, and that a lawyer who defends a criminal is himself sympathetic to crime.

That phrase in the second sentence, "as far as we know," is curious. It implies strongly that the only conceivable explanation of the Committee's attitude is the action of the Guild in providing lawyers to defend indicted Communists, and that there is no public information which gives plausibility to the Committee's belief that the Guild is a "front" organization, controlled and run by Communists. On the contrary, however, "as far as we know," and we know much further than Professor Commager suggests, the Lawyers' Guild is a Communist creation that, as A. A. Berle stated when he resigned from it in 1940, "is not prepared to take any stand which conflicts with the Communist party line." Moreover, the House Committee on Un-American Activities has collected and published sufficient evidence to demonstrate this beyond cavil—which leads one to think that if Professor Commager spent nearly as much time reading the records of Congressional hearings as he does denouncing them, we should all be better off.

The entire third sentence is even more curious: "We need not inquire into the accuracy of this charge or into the degree of zeal displayed by the Lawyers' Guild." If we take "zeal" to mean pro-Communism (in the context, that is all it can mean), then the degree of this zeal and the accuracy of the charge of pro-Communism are precisely what we *do* need to inquire into. How can we know whether to sanction or condemn the Committee's investigation of the Guild as a pro-Communist organization unless we make an effort to find out if the Guild is or is not, in fact, a pro-Communist organization? Even Professor Commager surreptitiously ignores his own disclaimer, as the last two sentences of his paragraph show. Obviously, the two "logical conclusions" flow not from the Committee's premise, but his own: namely, that the Lawyers' Guild is neither pro-Communist nor subversive. From the Committee's own premise, quite other logical conclusions may be inferred—one of them being that the Committee is engaged in showing up Communist fronts for what they are. Professor Commager's "logic" is a sleight-of-hand whereby premises that are prejudiced in favor of the Communist interpretation of affairs are made to pass for natural conclusions.

In the same vein, there is a liberal rhetoric of insinuation that works under cover of a high moral posture. Its net effect is to give a backhanded credence to the Communist assertion that it is impossible to oppose Communism vigorously without walking into the arms of Black Reaction. It is the kind of thing represented in the following observation of Alan Barth's:

In the New York trial of eleven Communist Party leaders in 1949, a number of FBI undercover operatives who had joined the party appeared as prosecution witnesses. How widely such agents have been dispersed in labor unions, in lawful voluntary associations, and in political groups is a matter of mere conjecture. But it is certainly a matter of legitimate concern to Americans who care about preservation of the traditional rights of privacy.

A noble sentiment, and the unwary reader assents—who is against the right to privacy, and who is not prepared to be concerned with its violation? Only the exceptionally attentive will note that the supposed threat to "the traditional rights of privacy" is "a matter of mere conjecture." Whose conjecture? We are not told. Is there any ground for such a conjecture? We are not told that either. Is Mr. Barth against the use of undercover agents in principle? He does not say so. Is he against the use of undercover agents in Communist organizations? He does not say this, either. He would seem to be against dispersing FBI agents in bona fide labor unions, lawful voluntary associations, and political groups, and reminds us of the consequences. But who is for it? The answer, which he does not bother to give, is: nobody—and that is why the FBI is doing no such thing and why the whole business is a "matter of mere conjecture." In the course of Mr. Barth's innuendoes, however, the onus has been neatly shifted from the Communist conspirators to the FBI agents who identified them.

The same technique of persuasion is at work in such a statement as this one by Professor Commager: "It will be useful to determine, a generation from now, whether those universities that have purged their faculties are actually stronger than they were before the purges occurred—stronger in those essentials that go to make a university." This has about it so trembling an air of bittersweet wisdom that it seems positively boorish to ask: just which universities would Professor Commager describe as "purged"? Surely Columbia is not one of them, for Professor Commager is not the kind of man who would retain his post on a "purged" faculty. Is it Yale? Princeton? Harvard? University of Chicago? The list could be extended indefinitely, for there is not a single university in the United States that can be said to have been, in any meaningful sense of the word, "purged." There has been no more than a handful of cases where Communist college teachers have been dismissed, and less than a handful of cases where non-Communists have been unjustly fired as "Reds." To call this a "purge"—even regardless of whether or not one thinks Communists have a right to teach in colleges —is to echo Communist propaganda.

Perhaps Professor Commager had in mind the University of California, where several dozen (out of a total of more than a thousand) teachers found the idea of a special loyalty oath—the content of which was irrelevant to their action—so offensive and intolerable that they exercised their constitutional right to refuse to swear it, and consequently had to seek other employment. Granting that the notion of a special oath for teachers is obnoxious, and even conceding that this minority was correct and courageous in its particular reaction to it—is it the part of sobriety to insist, as Professor Commager goes on to do, that the philosophy behind the actions of California's Board of Regents does not differ "in any essentials" from the philosophy behind the totalitarian control of university teaching? One swallow does not make a spring, or one injustice an apocalypse.

Despite their fondness for clichés of Communist manufacture, all these liberal spokesmen are sincerely anti-Communist—otherwise, what they have to say would be of little interest to anyone. But their rejection of Communism has all the semblance of a preliminary gesture, a repudiation aiming to linger in the memory as a floating credential. It has little relation to all the ensuing scenes of the political drama, where bad conscience and stubborn pride join to guide the liberal through his role.

Did not the major segment of American liberalism, as a result of joining hands with the Communists in a Popular Front, go on record as denying the existence of Soviet concentration camps? Did it not give its blessing to the "liquidation" of millions of Soviet "kulaks"? Did it not apologize for the mass purges of 1936–38, and did it not solemnly approve the grotesque trials of the Old Bolsheviks? Did it not applaud the massacre of the non-Communist left by the GPU during the Spanish Civil War? All this carries no weight with Alan Barth, who knows that, though a man repeat the Big Lie, so long as he is of a liberal intention he is saved. On the participation of non-Communists in Communist fronts during the 1930's, he writes: "In the main, their participation, while it lasted, was not only innocent but *altogether* praiseworthy." (My italics.)

Even Francis Biddle, who is generally cautious, remarks in his book *The Fear of Freedom*: "What makes an organization subversive? If a vast majority of its members are Communists but its conduct has always been exemplary, advocating desirable social reforms which Communists usually back, it can hardly fit the description."

One surmises that Mr. Biddle is not really so politically naive as this statement, on the face of it, would lead one to believe. He must know what it means to be "subversive," since it was he who, as Attorney General, sent eighteen members of a minuscule Trotskyist sect to jail in 1942 for being just that; he must know how Communists work, how front organizations act as an ancillary to the Communist party apparatus, since this is a matter of common knowledge and Mr. Biddle is uncommonly literate and intelligent. No, it was no elevated unsophistication that urged him on, but rather a sense of shame and a cowardliness to confess that shame. Mr. Biddle, like Mr. Barth, refuses to admit what is now apparent: that a generation of earnest reformers who helped give this country a New Deal should find themselves in retrospect stained with the guilt of having lent aid and comfort to Stalinist tyranny. This is, to be sure, a truth of hindsight, an easy truth. But it is the truth nonetheless, and might as well be owned up to. If American liberalism is not willing to discriminate between its achievements and its sins, it only disarms itself before Senator McCarthy, who is eager to have it appear that its achievements *are* its sins.

The problem of fighting Communism while preserving civil liberties is no simple one, and there is no simple solution. A prerequisite for any solution, however, is, firstly, a proper understanding of Communism for what it is, and secondly, a sense of proportion. So long as liberals agree with Senator McCarthy that the fate of Communism involves the fate of liberalism, and that we must choose between complete civil liberties for everyone and a disregard for civil liberties entirely, we shall make no progress except to chaos. So long as one is either for or against "guilt by association," it is hopeless to try to distinguish between a sober and silly definition of that concept—sober when it is taken to mean, as for instance the Canwell Committee of the State of Washington took it to mean, that anyone who is a member of three or more organizations officially declared subversive is to be considered a Communist; silly when it is taken to mean, as many government loyalty boards take it to mean, that if you have a friend or a relation who is sympathetic to Communism, you are a "bad security risk." So long as Senator McCarthy and the liberals agree that the right of a Communist to teach or be a government employee is a matter of principle, we shall remain distant from that intelligent discrimination between one case and another, and one situation and another, which alone can give us our true bearings.

Inevitably, liberals will disagree among themselves about the appropriateness of specific actions with regard to Communism and Communists. Inevitably, too, there will always be a basic division and antagonism between liberalism (which is solicitous of freedom) and McCarthyism (which is not). But if a liberal wishes to defend the civil liberties of Communists or of Communist fellow-travelers, he must enter the court of American opinion with clean hands and a clear mind. He must show that he knows the existence of an organized subversive movement such as Communism is a threat to the consensus on which civil society and its liberties are based. He must bluntly acknowledge Communists and fellow-travelers to be what they are, and then, if he so desires, defend the expediency in particular circumstances of allowing them the right to be what they are. He must speak as one of *us,* defending *their* liberties. To the extent he insists that they are on our side, that we can defend our liberties only by uncritically defending theirs, he will be taken as speaking as one of them.

GUIDES FOR READING AND DISCUSSION

1. During most periods of crisis in the United States, anti-libertarian movements have gained strength. Why should this be so? What other factors, apart from crises, give support to such movements?

2. How does the current state of political liberty in your community compare with the McCarthy period as pictured by Barth? By Roche? How would one go about establishing which appraisal of the recent past is more accurate?

3. Kristol argues that liberals by and large failed to admit the real and serious threat that Communism posed, and that they thus prepared the way for a demagogue like McCarthy. Can a man with Kristol's views be considered a liberal? Does his argument suggest that "liberal" may be too all-inclusive a term?

SUGGESTED ADDITIONAL READINGS

Jack Anderson and Ronald W. May, *McCarthy: The Man, the Senator, the "Ism"* (Boston: Beacon, 1952).

Daniel Bell, ed., *The New American Right* (New York: Criterion, 1955).

Zechariah Chafee, *The Blessings of Liberty* (New York: Lippincott, 1956).

Sidney Hook, *Political Power and Personal Freedom* (New York: Criterion, 1959).

Paul F. Lazarsfeld and Wagner Thielens, Jr., *The Academic Mind: Social Scientists in a Time of Crisis* (Glencoe, Ill.: Free Press, 1958); see also review articles by Everett C. Hughes and Robert K. Carr, in *American Sociological Review*, August 1959; by Ernest van den Haag, in *Commentary*, February 1959.

Edward A. Shils, *The Torment of Secrecy* (Glencoe, Ill.: Free Press, 1955).

Samuel A. Stouffer, *Communism, Conformity, and Civil Liberties* (New York: Doubleday, 1955).

Telford Taylor, *Grand Inquest* (New York: Simon and Schuster, 1955).

Adam Yarmolinsky, *Case Studies in Personnel Security* (Washington: Bureau of National Affairs, 1955).

HAS THE SUBURB CREATED
A NEW AMERICAN?

During most of this country's history, the trend of urbanization was toward greater and greater concentration. From about 1920 on, however, the rural-urban migration has been countered by an out-migration from the central cities of metropolitan areas to their suburbs. Between 1950 and 1960, thus, while the population of many of the central cities actually decreased, that of the metropolitan "rings" increased by almost half. Well over 60 per cent of the country's population now lives in its 192 metropolitan areas; and a large and increasing proportion of this majority are, in one sense or another, suburbanites. When one speaks today of "the quality of American life," therefore, one must pay particular attention to this sector. The portrait of the American as a conformist is closely linked to the emerging suburb. For many writers "the" suburbanite is the epitome of the conformist American.

Actually, however, we still know rather little about the "suburb." Even its definition is not agreed on, and those who work with Census Bureau data often prefer to avoid the term. Most analyses are by men who season their sociological findings with considerable imagination.

The first of the two selections included here, a summary of what a team of researchers from *Fortune* found in a small number of supposedly typical suburbs, emphasizes the homogeneity and conformity of the suburban way of life. The article by Professor Clark challenges these findings, less because he considers them inaccurate than because he doubts whether the communities studied are typical of all suburbs. He breaks down the omnibus *suburb* first by type, "packaged" versus random settlements; then according to the age of the community; and consistently according to the dominant social class of the residents. The two antagonists would agree that Whyte's generalizations constitute a caricature, but for Whyte it is an accurate representation of the future. Clark disagrees; since Whyte's study did not take the enormous variation in present suburbia into account, it is a poor base from which to predict trends. According to Clark, many of today's suburbs are neither especially conformist nor very homogeneous in their population, and some seem to be growing less so.

THE NEW SUBURBIA

William H. Whyte, Jr.

Precut, pre-engineered, and prelandscaped, a new kind of suburbia is arising on the outskirts of our major cities. These suburbs are obviously important as a market, but they are even more important as a clue to the values and attitudes people will show in the decade ahead.

How valid are these new suburbs as an index? Some people have protested that the picture they give us is far too glossy or, according to the inclination of the reader, too appalling. They are artificial and synthetic communities, they protest, and thus are not representative. I raise the point because the validity of my remarks rests on the premise that these communities are not synthetic. They are a natural phenomenon. They are a response, a collision, if you will, to a host of changing economic and social realities. Accentuated, yes; but therein lies their value, for here—almost in caricature—we may have a preview of what is ahead.

Let me start with the question of mobility. Americans have always conceded that they are a nomadic people, but the customary picture of American society has been patterned on the traditional community—the community in which the Hill, local business ties, and interlocking family relationships firmly fix the individual's position. He can move upwards from, say, the upper-middle to the lower-upper class (from the Elks to the country club) only by sanction of the next upper group.

It is a premise of this paper that the man who leaves home is not the exception to American society but the key to it. We have come to the age of the large organization—the corporation, the Atomic Energy Commission, the armed services, and so on; and this way of life has inevitably meant mobility. Management man, for example, is almost by definition a man who left home and, like the man who went from the Midwest to Harvard, kept on going. There are now so many of him that those who stayed put are as much affected by the migration as those who leave. As many of us know from personal experience, in small- and medium-sized cities all over the country there have been so many departures and, at the same time, so many new faces that the local citizenry now find themselves in the position of being abroad at home.

The magnitude of this transiency has yet to be grasped.

Several of my colleagues looked into the developments outside ten of our largest cities. I went to Park Forest, outside Chicago, then to Park Merced, San Francisco. And what we found was that in varying degrees these developments were a stepping stone. The key fact about them was that the single largest group were transients, and the reason these people were transient was that they were organization people—corporation "junior executives," A.E.C. researchers, Army and Navy officers, and the like.

Abridged from William H. Whyte, Jr., "The Consumer in the New Suburbia," in Lincoln H. Clark, ed., *Consumer Behavior* (New York: New York University Press, 1954), pp. 1–14. Reprinted by permission of the author and the publisher. Mr. Whyte, a past editor of *Fortune*, has written on corporation structure, the new middle classes, and conservation.

The other key fact was the suburbs' extraordinary homogeneity. From suburb to suburb the statistics varied little: average income, about $5,700; average husband's age, 31; children, one born and one on the way; politics, 68 per cent Republican.

For the bulk of our research we picked a suburb that encompassed in one package most of the features of the new suburbia. You could not call it typical. You might say that it is like the others, only more so.

Park Forest, Illinois, our suburb, is not unlike the Fournier and Owenite communities of the early 1800's. But it is likely to last a lot longer. It was not planned as a venture in Utopia but, simply, as a shrewd way to capitalize on some current facts of American life. After the war, there was in Chicago, as elsewhere, a great floating population of young people with children, a taste for good living, and not much money. Why not, figured a group of businessmen, build a whole new community for these people? The group bought up 2,400 acres in the cornland 30 miles south of Chicago and proceeded to do so.

The final plan was to build clusters of rental garden apartments (rent for two-bedroom duplex: $92) around a central shopping center and then, as time went on, to build ranch-type houses for sale ($11,995) on the periphery of the area. They would be merchandised at bargain rates. The real money would come from the waterworks and the company's cut (ranging up to 10 per cent) of every dollar spent in the shopping center. In effect, a city was being built to provide a market—a constantly rotating, nonsatiable market of 30,000 people, many of whom would ever be poised at that stage when families just begin to lay up possessions.

As early as possible the government of the town would be turned over to the residents. This, plus the isolation of the community, is what made it so valuable for our study. The way the town is governed, its schools, its churches—all these would reflect not tradition, the hegemony of elders, but the wants and needs of its young population.

The first wave of colonists was heavy with academic and professional people—the place, it appeared, had an extraordinary affinity for Ph.D.'s. Since Chicago is the nexus of America's business migration, another kind of affinity has proved even stronger; Park Forest quickly became a haven for the corporation's young transients.

The most permanent feature of Park Forest has been impermanence. In the rental courts turnover has been roughly 35 per cent annually; even in the homes area, the figure runs between 20 per cent and 25 per cent. Clearly, transfer is the basic cause: 66 per cent of all "move-outs" are people being sent elsewhere by their organizations (12 per cent service; 55 per cent corporation).

When the developers were figuring how best to advertise the new homes for sale, their advertising agency sent two girls out to interview some of the settlers. Then a panel of psychiatrists analyzed the interviews for motivation. The analysis was very interesting, and it produced one high-pulling advertisement—a pair of outstretched arms and the slogan "At Park Forest, YOU BELONG." Nowhere in the analysis, however, did one simple fact obtrude: that many, many people were not looking to sink permanent roots, to identify themselves with the land, and so on; they were looking for something to house them until, two or three years hence, they would have to pack up and move on. Actually, buying a $12,000 house, if one has the necessary $1,000 down payment, is a far cheaper proposition for such people than renting. So far, however, no advertisement has capitalized on this possibly quite compelling appeal.

This transiency has had a great effect on the individual's relations with the group. Thus we arrive at another point: the increasingly communal nature of American life.

Let us take as an example a couple we shall call Dot and Charlie Adams. Charlie, a corporation trainee, is uprooted from the Newark office, arrives at Apartment 8, Court M-12, in Suburbia. The kids are crying, Dot is half sick with exhaustion, and the movers won't be finished till late.

But soon, because M-12 is a "happy" court, the neighbors will come over to introduce themselves. Some will help them unpack, and around suppertime two of the girls will come over with a hot casserole and another with a percolator full of hot coffee. Within a few days, the children will have found playmates, Dot will be kaffeeklatsching and sunbathing with the girls like an old-timer, and Charlie, who finds that Ed Robey in Apartment 5 went through officers' training school with him, will be enrolled in the court poker club. The Adamses are, in a word, IN—and someday soon, when another new couple, dazed and hungry, move in, the Adamses will express their thankfulness by helping them to "get in."

In the court, they find, their relationships with others transcend mere neighborliness. Except for the monastic orders and the family itself, there is probably no other social institution in America in which there is such a communal sharing of property as in the new suburbia. For these are a people without capital; a people, furthermore, that do not think in terms of capital. Except for the $200 or $300 put aside for the next baby, few of the transients have as yet been able to accumulate much in the way of worldly possessions, and in their desk drawer are several little books with twelve or sixteen or eighteen or more monthly-payment coupons to fill out. But they do not worry. This is the normal state in our economy, they know, and their bond with the Organization is their disaster insurance.

In the meantime, they share to make the best of it. One lawn mower (with each man doing his allotted stint) may do for the whole court. For the wives there is a baby-sitting "bank." When one wife baby-sits for another she is credited with the time, and, when she wishes to draw on it, one of the wives who has a debit will sit for her. To hoard possessions is frowned upon. Books, silverware, and tea services are constantly rotated, and the children feel free to use each other's bicycles and toys without bothering to ask. "We laughed at first at how the Marxist society had finally arrived," one transient told me, "but I think the real analogy is to the pioneers."

This responsiveness to the group, it is important to note, is a factor of which residents in these communities are very much aware, and they discuss it with such sophistication that at times it almost seems as if every man is his own resident sociologist. In bull sessions, words like "permissive" and "sociocultural groups" are frequently tossed about, and in the most casual conversation you are likely to hear "outgoing" time and again. Even their wisecracks are, to borrow a word, socio-economic; their suburbs they describe as "a Russia, only with money"; "a womb with a view."

The court life is the "outgoing" life, and if one isn't outgoing, people stand ready to help. In every court you'll find several social activists who make a special point of "bringing out" shy people. The education "takes," and those who have been "brought out" like to dwell on their transformation. They speak enthusiastically, and, if their experiences had to be summed up in a phrase, it would boil down to one heartfelt note of joy: *They weren't introverts after all.*

More than ever before, the newcomers get in the habit of doing things with other people. Civic activity is rife, but this is a fraction of the energies expended in group activity. Court social life throbs with bridge and canasta, bring-your-own-bottle parties, and teas; and, when spring brings everyone outdoors, the tempo of activity becomes practically nonstop.

With communication so intensive, everyone has a stake in the equilibrium of the court. Individual spats or feuds threaten the whole court; and the court, like all informal groups, reacts to discipline the errant. The sanctions are not obvious; but the look in the eye, the absence of a smile, the inflection of a hello can be exquisite punishment; and they have brought more than one to a nervous breakdown.

The problem of personal morals is similarly critical. Young suburbanites talk an awful lot about sin, and in their parties they discuss conjugal sex in almost clinical terms. Notwithstanding, as far as morals are concerned, places like Park Forest are possibly the greatest invention since the chastity belt. There have been, to be sure, affairs here and there. The evidence is strong, however, that there is less philandering among Park Foresters than among their contemporaries in more traditional communities.

For one thing, it is practically impossible to philander without everyone's knowing about it. One's callers are observed, and, if neighbors feel there is anything untoward, Park Forest's phenomenal grapevine will speed the news. This is not mere venom. In a web of relationships as delicate as that of the court, an affair can harm not only two marriages—it can upset the whole court applecart. And everyone knows it.

More important, the sustenance of the group fills a void in the life of the young wife that is not always filled elsewhere. The group is a deterrent to divorce. Few people in Suburbia get divorces until they break with their groups. In the estimation of ministers, the fact that it is so hard to break with a group in Suburbia has had a lot to do with keeping some marriages from going on the rocks.

Now it might be argued that this sensitivity to the group is merely temporary. In the matter of degree, yes; court life does intensify the attitudes. But the basic attitude is not temporary. In scores of ways the young suburbanites indicate that, to them, adjusting to others has become akin to a moral duty and is a precept to be articulated and passed on.

This is not the place to expand on Park Forest's educational philosophy. However, two facts about it are pertinent to our subject. First, the schools are a prototype of what is coming to be termed "the life-adjustment curriculum." Second, the majority of parents are in favor of it. In a recent survey of parent sentiment conducted by the high school, most parents wrote that the prime aim of the school should be to teach people how to get along with other people.

Not only for their children but also for themselves, Park Foresters rationalize necessity into a virtue. Consider for a moment their attitude towards privacy. They are well aware they have little. From the eye of the court there is no escape; like the double bed, it enforces intimacy, and isolation becomes psychologically impossible. Not even the apartment is a redoubt. People don't bother to knock, and they come and go furiously. The lack of privacy, furthermore, is retroactive. As one resident puts it, "They ask you all sorts of questions about what you were doing. 'Who was that that stopped in last night?' 'Who were those people from Chicago last week?' You're never alone, even when you think you are."

Yet they like this more than they hate it. "It's wonderful," says one young wife. "You find yourself discussing all your personal problems with your neighbors—things that back in South Dakota we would have kept to ourselves." As time goes on, this capacity for self-revelation grows; and, on the most intimate details of family life, people once shy become amazingly frank with each other. No one, they point out, ever need face a problem alone.

With all this coming and going, ever to get oneself alone is a major operation. Such a purely negative response as not answering the phone is not enough. To gain privacy one has to *do* something. One court resident, for example, moves his chair to the front rather than the court side of his apartment to show he doesn't want to be disturbed. Often a whole court or wing of it will develop such a signal. A group in one Drexelbrook court has decided that, whenever one of them feels he or she has finally had it, the venetian blinds should be drawn all the way down to the bottom of the picture window. Since this position is an unusual one, the others spot it as a plea to be left alone.

But there is an important corollary of such efforts at privacy. People feel a little guilty about making them. Except very occasionally, to shut oneself off from others like this is regarded as either a childish prank or, more likely, an indication of some inner neurosis. The individual, not the group, has erred. So, at any rate, many errants seem to feel, and they are often penitent about what elsewhere would be regarded as one's own business, and rather normal business at that. "I've promised myself to make it up to them," one court resident recently told a confidant. "I was feeling bad and just plain didn't make the effort to ask the others in later. I don't blame them, really, for reacting the way they did. I'll make it up to them somehow."

Privacy has become clandestine. Not in solitary and selfish contemplation but in doing things with other people does one fulfill oneself. Nor is it a matter of overriding importance just what it is that one does with other people; even watching television together—for which purpose, incidentally, several groups have been organized—helps make one more of a real person.

Unsettling as this adjustment may be, there is one very good side to it. For these people could not meet as they do except at the expense of regional, racial, and class barriers that have long fragmented us. Almost because the suburbs are a haven for the basically middle-class organization man, they provide a forced-draft education in new values for many others. For one thing, these communities speed up potential switches in religious affiliations;

and the couple from, say, a small Ozark town are likely to leave a funda-mentalist allegiance to become Methodists or Presbyterians. Not so inci-dentally, many "mixed-marriage" couples have come to Park Forest, for here, they have correctly sensed, is a refuge from the conflicting loyalties that would beset them elsewhere.

People from big-city Democratic wards tend to become Republicans and, if anything, more conservative than the people whose outlook they are un-consciously adopting. Personal tastes change more slowly, though the wives are rather quick to pick up the right cues, and their clothes, whether they are slacks or cardigans and pearls, show it.

It is in the more subtle field of family background that one finds the most energetic kind of tolerance. Park Foresters are egalitarian, but not unconsciously so. They miss few of the clues of family background pro-vided by slips in speech or peculiarities of taste, and in almost every block there is someone—to use a favored euphemism—that the others say "has not had all the advantages some people have had." Such a person is not snubbed. Quite the opposite; the others will go out of their way to make him feel at home and through a sort of osmosis educate him in the values of the group.

Park Forest is a melting pot in other respects also. The intellectuals like-wise receive an education. "When I first came here I was pretty rarefied," a self-styled "egghead" explained to a recent visitor. "I remember how shocked I was one day when I told the girls in the court how much I had enjoyed listening to *The Magic Flute* the night before. They didn't know what I was talking about. I began to learn that diaper talk is a lot more important to them. I still listen to *The Magic Flute,* but now I realize that for most people other things in life seem as important."

What we have, then, is an active seeking of common denominators. Just as the bunco player may put his mind to mastering bridge, so the Ph.D.'s wife learns to have fun at a kaffeeklatsch. Just as the fundamentalist learns to unbend with a tentative risqué story and a beer now and then, so his neighbor tones down his stories.

Bridge scores are another case in point. The reader may recall how in William Foote Whyte's study of a street-corner gang, the members' bowling scores tended to correspond with their rank in the group. At Park Forest you find a twist on this phenomenon. In bridge groups in traditional com-munities, there is usually a pronounced ranking of the players. A perform-ance chart of the number of times members of two particular Park Forest bridge clubs have won prizes shows an opposite result. Per number of games, everyone wins about as many times as everyone else.

But the pot melts just so much. There is no class structure in the new suburbia. There is, however, one dividing line of considerable importance: transiency. This shows poignantly in some residents' attitude toward the community. The usual transient affects an attitude of fond detachment—swell place, lots of kicks, but, after all, the sort of place you graduate from. For some, however, the place is less a way station than the end of the road. The permanence of the community, not its impermanence, is what they want to see, and for them the moving van can be an unsettling reminder of a transiency they are not going to share. Then, for others, the new suburb is too much of a personal achievement to take with anything but deadly seriousness, and they are extraordinarily sensitive to any references that might be invidious. "Those pictures are absolutely disgraceful," one resident recently said of some published pictures of her area. "The way they angled them, it makes it look as though this was a development!"

The intensity of feeling that many people in this situation develop is no joking matter. Their social enfranchisement is a great achievement of our expanding society, but the process, it is important to remember, is psychologically nonreversible. Of all the groups in America, none is so ill equipped emotionally as the new white-collar group to adjust to a severe economic downturn, and, if our society has an Achilles' heel, this might be it. Not without a fight, and one that could become collectively ugly, would they be pushed back across the tracks.

The concrete implications of this meshing of values were brought home to us by the patterns of friendship. We selected one court and spent four weeks checking, first, the friendship pattern that day-to-day behavior revealed and, second, the individuals themselves. By the time we were done, we had a considerable pile of data on religion, occupation, age, and so on. When we tried to correlate these data with the friendship patterns, we found we were right back where we started. Individual considerations often affected friendships—age especially—but, by and large, it was clear that physical layout was the great determinant.

The way physical design influences social traffic is sometimes capricious. Some people are so ambiguously located that they can never quite be sure whom they should select for friends. By and large, however, the social traffic follows a logical pattern.

It begins with the children. The new suburbs are matriarchies, yet the children are in effect so dictatorial that a term like filiarchy would not be entirely facetious. It is the children who set the basic design. Their friendships are translated into the mother's friendships, and these, in turn, into the family's. Fathers just tag along.

The children are a key factor in determining court behavior. With their remarkable sensitivity to social nuance, the children are a highly effective communication net, and parents sometimes use them to transmit sentiments that custom dictates elders cannot say face to face. "One newcomer gave us quite a problem in our court," says a resident in an eastern development. "He was a Ph.D., and he started to pull rank on some of the rest of us. I told my kid he could tell his kid that the other fathers around here had plenty on the ball. I guess all we fathers did the same thing; pretty soon the news trickled upward to this guy. He isn't a bad sort; he got the hint— and there was no open break of any kind."

So pervasive are the concerns of parenthood that adjustment to court life is almost impossible for childless couples. Unless the wife patently loves children—unless she is the kind, for example, who keeps a cooky jar for the neighbors' kids—her daily routine is painfully out of kilter with the others'. Understandably, the recourse of adopting a child is sought very frequently. Equally understandable, adoption agencies look on Park Forest couples as particularly good bets.

Who are the deviates? Basically there are four categories of residents. First, there are the members of the group—the great majority. Second, there are those whose friendships, through community-wide activities, tend to cut across the whole community rather than to be concentrated in one geographic area. Third, there are those intrinsically antisocial people who would not get along with anybody anywhere. Fourth, there are those who are almost pathetically eager to be members of the group, but who somehow bring out all the bullying instincts in those about them.

If the deviate is at the end of a block or is otherwise isolated physically, he may remain ignorant of what he is missing. In a more central and thereby exposed position, the result is different.

How, the stranger wonders, does one tell rank in a place like Park Forest—or, for that matter, "pull" it? The higher-rent two-apartment buildings, which are sited individually on roads rather than arranged in court fashion, rent for $117, versus $92 to $104 for court apartments, and constitute something of a local gold coast. But, aside from these, the houses and apartments differ little in cost, and physically they are distinguished from each other largely by changes in façade. One's location in the courts, furthermore, is determined largely by chance rather than by personal selection.

Cars are not much help either. Of the thousands that lie in the parking bays, few are more expensive than the Buick Special, and rakish touches are not too frequent. Only in nearby industrial towns do people show exuberance in the captainship of the American car: foxtails and triumphant pennants, like Cyrano's white plume, fly defiantly on cars there, and occasionally from the radiator a devil thumbs his nose at the passing mob. Not at Park Forest; whatever else it has, it has no panache.

The fact that the transients do not have much money is, of course, part of the story—but only part. "There is no keeping up with the Joneses here" is an observation so often and so emphatically voiced as to indicate that these people are united in a code of inconspicuous consumption.

The job is not so much to keep up with the Joneses; it is to keep down with them. When a resident sees his neighbor vaunting worldly goods, he sees this as an offense not simply to him but to the community as well. Interestingly enough, when people comment about display, they usually make the point that they themselves see nothing wrong with it, but that other people might, and that therefore the purchase is ill advised.

For all the apparent sameness of consumption, to the resident there is great diversity. The more one becomes acclimated to the homogeneity, the more sensitized one becomes to the small differences. At Levittown, Pennsylvania, for example, residents are very much aware of who has which "modification" of the basic ranch-house design; and one house on which the owner has mounted a small gargoyle has become so famous a "sight" that many residents drive out of their way to show it to visitors. Similarly, people have a sharp eye for the smaller variations from the norm of home furnishings, and the acquisition of a new automatic dryer or an unusually good television set is always cause for notice. Lack of such amenities, conversely, is also noted. In one suburb, to cite a rather extreme example, a couple were so sensitive about the bareness of their living room that they smeared their windows with Bon Ami—and kept them that way until a dinette set arrived.

The leveling process is just that, leveling, and those financially above the norm who let the fact be visible are risking trouble. Though neighbors speak kindly of someone who "has not had all the advantages," the words "they are more fortunate than the rest of us" are likely to be spoken with a real bite.

Just how much bite depends on how happy the group is. The more happiness, the more bite. For, the more vigorous the search for common denominators, the stronger is the pressure to alikeness. Sometimes this extends even to house design. The architects have tried to vary the façades of the houses; and one might assume that in putting up aluminum awnings, making alterations, repainting, and the like, residents would try hard to enlarge the differences. This is not always so. In some areas residents have apparently agreed to unify the block with a common design and color scheme for garages and such.

In such blocks an otherwise minor variation becomes blatant deviance. A man who paints his garage fire-engine red in a block in which the rest of the garages are white has psychologically made himself a marked man. So it is with fences. If they are obviously designed to keep the children safe, eyebrows are not raised. But, if the height or elaborateness of the fence indicates other motives, there will be feeling.

Lawns are another good clue. A lawn notably less manicured than the others in a block is a strong indication that all is not well between its owner and the others. It is not merely that the state of the lawn itself has provoked feeling. The lawn is an effect as well as a cause, and in talking to owners of neglected lawns one gets the suspicion that they have subconsciously used them as a weapon against the others. "I suppose I should do more about it," says one resident, waving to a rather weedy expanse outside, "but my wife and I think there are other things more important in life."

Let me recapitulate a bit: In part because of the great increase in transiency among Americans, the oncoming generations have had to develop a new kind of roots. They no longer have the firm support of close kin and home community ties. But they have found compensations. They have found a kind of interchangeable roots through the kind of fraternity life we have been talking about. They have developed ties, and, when they sever these and pack up to go elsewhere, they can repeat the process all over again. The roots are shallow, perhaps, but, like those of the redwood tree, a lot of shallow roots can give a great deal of support.

Now, in this constant tuning in, this constant searching for denominators, to bind oneself with others, there is a strong force against the expression of individual taste. When one is trying to identify himself with a group, the emphasis is on what is similar, not on what is dissimilar.

Most of the critical tensions found in the courts and the blocks are problems of leisure time. On such matters as car pools, housework, and the like, there is great consensus; it is not until we get to two o'clock in the afternoon, to the cocktail hour on a Saturday, that we come to that area in which people are not quite sure what the standard should be. Accordingly, they are supersensitive to cues. What, the question constantly recurs, is right? And who dares to lead?

To oversimplify a bit, let me divide Park Forest into three categories. At the bottom we have those people for whom complete sublimation in the group is fulfillment—and for whom the group standards represent an improvement over their past ones. In the middle, there is a very sizable number of people who are torn between their desire for the warmth and approbation of the group and their own unfulfilled cultural impulses. Then, at the top, there are the "eggheads."

The term "egghead" is used for want of a better designation. It is not used in the political sense. Perhaps Russell Lynes's "upper-middlebrow" is more to the mark. In any event, the one thing that most characterizes Park Forest leadership is an affinity, sometimes a strenuous search, for cultural expression. At first it appeared as if the high-fidelity set, the California Frank Schoonmaker wine with dinner, and the intense bull sessions—in short, the eggheadism—was restricted to a very small minority, mostly lawyers and university people. As far as intensity goes, that is true. But as we got to know more people we began to grasp how very deep was the urge among many, many others for this same kind of expression. Even among the most resolutely philistine there is great pride that Park Forest is so "cultural." Talk to, say, a carpenter's wife who has just made that tremendous jump from Chicago Heights one mile away, and she will tell you first off how many Park Foresters are college people—and how many writers, Ph.D.'s, and artists they have there.

Let us look at the "junior executives." In most cases, the successful junior executive was measurably more inclined than his contemporaries toward what is usually called "culture." He had more and better books on his bookshelves, more and better magazines, and usually a good record collection. His tastes were by no means so highbrow as those of the more culturally intense academic and professional people—Strauss and concertos, you might say, rather than Schönberg and quartets, were the rule. Between the successful and the run-of-the-mill junior executive, however, the difference was so great that it is fair to conclude that the "impractical" is more closely related to the attributes of leadership than many businessmen suspect.

Let us look at another kind of leader—the members of the League of Women Voters. There is a very strong correlation between League membership and community leadership, and there is also a rather strong correlation between community leadership and interest in cultural pursuits. Yet, in a sense, League members seem atypical. Compared with, say, the members of the community women's club—an organization, by the way, about which League people are loftily condescending—League women are likely to be somewhat absent-minded about their clothes and their housekeeping, and often they tend to be a little bit on the scrawny side. League women themselves like to point this out. They explain they are too busy doing things that "count" to have time for coffee and doughnuts.

Now, we seem to have something of a conflict here. On one hand, there is the tightly knit, gregarious group, militating against anything that rises too much above the common denominator. On the other hand, most of the people in leadership positions of one kind or another are demonstrably more catholic in their leisure-time pursuits than their contemporaries.

One explanation, of course, is that the group can be tyrannous only to those who let it be. To put it another way: the woman who wants desperately to be a member of the gang often seems to bring out all the "bullyness" and cruelty latent in the group. The League of Women voters type does not care much. Ordinarily she is careful about the neighborly graces—the baby-sitting, the lending of the meat slicer, and so on. But she keeps a certain detachment, a certain buffer zone. Like the wise shipboard traveler, she doesn't get too involved. The result is that the group, whether they quite say so or not, tend to look up to her. The more cultural types would hate to concede this, but I think I am safe in saying that at least eight out of every ten persons talked to at Park Forest always made the remark, "Isn't it a shame, all this conformity"; and they did not care whether people thought they were "screwball" or not, someone had to be an individualist.

One very attractive woman, about forty years old, rather good-naturedly told me that she had come to be considered quite eccentric in her court. In the afternoons, instead of sunbathing on the back stoop so that she could kaffeeklatsch with the girls, she moved her chair around to the front, as a sort of signal that she would rather read undisturbed. The others were curious but they respected her wish. Then, one day, one of them took a shortcut across her lawn. "What you reading, hon?" she asked. The older woman told me, "You might have known it would have to be Plato that day." Her visitor was incredulous, and the older woman was sure that she would now be known as a real deviate.

The story is relevant because that was not true. I talked to no one in the court who made fun of her or showed her anything but respect, if often a bit grudgingly.

Is it possible to cultivate, to encourage, this kind of cultural leadership, this widening of choice? Of course it is. Let me try to document this in reverse. One moral that planners and architects sometimes draw from our increasing knowledge about the relationship between design and social life is that the architect is now in a position to design the optimum happy block.

Noting how certain physical arrangements make for more intense neighborliness, these people reason that by simply reproducing these conditions they can deliberately create a higher measure of group cohesion. They are probably right. However, one question obtrudes: What kind of happiness is the result? As we have already seen, the more social the block, the rougher it is on those who cannot make the grade, and in some cases it is questionable if the *Gemütlichkeit* of the gang compensates for the misery of the deviate.

But there is a more important question than this: How does this happiness affect behavior in regard to leisure time?

When we first started out on our study we assumed that those courts that were month in and month out the most social, the most close-knit, would be the ones producing most of the community leadership. We began to plot the location of the leaders of all Park Forest's seventy-odd organizations. We plotted them for 1951 and for late 1952. We found that, in spite of the turnover, certain courts were producing a disproportionate share of Park Forest leadership.

But they were not, we found, the social courts. They weren't the other extremes either—that is, the courts chronically producing the greatest number of ambulance and police calls, feuds, and so forth. Socially they were just sort of average. But in these courts where the group cohesion is not intense, there is more tolerance—not to mention time—for the expression of individual urges.

The homes area also demonstrates this. About the most social block in the whole area—more bridge parties, afternoon kaffeeklatsches, barbecue get-togethers per capita than any other block—is also without much representation in the civic and cultural life of the community.

Is it simply that these people have no urge for civic and cultural activity? Not at all. One woman there is a good case in point. She is one of the three most active social leaders and ostensibly enjoys her role very much. Yet she is very frustrated in some respects. She would like to be a member of the Human Relations Commission of Park Forest. She has also toyed with the idea of joining an art group. She has done neither, for she correctly senses that to do this would inevitably drive something of a wedge between her and the group. Therefore, she and many others like her keep on their social way, imprisoned in brotherhood.

To be fair, we must note that the young transients' adaptability is not, as some observers assume, a reversal of our national character. The American genius has always lain, in good part, in our adaptability, in our distrust of dogma.

Some observers fasten their eyes on the new suburbia and see it as the avenue to *1984*. But this homogeneity is not the real issue. The external similarities in the way of life revealed by the new suburbia are dictated by economic necessity, and it is intellectually irresponsible to bemoan them without facing up to the lack of a reasonable alternative. Rows and rows of identical houses are not in themselves a force for conformity—any more than, say, rows of identical Park Avenue apartments or rows of city houses built at the turn of the century, or, for that matter, some of the identical brick fronts of eighteenth-century America.

It is not in the material similarities that so preoccupy some observers that the problem lies; nor is it even in the similarities of behavior that mark the young transients. The problem lies in the transients' *attitude* toward these similarities.

THE SOCIETY OF SUBURBIA

S. D. Clark

This paper argues a case. It might well have been given the title "In Defense of Suburbia." Though much has been written in recent years about the phenomenon of suburbanism, very little has had anything good to say about the suburban community. Sometimes the bias is hidden; very often it is openly expressed. A dislike for the suburbs is clearly assumed to be a mark of good judgment. Thus could David Riesman write, in the

From S. D. Clark, "The Suburban Community," in S. D. Clark, ed., *Urbanism and the Changing Canadian Society* (Toronto: University of Toronto Press, 1961), pp. 20–38. Revised version, approved by the author and reprinted by permission of the author and the publisher. S. D. Clark, a professor of sociology at the University of Toronto, is the author of books and articles on social history, religions, and urbanism.

opening sentence of a paper on the suburban way of life: "I speak in this paper from the perspective of one who loves city and country, but not the suburbs."[1] To have confessed to the opposite bias would have been almost unthinkable.

A generation ago, the student of American society, typically rural in origin, could find in the big city all that was evil, depraved, and corrupt in the American way of life. A highly romantic picture of rural society, the product of not a little nostalgia, served to bring into sharp relief the undesirable qualities of urban society. In the quarter-century or so that has since passed, however, the student of American society has learned to love the city in the manner that he has for long loved the country; and now suburbia —portrayed in terms of slavish conformity, fetish of togetherness, and craze for organization—is set over against a romantic image of the city, with its narrow and cluttered streets, its quaint shops and picturesque tenements, its strange and ever changing assortment of people of many colors, nationalities, and languages, producing a way of life which seemingly brings out all that is worthwhile in man.

It may be difficult to believe that such as Riesman know better the suburbs they profess to dislike than "the country" they profess to love, but the suburbia myth cannot be dismissed as the product simply of the imagination of those students of American society intent on finding in the suburban way of life the symptoms of "the sickness of our times." Interest in the phenomenon of surburbanism has led to much research and faithful reporting of research findings.[2] So deeply imbedded in thinking, however, has become the suburbia myth that it has determined in large degree the very design of the research which has been undertaken.[3] Students of suburbia have gone from reading Riesman (and Whyte and Fromm) to reading Parsons, and nothing to them could have appeared more sociologically righteous than the effort to discover in the suburban society a basic personality type, a dominant ethos or outlook on life. Here, indeed, was a society which seemed to exemplify to a high degree the character of the socializing process at work in all societies. The very emphasis upon values of child-rearing in suburbia reflected, it could be assumed, the underlying concern of human beings for the creation of the conditions of consensus and social integration.

By concentrating attention upon certain kinds of suburban areas, it has

[1]David Riesman, "The Suburban Sadness," in William M. Dobriner, ed., *The Suburban Community* (New York: Putnam, 1958), pp. 375–408.
[2]Of books on suburbia, William H. Whyte, Jr., *The Organization Man* (New York: Simon and Schuster, 1956), is the one which has attracted the most attention; Part VII is devoted to the suburbs. It would serve no useful purpose to attempt to list the very great number of articles on suburbia appearing in popular and semipopular journals and magazines.
[3]Very much an exception is Bennett M. Berger, *Working-Class Suburb* (Berkeley: University of California Press, 1960). In this study of a suburban community made up of auto workers, Berger does a masterful job of exposing "the myth of suburbia." His findings agree almost completely with mine. Berger, however, emphasizes the negative aspects of suburban life. What he is concerned in showing is that the way of life of the population he studied grows in large part out of its working-class culture and not out of its suburban situation. What I argue in this paper is that there is a difference, however, between the suburban and urban society but the difference is to be accounted for simply on the grounds that the suburban society is new. This aspect of the problem is not developed by Berger.

not been difficult in the findings of research to build up a particular image or stereotype of suburbia. Thus, for instance, from the picture presented in *Crestwood Heights*,[4] a suburb of Toronto, clearly identifiable as Forest Hill Village, much could be made of the kinds of social pressures making for conformity considered characteristic of suburban life. Had those who have thus used this study known Toronto better, however, had they known something about the hundreds of subdivisions spreading east, north, and west at least 30 miles, housing a population very different from that found in Forest Hill Village, they would have realized how little characteristic of suburban society this society was. What was being studied here was not the social process of suburbanism but the culture of a particular urban social class and, in large degree, ethnic group.

A good many of those residential areas selected for investigation by the student of suburbia have characteristics not unlike those of Forest Hill Village. They have tended to have a population of above average means or, if not, one that aspired strongly to improve its social position. Very often, they have been heavily populated by an ethnic minority anxious to find in the suburbs a social world where it could be sheltered from the assimilative or culturally disintegrative forces of an urban environment. Almost all of them have had something of a ready-made quality. Residential communities like Park Forest or the Levittowns did not simply grow up. They were created, often on the initiative or under the direction of one man. They were, indeed, "packaged" communities, residential developments designed to offer everything that was required by people in order to live a full community life. Such suburban communities thus had something of the character of social oases, residential areas cut off not only from old established urban areas but also from other residential areas growing up.

Why areas like these have been selected for analysis is not at all hard to understand. The very isolation of such residential areas from the built-up sections of the urban community, their physical compactness, and their development around well-defined centers make them easy to study. They have clearcut boundaries, and there is an orderliness in the structure of their social life. They appear to have some sort of ethos or character, and they appear to produce a distinctive personality type; such can scarcely fail to be so since only certain kinds of people choose to settle in them. In areas like these the sociologist finds a society which can be described and analyzed in the same manner as the anthropologist describes and analyzes a primitive society. The characteristics of the population can be readily determined, sampling techniques employed without difficulty, patterns of behavior searched out and meaningfully related to the values and goals of the group as a whole, processes of socialization identified and measured, and the major institutions of the society fitted together into something that appears to have the characteristics of a social system. In methodological terms, indeed, the packaged suburban residential community offers almost a perfect sociological laboratory for investigation and analysis.

What the study of such suburban areas has meant, however, is that a bias has been built into the sociological conception of suburbanism. A high

[4]J. R. Seeley, R. A. Sim, and E. W. Loosley, *Crestwood Heights* (Toronto: University of Toronto Press, 1956).

degree of order has been found characteristic of suburban society, but it has been those suburban societies displaying a high degree of order that were selected for investigation. With theoretical tools borrowed largely from the anthropologist and psychologist, the sociologist in studying suburban society has been looking for a system of order, and nowhere has he been better able to find such a system than in the packaged type of suburban community.

Of course, where the sociological interest is to examine such processes as socialization, there can be no quarrel with the selection. There is an order in suburban society as in all societies, and its nature can certainly be most clearly discerned in those suburban communities that are largely a product of planning and direction. But suburbanism is not only an order, it is also a process; and to analyze suburbanism as a process, one should look at those suburban areas where a sense of order is not the most, but the least, prominent. It is in these areas, not those produced by planning and direction, that the dynamics of suburban growth are to be discovered. The pattern of suburban development is away from as well as toward a state of order, since what suburban development essentially means is the process of transformation of the country into the city. It is in the nature of this transformation that the characteristics of the suburban society are to be found.

It is not possible here to examine in all its complexity the movement of population from the city to the country and the creation in the country of an urban type of society. In general terms, two fairly distinct phases of suburban development can be distinguished. The first is characterized by the efforts of individual urban families and of certain special kinds of urban social groups to take advantage of the opportunity offered by the open countryside to escape the burdens of life in the large city, to try to realize a way of life no longer possible in an urban environment. Where a collective effort is possible, this search for a new way of life in the suburbs, for a utopia, can lead to the construction of whole new residential communities, conceived and developed so as to realize a very distinctive, and clearly held, set of social values. Thus has developed the packaged type of surburban residential community, in which much of the structure of a society is established from the very beginning.[5]

But in this early phase of suburban development there is not only a type of settlement with a good deal of direction and control but also one with an almost complete absence of direction and control. Individual families have simply moved out into the country on their own, settling wherever opportunity offered, along some back road, on the outskirts of old established villages or towns, or in hidden pockets of the open country where land is of such poor quality that it cannot be profitably farmed. This is the ribbon or leapfrog kind of development, long the despair of the community planner, in which urban residents spread out into areas far distant from

[5]Not all of the residential developments of the packaged type, it should be pointed out, are made up of people of above-average income. The development may result from the cooperative efforts of a group of working-class people, for instance, or it may be sponsored by an industrial firm which has moved out from the city and brought its workers with it. An alternative way of describing these developments might be to call them "collectively sponsored."

the city and create a society which, though neither rural nor urban, possesses some of the qualities of both. In contrast with packaged surburbs of the Park Forest type, thus, there are these very different residential areas, created by the completely haphazard dispersion from the city of individual families, ranging from the very rich to the very poor, and differing as much in social values as in material possessions.

In this first phase of suburban development, the city, in terms of all the population types represented, may be thought of as seeking to reproduce itself in the country. But this it can do only to a degree so long as the conditions persist which place a sharp limit on urban growth. This is a phase of selective growth: not everyone is tempted to move into the suburbs. Indeed, for the vast majority of persons seeking residential accommodations the suburbs have little to offer during this early phase of development. For financial or other reasons, many are not prepared to locate in a packaged residential development; and settlement along a country highway, on the outskirts of a country village, or in some distant rural area can also have little appeal. Thus, the movement from the city during this first phase of suburban development is characterized by what seems to be haphazard occupation of country areas, with the over-all pattern of growth determined by differences in the price of land and the availability of public services, and in particular of roads to the city. Here and there, as the result either of careful planning or of no planning at all, small clusters of urban residents appear, while a few urban families scatter along highways reaching into the country or about country villages. But vast stretches of open countryside yet remain to be occupied; rural society still is far from being transformed. Urbanization comes only with a very different type of development, in which the urban population overruns the countryside and occupies all at once great stretches of farm land.

Yet it is this earlier phase of development which creates the conditions for the later. The mass movement into the suburbs comes only with the production of the kind of housing that reaches a mass market, and before this can happen the occupation of the countryside must have become great enough to support a certain level of urban services. Once this breakthrough is reached, however, there is virtually no intrinsic limit to the residential growth that can take place; and private enterprise, in the mass assembly of land and mass building of homes, takes advantage of the opportunity to reach a suddenly widened housing market. In the early phase of suburban development, the settlement of any particular area is limited by the maximum burden that can be borne by long-established public services, except in the packaged type, where the occupation is accompanied by the establishment of such services by the new residents. In this later phase, however, the economies of settlement demand the full occupation of newly serviced areas in the shortest possible time. Movement into the suburbs thus becomes a great wave, sweeping all before it. In this manner, in the years since World War II, much of the countryside around our larger cities has been occupied.

This development, it must be emphasized, is nonselective with respect to the kinds of people involved. It is truly a mass movement of population. Among those settling in the suburbs can be found still many well-to-do and many very poor, and along country roads even farther from the city there are families willing to sacrifice urban services for the advantages of country life. But those overrunning the vast countryside are much less distinctive—the city's great house-hungry population which can find space only by spreading beyond the limits of the urban community.

If there is a suburban society, those settling in these mass-produced housing areas are its creators. But this society clearly does not conform to the stereotype of suburbia. It has no form—indeed, no determinate boundaries. It cannot be studied in the same ways, therefore, as a Forest Hill Village or a Park Forest. In this undifferentiated mass of dwellings, street blocks, and subdivisions, beginning and ending nowhere that can be seen clearly, the inhabitants seem to be as little differentiated as the areas themselves. People *choose* to live in a Forest Hill Village or Park Forest; they seek, and are prepared to pay for, the particular way of life that such residential areas appear to offer. But for those who move into the mass-produced housing areas, there is generally no such choice. What such people seek primarily is a house, and they move where they do because it is there they can find one they can afford. This is essentially as true of the person buying a $20,000 house as of one buying a $12,000 house.[6] Though residential areas are differentiated by price, and their populations thus by income, the individual chooses simply according to his capacity to pay. A house is being bought, not a social environment; and this characteristic of large-scale residential development means that it is a mass market.

The failure to see the packaged suburban community in the perspective of this much more extensive kind of mass-produced housing accounts for many of the misconceptions concerning the nature of suburban society. There is no completely new and different kind of society being created; nothing about the way suburbia develops distinguishes it from any other society. Indeed, the pattern of settlement of an area like the Great Plains is strikingly similar. The West had its pioneers, families moving far beyond settled areas to wait, perhaps for years, until the region filled up enough to support a form of community life; it had its experiments in community building, backland utopias created out of the dreams of the visionary or out of the determination of certain people (often of a particular religious faith or ethnic attachment) to preserve their way of life; and it had its half-hidden settlements of the impoverished, the economic cast-offs of older societies. While these types of farm settlements characterized the early development of the Great Plains, their real occupation came only when this selective settlement gave way to the mass movement of land-hungry people. To have delineated the typical "Westerner" from among the people making up one or another of these little ethnic, religious, or other such colonies scattered over the Great Plains in the early years of settlement would have been as justified as the search for the typical "suburbanite" among the residents of one or another of the planned experiments in community building characteristic of the early phase of suburban growth.

This is not to say that the population moving into the mass-produced housing areas outside the city has no distinctive characteristics. For one

[6]But not of the person buying a $30,000 house. Homes in this price range are not built for a mass market, and they are built only where there has been sufficient planning to protect property values. Thus the purchaser of such a property buys a social environment as well as a house, and is prepared to pay $30,000 or more for it. No precise line can be drawn, of course, between these two different kinds of market.

thing, it is a very young population.[7] For another, it is a population with no previous experience of home ownership.[8] It can well be described as a foot-loose population. The typical movement has been from an apartment to a house in the suburbs, with no previous identification with a way of life, no putting down of roots in a community. Before the purchase of the house, the total investment was in marriage and the founding of a family.

Such a population produces a certain kind of society. Baby-sitting, for instance, becomes a major concern, as does education at the elementary level; and all sorts of social stratagems are developed to meet problems like these. But the resulting patterns of social behavior can in no way be described as distinctly suburban. With variations in small matters of detail, they are the patterns of behavior of all populations that move—of the population, for instance, of the Great Plains in the early years of settlement, or of the new mining towns growing up today in northern Canada.

In the mass-produced suburban housing areas, these young people are suddenly faced with the task of building a community without outside help. The effort to keep the price of each house within the reach of the mass buyer determines not only the site of the projects—beyond the belt immediately surrounding the city, where real-estate speculation pushed up the price of land—but also the nature of the development: all homes in the subdivided area are constructed and sold at the same time. Thus there can be no easy extension of the social structure of old residential areas into the new; nor can there be, where all take up residence at once,. any reliance upon the accomplishments or the experience of those already there. The suburban society is created almost literally overnight, and out of only those limited materials the newcomers brought with them.

Such a society has much, certainly, that a Riesman or Whyte can deplore, as there was much they could have deplored in the society of the Great Plains in the early years of settlement. The suburban is a society that can boast no strong interest in public affairs, in cultural activities, or in the development of gracious forms of living. People are concerned rather about matters related to the immediate struggle to establish a home and raise a family: mounting property taxes, roads that break up with the spring thaw, water-filled ditches along streets which are a hazard to children playing, basements that leak and plaster that cracks, classrooms that are crowded. An intense dissatisfaction concerning matters that an outsider may see of little importance is joined with a general complacency toward issues of great public significance.

But it must be remembered that this is a young population, undertaking for the first time to make a home and community for itself. It is treacherously

[7]In contrast not only to the population of the city but to the population involved in the earlier phase of residential development. The contrast to the population of the city is striking. In a typical subdivision development outside the city of Toronto, for instance, of the total population aged 20 and over in 1956, 46 per cent were in the age-group 25–34; 76 per cent, in the age-group 25–44. In a typical residential area in the city of Toronto, in contrast, only 15.8 per cent of the total adult population were in the age-group 25–34; and only 32.6 per cent, in the age-group 25–44. The age structure of the population in the packaged residential area is somewhere between that of the city and that of the mass-produced development.

[8]Of the 379 families settling in Regency Acres, a typical subdivision outside Toronto, only 16.3 per cent had previously owned homes. However, in Thorncrest Village, a typical packaged community, the comparable figure was 57.6 per cent.

easy for the well-established 50-year-old to pass judgment on how the 25-year-old ought to live, but fortunately for the progress of the human race his judgment does not always prevail. The well-established 50-year-old has a stake in the community; his status is closely identified with its organizational life and the system of values upon which this depends. Thus a community with a high degree of social participation comes to be perceived as the ideal community. Public spirit is judged a social good. Yet most of the young people moving into suburbs clearly do not want to live in this kind of community at all; they couldn't care less for the kinds of things offered by packaged residential areas like Park Forest. What they seek, rather, if they seek anything at all, is an escape from the kinds of demands that an old established community would place upon them.

These migrants do not, of course, clearly recognize what it is they are escaping from. They are intent only on the business at hand: the acquisition of a home in which to raise a family. But this means a very strong reluctance to get caught up in the network of obligations normal to an old established society.

The attributes identified as suburban in so much of the literature on the subject are thus the very ones most conspicuously absent. Packaged residential areas have a great deal of "neighboring." Their residents carefully observe the conduct of their fellows and conform to what appear to be group values. Public spirit is much in evidence. But these people moved into such areas precisely in order to find a rich community life. Where the investment in the home also represents an investment in a particular way of life, community improvement is a means of protecting property values. Active participation in community life is an obligation readily accepted and, given the selective character of the population, one which imposes no great burden.

The mass-produced housing development, however, has no such neighboring, or participation in organizational activity, or conformity to the values of the group. These young people, excited by the fact of home ownership, take their responsibilities as parents very seriously; but, contrary to the stereotype, they are not anxious to become involved with neighbors, to join organizations or attend meetings, to accept public office, or to try to "keep up" with others in the community. Where the only concern was to find a home priced within reach, there can be no protecting property values by community improvement. Almost wholly lacking here is that drive to upward mobility, so much stressed by Whyte, which leads to the careful selection of one place to live, and its ready abandonment for another, in terms of one's established status and aspirations.

All that has been said applies, of course, to the suburban community only just come into being. In actual fact, no suburban community is so completely new that it displays only these characteristics. From the very beginning, the old society intrudes on the new, even if only a little; however isolated mass-produced residential developments, they do not grow up completely apart from older residential areas. And in time, homes change hands; people move out and others move in. Though the difference between the original and the later home owners may not be great, there is a difference. Moreover, even where no change of ownership takes place, the very passing of time produces a different people. Families begin to grow up, savings accumulate, the equity in the house becomes larger; and with such changes in family circumstances, the stake in the community becomes greater. A pride develops in the home and in the neighborhood. Concern shifts from problems narrowly centered in the house and family to those of the larger social world, in which the suburban resident finds himself becoming increasingly involved. The taxpayers' association withers away, its place taken by the community association or service club; neighborhoods develop a new self-consciousness on the basis of social class or ethnic identity; an increasing proportion of the suburbanite's time and energy is consumed in the social life of the larger community. Vast differences separate a suburban community ten years old from one newly born.

Indeed, the social life of some of these ten-year-old communities may not be unlike that generally identified with suburbia. If this is the case, however, the reason is not that these communities are suburban but that they are becoming urban. Probably no more highly urbanized area could have been found than the one selected by Seeley, Sim, and Loosley for study. The people who moved into Forest Hill Village could afford from the beginning to maintain the whole gamut of urban services and, with it, the social supports of an urban way of life. Indeed, the Village was created in order to preserve urban values, or more specifically the values of an urban middle class, from the destructive forces of urban growth. The later selective migrations, which brought about a very substantial change in the ethnic composition, accentuated the urban character; it was a highly urbanized people who replaced the original home owners. To some degree, selection by such a differential identification with a particular set of urban values characterizes the migration to any suburban area, which means that something of the urban social structure is transferred to even the most undifferentiated and unplanned of residential developments. It is nonetheless significant that this is very much less true of mass-produced than of packaged housing, and that in the mass-produced type, only with the passing of time do urban values become prominent in the structuring of the society. At that point, but only then, the packaged residential development, built from the beginning in accordance with the values of the urban middle class, may become indistinguishable from the larger complex of suburban middle-class society.

To say that the suburban becomes a part of the urban community does not mean that the whole of it acquires the characteristics of urban middle-class society. By the time the countryside surrounding the city is fully occupied, the city has reproduced itself, so that scarcely any element of the urban population is not represented in the suburban. Besides the new middle-class societies that the city has brought into being are new exclusive residential areas, working-class districts, ethnic colonies, slums, criminal underworlds, and even bohemias. To find here the "other-directed" or "organization" man would not be difficult, among all the various types produced by a highly diversified urban society. The society of "suburbia" disappears, but in reality such a society existed only in the imagination of those who— specifying the social characteristics associated with bureaucratic organization and mass communication and discovering these in certain kinds of suburban areas—created the stereotype.

To say this and nothing more about suburban development, however, is to skirt one of the main problems of such development. While suburban society may have none of the characteristics it has been made out to have, its development nevertheless does pose problems regarding the future welfare of urban society at large. The countryside surrounding the city is being overrun by an urban population[9] in a manner that appears highly wasteful both economically and socially. It is not difficult to estimate some of the economic costs involved: the provision of transportation, sewerage, water, fire protection, education, shopping, police, and other such services, in areas far removed from the main concentrations of population. The social costs, though less readily measured, are probably no less great. Society is poorer by the deprivation suffered by a suburban population—its isolation, the weakening of kinship ties, the age imbalance, the expenditure of its energy in the struggle to provide itself with housing and in commuting, its incapacity to support forms of intellectual or cultural expression. Indeed, it is scarcely possible to escape the feeling there is something almost fraudulent about the whole vast enterprise directed to the object of persuading people to move into the suburbs. Many of the real costs of such a movement are hidden: by municipal councils, in passing on to future taxpayers a part of the cost of providing new services; by the new residents themselves, in postponing the charge of the house purchase on their earnings through first and, even more, second mortgages; by a federal government, in using financial aid to housing as a fiscal device; and by society at large, which in the end must suffer the economic and social losses suburban development has entailed.

But the real question is not whether there are such losses but whether they are worth suffering; to this question no final answer can be given, for it must be based on values about which there is no agreement. Indeed, the very use of such terms as "urban sprawl" indicates the biases in much of the discussion of urban growth. Those who view with alarm the way our cities are being permitted to grow are too often people, like C. Wright Mills, for instance, who believe strongly in the virtues of planning, and who consequently find no good in unplanned growth.

Under different conditions of development, would the economic and social losses resulting from urban growth be lessened? In seeking an answer to this question, we must keep two facts clearly in mind. First, most families moving into the suburbs cannot afford homes more expensive than those made available under present conditions of development. Under more exacting conditions of planning, would it be possible to provide housing within the reach of as many people, for instance, and prevent the rise of subdivisions beyond the belt of undeveloped land surrounding the city, or insist on a greater variety in housing designs or on a more imaginative street lay-out? If not, the effect would be to eliminate from the housing market some who are now able to buy homes.

It can be argued, of course, that many of those buying suburban homes should be discouraged by price from doing so. If esthetic values had been

---

[9]And by urban industry and commercial establishments, but discussion of this larger aspect of the problem lies beyond the scope of this paper.

the only consideration, one would have quickly settled for the Park Forest model in the planning of the expansion of our cities, even if it had meant that only half as many people would have been housed in the suburbs as is now the case. But the social consequences of such a restriction cannot be overlooked. In the years since World War II, many thousands of impoverished families situated in the overcrowded sections of our larger cities have been able to secure homes for themselves by moving far out into the country, where land was cheap and substandard housing could be secured at little cost. Such areas would quickly have been condemned by city planning and welfare departments, had their jurisdiction reached so far. Their creation and continued existence have depended upon the tolerance of municipal councils made up of farmers or people with a rural outlook. These residential areas have no paved streets, well-cared-for lawns, public playgrounds for children, shopping centers, or homes that would pass even the most careless building, fire, and health inspections. In short, the housing and public services do not meet any generally accepted minimum standard of decency. Yet one cannot escape asking whether the people settled in these areas would have been as well off had they been unable to move out of the city. Here at least they escape smoke-laden air and shared housing, and children have open playing areas. By taking advantage of the opportunity to secure housing within their price range, poor people have been able to build for themselves homes and communities in a way impossible in the city. Such people, of course, could have been provided with more adequate housing less wastefully if society had been prepared to bear the cost.

But, and this is the second fact that must be kept in mind, the home owners of the mass-produced housing areas outside the city have very definite preferences concerning how they want to live, or perhaps rather how they do not want to live. That is not to say that they have precise ideas about housing designs, street lay-outs, or community plans; but most people moving into the suburbs seemingly want to live as they are in fact living. They want a home of their own and, if more than this, they want to be away from the confusion and the congestion of the big city, to be able to look out on open fields—even knowing that they will soon disappear; and they want the anonymity of the big, unplanned residential development. They may not fully count the costs—the fatiguing and expensive daily trip to work, the onerous burden of mortgage payments and property taxes, the loneliness of subdivision life, the tribulations of keeping a shabbily built house in repair, the lack of recreational facilities for children who have passed beyond school age. Yet they are ready to accept such disadvantages for the sake of the advantages of suburban life. In another society—urban Europe, for instance—people may want to live differently, and what our society sees as the good life the European might thus consider intolerable. We can learn much from the experience of city-building in other lands, but only if we recognize the differences as well as the similarities.

To urge that such considerations are important is not to argue that planning is bad, or that city growth could not have been better planned. The unrestricted growth of urban centers in past years has resulted in appalling waste of material and human resources. Indeed, much urban energy is devoted to clearing up the mess left them by those who have gone before, and this has always been so. But while the costs of unrestricted development are readily measurable, the costs of planning and control are largely hidden and often biased. Even discussion of the process of urban growth seldom completely avoids the stereotype of suburbia, so that it is hard not to believe that life in the suburbs is less desirable than in the city. Ostensibly the objection to suburban development may be esthetic, but under it is a deeper conviction that suburban people are not living as they should.

Critics of suburbia could not be expected, perhaps, to ask whether people in the suburbs are living as they want to. But one might expect such critics to pose more seriously the question whether people in the suburbs are really living as they are made out to be. The stereotype of suburbia has done more than simply amuse the reader of the popular magazine or paperback book. It has markedly influenced thinking about how our cities should be planned, to assure a more satisfying urban way of life. To the extent that the stereotype is empirically false, its effect has been to becloud the issues of urban growth and development.

GUIDES FOR READING AND DISCUSSION

1. What important characteristics distinguish one type of suburb from another? What kind of suburb most closely approximates the portrait drawn by Whyte, and which departs from it most dramatically? Is Whyte or Clark more nearly correct concerning the probable future of suburbia?

2. In the 1920's the suburb was often viewed as a utopian synthesis of urban and rural life; currently it is portrayed as a nightmare of conformity. What factors, in your opinion, account for this radical shift in intellectuals' assessment of suburban life?

3. In what ways does suburban life incorporate elements of rural life? Of urban life?

4. By definition, every society demands that its members conform to the minimum norms that define that particular culture, and in fact there is always some deviation from those norms. What does it mean, then, to say that American society is "conformist" or to advocate unspecified "dissent"? In your opinion, do Americans "conform" more than, say, Englishmen, or Italians, or Latin Americans? How can one make such a question more meaningful?

SUGGESTED ADDITIONAL READINGS

Bennett M. Berger, *Working-Class Suburb: A Study of Auto Workers in Suburbia* (Berkeley: University of California Press, 1960).

William M. Dobriner, ed., *The Suburban Community* (New York: Putnam, 1958.)

David Riesman *et al., The Lonely Crowd* (New Haven: Yale University Press, 1950).

John R. Seeley, R. Alexander Sim, and Elizabeth Loosley, *Crestwood Heights* (Toronto: University of Toronto Press, 1956).

William H. Whyte, Jr., *The Organization Man* (New York: Doubleday-Anchor, 1957).

Robert C. Wood, *Suburbia: Its People and Their Politics* (Boston: Houghton Mifflin, 1958).

Several centuries ago, when the great mass of Europe's population was illiterate and—by modern standards—abysmally poor, the high culture of the Western world was carried by a small minority. By the perspective of that time, this monopoly was inevitable, part of the state of nature. The social philosophers of the eighteenth century, however, dreamed of a future when every adult would be able to read and thus have access to the best writings. In one sense this seemingly utopian fantasy has been realized: in the Western world, illiteracy is now an anomaly; and especially in the United States, the masses can choose from a stupendous range of cultural commodities. From a democrat's point of view, this transformation would seem to have been an indisputable gain, but some believe that its cost has been too great.

American intellectuals have always been unhappy about the state of the arts in their country. In the nineteenth century, when European literati ordinarily looked down their noses at the frontier products from the New World, their American counterparts often accepted this appraisal as just. Now American culture has burgeoned overseas in such forms as television, Hollywood movies, rock 'n' roll, vulgar automobiles, cheap novels; and American intellectuals are again inclined to be apologetic for what is seen as a peculiarly American phenomenon.

The broader base of present-day education means, obviously, that many who participate in high culture have no family tradition to guide them; and such types may stimulate a demand for mediocrity or trash. By one interpretation, here represented by Mr. Macdonald's article, this intrusion of the half-educated threatens all authentic art forms, whether of high or of folk culture. Professor Shils suggests, on the contrary, that "mass culture" is a transitional phase. For a democrat, he argues, the democratization of culture can be interpreted as degenerative only by romanticizing the provincial, grubby existence of the masses in pre-industrial societies.

A THEORY OF MASS CULTURE

Dwight Macdonald

For about a century, Western culture has really been two cultures: the traditional kind—let us call it "High Culture"—that is chronicled in the textbooks, and a "Mass Culture" manufactured wholesale for the market. In the old art forms, the artisans of Mass Culture have long been at work: in the novel, the line stretches from Eugène Sue to Lloyd C. Douglas; in music, from Offenbach to tin-pan alley; in art, from the chromo to Maxfield Parrish and Norman Rockwell; in architecture, from Victorian Gothic to suburban Tudor. Mass Culture has also developed new media of its own, into which the serious artist rarely ventures: radio, the movies, comic books, detective stories, science fiction, television.

It is sometimes called "Popular Culture,"[1] but I think "Mass Culture" a more accurate term, since its distinctive mark is that it is solely and directly an article for mass consumption, like chewing gum. A work of High Culture is occasionally popular, after all, though this is increasingly rare. Thus Dickens was even more popular than his contemporary G. A. Henty, the difference being that he was an artist, communicating his individual vision to other individuals, while Henty was an impersonal manufacturer of an impersonal commodity for the masses.

The historical reasons for the growth of Mass Culture since the early 1800's are well known. Political democracy and popular education broke down the old upper-class monopoly of culture. Business enterprise found a profitable market in the cultural demands of the newly awakened masses, and the advance of technology made possible the cheap production of books, periodicals, pictures, music, and furniture, in sufficient quantities to satisfy this market. Modern technology also created new media like the movies and television, which are specially well adapted to mass manufacture and distribution.

The phenomenon is thus peculiar to modern times and differs radically from what was hitherto known as art or culture. It is true that Mass Culture began as, and to some extent still is, a parasitic, a cancerous growth on High Culture. As Clement Greenberg pointed out, "The precondition of kitsch [a German term for "Mass Culture"] is the availability close at hand of a fully matured cultural tradition, whose discoveries, acquisitions, and perfected self-consciousness kitsch can take advantage of for its own ends."[2] The connection, however, is not that of the leaf and the branch but rather that of the caterpillar and the leaf. Kitsch "mines" High Culture the way improvident frontiersmen mine the soil, extracting its riches and putting

Reprinted from Dwight Macdonald, "A Theory of Mass Culture," *Diogenes,* No. 3 (Summer 1953), pp. 1–17, by permission of the author and the publisher. Mr. Macdonald, a past editor of *Fortune, Partisan Review,* and *Politics,* has written books and articles on politics and, more recently, on literature and popular culture.

[1]As I did myself in "A Theory of Popular Culture" (*Politics,* February 1944), parts of which have been used or adapted in the present article.
[2]Clement Greenberg, "Avant Garde and Kitsch," *Partisan Review* (Fall 1939).

nothing back. Also, as *kitsch* develops, it begins to draw on its own past, and some of it evolves so far away from High Culture as to appear quite disconnected from it.

It is also true that Mass Culture is to some extent a continuation of the old Folk Art which until the Industrial Revolution was the culture of the common people, but here, too, the differences are more striking than the similarities. Folk Art grew from below. It was a spontaneous, autochthonous expression of the people, shaped by themselves, pretty much without the benefit of High Culture, to suit their own needs. Mass Culture is imposed from above. It is fabricated by technicians hired by businessmen; its audiences are passive consumers, their participation limited to the choice between buying and not buying. The Lords of *kitsch,* in short, exploit the cultural needs of the masses in order to make a profit and/or to maintain their class rule—in Communist countries, only the second purpose obtains. (It is very different to *satisfy* popular tastes, as Robert Burns's poetry did, and to *exploit* them, as Hollywood does.) Folk Art was the people's own institution, their private little kitchen-garden walled off from the great formal park of their masters' High Culture. But Mass Culture breaks down the wall, integrating the masses into a debased form of High Culture and thus becoming an instrument of political domination. If one had no other data to go on, the nature of Mass Culture would reveal capitalism to be an exploitative class society and not the harmonious commonwealth it is sometimes alleged to be. The same goes even more strongly for Soviet Communism and *its* special kind of Mass Culture.

"Everybody" knows that America is a land of Mass Culture, but it is not so generally recognized that so is the Soviet Union. Certainly not by the Communist leaders, one of whom has contemptuously observed that the American people need not fear the peace-loving Soviet state which has absolutely no desire to deprive them of their Coca-Cola and comic books. Yet the fact is that the U.S.S.R. is even more a land of Mass Culture than is the U.S.A. This is less easily recognizable, because their Mass Culture is *in form* just the opposite of ours, being one of propaganda and pedagogy rather than of entertainment. None the less, it has the essential quality of Mass, as against High or Folk, Culture: it is manufactured for mass consumption by technicians employed by the ruling class and is not an expression of either the individual artist or the common people themselves. Like our own, it exploits rather than satisfies the cultural needs of the masses, though for political rather than commercial reasons. Its quality is even lower: our Supreme Court building is tasteless and pompous but not to the lunatic degree of the proposed new Palace of the Soviets, a huge wedding-cake of columns mounting up to an eighty-foot statue of Lenin; Soviet movies are so much duller and cruder than our own that even the American comrades shun them; the childish level of *serious* Soviet magazines devoted to matters of art or philosophy has to be read to be believed, and as for the popular press, it is as if Colonel McCormick ran every periodical in America.

The separation of Folk Art and High Culture in fairly watertight compartments corresponded to the sharp line once drawn between the common people and the aristocracy. The eruption of the masses onto the political stage has broken down this compartmentation, with disastrous cultural results. Whereas Folk Art had its own special quality, Mass Culture is at best a vulgarized reflection of High Culture. And whereas High Culture could formerly ignore the mob and seek to please only the *cognoscenti,* it must now compete with Mass Culture or be merged into it.

The problem is acute in the United States and not just because a prolific Mass Culture exists here. If there were a clearly defined cultural elite, then the masses could have their *kitsch* and the elite could have its High Culture, with everybody happy. But the boundary is blurred. A significant part of the population, I venture to guess, is chronically confronted with a choice between going to the movies and to a concert, between reading Tolstoy and a detective story, between looking at old masters and a TV show; i.e., the pattern of their cultural lives is "open" to the point of being porous. Good art competes with *kitsch,* serious ideas compete with commercial formulas —and the advantage lies all on one side. There seems to be a Gresham's Law in cultural as well as monetary circulation: bad stuff drives out the good, since it is more easily understood and enjoyed. It is this facility of access which at once sells *kitsch* on a wide market and also prevents it from achieving quality.[3] Clement Greenberg writes that the special esthetic quality of *kitsch* is that it "predigests art for the spectator and spares him effort, provides him with a shortcut to the pleasures of art that detours what is necessarily difficult in genuine art" because it includes the spectator's reactions in the work of art itself instead of forcing him to make his own responses. Thus "Eddie Guest and the Indian Love Lyrics are more 'poetic' than T. S. Eliot and Shakespeare." And so, too, our "collegiate Gothic" like the Harkness Quadrangle at Yale is more picturesquely Gothic than Chartres, and a pin-up girl smoothly airbrushed by Petty is more sexy than a real naked woman.

When to this ease of consumption is added *kitsch's* ease of production because of its standardized nature, its prolific growth is easy to understand. It threatens High Culture by its sheer pervasiveness, its brutal, over-whelming *quantity.* The upper classes, who begin by using it to make money from the crude tastes of the masses and to dominate them politically, end by finding their own culture attacked and even threatened with destruction by the instrument they have thoughtlessly employed.

Like nineteenth-century capitalism, Mass Culture is a dynamic, revolutionary force, breaking down the old barriers of class, tradition, taste, and dissolving all cultural distinctions. It mixes and scrambles everything together, producing what might be called homogenized culture. It thus destroys all values, since value judgments imply discrimination. Mass Culture is very, very democratic: it absolutely refuses to discriminate against, or between, anything or anybody. All is grist to its mill, and all comes out finely ground indeed.

Consider *Life,* a typical homogenized mass-circulation magazine. It appears on the mahogany library tables of the rich, the glass end-tables of

<hr />

[3] The success of *Reader's Digest* illustrates the law. Here is a magazine that has achieved a fantastic circulation—some fifteen millions, much of which is accounted for by its foreign editions, thus showing that *kitsch* by no means appeals only to Americans—simply by reducing to even lower terms the already superficial formula of other periodicals. By treating a theme in two pages which they treat in six the *Digest* becomes three times as "readable" and three times as superficial.

the middle class, and the oilcloth-covered kitchen tables of the poor. Its contents are as thoroughly homogenized as its circulation. The same issue will contain a serious exposition of atomic theory alongside a disquisition on Rita Hayworth's love life; photos of starving Korean children picking garbage from the ruins of Pusan and of sleek models wearing adhesive brassieres; an editorial hailing Bertrand Russell on his eightieth birthday ("A GREAT MIND IS STILL ANNOYING AND ADORNING OUR AGE") across from a full-page photo of a housewife arguing with an umpire at a baseball game ("MOM GETS THUMB"); a cover announcing in the same size type "A NEW FOREIGN POLICY, BY JOHN FOSTER DULLES" and "KERIMA: HER MARATHON KISS IS A MOVIE SENSATION"; nine color pages of Renoirs plus a memoir by his son, followed by a full-page picture of a roller-skating horse. The advertisements, of course, provide even more scope for the editor's homogenizing talents, as when a full-page photo of a ragged Bolivian peon grinningly drunk on coca leaves (which Mr. Luce's conscientious reporters tell us he chews to narcotize his chronic hunger pains) appears opposite an ad of a pretty, smiling, well-dressed American mother with her two pretty, smiling, well-dressed children (a boy and a girl of course—children are always homogenized in American ads) looking raptly at a clown on a TV set ("RCA VICTOR BRINGS YOU A NEW KIND OF TELEVISION—SUPER SETS WITH 'PICTURE POWER' "). The peon would doubtless find the juxtaposition piquant if he could afford a copy of *Life,* which, fortunately for the Good Neighbor policy, he cannot.

Until about 1930, High Culture tried to defend itself against the encroachment of Mass Culture in two opposite ways: Academicism, or an attempt to compete by imitation; and Avantgardism, or a withdrawal from competition.

Academicism is *kitsch* for the elite: spurious High Culture that is outwardly the real thing but actually as much a manufactured article as the cheaper cultural goods produced for the masses. It is recognized at the time for what it is only by the Avantgardists. A generation or two later, its real nature is understood by everyone and it quietly drops into the same oblivion as its franker sister-under-the-skin. Examples are painters like Bougereau and Rosa Bonheur, critics like Edmund Clarence Stedman and Edmund Gosse, the Beaux Arts school of architecture, composers like the late Sir Edward Elgar, poets like Stephen Phillips, and novelists like Alphonse Daudet, Arnold Bennett, James Branch Cabell, and Somerset Maugham.

The significance of the Avantgarde movement (by which I mean poets like Rimbaud, novelists like Joyce, composers like Stravinsky, and painters like Picasso) is that it simply refused to compete. Rejecting Academicism— and thus, at a second remove, also Mass Culture—it made a desperate attempt to fence off some area where the serious artist could still function. It created a new compartmentation of culture, on the basis of an intellectual rather than a social elite. The attempt was remarkably successful: to it we owe almost everything that is living in the art of the last fifty or so years. In fact, the High Culture of our times is pretty much identical with Avantgardism. The movement came at a time (1890–1930) when bourgeois values were being challenged both culturally and politically. (In this country, the cultural challenge did not come until World War I, so that our Avantgarde flourished only in the twenties.) In the thirties the two streams mingled briefly, after each had spent its real force, under the aegis of the Communists, only to sink together at the end of the decade into the sands of the wasteland we still live in. The rise of Nazism and the revelation in the Moscow Trials of the real nature of the new society in Russia inaugurated the present period, when men cling to the evils they know rather than risk possibly greater ones by pressing forward. Nor has the chronic state of war, hot or cold, the world has been in since 1939 encouraged rebellion or experiment in either art or politics.

In this new period, the competitors, as often happens in the business world, are merging. Mass Culture takes on the color of both varieties of the old High Culture, Academic and Avantgarde, while these latter are increasingly watered down with Mass elements. There is slowly emerging a tepid, flaccid Middlebrow Culture that threatens to engulf everything in its spreading ooze. *Bauhaus* modernism has at last trickled down, in a debased form, of course, into our furniture, cafeterias, movie theaters, electric toasters, office buildings, drug stores, and railroad trains. Psychoanalysis is expounded sympathetically and superficially in popular magazines, and the psychoanalyst replaces the eccentric millionaire as the *deus ex machina* in many a movie. T. S. Eliot writes *The Cocktail Party* and it becomes a Broadway hit. (Though in some ways excellent, it is surely inferior to his *Murder in the Cathedral,* which in the unmerged thirties had to depend on the WPA to get produced at all.)

The type creator of *kitsch* today, at least in the old media, is an indeterminate specimen. There are no widely influential critics so completely terrible as, say, the late William Lyon Phelps was. Instead we have such gray creatures as Clifton Fadiman and Henry Seidel Canby. The artless numbers of an Eddie Guest are drowned out by the more sophisticated though equally commonplace strains of Benét's *John Brown's Body.* Maxfield Parrish yields to Rockwell Kent, Arthur Brisbane to Walter Lippmann, Theda Bara to Ingrid Bergman. We even have what might be called *l'avantgarde pompier* (or, in American, "phoney Avantgardism"), as in the buildings of Raymond Hood and the later poetry of Archibald MacLeish, as there is also an academic Avantgardism in belles lettres so that now the "little" as well as the big magazines have their hack writers.

All this is not a raising of the level of Mass Culture, as might appear at first, but rather a corruption of High Culture. There is nothing more vulgar than sophisticated *kitsch*. Compare Conan Doyle's workmanlike and unpretentious Sherlock Holmes stories with the bogus "intellectuality" of Dorothy M. Sayers, who, like many contemporary detective-story writers, is a novelist *manquée* who ruins her stuff with literary attitudinizing. Or consider the relationship of Hollywood and Broadway. In the twenties, the two were sharply differentiated, movies being produced for the masses of the hinterland, theater for an upper-class New York audience. The theater was High Culture, mostly of the Academic variety (Theater Guild) but with some spark of Avantgarde fire (the "little" or "experimental" theater movement). The movies were definitely Mass Culture, mostly very bad but with some leaven of Avantgardism (Griffith, Stroheim) and Folk Art (Chaplin and other comedians). With the sound film, Broadway and Hollywood drew closer together. Plays are now produced mainly to sell the movie rights, with many being directly financed by the film companies. The merger has standardized the theater to such an extent that even the early Theater Guild seems vital in retrospect, while hardly a trace of the "experimental" theater is left. And what have the movies gained? They are more sophisticated, the acting is subtler, the sets in better taste. But they too have become standardized: they are never as awful as they often were in the old days, but they are never as good either. They are better entertainment and worse art. The cinema of the twenties occasionally gave us the fresh charm of Folk Art or the imaginative intensity of Avantgardism. The coming of sound, and with it Broadway, degraded the camera to a recording instrument for an alien art form, the spoken play. The silent film had at least the *theoretical possibility,* even within the limits of Mass Culture, of being artistically significant. The sound film, within those limits, does not.

The whole field could be approached from the standpoint of the division of labor. The more advanced technologically, the greater the division. Cf. the great Blackett-Semple-Hummert factory—the word is accurate—for the mass production of radio "soap operas." Or the fact that in Hollywood a composer for the movies is not *permitted* to make his own orchestrations any more than a director can do his own cutting. Or the "editorial formula" which every big-circulation magazine tailors its fiction and articles to fit much as automobile parts are machined in Detroit. *Time* and *Newsweek* have carried specialization to its extreme: their writers don't even sign their work, which in fact is not properly theirs, since the gathering of data is done by a specialized corps of researchers and correspondents and the final article is often as much the result of the editor's blue-penciling and rewriting as of the original author's efforts.

Such art workers are as alienated from their brain-work as the industrial worker is from his hand-work. The results are as bad qualitatively as they are impressive quantitatively. The only great films to come out of Hollywood, for example, were made before industrial elephantiasis had reduced the director to one of a number of technicians, all operating at about the same level of authority. Our two greatest directors, Griffith and Stroheim, were artists, not specialists; they did everything themselves, dominated everything personally: the scenario, the actors, the camera work, and above all the cutting (or montage). Unity is essential in art; it cannot be achieved by a production line of specialists, however competent. There have been successful collective creations (Greek temples, Gothic churches, perhaps the *Iliad*), but their creators were part of a tradition which was strong enough to impose unity on their work. We have no such tradition today, and so art— as against *kitsch*—will result only when a single brain and sensibility is in full command. In the movies, only the director can even theoretically be in such a position; he was so in the pre-1930 cinema of this country, Germany, and the Soviet Union.

Griffith and Stroheim were both terrific egoists—crude, naive, and not without charlatanry—who survived until the industry became highly enough organized to resist their vigorous personalities. By about 1925, both were outside looking in; the manufacture of commodities so costly to make and so profitable to sell was too serious a matter to be entrusted to artists.

"One word of advice, Von," Griffith said to Stroheim, who had been his assistant on *Intolerance,* when Stroheim came to him with the news that he had a chance to make a picture himself. "Make your pictures in your own way. Put your mark on them. Take a stand and stick to your guns. You'll make some enemies, but you'll make good pictures." Could that have been only thirty years ago?

The homogenizing effect of *kitsch* also blurs age lines. It would be interesting to know how many adults read the comics. We do know that comic books are by far the favorite reading matter of our soldiers and sailors, that some forty million comic books are sold a month, and that some seventy million people (most of whom must be adults, there just aren't that many kids) are estimated to read the newspaper comic strips every day. We also know that movie Westerns and radio and TV programs like "The Lone Ranger" and "Captain Video" are by no means enjoyed only by children. On the other hand, children have access to programs for adults in the movies, radio, and TV. (Note that these newer arts are the ones which blur age lines because of the extremely modest demands they make on the audience's cultural equipment; thus there are many children's books but few children's movies.)

This merging of the child and grown-up audience means (1) infantile regression of the latter, who, unable to cope with the strains and complexities of modern life, escape via *kitsch* (which in turn confirms and enhances their infantilism); (2) "overstimulation" of the former, who grow up too fast. Or, as Max Horkheimer well puts it: "Development has ceased to exist. The child is grown up as soon as he can walk, and the grown-up in principle always remains the same." Also note (1) our cult of youth, which makes 18–22 the most admired and desired period of life, and (2) the sentimental worship of Mother ("Momism") as if we couldn't bear to grow up and be on our own. Peter Pan might be a better symbol of America than Uncle Sam.

Too little attention has been paid to the connection of our Mass Culture with the historical evolution of American society. Leo Lowenthal compared the biographical articles in *Colliers* and *The Saturday Evening Post* for 1901 and 1940–1 and found that in the forty-year interval the proportion of articles about business and professional men and political leaders had declined while those about entertainers had gone up 50 per cent.[4] Furthermore, the 1901 entertainers are mostly serious artists—opera singers, sculptors, pianists, etc.—while those of 1941 are *all* movie stars, baseball players, and such; and even the "serious" heroes in 1941 aren't so very serious after all: the businessmen and politicians are freaks, oddities, not the really powerful leaders as in 1901. The 1901 *Satevepost* heroes he calls "idols of production"; those of today, "idols of consumption."

Lowenthal notes that the modern *Satevepost* biographee is successful not because of his own personal abilities so much as because he "got the breaks." The whole competitive struggle is presented as a lottery in which a few winners, no more talented or energetic than anyone else, drew the lucky tickets. The effect on the mass reader is at once consoling (it might have been me) and deadening to effort, ambition (there are no rules, so

[4]Leo Lowenthal, "Biographies in Popular Magazines," in Paul F. Lazarsfeld and Frank Stanton, eds., *Radio Research, 1942–43* (New York: Columbia University, Bureau of Applied Social Research, 1944).

why struggle?). It is striking how closely this evolution parallels the country's economic development. Lowenthal observes that the "idols of production" maintained their dominance right through the twenties. The turning point was the 1929 depression when the problem became how to consume goods rather than how to produce them, and also when the arbitrariness and chaos of capitalism was forcefully brought home to the mass man. So he turned to "idols of consumption," or rather these were now offered him by the manufacturers of Mass Culture, and he accepted them.

They seem to lead to a dream world of the masses, who are no longer capable or willing to conceive of biographies primarily as a means of orientation and education. . . . He, the American mass man, as reflected in his "idols of consumption," appears no longer as a center of outwardly directed energies and actions on whose work and efficiency might depend mankind's progress. Instead of the "givers" we are faced with the "takers." . . . They seem to stand for a phantasmagoria of worldwide social security—an attitude which asks for no more than to be served with the things needed for reproduction and recreation, an attitude which has lost every primary interest in how to invent, shape, or apply the tools leading to such purposes of mass satisfaction.

The role of science in Mass Culture has similarly changed from the rational and the purposive to the passive, accidental, even the catastrophic. Consider the evolution of the detective story, a genre which can be traced back to the memoirs of Vidocq, the master detective of the Napoleonic era. Poe, who was peculiarly fascinated by scientific method, wrote the first and still the best detective stories: *The Purloined Letter, The Gold Bug, The Mystery of Marie Roget, The Murders in the Rue Morgue.* Conan Doyle created the great folk hero, Sherlock Holmes, like Poe's Dupin a sage whose wizard's wand was scientific deduction (Poe's "ratiocination"). Such stories could only appeal to—in fact, only be *comprehensible* to—an audience accustomed to think in scientific terms: to survey the data, set up a hypothesis, test it by seeing whether it caught the murderer. The very idea of an art genre cast in the form of a problem to be solved by purely intellectual means could only have arisen in a scientific age. This kind of detective fiction, which might be called the "classic" style, is still widely practiced (well by Agatha Christie and John Dickson Carr, badly by the more popular Erle Stanley Gardner) but of late it has been overshadowed by the rank, noxious growth of works in the "sensational" style. This was inaugurated by Dashiell Hammett (whom André Gide was foolish enough to admire) and has recently been enormously stepped up in voltage by Mickey Spillane, whose six books to date have sold thirteen million copies. The sensationalists use what for the classicists was the point—the uncovering of the criminal—as a mere excuse for the minute description of scenes of bloodshed, brutality, lust, and alcoholism. The cool, astute, subtle Dupin-Holmes is replaced by the crude man-of-action, whose prowess is measured not by intellectual mastery but by his capacity for liquor, women, and mayhem (he can "take it" as well as "dish it out"—Hammett's *The Glass Key* is largely a chronicle of the epic beatings absorbed by the hero before he finally staggers to the solution). Mike Hammer, Spillane's aptly named hero, is such a monumental blunderer that even Dr. Watson would have seen through him. According to Richard W. Johnston, "Mike has one bizarre and memorable characteristic that sets him apart from all other fictional detectives: sheer incompetence. In the five Hammer cases, 48 people have been killed, and there is reason to believe that if Mike had kept out of the way, 34 of them—all innocent of the original crime—would have survived."[5] A decade ago, the late George Orwell, apropos a "sensationalist" detective story of the time, *No Orchids for Miss Blandish,* showed how the brutalization of this genre mirrors the general degeneration in ethics from nineteenth-century standards. What he would have written had Mickey Spillane's works been then in existence I find it hard to imagine.

The real heirs of the "classic" detective story today, so far as the exploitation of science is concerned, are the writers of science fiction, a genre begun by Jules Verne and H. G. Wells that has of late become very popular. Or at least of the more sophisticated kinds of science fiction, where the marvels and horrors of the future must always be "scientifically possible"— just as Sherlock Holmes drew on no supernatural powers. This is the approach of the bourgeoisie, who think of science as their familiar instrument. The masses are less confident, more awed in their approach to science, and there are vast lower strata of science fiction where the marvelous is untrammeled by the limits of knowledge. To the masses, science is the modern *arcanum arcanorum,* at once the supreme mystery and the philosopher's stone that explains the mystery. The latter concept appears in comic strips like "Superman" and in the charlatan science exploited by "health fakers" and "nature fakers." Taken this way, science gives man mastery over his environment and is beneficent. But science itself is not understood, therefore not mastered, therefore terrifying because of its very power. Taken *this* way, as the supreme mystery, science becomes the stock-in-trade of the "horror" pulp magazines and comics and movies. It has got to the point, indeed, that if one sees a laboratory in a movie, one shudders, and the white coat of the scientist is as blood-chilling a sight as Count Dracula's black cloak. These "horror" films have apparently an indestructible popularity: *Frankenstein* is still shown, after 21 years, and the current revival of *King Kong* is expected to gross over two million dollars.

If the scientist's laboratory has acquired in Mass Culture a ghastly atmosphere, is this perhaps not one of those deep popular intuitions? From Frankenstein's laboratory to Maidenek and Hiroshima is not a long journey. Was there a popular suspicion, perhaps only half-conscious, that the nineteenth-century trust in science, like the nineteenth-century trust in popular education, was mistaken, that science can as easily be used for anti-human as for pro-human ends, perhaps even more easily? For Mrs. Shelley's Frankenstein, the experimenter who brought disaster by pushing his science too far, is a scientific folk hero older than and still as famous as Mr. Doyle's successful and beneficent Sherlock Holmes.

Conservatives like Ortega y Gasset and T. S. Eliot argue that since "the revolt of the masses" has led to the horrors of totalitarianism (and of California roadside architecture), the only hope is to rebuild the old class walls and bring the masses once more under aristocratic control. They think of the popular as synonymous with the cheap and vulgar. Marxian radicals and liberals, on the other hand, see the masses as intrinsically healthy but as the

[5]*Life,* June 23, 1952.

dupes and victims of cultural exploitation by the Lords of *kitsch*. If only the masses were offered good stuff instead of *kitsch*, how they would eat it up! How the level of Mass Culture would rise! Both these diagnoses seem to me fallacious: they assume that Mass Culture is (in the conservative view) or could be (in the liberal view) an expression of *people*, like Folk Art, whereas actually it is an expression of *masses*, a very different thing.

There are theoretical reasons why Mass Culture is not and can never be any good. I take it as axiomatic that culture can only be produced by and for human beings. But in so far as people are organized (more strictly, disorganized) as masses, they lose their human identity and quality. For the masses are in historical time what a crowd is in space: a large quantity of people unable to express themselves as human beings because they are related to one another neither as individuals nor as members of communities—indeed they are not related *to each other* at all but only to something distant, abstract, non-human: a football game or bargain sale in the case of a crowd; a system of industrial production, a party, or a state in the case of the masses. The mass man is a solitary atom, uniform with and undifferentiated from thousands and millions of other atoms who go to make up "the lonely crowd," as David Riesman well calls American society. A folk or a people, however, is a community, i.e., a group of individuals linked to each other by common interests, work, traditions, values, and sentiments; something like a family, each of whose members has a special place and function as an individual while at the same time sharing the group's interests (family budget), sentiments (family quarrels), and culture (family jokes). The scale is small enough so that it "makes a difference" what the individual does, a first condition for human—as against mass—existence. Human creativity is nourished by a rich combination of individualism and communalism. (The great culture-bearing elites of the past have been communities of this kind.) In contrast, a mass society is so undifferentiated and loosely structured that its atoms tend to cohere only along the line of the least common denominator; its morality sinks to that of its most brutal and primitive members, its taste to that of the least sensitive and most ignorant. And in addition to everything else, the scale is simply too big, there are just *too many people*.

Yet this collective monstrosity, "the masses," "the public," is taken as a human norm by the scientific and artistic technicians of our Mass Culture. They at once degrade the public by treating it as an object, to be handled with the lack of ceremony and the objectivity of medical students dissecting a corpse, and at the same time flatter it, pander to its level of taste and ideas by taking these as the criterion of reality (in the case of questionnaire-sociologists and other "social scientists") or of art (in the case of the Lords of *kitsch*). When one hears a questionnaire-sociologist talk about how he will "set up" an investigation, one feels he regards people as a herd of dumb animals, as mere congeries of conditioned reflexes, his calculation being which reflex will be stimulated by which question. At the same time, of necessity, he sees the statistical majority as the great Reality, the secret of life he is trying to find out; like the *kitsch* Lords, he is wholly without values, willing to accept any idiocy if it is held by many people. The aristocrat and the democrat both criticize and argue with popular taste, the one with hostility, the other in friendship, for both attitudes proceed from a set of values. This is less degrading to the masses than the "objective" approach of Hollywood and the questionnaire-sociologists, just as it is less degrading to a man to be shouted at in anger than to be quietly assumed to be part of a machine. But the plebs have their dialectical revenge: complete indifference to their human *quality* means complete prostration before their statistical *quantity,* so that a movie magnate who cynically "gives the public what it wants"—i.e., assumes it wants trash—sweats with terror if box-office returns drop 10 per cent.

The conservative proposal to save culture by restoring the old class lines has a more solid historical base than the Marxian hope for a new democratic, classless culture, for, with the possible (and important) exception of Periclean Athens, all the great cultures of the past were elite cultures. Politically, however, it is without meaning in a world dominated by the two great mass nations, U.S.A. and U.S.S.R., and becoming more industrialized, more mass-ified all the time. The only practical thing along those lines would be to revive the *cultural* elite which the Avantgarde created. As I have already noted, the Avantgarde is now dying, partly from internal causes, partly suffocated by the competing Mass Culture, where it is not being absorbed into it. Of course this process has not reached 100 per cent, and doubtless never will unless the country goes either Fascist or Communist. There are still islands above the flood for those determined enough to reach them, and to stay on them: as Faulkner has shown, a writer can even use Hollywood instead of being used by it, if his purpose is firm enough. But the homogenization of High and Mass Culture has gone far and is going farther all the time, and there seems little reason to expect a revival of Avantgardism. Particularly not in this country, where the blurring of class lines, the absence of a stable cultural tradition, and the greater facilities for manufacturing and marketing *kitsch* all work in the other direction. The result is that our intelligentsia is remarkably small, weak, and disintegrated. One of the odd things about the American cultural scene is how many brain-workers there are and how few intellectuals, defining the former as specialists whose thinking is pretty much confined to their limited "fields" and the latter as persons who take all culture for their province. Not only are there few intellectuals, but they have very little sense of belonging to a community; they are so isolated from each other they don't even bother to quarrel—there hasn't been a really good fight among them since the Moscow Trials.

If the conservative proposal to save our culture via the aristocratic Avantgarde seems historically unlikely, what of the democratic-liberal proposal? Is there a reasonable prospect of raising the level of Mass Culture? In his book, *The Great Audience,* Gilbert Seldes argues that there is. He blames the present sad state of our Mass Culture on the stupidity of the Lords of *kitsch,* who underestimate the mental age of the public; the arrogance of the intellectuals, who make the same mistake and so snobbishly refuse to work for mass media like radio, TV, and movies; and the passivity of the public itself, which doesn't insist on better Mass Cultural products. This diagnosis seems to me superficial in that it blames everything on subjective, moral factors: stupidity, perversity, failure of will. My own feeling is that, as in the case of the alleged responsibility of the German (or Russian) people for the horrors of Nazism (or Soviet Communism), it is unjust to blame social groups for this result. Human beings have been caught up in the inexorable workings of a mechanism that forces them, with a pressure only heroes can resist (and one cannot *demand* that anybody be a hero, though one can *hope* for it), into its own pattern. I see Mass Culture as a reciprocating engine, and who is to say, once it has been set in motion, whether the stroke or the counterstroke is "responsible" for its continued action?

The Lords of *kitsch* sell culture to the masses. It is a debased, trivial culture that voids both the deep realities (sex, death, failure, tragedy) and also the simple, spontaneous pleasures, since the realities would be too real and the pleasures too *lively* to induce what Mr. Seldes calls "the mood of consent": i.e., a narcotized acceptance of Mass Culture and of the commodities it sells as a substitute for the unsettling and unpredictable (hence unsalable) joy, tragedy, wit, change, originality, and beauty of real life. The masses, debauched by several generations of this sort of thing, in turn come to demand trivial and comfortable cultural products. Which came first, the chicken or the egg, the mass demand or its satisfaction (and further stimulation) is a question as academic as it is unanswerable. The engine is reciprocating and shows no signs of running down.

Indeed, far from Mass Culture getting better, we will be lucky if it doesn't get worse. When shall we see another popular humorist like Sholem Aleichem, whose books are still being translated from the Yiddish and for whose funeral in 1916 a hundred thousand inhabitants of the Bronx turned out? Or Finlay Peter Dunne, whose Mr. Dooley commented on the American scene with such wit that Henry Adams was a faithful reader and Henry James, on his famous return to his native land, wanted to meet only one American author, Dunne? Since Mass Culture is not an art form but a manufactured commodity, it tends always downwards, towards cheapness—and so standardization—of production. Thus, T. W. Adorno has noted, in his brilliant essay "On Popular Music,"[6] that the chorus of every popular song *without exception* has the same number of bars, while Mr. Seldes remarks that Hollywood movies are cut in a uniformly rapid tempo, a shot rarely being held more than 45 seconds, which gives them a standardized effect in contrast to the varied tempo of European film-cutting. This sort of standardization means that what may have begun as something fresh and original is repeated until it becomes a nerveless routine; *vide* what happened to Fred Allen as a radio comedian. The only time Mass Culture is good is at the very beginning, before the "formula" has hardened, before the money-boys and efficiency experts and audience-reaction analysts have moved in. Then for a while it may have the quality of real Folk Art. But the Folk artist today lacks the cultural roots and the intellectual toughness (both of which the Avantgarde artist has relatively more of) to resist for long the pressures of Mass Culture. His taste can easily be corrupted, his sense of his own special talent and limitations obscured, as in what happened to Disney between the gay, inventive early Mickey Mouse and "Silly Symphony" cartoons and the vulgar pretentiousness of *Fantasia* and heavy-handed sentimentality of *Snow White*; or to Westbrook Pegler, who regressed from an excellent sports writer, with a sure sense of form and a mastery of colloquial satire, into a rambling, coarse-grained, garrulous political pundit. Whatever

[6]*Studies in Philosophy and Social Science*, No. 1 (New York, 1941).

virtues the Folk artist has, and they are many, staying power is not one of them. And staying power is the essential virtue of one who would hold his own against the spreading ooze of Mass Culture.

DAYDREAMS AND NIGHTMARES

Edward Shils

The well-wishers of the human race who laid the foundations of our present outlook looked forward to a time when man would be free from the brutish ignorance and squalor in which he then lay, and from the shadows which darkened his mind. The easing of burdens, a more universal opportunity, a heightened respect would, they thought, open man's spirit to the great heritage of literature, philosophy, and art. Revolutionaries, Marxist and otherwise, extended and made more intense this dream of philanthropic liberalism.

The present century has, at least for the time being, belied these hopes. Universal education, the alleviation of physical misery, the drift of equality have not brought with them that deepening and enrichment of the mind to which liberals and revolutionaries alike aspired. The silliness of television, the childishness of the comic strips, the triviality of the press, the meanness of the luridly bound "paperbacks" are now taken as signs that Western humanity has turned off the road which for a time seemed to lead into the broad sunlit uplands of a discriminating appreciation and is rushing into the swamps of vulgarity. Beyond the swamps many now perceive the sea of a base and unredeemable vulgarity. The sea has never been in such flood, and never has it so threatened not only the lowlands in which the populace lives but the heights of the high culture of the West.

In the United States, in Great Britain, on the continent of Europe, or at least in the parts of Europe where the custodians and consumers of the traditional culture of the educated classes are free to express their views, there is a feeling of consternation and bewilderment, deliberate complacency, guilty enthusiasm, and apologetic curiosity about the phenomenon of mass culture.

Between the wars, the voices were few and their focus was scattered. The late Wyndham Lewis and Ortega y Gasset, and Dr. F. R. Leavis and his circle criticized the culture of the neo-literate and for their pains they were either called Fascists or were passed over in silence. Since the end of the Second World War, the criticism has gained in force, volume, and

Abridged from Edward Shils, "Daydreams and Nightmares: Reflections on the Criticism of Mass Culture," *Sewanee Review*, 65 (Autumn 1957), 597–608. Copyright © 1957 The University of the South. Reprinted by permission of the author and the publisher. Edward Shils is a professor of sociology and social thought, Committee on Social Thought, University of Chicago, and a Fellow of King's College, Cambridge. He is the author of books and articles on social theory, intellectuals, and the sociology of culture.

coherence of focus. The majority of the writers are now resident in America, where popular culture has made itself more visible to the educated, but British and Continental authors have been no less alarmed. The earlier critics of mass culture were aristocratic and esthetic in their outlook. Wyndham Lewis, Ortega y Gasset, and the Leavises feared the preponderance of poor taste and judgment. Ortega's viewpoint was only a subtle extension into the moral and esthetic sphere of a conception of the coarseness and indiscipline of the lower classes which had prevailed among the opponents of political democracy since early in the nineteenth century. The Leavis argument had nothing political about it; it was entirely concerned with the obstacles to the diffusion of discrimination in literary judgment. The new critique of mass culture takes over many of the aristocratic and esthetic arguments and the anti-bourgeois attitudes of nineteenth-century Europe. Its point of departure is, however, different.

It is not accidental that most of the recent critics of mass culture are, or were, Marxian socialists, some even rather extreme, at least in their past commitment to the socialist ideal. Mr. Dwight Macdonald,[1] who, as editor of *Politics,* did more than any other American writer to bring this interpretation of mass culture to the forefront of the attention of the intellectual public, was a former Trotskyite Communist, whose zeal had waned and since then has entirely disappeared. Prof. Max Horkheimer,[2] who is the leading exponent of the "critical" philosophy of the Frankfurt circle, is an apolitical Marxist whose Hegelian sociological terminology obscures his Marxism. Prof. T. Wiesengrund-Adorno[3] and Prof. Leo Lowenthal,[4] the former at Frankfurt University, the latter at the University of California, are both leading adherents of this school in which a refined Marxism finds its most sophisticated expression. Dr. Erich Fromm[5] was a psychoanalyzing Marxist. Karl Bednarik[6] is an Austrian socialist. Czeslaw Milosz[7] is a Polish poet who served the Stalinist Polish Government as a cultural official for some years, then adumbrated the recent break-up of Polish Stalinism by quitting his post and going to live abroad while still adhering to the ideals which made him a Communist. Richard Hoggart[8] is a socialist of the Laborite persuasion. Irving Howe and Bernard Rosenberg[9] are socialists in the tradition of Trotsky, and moving spirits of *Dissent.*

[1]Dwight Macdonald, "A Theory of Mass Culture," *Diogenes,* no. 3 (Summer 1953); reprinted in Bernard Rosenberg and David White, eds., *Mass Culture: The Popular Arts in America* (Glencoe, Ill.: Free Press, 1957) [and also above, pp. 317–329].
[2]Max Horkheimer and T. W. Adorno, *Dialektik der Aufklärung* (Amsterdam: Querido Verlag, 1947); Horkheimer, "Art and Mass Culture," *Studies in Philosophy and Social Science,* vol. 9 (1941).
[3]Adorno, "On Popular Music," *Studies in Philosophy and Social Science,* vol. 9 (1941); and "Television and the Patterns of Mass Culture," *Quarterly of Film, Radio, and Television,* vol. 8 (1954), reprinted in *Mass Culture.*
[4]Leo Lowenthal, "Historical Perspectives of Popular Culture," *American Journal of Sociology,* vol. 55 (1950), reprinted in *Mass Culture.*
[5]Erich Fromm, *Escape from Freedom* (New York: Farrar & Rinehart, 1941).
[6]Karl Bednarik, *The Young Worker* (London: Faber & Faber, 1955; Glencoe, Ill.: Free Press, 1956).
[7]Czeslaw Milosz, "Bielinski and the Unicorn," *Papers of the Milan Conference on the Future of Freedom* (Paris: Congress of Cultural Freedom, 1955).
[8]Richard Hoggart, *The Uses of Literacy* (Fair Lawn, N.J.: Essential Books, 1957).
[9]Bernard Rosenberg, "Mass Culture in America," in *Mass Culture;* Irving Howe, "Notes on Mass Culture," in *Politics,* 1948, reprinted in *Mass Culture.*

None of these socialists and former socialists is an orthodox Marxist, and some of them no longer think of themselves as Marxists at all. The names and terminology of Marxism scarcely appear on their pages. Yet Marxism has left a formative imprint on their thought about mass culture. Their earlier economic criticism of capitalistic society has been transformed into a moral and cultural criticism of the large-scale industrial society. They no longer criticize the ruling class for utilizing the laws of property and religion to exploit the proletariat for the sake of surplus value; instead they criticize the "merchants of *kitsch*" who are enmeshed in the machine of industrial civilization and who exploit not the labor but the emotional needs of the masses—these emotional needs themselves produced by industrial society. They no longer criticize modern society for the hard life which it imposes on the majority of its citizens. They criticize it for the uninteresting and vulgar life which it provides. They criticize the esthetic qualities of a society which has realized so much of what socialists once claimed was of central importance, which has, in other words, overcome poverty and long arduous labor. The indissoluble residue of their Marxism shows itself particularly in the expectations which form the standard of judgment which they apply to mass culture.

As Marxists they once thought that the working classes—as Engels said of the German proletariat—were destined to be "the heirs of classical philosophy," by which was meant that the working class had a special receptiveness for the highest manifestations of the "objective spirit." They shared the Feuerbachian conception of man elevated to the condition of full humanity, in which all share in the greatest discoveries and creations of the human mind. They believed that in the "realm of freedom," which socialism would bring about, the freedom of each man from the dominion of others and particularly from the dominion of the propertied, and the sufficient wealth and leisure which the realm of freedom would carry with it, would emancipate the mind, free it from prejudice and superstition and make it master of itself. Knowledge would be universally diffused, and taste would be refined. Their hopes were the hopes of Trotsky, who, while Marxism was descending from its heroic phase to the depths of tyrannical and bureaucratic dogmatism, still retained enough of the old spirit of the French and German Enlightenment and of German idealism to envisage a future in which "the average human type will rise to the heights of an Aristotle, a Goethe, or a Marx. And above this ridge, new peaks will rise."[10]

Now they are affronted by the waywardness of the mass of the population, in whom they once thought they found the chief agent and the greatest beneficiary of progress. That section of the population from which they expected heroic action on behalf of great far-distant goals has turned out to be interested in wasting its time in self-indulgent and foolish pleasures. Instead of reading Shakespeare, Goethe, and Tolstoi, it reads comic books, sensational newspapers and magazines which concentrate on illicit sexual activity and crimes of violence. Those classes from whom intellectuals expected a heroic awareness of grandiose events, and an eagerness to participate in them, concern themselves at best with the routine philistine life of bourgeois politics, and often not even with that. Instead of high aspira-

[10]Leon Trotsky, *Literature and Revolution* (London, 1925), p. 256.

tions they immerse themselves in their immediate situations or in cultural creations which are either only slight extensions of their private situations or else wholly unrealistic dream-worlds. Those from whom it was believed a hitherto hidden appreciation of the sublime and the beautiful would emerge are attracted by the trivial, the sensational, and the gruesome.

The working classes, even where, as in Britain and Germany, they have become socialists, or as in Italy and France, Communists, are uninterested in revolution, in the moral transformation of themselves and the rest of the human race. Instead of rising to the highest levels of the human spirit, to which their prophets had summoned them, they are satisfied to take life as it comes and to seek pleasures which are alien to the great dream of a transfigured humanity.

The indulgence in mass culture is not only esthetically and intellectually degrading but, according to its critics, it prevents its victims from striving to achieve the socialist ideal. One of the gravest charges against mass culture is that it deadens and deforms the capacity to conceive of a better world, i.e., to participate in revolutionary movements.[11]

It is assumed by many of these ex-Marxists that there is really only one reasonable social ideal—namely, socialism. All activities which do not strive to establish socialism, if they are not of the stuff of high culture, are "escapist."[12]

Few of the critics of the new culture of the lower classes have had first-hand contact with those classes; their hopes were derived from an image which was almost entirely doctrinal. Writers like Richard Hoggart are exceptional for their vivid and affectionate first-hand recollections of lower-class life. These give an especial poignancy to his regrets for the fading of an independent and lively pattern of life. But since the hopes were the same, the disappointment is essentially the same. He, as well as the more doctrinal critics of mass culture, is disappointed that instead of ascending to the heights of the greatest cultural achievements of aristocratic and bourgeois societies, the working classes are content to accept the infiltration of the advertising man's culture, cheap films, machine-fabricated popular songs, the insipid or sensational entertainment of television.

There is a shock of pain in their perceptions and an element of revenge in their disclosure of the corruptibility and actual corruption of those whom they once loved. Part of the preoccupation with mass culture is the obsessiveness of the disappointed lover who, having misconceived his beloved when their love was blooming, now feels that she deceived him and he now has no eye for anything but her vices and blemishes. Her present vices are magnified by the past exaggeration of her virtues, and she cannot be forgotten.

[11]"Wherever revolutionary tendencies show a timid head, they are mitigated and cut short by a false fulfillment of wish-dreams, like wealth, adventure, passionate love, power and sensationalism in general." Lowenthal, "Historical Perspectives," *Mass Culture*, p. 55.

[12]Nothing shows the persistence of puritanical Marxism in the writings critical of popular culture as much as the idea that popular culture is "escapist." Underlying it is the belief that man's first obligation is to understand his environment in order to transform it into the socialist society. Expressive dispositions, the need for phantasy, the play of imagination are disregarded by this standpoint. The same hostility against "art for art's sake" which was characteristic of Marxist literary criticism reappears here in another guise and context.

The transmogrified Marxism of the disappointed manifests itself in another way. They still believe, as they once believed, under the auspices of their pristine Marxist outlook, in the existence of a crisis of culture. Creative high culture is still endangered by the pressure of society, but whereas before it was the specific pressure of the contradictions and crises of capitalism, now it is the result of modern industrial society—namely, mass culture—which endangers high culture. The once prospective heirs of high culture have turned out to be a menace to its survival.

Mass culture threatens to destroy high culture. Mr. Dwight Macdonald, Prof. Van den Haag, and the others are at one in their diagnosis of the dangers. Mass culture, by its remunerative market, exerts a great pull on artists who are nowadays "more market-oriented than taste-oriented. They create for anonymous consumers rather than for the sake of creation."[13] The opportunity to write for the films, television, for *Reader's Digest* or *Life* is so attractive that artists become corrupted in their standards. "There are some," Prof. Van den Haag concedes, "who doggedly insist on being themselves but the temptations are infinite, infinitely disguised, and insinuating. The psychological burden of isolation has drawbacks affecting creation. The ability and will to create are impaired if there is no public and the defense against the temptations of popular culture uses much of the energy needed for creation. The artist who, by refusing to work for the mass market, becomes marginal cannot create what he might have created had there been no mass market." Mr. Macdonald, believing that "all the cultures of the past were elite cultures," thinks that there is little chance for high culture to survive in America where class lines are blurred, stable cultural traditions are lacking, the intellectuals as a group are incoherent, and the manufacture and distribution of *kitsch* have so much greater resources. There is something "inexorable" in the mechanism by which mass culture is killing high culture, and only a few heroes can hold out.[14]

Of course, the frustration of socialist expectations is not the sole reason for the aggrieved preoccupation with mass culture. It is obtrusive, garishly visible, and blatantly audible; and one would have to be blind and deaf and very withdrawn not to be aware of it—especially in America. There are also some other important reasons why it draws the attention of intellectuals. The institutions of mass culture offer well-paid employment which many accept in advertising, radio, television, films, and market research, and this troubles the conscience and disturbs the equanimity of those who are inside as well as outside these institutions. Some of the most savage criticism of mass culture is produced by those who are engaged in creating or promoting it.[15]

Moreover, the bulk of the literature which defends popular culture shares many of the convictions of the more hostile criticisms. It regards

[13]Ernest van den Haag, *Mass Culture*, p. 520.
[14]Macdonald, *Mass Culture*, p. 71.
[15]And on the other side, some of the defensive literature is no more than special pleading by persons who, having found a niche in life in the professions connected with mass culture, seek to give respectability to their work. Often they are a little guilty because neither they nor the intellectual circles in which they grew up really approve of mass culture, and yet, because they are very well paid or because they have an intense pleasure in what they disapprove of simply because it is what they are doing, strive to give their work and pleasure a dignity which they sometimes inwardly doubt.

the widespread pleasure which television, films, radio, comic strips and books, and novels of violence bring, as a misuse of leisure time. It asserts that the great audience does not know how to use its leisure time properly and that the producers of popular culture do not, on the whole, serve it well. It thinks that the masses are ill-advised to spend their time in the way they do. The great difference between the negative and the affirmative standpoints is that the former regards mass culture as an unqualified catastrophe, the latter as a misfortune which still has a chance of correction, and which in any case does little harm. They agree in morals and esthetics but they differ in their fundamental political expectations.

The critical interpretation of mass culture rests on a distinct image of modern man, of modern society, and of man in past ages. This image has little factual basis. It is a product of disappointed political prejudices, vague aspirations for an unrealizable ideal, resentment against American society and, at bottom, romanticism dressed up in the language of sociology, psychoanalysis, and existentialism.

If one were to take seriously the two fountainheads of the interpretation of mass culture, namely, the Frankfurt *Institut für Sozialforschung,* led by Professor Horkheimer, and *Politics,* under the editorship of Mr. Macdonald, one would believe that the ordinary citizen who listens to the radio, goes to films, and looks at television is not just *l'homme moyen sensuel* known to past ages. He is something new in the world. He is a "private atomic subject," utterly without religious beliefs, without any private life, without a family which means anything to him;[16] he is standardized, ridden with anxiety, perpetually in a state of "exacerbated" unrest, his life "emptied of meaning," and "trivialized," "alienated from his past, from his community, and possibly from himself," cretinized and brutalized.[17] The ordinary man has, according to this view, been overwhelmed by the great society; he had lost his roots in his organic communities of territory and kinship, craft and faith. Man in modern society lacks individuality and yet he is terribly lonely. Instead of developing the rich individuality for which his well-wishers idly hoped, he has lost his apparently once-existent individuality through the anonymity of modern institutions. He has been depersonalized and degraded to the point where he is a cog in an impersonal industrial machine. The mass-produced nature of his culture—which is necessary if he and his kind are to be satisfied in sufficient quantity and cheapness—prevents him from developing his tastes and intelligence. Instead of rising to the heights of sensitivity and awareness, as socialist doctrine led its adherents to expect, the majority of the population voluntarily impoverishes its own existence, welcomes the "distractions from the human predicament"[18] which mass culture provides, and yet, it finds no contentment. Modern man is incapable of having genuinely affectionate relationships with other persons. He can no longer love.[19] Mass culture is welcomed by this unfortunate being because it "adjusts" him to an unworthy reality

[16]Horkheimer, *Mass Culture,* pp. 292–294.
[17]Bernard Rosenberg, *Mass Culture,* pp. 4, 5, 7. The words are Mr. Rosenberg's but the ideas are the common property of the critics.
[18]Irving Howe, in *Mass Culture.*
[19]Erich Fromm, *The Art of Loving* (New York, 1956), pp. 83–106.

by "helping us to suppress ourselves." Lacking religion, man can find surcease from his burdens only in the movie theaters.[20]

This interpretation of life in modern society has a corollary in the picture of society before modern industrialism burst in upon us. Art and the works of culture in this legendary time were vitally integrated into everyday life, the artist was aware of his function, man was in a state of reposeful self-possession. The mass of the population naturally did not have access to the works of high culture but it had its own art, namely, folk art, created by itself and genuinely expressing its own relationship to the universe. Peasant society and aristocratic society had no problem of mass culture. They were societies in which nothing factitious or meretricious existed. Taste had nothing vulgar about it. The educated classes were genuinely educated and, despite the rigors of a fundamentally exploitative society, religious faith was genuine, artistic taste was elevated, and important problems were thought about with true sincerity. Men did not seek to "escape." If we are to believe what Professors Horkheimer and Van den Haag say, pre-modern man was autonomous; he was spontaneous; his life had continuity and distinction. His existence felt none of the pressures which are dehumanizing modern man.[21] Genuine individuality flourished, in which there was no alienation of man from man or of man from himself.

What is the source of this picture of the past and present of the American and European sections of the human race? Is it systematic firsthand observation, is it deep historical scholarship, is it a wide experience of life, or a facility to enter into intimate contact with all sorts and conditions of men? It is none of these.

Its intellectual history can be traced to the early writings of Marx and to German sociological romanticism.[22] The transformation of Hegel's philosophy of the spirit into a doctrine of criticism, directed against the existing institutions of civil society, laid special stress on the phenomenon of alienation, on the condition of man when he is not permeated by the "spirit." German sociological romanticism, which found its decisive expression in Ferdinand Tönnies' *Gemeinschaft und Gesellschaft* (1887), in Georg Simmel's numerous works, especially in *Die Philosophie des Geldes* (1900) and *Über soziale Differenzierung* (1890), and in Werner Sombart's early quasi-Marxist writings on capitalist society, had at the very center of its conception of the world a picture of a pre-modern peasant

[20]Howe, *Mass Culture*, pp. 498, 497. This, it should be noted, comes from a leftist without sympathy for religion. Mr. Howe accepts, however, the conventional romantic sociological critique of modern society which stresses among other things its religious faithlessness. He notes no contradiction between that and his socialist convictions which are entirely "secular."

[21]These phantasies about the qualities of the happy pre-mass culture have been very fairly and cogently criticized by Professor Denis Brogan: "The Problem of High Culture and Mass Culture," *Diogenes*, no. 5 (Winter 1954), pp. 1–13, and by Mr. Henry Rabassiere, "In Defense of Television," *Mass Culture*, pp. 368–374.

[22]The criticism of popular culture, and the outlook from which it is derived, have much in common with the criticisms of modern society which emanate from other intellectual milieux. The Roman Catholic romanticism of Chesterton and Belloc, the French Monarchists, the classicism and the admiration for heroic violence of T. E. Hulme, the Southern Agrarians, the heroic puritanism of Georges Sorel come from intellectual sources as diverse as Cobbett, Proudhon, Comte, Le Play, and Jefferson. The common feature is their dislike of urban society and of bourgeois individualism and hedonism. They were all ideologists, hostile to human beings as they are, and this they share with Marxism.

society in which men lived in the harmonious mutual respect of authority and subordinate, in which all felt themselves integral parts of a community which in its turn lived in continuous and inspiring contact with its own past. Traditions were stable, the kinship group was bound together in unquestioned solidarity. No one was alienated from himself or isolated from his territorial community and his kin. Beliefs were firm and were universally shared. This is the phantasy which lies at the basis of the criticism of modern society which allegedly hard-headed publicists and scientific sociologists have accepted without critical examination. This idyll was juxtaposed against a conception of modern urban society which is much like the state of nature described by Hobbes, where no man is bound by ties of sentimental affection or moral obligation or loyalty to any other man. Each man is concerned only with his own interest, which is power over others, their exploitation and manipulation. The family is dissolved, friendship dead, religious belief evaporated. Impersonality and anonymity have taken the place of closer ties. This is the picture of life in the great cities of the West which flourished in German sociology from the time of Ferdinand Tönnies and Georg Simmel and it found many adherents in America[23] and France. The refined Marxism of the earlier, more romantic writings of Marx and Engels formed a perfect companion piece to this academic romanticism. It was left, however, for the *Institut für Sozialforschung,* attached to the University of Frankfurt before 1933 and to Columbia University during the late 1930's and early 1940's, and to the *Politics* circle, which came under its influence, to effect the synthesis. The Marxism of the *Institut* was never the Marxism of the parties and barricades, and it never felt bound by the arid dogmas of the Marxist parties. In a series of important collaborative works—which included *Autorität und Familie* (Paris, 1934), *The Authoritarian Personality* (New York, 1948), and a variety of other equally characteristic books like Fromm's *Escape from Freedom,* Neumann's *Behemoth,* Horkheimer's *Eclipse of Reason,* and most recently Marcuse's *Eros and Civilization*—an ingenious, courageous, and unrealistic point of view was promulgated and applied to modern society. A fusion of Hegelian Marxism, psychoanalysis, and esthetic repugnance for industrial society, each freely and imaginatively adapted to the underlying philosophy of the *Institut,* dominated their point of view.

The *Institut's* point of view was formed in its most general outlines in Germany and in the first years of exile in Europe but it developed into a critique of mass culture only after the immigration to the United States. Here they encountered the "mass" in modern society for the first time. Their anti-capitalistic and, by multiplication, anti-American attitude found a traumatic and seemingly ineluctible confirmation in the popular culture of the United States. Whereas in Europe, an educated person of the higher classes could, and even now still can, avoid awareness of the life of the majority of the population, this is impossible in the United States. What is a vague disdain in Europe must become an elaborate loathing in America.

[23]In American sociology, it found its fullest expression in the writings of Robert Park, who had been a pupil of Simmel, and in "Urbanism as a Way of Life" by the late Louis Wirth. The latter essay appeared originally in the *American Journal of Sociology,* 44 (July 1938), 1–24, and has been frequently reprinted.

The *Institut* had responded to the terrible experience of the rise and temporary triumph of National Socialism with a strenuous effort to understand why it had happened. It tried to discern trends towards the spread of totalitarianism to other Western countries. Orthodox Marxism, to which the *Institut* had in any case never been bound, was not adequate to the task. It might explain why the property-owning classes welcomed National Socialism but it could not explain why there was so much voluntary and enthusiastic submission on the part of those who might have been expected, on the basis of an attachment to the ideals of liberalism and socialism, to resist. Why had the working classes not been true to the revolutionary vocation with which Marxism had endowed them? Here German romanticism, brought up to date by sociology and psychoanalysis, appeared to offer an answer.

It was because man was alienated and uprooted that he so eagerly accepted the cruel and spurious ethnic community proffered by National Socialism. The same factors which led them to National Socialism are responsible for modern man's eager self-immersion into the trivial, base, and meretricious culture provided by the radio, the film, the comic strips, the television, and mass-produced goods. It is therefore to be expected that the mass culture which has been created to meet the needs of alienated and uprooted men will further the process, exacerbate the needs, and lead on to an inevitable culmination in fascism. According to Mr. Rosenberg, who is not a member of the *Institut* but who speaks with its voice, "mass culture threatens not merely to cretinize our taste and to brutalize our senses," it paves "the way to totalitarianism."[24] The fact that fascism triumphed in Germany, Italy, and Spain before the "masses" in these and other countries began to enjoy the benefits of mass culture raises no questions in the minds of these writers.[25]

These arbitrary constructions emerge from the minds of speculative sociologists, existentialist philosophers, publicists, and literary critics. The chaos of motives and the lack of intellectual discipline render understandable the arbitrary and melodramatic nature of their conclusions. But empirical sociologists are also involved in the analysis of mass culture. Do they not bring a sobering influence into the discussion? Do they not control their observations and judgments by a systematic discipline?

The reply must be equivocal. Precise and orderly as their observations might be, they are made outside a matrix of intimate experience, without the sense of empathic affinity which would enable the events which they observe to be understood as they actually occur in the lives of those who experience them. One frequently feels, in reading the sociological reports on the cultural interests and activities of the populace, that the observers are from Mars and that they know only of the listening or viewing or buying activities of their subjects. Their other interests and activities fade

[24]*Mass Culture*, p. 9.
[25]Nor does the fact that the United States, where mass culture is so developed and where according to the research of Professor Adorno and his collaborators in *The Authoritarian Personality* so many Americans are proto-fascists, is the scene of a thriving democracy arouse any doubts about their theory of the nature and consequences of mass culture.

into the background, not because they are actually inconsequential, but because the particular techniques of inquiry bring the contact with mass communication so sharply into the foreground.[26] The inquirers often, and the interpreters of the inquiries not less frequently, go far beyond the limits set by their observations and assume that reading or seeing is evidence of a close correspondence between the content of what is seen, as interpreted by the sociologist, and the mind of the person who comes into contact with it. Most of the discussion goes even further and assumes, without any basis, the full assimilation into the depths of consciousness and unconsciousness of the latent content of films, radio and television broadcasts. Too often, the observations are very limited in scope, and the "interpretation," which goes far beyond them, introduces utterly baseless prejudices.

"Content analyses" are regarded by many students of popular culture as providing a direct and unquestionable path of entry into contact with the depths of the mind. The nature of the person who reads or sees or hears some work of popular culture is inferred from the content of the work, on the assumption that every image, every event corresponds to some deep and central need in the personality of the reader, viewer, or listener. There is no reason whatever to think that this is so, and yet this assumption lies near the heart of much of the treatment of mass culture.[27]

Orderly and realistic sociological research could tell us much about "modern man" and his relations with the roaring ocean of "mass culture." It is still to be undertaken. There is no reason at present to believe that men and women in modern Western society or that Americans in particular have much resemblance to the picture of them presented in the works of contemporary social scientists. There is far too much arbitrariness in these inquiries, far too little direct and intimate contact, far too little empathy in a matrix of the sense of affinity to justify in any convincing way the general and melodramatic interpretations which are made by the critics of mass culture. The sociological study of mass culture is the victim of the culture of sociological intellectuals.

It would, of course, be frivolous to deny the esthetic, moral, and intellectual unsatisfactoriness of much of popular culture or to claim that it shows the human race in its best light. The major error of the analysts of popular culture, however, is their belief that it has succeeded to something which was intrinsically worthy, that man has sunk into a hitherto unknown mire because of it, and that this is a necessary prelude to the further degradation, and perhaps ultimate extinction, of high culture.

[26]One should perhaps except from this the report by Mr. Leo Bogart on his inquiry into the response of adult readers to comic strips (*Mass Culture*, pp. 189–198).
[27]It would be more conducive to the understanding of the reasons for the concern about mass culture if sociologists, psychologists, and critics were to examine the producers of the works of mass culture—the film writers and producers, the authors of radio scripts, etc. Much of value concerning the producer's attitude towards his prospective audience and his underlying sentiments about his fellow countrymen would emerge from such studies. It is quite conceivable that they would reveal the circularity and the arbitrariness of much of the concern about mass culture. The producers and authors of works of mass culture make certain assumptions about the needs and desires of their audience, and then produce the work. Sociological investigators then proceed to study the works and from this draw inferences regarding the nature of the personalities who listen to it. These analyses then enter the atmosphere of intellectual opinion and provide allegedly scientific evidence to those who promote such production that their assumptions are correct.

Most of the analysts of popular culture make a mistake when they fail to see the great volume of output of popular culture as more than the expansion of a stream which has never been absent from Western society. They forget that up to the nineteenth century when a great change was brought about by the confluence of economic progress, a new sentiment of the value of human life, and the efforts of liberal and humanitarian reformers, the mass of the human race lived a degraded life. It is sheer romanticism when Prof. Van den Haag says "industry has impoverished life."[28] The contrary is true. Hunger and imminence of death, work such as we in the West would now regard as too burdensome even for beasts, over very long hours, prevented the development of individuality, of sensitivity or refinement in any except those very few in the lower classes who were either extremely strong personalities or extremely talented or extremely fortunate in forming a connection with the aristocratic or mercantile classes, or all three together.

The culture of these strata, which were dulled by labor, illness, and fear, and which comprised a far larger proportion of the population than they do in advanced societies in the twentieth century, was a culture of bear-baiting, cock-fighting, drunkenness, tales of witches, gossip about the sexual malpractices of priests, monks, and nuns, stories of murders and mutilations. The story of Sweeny Todd, the demon barber of Fleet Street, who ran a profitable business in meat pies made with the flesh of the victims dropped through the trapdoor of his barber shop, is not a creation of modern mass culture. It dates from the Middle Ages. The *fabliaux* were about the best that folk literary culture could offer in the Middle Ages and they were certainly not very salubrious. The *"littérature du colportage"* (or, trashy books sold by itinerant book-sellers) was not a literature in the style of Jane Austen or Gustave Flaubert. It was much closer and much inferior to Eugène Sue. The present pleasures of the working and lower middle classes are not worthy of profound esthetic, moral, or intellectual esteem but they are surely not inferior to the villainous things which gave pleasure to their European ancestors from the Middle Ages to the nineteenth century.

Only ignorance and prejudice, impelled by a passionate and permeative revulsion against their own age and their own society, can explain why contemporary intellectuals, who pride themselves on being socialists or liberals and democrats, wish to believe that the aristocracy and gentry in European societies of the seventeenth and eighteenth centuries lived an elevated cultural life, or that the spiritually numbed peasantry lived a coherent and dignified existence. Only a very small minority of the upper classes of the first four centuries of the modern era read a great deal, and a great deal of what they read was worthless from any point of view except that much of it was harmless. No one who has spent many hours in old libraries or in antiquarian bookshops can evade the conclusion that the vast majority of books produced in the seventeenth and eighteenth centuries, to say nothing of the nineteenth century, were of no consequence from an esthetic, moral, or intellectual point of view. The high culture of the seventeenth century included not only Shakespeare, Jonson, Bacon, Hobbes, Racine, Pascal, La Rochefoucauld, et al., but a far greater number of

[28]Van den Haag, *Mass Culture*, p. 531.

absolutely worthless writers, authors of spurious philosophical works, of foolishly mean-spirited and trivial theological treatises, of tales as vapid as the choices of the Book-of-the-Month Club and of poems which would try even the insensate patience of a Ph.D. candidate in English literature. It was not different in the eighteenth and nineteenth centuries.

This is not to take the modernist side in the battle of the books, or to claim that our contemporary philosophic, artistic, and literary genius is as rich as it was in the three preceding centuries. It is intended only to correct the utterly erroneous idea that the twentieth century is a period of severe intellectual deterioration and that this alleged deterioration is a product of a mass culture which is unique in all respects to this unfortunate century.

Indeed, it would be far more correct to assert that mass culture is now less damaging to the lower classes than the dismal and harsh existence of earlier centuries had ever been. The reading of good books, the enjoyment of superior music and painting, although perhaps meager, is certainly more widespread now than in previous centuries, and there is no reason to believe that it is less profound or less genuine. Only the frustrated attachment to an impossible ideal of human perfection, and a distaste for one's own society and for human beings as they are, can obscure this.

The root of the trouble lies not in mass culture but in the intellectuals themselves. The seduction and corruption of intellectuals are not new, although it is true that mass culture is a new opportunity for such degradation. Intellectuals are not required to read comic strips and then to blame others for doing so. They can skip the first and accept the second as an inevitable manifestation of "the old Adam." It is not popular literacy and leisure which force university professors to spend their leisure time in reading crime stories or looking at silly television programs. If they lower their own standards, they should not blame those who have not had the privilege of living within a tradition of high standards such as they themselves enjoy or could enjoy if they cared to do so.

Intellectuals do not have to work in the mass media, and even if they do, there is no unavoidable requirement for them to yield their standards as easily as they do, either in their work or outside it. Much but not all the wretched quality of the products of popular culture is a result of the producers' and authors' contempt for the tastes of the prospective audience and of their own *nostalgie de la boue* (or, "yearning for the mire"). There are certainly limitations in what the producers and authors in these occupations can accomplish because their employers are often convinced that only intellectual and esthetic products which we regard as inferior will find a large audience; there are probably also inherent limitations in the capacity of the audiences of the working and lower middle classes to respond appreciatively to works of good quality. It is far from certain, however, that the range of those limits has been definitely established and that the best possible has been done within them.

The uneasiness of Mr. Macdonald and of Prof. Van den Haag is not entirely without foundation. Populism, popularity, commercial criteria, expediency, are all impediments to great, if not to good, cultural achievements. But there are other factors which have little to do with mass culture and which are at least as important, and they do not consider these.

Excessive educational and professional specialization seems to me to be more injurious to the cultural life of the educated classes than popular culture, and indeed it prepares the way to resort to popular culture. The squandering by our educational system of the opportunities for creating a foundation for general cultural responsiveness among our more gifted boys and girls and young men and women between the ages of five and twenty-one is certainly far more damaging to high culture in America than the availability of popular culture to the mass of the less gifted. The readiness of university teachers and literary publicists to lower their own standards in their teaching and writing is more pernicious in its effects on high culture than Hollywood or the radio industry.

Naturally there are intellectuals who feel guilty for not acting up to the standards of cultural life which they know to be right. That is no reason why they should take it out on others who come from strata which only now in the twentieth century have for the first time in history the possibility of becoming full members of their society, of living a human life with some exercise of cultural taste, and the means to acquire or to come into contact with the objects of their taste. Nor are their own shortcomings a good reason why intellectuals should, with such *Schadenfreude*, proclaim and encourage the dilapidation of the high intellectual tradition to which they claim to be devoted.

Finally, it should be said that the strata which have just emerged from an immemorially old, clod-like existence cannot be reasonably expected to have good taste or discriminating judgment. It is quite likely that the majority never will be able to develop such taste and judgment. It is also, however, quite possible that a substantial minority, after several generations, will be assimilated as producers or consumers into one of the various traditions of high culture, and that they will serve as a leaven among their fellows. The chances for this to occur will naturally diminish if the bearers of high culture strike their own flags and scuttle their own ships. All the more reason, therefore, why intellectuals should not, out of impossible political zeal or out of furtive indulgence in pleasures which they know to be unworthy of their own traditions, blame these newly-born strata for ruining what is neither yet ruined nor necessarily ruined. The seed of the cultural health of the intellectuals lies within themselves.

GUIDES FOR READING AND DISCUSSION

1. Mr. Macdonald distinguishes among high, mass, and folk cultures. By what criteria does he define these types; does he apply the criteria consistently? Is the distinction between "mass culture" and "high culture" ultimately a matter of individual taste? If not, what other factors apply?

2. Is a mass medium necessarily at a low level? If not, what determines the level? May the government legitimately intervene to raise artistic standards in such mass media as radio and television; or does this contravene constitutional guarantees?

3. Is the quality of public education in the United States related to the content of mass culture? Is the general mass of the people educable not only in the sense of being able to learn to read, but also of being able to learn to appreciate complex and subtle art forms?

SUGGESTED ADDITIONAL READINGS

Kingsley Amis, *New Maps of Hell* (New York: Ballantine, 1960).

Martin Green, *A Mirror for Anglo-Saxons* (New York: Harper, 1960).

Leo Lowenthal, *Literature, Popular Culture, and Society* (Englewood Cliffs, N.J.: Prentice-Hall, 1961).

Dwight Macdonald, *Masscult & Midcult* (New York: Partisan Review, 1961).

"Mass Culture and Mass Media," *Daedalus,* Spring 1960, entire issue.

Bernard Rosenberg and David M. White, eds., *Mass Culture: The Popular Arts in America* (Glencoe, Ill.: Free Press, 1956).

Ralph Ross and Ernest van den Haag, *The Fabric of Society* (New York: Harcourt, Brace, 1957), ch. 15.